Peacemaking, Religious Belief and the Rule of Law

This book offers a new way of understanding the role of t[illegible]eaching parties the interrelationship between sustainable peace, forgiveness, and international justice. It argues that the arrival of social media presents new opportunities for reaching sustainable peace agreements, through their use in gathering the detailed information that can match victims and perpetrators of past atrocities.

The author aims to advance a more expansive understanding of the subjects and limitations of making peace in the shadow of international law by examining the concepts of mediation and forgiveness that exist alongside law. To that end, the book offers an account of the role of the mediator that emerges from the interplay between Ricouerian imagination and forgiveness and predicts ever-greater opportunities for making peace and protecting human rights that can be facilitated by a harnessing of social media as a tool for making peace with justice.

The author also aims to examine how strategies for sustaining the peace must combat the inevitable frustrations with democracy that can lead to a slide into dictatorship. Assad, Obama, and the UN leadership and their decisions concerning making and maintaining peace in Syria are used as case studies to examine the interplay between a leaders' religious beliefs, faith in democracy and the rule of law, and impulses towards totalitarianism.

Paul J. Zwier is Professor of Law and Director of the Center for Advocacy and Dispute Resolution at Emory University School of Law.

Routledge Research in International Law

For a full list of titles in this series, visit www.routledge.com/Routledge-Research-in-International-Law/book-series/INTNLLAW

Available

Nationalization, Natural Resources and International Investment Law
Contractual Relationship as a Dynamic Bargaining Process
Junji Nakagawa

Queering International Law
Possibilities, Alliances, Complicities, Risks
Edited by Dianne Otto

Sovereignty Conflicts and International Law and Politics
A Distributive Justice Issue
Jorge E. Núñez

The Rule of Law in the United Nations Security Council Decision-Making Process
Turning the Focus Inwards
Sherif Elgebeily

Universal Jurisdiction in International Criminal Law
The Debate and the Battle for Hegemony
Aisling O'Sullivan

The Right to Democracy in International Law
Between Procedure, Substance and the Philosophy of John Rawls
Khalifa A Alfadhel

Latin America and the International Court of Justice
Contributions to International Law
Edited by Paula Wojcikiewicz Almeida and Jean-Marc Sorel

Fragmentation vs the Constitutionalisation of International Law
A Practical Inquiry
Edited by Andrzej Jakubowski and Karolina Wierczyńska

Peacemaking, Religious Belief and the Rule of Law

The Struggle Between Dictatorship and Democracy in Syria and Beyond

Paul J. Zwier

Routledge
Taylor & Francis Group
LONDON AND NEW YORK

First published 2018
by Routledge

2 Park Square, Milton Park, Abingdon, Oxfordshire OX14 4RN
52 Vanderbilt Avenue, New York, NY 10017

Routledge is an imprint of the Taylor & Francis Group, an informa business

First issued in paperback 2020

British Library Cataloguing-in-Publication Data
A catalogue record for this book is available from the British Library

Library of Congress Cataloging-in-Publication Data
Names: Zwier, Paul J., 1954– author.
Title: Peacemaking, religious belief, and the rule of law : the struggle between dictatorship and democracy in Syria and beyond / Paul J. Zwier.
Description: Abingdon, Oxon [UK] ; New York : Routledge, 2018. | Series: Routledge research in international law | Includes index.
Identifiers: LCCN 2017039486 | ISBN 9781138220799 (hardback)
Subjects: LCSH: Mediation, International. | Pacific settlement of international disputes. | Syria—History—Civil War, 2011– | Government, Resistance to—Syria. | Reconciliation (Law)—Syria. | Restorative justice. | Forgiveness. | Rule of law—Syria. | United States—Foreign relations—Syria. | Syria—Foreign relations—United States. | Dictatorship—Syria.
Classification: LCC KZ6045 .Z85 2018 | DDC 956.9104/231—dc23
LC record available at https://lccn.loc.gov/2017039486

ISBN: 978-1-138-22079-9 (hbk)
ISBN: 978-0-367-59358-2 (pbk)

Typeset in Galliard
by Apex CoVantage, LLC

Contents

Preface vii

PART I
The US, the UN, and the Syrian conflict: the role of religion and the dictator/democracy dilemma 1

1 The history of US–Syrian relations: the role of Bashar al-Assad 3

2 The history of US relations with Syria: the role of Obama – and now Trump 34

3 UN and NGO peacemaking efforts 66

4 Options for a constitution-based transition in Syria: the Russian draft and a problem-solving approach 98

PART II
A moral theory for peacemaking with justice: history, imagination, and forgiveness on an international stage 129

5 History and imagination: the hermeneutics of Paul Ricoeur 131

6 Justice and forgiveness 152

PART III
The potential impact of social media on peacemaking in Syria 181

7 Social media and conflict mapping in Syria: implications for peacemaking, international criminal prosecutions, and for TRC processes 183

8 Conclusion 219

Index 227

Preface

It is early winter, 2013. Jamal is walking one morning in the Damascus suburb in the Mezze 86 district. Mezze, sometimes spelled Mezzeh, is a sprawling area on the western edge of Damascus, one of the first city panoramas that greets visitors arriving on the Damascus–Beirut highway, named for Hafez al-Assad, the president's father, who ruled for 30 years.

Jamal has left the West Villas section of Mezze, a neighborhood of stand-alone houses across the highway from a military airport. It is home to wealthy Syrians of a mix of ethnic backgrounds and political persuasions, many of whom lead cosmopolitan lives and have business connections or family abroad. He has taken a turn to Mezze 86, where he plans to see a friend.

Mezze 86 is a less wealthy area than the West Villas section and is home to many members of President Assad's minority Alawite sect, members of the security forces and, some residents say, the pro-government gangs known as *shabiha* that have been unleashed against the opposition. The housing is four- to five-story apartment complexes, running side by side on both sides of the street. Laundry hangs from the balconies. The facades of the buildings are dirty and scarred.

Jamal knows that Mezze 86 borders on the location of an interrogation facility and prison complex.

The wind rises and Jamal smells black smoke coming from the direction of the prison complex. At first he thinks it smells like burning tires, but then he recognizes the smell as something different, more chilling. He had smelled it a few months earlier, when Syrian security force burned the bodies of civilians in the streets after a massacre. The smell of burning hair in particular seemed to pierce through, as it was the smell of something he never hoped to have to smell again.

Jamal has a connection to a friend in Beirut, who is a member of the expatriate community there. This friend, Abdullah, was a human rights lawyer before spending close to a month in one of Assad's prisons, where he was humiliated and tortured. When he got out, he packed up his family and pregnant wife and fled, outraged that his loyalty to human rights in Syria made him an enemy of the state. Abdullah put Jamal in touch with a friend at Human Rights Watch.

Jamal is certainly not the only one; indeed, starting in the winter of 2013, others had also begun to recognize the smells and to report them to the international human rights community. But it was not until 16 May 2017 that Nikki S. Haley, the American ambassador to the United Nations, made an assertion that the Syrian government had built a crematorium in the Sednaya prison complex. She asserted that the purpose of the crematorium was to burn bodies of the prisoners the Syrian security forces had tortured and killed. The US had satellite photos that it said showed the crematorium. It knew it was a crematorium because the photos, some taken in the winter of 2013, showed the other buildings covered in snow, while the one with smoke billowing out of chimney structures was not. This of course indicated extreme heat coming from inside the building, a heat consistent with ovens that burned at very high temperatures.

Some Syrian observers wanted to know why the US was only disclosing this now. UN ambassador Haley was not shy about her purpose. The US was trying to get Russia to back away from its support for the Syrian government as well as using evidence of Syrian atrocities to make more negotiating room for the parties already engaged in peace talks. As of May 2017, the Syrian government was taking an extremely hardline approach in its negotiations with moderate rebels. Perhaps, if the Russians would back away from Assad, just a little, a more reasonable and good faith negotiation could take place over the future of Syria.

Yet, beyond her stated purpose, what exactly was the reasoning behind her assertions? Was the US shifting its policy toward Syria? President Trump was sending mixed messages. On one hand, he had signaled since coming to power that he was more willing to negotiate with foreign powers than make pronouncements about human rights.[1] At the same time, the president seemed genuinely troubled by scenes of Syrian children dying after having been gassed by the Syrian government.

It was not as if the conflict was new or that other war crimes had not been alleged against Assad. The facts were already familiar to Syrian observers. During the Obama administration, policy makers had been divided by the conflict. Its start in 2010–11 coincided with other Arab spring pro-democracy movements in Egypt and Tunisia. At first the US took a hands-off approach, worrying that it not repeat the mistakes it had made in Iraq.

Then there was Benghazi and the Libyan catastrophe that resulted from the power vacuum left by the removal of Muammar Gaddafi. Again, the Obama administration worried that if it acted to remove a leader like it had with Gaddafi, it might create a power vacuum that could lead to even more instability, an even greater flood of refugees, and more atrocities by various insurgent groups trying to establish control in the setting of a failed state. While it wanted to encourage and support the democracy movement, it also wanted to make sure that it did not end up making things worse.

Then, there arose ISIS, otherwise known as DAESH, or ISIL. And the US was put into the dilemma of whether to act militarily and back a particular moderate rebel group, or the Kurds, or to sit on the sidelines and try to remain neutral as Syrians themselves sorted out how to best deal with ISIS on the one side and Assad on the other.

Then, in 2012, Assad used chemical weapons on his own people. Assad got the US's and the UN's full attention. The international community united in condemnation of the use of chemical weapons and called for sanctions. The US and Russian negotiators were able to negotiate with Assad, and he committed to destroying his chemical weapons stockpile. He even allowed for international inspections to verify the destruction of the chemicals. The inspectors not only were able to conclude that chemical weapons were used – attributing no responsibility – but then also assisted in and attempted to verify disposal of chemical weapons in Syria.[2]

The Obama administration continued its humanitarian aid in Syria but did not engage in direct military actions supporting any one military group. Most troubling, the US seemed to go back on a commitment it had made to not stand idly by while war crimes were being committed against civilians, even when done by those civilians' own government in the name of fighting terrorism. Violating clearly stated policies for military engagement, the US chose instead to negotiate rather than use military force. It worried that its involvement would create a reason for other rebel groups to join ISIS or Assad. Again, its experience in Iraq showed the dangers of backing Shias over Sunnis, or vice versa. The US continued to stay on the sidelines and to call for an end to Assad's presidency. Over time, it gradually increased its involvement by providing "non-lethal" military support to rebel groups it had grown to know and trust. Yet, initially, ISIS had its way in Syria, and the dangers that US arms would fall into the hands of ISIS caused the US to suspend even its non-lethal weapons support in 2014.

Then, Russia entered the conflict at the request of Syria in December 2015. Its involvement was pooh-poohed by the Obama administration as being a fool's errand. But there is no doubt that the Russian have complicated things greatly for peacemakers, as the Russians now seem completely committed to protecting the Assad regime and to supporting his forces in their attempts to retake Syria. Fighting both ISIS and other rebel groups, not only has Assad been fortified, but the war has also now taken a more sectarian turn. Iranian militia, including Hezbollah, have become more prominently involved on the side of Assad. The Saudis now actively support Sunni-aligned groups out of a concern that Shi'ite groups will in fact prevail.

Then, Trump was elected president. What does it portend for US's policy toward Syria and the Middle East? His first signal, that he meant to act on an "America first" agenda, led to the institution of a highly criticized temporary immigration ban from Muslim-majority countries.[3] Many argued that using one's religion as a basis to ban a person trying to enter the country was unconstitutional. Was it too early to worry about the US itself and its own faith in democracy?

Violating constitutional norms, his administration signaled a willingness to act on the international stage by putting a perception of national security ahead of principles. During the campaign, Trump had expressed admiration for Putin, among other so-called strong leaders who were willing to put national interest first in fighting terrorism, even if it meant violating human rights, free speech, using torture, or invading the privacy rights of individuals. As president-elect, Trump even wondered aloud what was the sense of having of nuclear weapons is if one was never willing to actually use them. Alarm bells started to ring when such statements were combined with an unwillingness to share his broader foreign policy strategies or protocols. He argued that the US should not tip its hand by describing what would trigger its use of military actions.

In his first trip abroad Trump continued to signal that he meant to act on his "America first" theory of foreign policy. He met with the Saudis and never mentioned their human rights record. He seemed to be ambivalent about the North Atlantic Treaty Organization (NATO), arguing that other members were not paying their share in providing military support. He weighed in on the side of the Saudis against Qatar, again without regard to the Saudi record on human rights. His reasoning was transparently signaling that human rights and the rule of law were not the issues, which was instead whether he could look good and take advantage of an argument that he was a great deal maker in the Middle East.

He decided the US should abandon the Paris climate accords: involvement didn't adequately serve US economic interests. He acted not unlike Putin, giving only lip service to liberal democratic principles while in fact pushing a nation-first agenda. Would the US, then, be willing to leave its principles aside in Syria and make a peace with Assad regardless of his war crimes?

On the other hand, it may be unfair to place this shift solely at the feet of Trump. After all there are additional forces that seem to be at work now as the US searches again for a coherent foreign policy in the Middle East and beyond. The US seems to have been shaken by its own experiences with democracy. Has the US been taken over by the despotism of democracy – that it is working only for the elites and exacerbating inequality while oppressing the poor and marginalized – by entrenching its own interests through controlling the rule of law and thereby entrenching its own interests?

Perhaps in seeing itself as far from perfect, some in the US have become more appreciative of "strong leadership" and more tolerant of dictatorship. And during the Cold War it has a history of backing dictators. Perhaps the US is becoming grudgingly appreciative of the economic success of China and Singapore, where strong leadership, even dictatorships, encourages economic development, even if liberties and human rights seemed to suffer. Its admiration for strong leadership may have blurred the differences between itself and foreign dictators. Additionally, a substantial portion of the voters seemed strangely untroubled by this. Perhaps these citizens no longer believe that democracy brings about the changes that make for them a meaningful life and so have lost faith that it can do so for others.

In contrast, in a speech she gave at Wellesley, Hilary Clinton made an appeal to a return to Enlightenment values of liberal democracy. She argued for reason, respect, and a renewed faith in liberal democratic values. Anxiety-producing to many of her supporters was the fact that the results of the election seemed to argue against putting much faith in the democratic processes. How could so many US voters reject the Enlightenment principles of a free press; equal opportunity regardless of age, race, sexual orientation, or gender; the protection of the environment; or the humane treatment of immigrants. How could so many favor a dangerous nationalism, long on feel-good promises and short on specifics of how jobs would actually return, or how a wall would protect against illegal immigration, or how gutting food stamps, Planned Parenthood, and public education would actually benefit lower- and middle-class white men?

What seems to have happened in America is a reaction to what Tocqueville had worried about in the mid-1800s but had hoped the US would be able to avoid. This worry was precisely the problem of democratic despotism. By democratic despotism, Tocqueville had meant a concern that democracy would gradually be taken over by the elites. These elites would then begin to assert their own interests through various bureaucratic institutions – the various regulatory bodies, courts, and administrative agencies that would reach into everyday life and impose the will of the elites on the masses. The post–French Revolution experience was telling to Tocqueville. Backed by well-meaning legislative actions, a sameness (brought about ironically by an emphasis on equality) that would creep into society through the regulatory agencies designed to enforce such legislative actions. Licensing for bars, certifications for growing wine, driving cars, disposing of waste, and so on would gradually raise the costs of competition, all in favor of the more established and well-financed actors. At stake were essential liberty interests that would inhibit risk taking, stifle innovation, and lock in existing structures of status and control. But most important, the result would be a stratification of society where lower classes would feel trapped and suffocate in the sameness of a society demanding too much equality.

On a scale of affirmative liberty, there seem to be fewer differences between nations, especially as they act on the international stage. By affirmative liberty, I am referring to what Isaiah Berlin describes as the freedom of each individual to define for herself what rules she wants to play by, thereby creating her own meaning in life. The importance of this affirmative liberty interest haunts the US's thinking about itself, about its very soul. How much will the US be able to sort out the right balance between liberty and equality? Will an overemphasis on equality and liberal democracy create its own brand of despotism? And will its own self-doubt lead the US to act on an international stage in the manner of an old-style imperialist nation without regard to the character of who it is partnering with? War crimes be damned; the rule of law be damned. The question for the US on an international stage would then become what the economic interests of the elite are and how the international situation can be taken advantage of to ensure the advancement of those interests.

As political philosopher Steven B. Smith says,

> [w]e live in a composite civilization made up of competing strands of both the Enlightenment and Counter Enlightenment that has made the emancipatory powers of reason and science seem increasingly illusory. The progressive narrative could never entirely slough off its doubles [that science has limits, and that humans are fundamentally driven by short term self interest, my addition). We remain perpetually gnawed at by our manifold discontents – and that is a good thing.[4]

Whether US policy is shifting on the whims of incompetence and impulsiveness or something more sinister, the Syrian conflict presents an important case study for the US and International Community. It will help us see if a shift in principles is underway and should be underway and if that shift should cause the US and UN to change their strategy in post conflict societies where their leadership has engaged in atrocities. Perhaps the US should change its approach toward Syria's Assad? Perhaps it should be more nuanced in its advocacy for the role that the rule of law plays in Syria. How one should approach peacemaking and make provisions for a lasting and sustainable peace?

Others have explored changes in US foreign policy on three different spectrums: (1) realism versus idealism, (2) imperialism versus neutral peacemaking,[5] and (3) national interest versus human rights. Some have seen these spectrums as related to the US's very identity, or the myths and narratives that impact how it sees itself. For example, David Brooks opines that the US is losing connection with its Exodus story, namely that it is a country of immigrants that left the oppression of Europe to found a new city set on a hill. This narrative comes complete with Judeo-Christian religious underpinnings: God in his providence is behind the US and its successes.

New narratives have begun to compete with this old and more classical narrative. One is a libertarian narrative that the US's greatness is related to its emphasizing individual liberties: in the market, as workers and taxpayers, and in business, one is globalized and that we provide the ideal setting for start-ups and lifelong learners, a setting that leads to technological fixes of some of the world's most pressing problems. Another narrative is multicultural, which makes us think less in terms of the individual and more in terms of the community as a whole. It is almost an intellectual narcissism that celebrates differences without being able to provide reasoned arguments that bring the different communities together. And now, in this age of Trump, a new narrative has emerged that is encapsulated by the seemingly ubiquitous phrase of "Make America Great Again." This narrative is backward-looking and pessimistic, filled with contempt for democratic norms and liberal values. It personalizes power, routinizes corruption and destabilizes the very idea of objective truth (David Brooks, *New York Times*, "The Four American Narratives," Friday, May 26, 2017). David Brooks adds two others: a mercantile model, where the US is in competition with China, Russia, and Europe, and a "talented community" model, which, like the ancient city of Athens, is a community of philosophers, poets, and dreamers, set apart to do the work of achieving progress for and on behalf of the world around it. (Of course, this last narrative flies in the face of American's reputation for being anti-intellectuals.)

Yet perhaps the bridges between liberal democracy, human rights, and national interests have long been crossed and are not in fact in competition with each other. Since the Vietnam War, the US has struggled to explain and to justify its actions on the world stage. If it wasn't fighting tyranny and making the world safe for democracy, and if it wasn't interested in imperial acquisitions of colonies, what defined its interests in places like the Middle East, or China, or Africa? For example, the US wasn't shy to say that its interest in the Middle East was oil. It needed a stable supply of oil to support its economy. Did that mean it would give up any insistence on human rights from governments that provided a steady supply of oil? The US's policies towards Iran, Saudi Arabia, and Bahrain seemed to say as much.

Recent administrations have struggled to balance the costs of the more aggressive of these policies with the moral imperatives to prevent genocide and other war crimes. For example, after leaving office, President Clinton expressed that one of his biggest regrets was not acting more aggressively in preventing the Rwandan genocide. Yet one of the principle failures of George W. Bush's administration was precisely its aggressive invasion of Iraq, which of course led to serious questions as to why no weapons of mass destruction were ever found. The Obama administration was no exception when it came to making decisions concerning when to use military force. On one hand, it seemed to be rather proud of its use of force to kill Osama bin Laden and its use of drones to carry out strategic strikes to combat terrorism. Obama was counseled by Samantha Powers, the author of *The Problem from Hell*, yet he found himself rejecting that counsel when it came to enforcing the "red line" in Syria. President Trump has already acted differently, showing that he is at least willing to take a targeted military response when Assad was later caught using chemical weapons on his own citizens.

One additional force in determining US foreign policy has been its relationship with the UN, which is at the very least the US's partner in taking on the responsibilities of peacemaking and the encouragement of sustainable governance. The UN has significant tools at its disposal. It now has an International Criminal Court, which can serve as a deterrent to war crimes. It has a peacekeeping authority, which can authorize a UN presence in conflict settings. But it is also restricted by its structure of governance: with Russia exercising its veto on the Security Council to block interventions in Syria, the UN has been neutralized as an independent force.

What really is the US's relationship to the UN as a force to prevent genocide, make peace, and build sustainable governance structures? Can the US delegate much of its role as the world policeman to the UN? The US contributes in US dollars more than $1 billion a year to the UN's regular budget and over $7.5 billion a year for all of its peacekeeping operations (28 percent of its overall programming). What rights does this financial support give the US in directing how that funding is to be used? Or is this really a drop in the bucket of what the US spends on peacekeeping around the world? Perhaps it still believes that independently of what it gets from the UN, the US's power and privilege in the world comes with responsibility. But, perhaps not. And what responsibility does it have for helping to establish international humanitarian law? Does it believe in reason enough to trust the UN to develop both its court and its peacemaking protocols, or does it finally believe more in its own power and right to define and protect itself, even if it will inevitably cause harm to its own principles and even to its own supporters?

Finally, the US's understanding of itself is shifting regarding its religious heritage and identity. Having long seen itself as a Christian nation, it now must confront the rise of Islam as being in legitimate competition with itself. The irony is that it also sees itself as a nation formed on freedom of religion and freedom of conscience. In creating room for difference within the Christian religion, even if some are suspicious of Catholicism, the US has used faith in the principles for liberty to evolve a belief in pluralism. Pluralism is united through a faith that civil discourse that will sort out the rough edges between people of different faiths. Until recently, in the US, belief in pluralism in the context of rational, non-violent discourse, has taken precedence over insistence on a particular version of religious nationalism.

But what if the competing religious faith does not believe in reason, let alone, civil discourse. What then? Is there room in some versions of more radical Islam for liberal democracy? Or will some versions of the faith inevitably clash with democratic principles that prioritize equality and human rights over religious laws?[6]

What is at stake here is clearly the US's very identity. Maybe it no longer believes it is fundamental to its role in the world that it use its military power to try to prevent genocide and other war crimes. Maybe some no longer believe in liberal democracy and the rule of law as foundational ideas in the development of sustainable government. Or maybe some in leadership positions have lost faith in the US's founding and basic principles, and are now willing to engage in old imperialist strategies as old as Machiavelli and honed by Kissinger, a policy of self-interest that encourages the rise and fall of foreign governments as long as US interests are being served. On a broader level, what would a shift to a more muscular and assertive role in Syria mean for US foreign policy mean for other disputes in the Middle East, and in North Korea? How would a willingness to become more assertive be financed and maintained in multiple disputes and in far-reaching settings?

This book seeks to explore US foreign policy and its relationship with the UN in a post-modern world. What I mean by a post-modern world is a world that seems to have lost its faith in the Enlightenment and is instead filled with skepticism, self-doubt, and even despair that governments can and should operate consistently with the precepts of liberal democracy. Yet, the US sees itself "as a country in which modernity has reached its fullest and most comprehensive expression."[7] It seems built on the theory that rational discourse protecting human rights and the basic freedoms of expression, of conscience, and of religion, is the best hope for sustainable government. If it gives up on these principles, in the pursuit of its political interests in the world, will it gain the world but, in the process, lose its soul?

The world seems more and more captured by the Counter-Enlightenment. Some seem willing to say that there is a certain amount of success that has developed in countries like Singapore, China, Russia, and Vietnam, countries that are virtually totalitarian and anti-democratic while nonetheless seeming to provide basic material prosperity to most of their people. What becomes clear is that a democratically elected president doesn't ensure religious freedom and the protection of human rights. Again, democracy, without rule-of-law protections for minority rights, including a commitment to those rights by legislative bodies and independent courts, can provide the means for a country to slide into tyranny and dictatorship.

Consider two troubling examples. Israel, for example, seems to be sliding away from its liberal democratic roots. Under the leadership of Netanyahu, backed by a conservative religious faction, it has promoted Jewish settlements in the West Bank. It has declared itself a Jewish state. It denied full rights to Palestinians, threatening its identity as a democracy, governed by the rule of law. It lives under legitimate fears of terrorism and existential attacks on its right to govern itself. Still, it has lived in a state of emergency for too long, and it is starting to get comfortable with itself as a Jewish state which discriminates against portions of its citizens based on religion and ethnicity.

And then there is Poland. Partly out of fear of Russia, and partly in the name of its right to be Christian and Catholic, Poland has rejected EU principles and their applications in its courts. They have called for the resignation of all existing judges, including those on its Supreme Constitutional Court. Poland is ruled by a democratically elected set of legislators and executive under the banner of a single political party, the Law and Justice Party. The Law and Justice candidates won the presidency and overwhelming majority of the legislature. The Law Justice party rose to prominence in 2014 in the context of fears arising from a refugee crisis caused, in part, by the conflict in Syria. Again, what this shows is that democracy is no long-term guarantor of minority rights. Without a commitment in these institutions to normative principles in the protection of religious freedom, the majority can easily assert itself, and override the independence of its courts, taking a country in the direction of unchecked power to the majority, as led by its executive.

Syria is the context of our discussion. The previously mentioned matters have important implications for a number issues faced by peacemakers in Syria. The first issue is a fair understanding and assessment of what has gone on before. Our method of examining this issue will be to look at two individuals, Bashar al-Assad and Barrack Hussein Obama, and then look at the role of UN as an institution. In examining the role of each of these actors in the ongoing crisis, I will attempt to combat the tendencies of some in the foreign policy community to be arrogant and condescending in their attitudes towards those previously in charge. The supposed experts of today are understandably trying to assert their own views in a way that makes them look superior to what has come before. It will help them gain purchase for their ideas. Unfortunately, the cycle of transitions of power often has a boomerang impact on policy, which is to say that the Obama foreign policy will overreact to Bush's and then Trump's to those of both Bush's and Obama's. What I will attempt is a more nuanced assessment of what has gone on before. So, for example, I will take the time to examine carefully what can be said about Bashar al-Assad, both in his favor and in the case against him. My method is like that of an adversarial court proceeding, leaving the final judgment to the court of international opinion. My judgments will be modest, and instead of automatically demonizing his decisions, I will attempt to understand and learn from them. The facts will matter. And before offering any tentative judgments or lessons, I will try to give a fair assessment of the surrounding considerations and the complexity of each issue faced. My method will also open up an examination of the role that religious belief plays in decision-making about the fight against terrorism and the use of military interventions to stop war crimes, prevent refugee crises, and even prevent genocide. I will show that for some, like Assad, religious oppression can be used to inspire supporters and proxies to defy opposition and demonize one's opponents. For others, like Obama, religious beliefs impact the way one even goes about making the decisions about intervention. It makes one question one's own motives, eschewing Churchillian rhetoric, and to negotiate even in the face of evil. For others, like some neoconservatives, religious beliefs are emboldening. They are to be trusted in determining whether one's opponent is good or evil and then used to galvanize support that force can and must be used to fight that evil. Finally, for others, like Trump, religious beliefs are an excuse for any action that one chooses to take, whether to ban immigrants or to use force. Some conservative Christians have seen Trump's willingness to use feelings of disrespect and religious fear as support for a more muscular Christianity." Other Christians see his actions in a different light, as having been made impulsively. They worry it will signal a falling of religious pluralism and a choice of one brand of Christianity over other dominations. They also see it as some Christians providing support for dictatorship over democracy. This attitude moves decision-making away from having a rational, or even democratic, basis into a basis of impulsively employed power.

Finally I will try to make a more nuanced connection between decisions leaders' efforts to make peace and the peace that is actually made. How will the UN's different roles in the international community – in particular, the workings of the International Criminal Court – impact its ability to make first a provisional and then a truly sustainable peace? Now, with the US joining 20 nations as part of a new Syria crisis group, and with the UN on the sidelines, Syria faces an important choice about how to transition to its future. How will the parties and their proxies demanding an end to the refugee crisis that is destabilizing the Middle East and Europe balance their own security interests versus the need for a future constitutional democracy in Syria. Calls for peace in Syria may impact decision-making concerning the whether a post-Soviet-style constitution is settled on for Syria. Ensuring some sort of election may not be enough for the future protection of human rights in Syria. And the rule-of-law protections and the capacity of the legislature and courts, as vital and viable checks on dictatorship, might end up being sacrificed in light of an international community's loss of faith in the importance of liberal democracy.

In addition, what role does the UN play as a mediator, and how does the supposed neutrality of this mediator potentially impact whatever peace is made, in conflict with the rule of law? Ricoeur's theories of mediation will also help us explore the role that religion may play in making peace in Syria. Moreover, the question of what role social media may play in complicating and undermining the legitimacy of any deal that maintains Hafez al-Assad in power will prove critical.

Acknowledgments. Much of what I have learned about negotiation and mediation comes from teaching with Joseph Harbaugh and Thomas Guernsey. I am also indebted to Hon. Anne C. Williams, (7th Cir. Ct of Appeals) whose grace and skill opened doors to the powers that be in so many contexts. I want to especially thank my research assistant Sergio Glajar, for his careful reading, editing, and research support during the writing of the book, Lila Lutfi, for her excellent research support, and also acknowledge the students in the Adv. International Negotiations Seminar, who teach me new insights about international negotiation theory and practice every day.

The book proceeds as follows.

Part I: the US, the UN, and the Syrian conflict: the role of religion and the dictator/democracy dilemma

Chapter 1: the history of US–Syrian relations: the role of Bashar al-Assad

This chapter will discuss the history of the US's foreign policy in its dealings in the Middle East and Syria, in particular. It will start with understanding Bashar al Assad and his responsibility for the choices made in fighting the civil war. We will try to look at the events in the context of the history of both Syria and Bashar al Assad himself. In the latter regard we will look at the role of religion and then his foreign policy doctrine and then how particular events give context to Assad's use of chemical weapons

Chapter 2: the history of US relations with Syria: the role of Obama – and now Trump

This chapter will look at Obama's decisions using the same organizational framework to understand Obama's actions in Syria. We will look at religion, doctrine, and events. Finally we examine Trump's early decisions to see what may emerge in this same regard. This chapter will consider the problem of evil and the scale and scope of the power of the modern dictator who acts to protect his power and survive as head of state. Dilemmas presented by the past war crimes of Charles Taylor of Liberia, President Omar Bashir of Sudan, and President Kenyatta of Kenya will also be discussed along with how the US dealt with these issues. This chapter will also outline the history of modern Syria and, more particularly, the Syrian conflict from its inception in 2010. It will also discuss the complex motivations of the parties, the rise of extremist groups, and the role that religion plays in complicating efforts at making peace.

Chapter 3: UN and NGO peacemaking efforts

This chapter will discuss the current efforts at making peace that have been attempted by the UN and the side role other NGOs have played in conducting negotiations with various representatives of the Syrian parties in Oslo. These efforts will allow us to see the creative and imaginative efforts already being discussed, the practical difficulties of making peace with justice, and the real obstacles presented by the potential intervention of the International Criminal Court (ICC). It will also discuss how old position-bargaining negotiation tactics present difficulties in getting the parties to discuss creative and imaginative solutions to making peace. It will show how such tactics keep the parties from discussing the necessary tradeoffs they must make between redressing past crimes, the need for meaningful input from the victims and their families, and the need to stop the conflict and end the violence. It will show how similar negotiations in similar situations in Liberia and Kenya have led to the use of Truth and Reconciliation Commissions (TRCs) that have not produced just results.

This chapter will also discuss the history of the ICC and its new role in indicting heads of state engaged in perpetrating war crimes. This chapter will also detail the UN's mediator role in Syria in its Geneva I and Geneva II conferences and how it is supporting further talks in the shadow of the Russian process.

Chapter 4: options for a constitution-based transition in Syria

Chapter 4 will discuss the various political options for Syria, post conflict. In particular, it will discuss the Russian draft of the Syrian constitution and the dilemmas facing peacemakers in making peace but providing for human rights, the rule of law, and deterring future war crimes. It will conclude that the hopes for what may emerge during the transition are two fold. The first is that these constituents realize that to be effective, there will need to develop some shared interests in the ends of the political process (democracy and rule of law). In addition the hope is that these parties develop the normative behavior, or shared sense of duty, for those given the responsibility to implement the political structures, that they put peace ahead of personal power.

Part II: a moral theory for peacemaking with justice: history, imagination, and forgiveness on an international stage

Chapter 5: history and imagination: the hermeneutics of Paul Ricoeur

How could the mediation and peacemaking efforts in Syria avoid the pitfalls of TRCs in Liberia, Kenya, and Sudan? Mediation on the international stage is, at its best, about transforming deadlocked negotiations into sustainable settlements. Three topics are critical to that goal and to this part of the book. The first is about history: the mediator's role in deconstructing and demystifying the parties' historical understanding of their dispute. The second is about avoiding the effects of position bargaining tactics. In other words, it will attempt to describe how mediators might facilitate the bargainers' imaginations: how a mediator can help the parties find in their narratives the imaginative spark that will facilitate their effort to identify a future-oriented approach to solving their problems and start them on the road to reconciliation with each other. Imagination is especially critical when the disputants' differences may be partly religious in nature. To help understand the role that both the history-focused theory of interpretation and the subsequent exercise of creative imagination play in an international mediation process, with religious overtones, this chapter will enlist the ambitious and challenging philosophy of Paul Ricoeur. In the process, the role that a mediator can play in transforming deadlock into more sustainable solutions can be better understood.

Chapter 6: justice and forgiveness

As helpful as Ricoeur's hermeneutics will be to the first two topics, a third topic will yet remain for the parties to work through in order to truly reach a just and sustainable settlement. This topic is particularly important for helping the parties design an appropriate and effective Truth and Reconciliation process. Where the parties have perpetrated atrocities on each other, it will be necessary to examine the topic most often raised in the imaginative spark of the renewed understanding of a group's identity narrative, that of the possibility that the parties offer forgiveness as part of a path to sustainable peace. On the topic of forgiveness this chapter will propose that Ricoeur's philosophy highlights the essential features of forgiveness: that it is outside the exchange or bargaining that typically drives peaceful settlements but nonetheless gives a future to the disputants past dealing with each other.

This chapter will also examine the necessary implications of forgiveness: that is that victims will most likely have to be engaged directly in the peace process or immediately thereafter in order for them to freely choose to forgive the perpetrators for atrocities that have been committed against them. Building on contributions from Ricoeur, it will be necessary for the mediator to better understand what impact the victim's choice to forgive may have on whether any settlement that is reached is ultimately just. Because meaningful forgiveness can only be voluntarily given by individual victims, a process that provides as much will need to be agreed to by party representatives. Such a process will insert fragility into the peace settlement.

This chapter will then examine whether a mediated peace process that relies on forgiveness can overcome the objection that forgiveness is incompatible with justice. It will show that these objections can be overcome but only if the parties understand the hard trade-offs they are making in choosing to forgive and if those making the peace ensure that any peace processes will involve victims in the final resolution of any lasting peace. In addition, it will show that as a matter of moral philosophy, such processes will have to involve a certain amount of fact-finding about the nature of the alleged atrocities and provide meaningful protections, much like those in play in formal legal processes, to ensure that any victim's or group of victims' choice to forgive will be meaningful.

Part III: the potential impact of social media on peacemaking in Syria

Chapter 7: social media and conflict mapping in Syria: implications for peacemaking, international criminal prosecutions, and for TRC processes

Synthesizing insights from the role that technology plays both in fomenting public dissent and in building democracy, this chapter will discuss the role that social media plays in gathering information before, during and after a conflict. It will first discuss how it has been seen as a tool in organizing dissent, but not, as yet, thought of as a way to provide information about disputants' acts during the conflict. The chapter will also discuss the mechanics of how such media might be harnessed by a non-governmental organization (NGO), like The Carter Center, to assist the UN and the parties in resolving the dispute in a way that is consistent with the requirements of sustainable peace through justice and meaningful forgiveness. It will discuss how social media (photos, videos, etc.) might be used by mediators and international courts/tribunals and its usefulness from a legal evidentiary standpoint. It will discuss how social media has the potential for providing accountability both for both regime and non-governmental (rebel group/ protesters/insurgents as well) actors.

Chapter 8: conclusion

This concluding chapter will make suggestions for peacemaking in post-conflict settings. It will also suggest some lessons to learn for the US, the UN, and the international NGO community in its future struggle between dictatorship and democracy.

I acknowledge this is a fast-moving area; the book was up to date in August 2017.

Notes

1 Julie Hirschfeld Davis and Mark Lander, "Trump Praises Erdogan as Ally in Terrorism Fight, Brushing Aside Tensions," *NYT*, May 16, 2017, www.nytimes.com/2017/05/16/world/middleeast/erdogan-turkey-trump.html?_r=0.

> White House officials have said that Mr. Trump has no interest in lecturing foreign leaders about human rights. He would prefer to make deals with them in areas of common interest, these officials said, believing that pressure on human rights generally backfires. Ibid.

2 Of course, we now know that all stockpiles were not destroyed, as there is substantial evidence they were used by Assad in April 2017 in an attack on the city of Khan Shaykhun in northwest Syria.

3 Students of history immediately worry about the similarity in Trump's slogan for his agenda with the Nazis slogan, "*Deutschland uber alles.*" And, in particular, "American first" as the slogan picked by Nazis sympathizers in protest of what it saw was Roosevelt's less-than-assertive response to socialism. Eric Rauchway, "Donald Trump's New Favorite Slogan Was Invented for Nazi Sympathizers: 'America First'

Was Charles Lindbergh's Motto in the 1930s," *Washington Post*, June 14, 2016, www.washingtonpost.com/posteverything/wp/2016/06/14/donald-trumps-new-favorite-slogan-has-a-nazi-friendly-history/?utm_term=.d541a078df65.

4 Steven B. Smith, *Modernity and Its Discontents: The Making and Unmaking the Bourgeois from Machiavelli to Bellow* (Yale and London: Yale University Press, 2016), 352.

5 Michael B. Oren, *Power, Faith and Fantasy, America in the Middle East 1776 to the Present* (New York, and London: W.W. Norton & Co., 2007).

6 Jeffrey Gettleman, *Love Africa: A Memoir of Romance, War and Survival* (New York: HarpersCollins, 2017), Chapter 7, Somalia, 2006.

7 Steven B. Smith, *Modernity and Its Discontents: The Making and Unmaking the Bourgeois from Machiavelli to Bellow* (Yale and London: Yale University Press, 2016), 352.

Part I

The US, the UN, and the Syrian conflict

The role of religion and the dictator/democracy dilemma

1 The history of US–Syrian relations

The role of Bashar al-Assad

A Syrian videographer, Adam Hussein records from a rooftop in Syria what initially caused him to start filming on April 4, 2017. He starts with a pan of the city of Khan Sheikhoun, Syria. It shows plumes of smoke following bombs that had been dropped from Syrian aircraft. But the plumes of smoke don't dissipate like they usually do. The smoke spreads out like a cloud of mist hanging in the air on a summer morning over the San Francisco Bay. But these are more yellow in color and don't burn off as the sun rises. He leaves his rooftop to get a closer look. He records a series of bodies lying in the mud. Then adults gasping for breath. Then children, one after another, doing the same. Some footage shows close-ups of children foaming at the mouth. Then shots of the hospital where he records scene after scene of gas victims, some children being taken in by a brother or a neighbor. Then scenes of patients of all ages, lying on stretchers. Then shrieks of grief from arriving family members.[1]

Clarissa Ward, for CNN, compiles other videos collected from those who witnessed what was going on. If this were a courtroom, her video would serve as an opening statement of proof in a case of the Syrian government's commission of war crimes on its own citizens. Here, the proof is compiled, complete with footage of families who bear witness to what had happened to their children, including footage of their sorrow and grief at the time of burial.[2]

How can this happen in 2017? How can it be allowed to happen? What role should the US play in stopping war crimes from happening? What role the does the UN play in US foreign policy decisions? To answer these questions, we need to take a close look at the Syrian civil war. We need to look at Bashar al-Assad, the president of Syria, and ask about his responsibility for what is happening there. What were the signals he gave that he might resort to war crimes, and how did the US react to these signals?

We next need to look at the US and its foreign policy, and what responsibility it bears for not preventing these atrocities. How has the US played a role in bringing about the situation in Syria? We will start by looking at Syria as a part of general US foreign policy in the Middle East following World War II. Then we will focus on the Obama administration, and the president, in particular, for keys to his reasoning to act or fail to act in Syria.

After all, the civil war has been going on since 2011. In a country of more than 20 million people, there has already been a displacement of close to 11 million of its citizens. Over 4 million are UN-registered refugees. Close to 500,000 Syrians have already died in the civil war. Thousands have been tortured. Fifty thousand have disappeared in Syrian prisons, with no word of their whereabouts. There has also been proof of earlier use of chemical weapons.[3] So why have the US and the UN been so slow to act? We will use the democracy and rule of law versus dictatorship dichotomies and the US's own ambivalence towards how important democracy really is to foreign policy as a lens through which to exam both presidents and their decisions concerning Syria. I will also describe the role that religious belief has in shaping individual decision-making of the various leaders. I will argue that religious belief can be used rather cynically to generate support from a particular political base or enlist the help of allies. It can also be used as an incentive to name parties in a conflict as evil and then justify the use of force, even brutal force, against the created backdrop of an apocalyptic battle between good and evil. Another way of using religious belief is found in Obama's decisions. As opposed to emboldening action, his belief in the evil of the world was turned internally as well as externally. It may have caused him to isolate Assad but then also caused a paralysis in the use of force that contributed to the rise of ISIS to Assad's later turning to Russia and to Assad's second use of chemical weapons and may have also contributed to the refugee crisis. These all made President Obama turn back to Congress for authority to use military force. But we are getting ahead of ourselves. We first need to look at Assad.

One narrative that tells how the US came to confront the dictator versus democracy dilemma starts in March 2011.

Bashar al-Assad's responsibility for committing war crimes. Ascribing intent from actions

As in any criminal case, one of the most difficult issues is determining the intent of the actor. For a jury to determine, absent a voluntary confession from the defendant that he killed the victim, whether the defendant acted with the requisite intent (that the actor was not insane and knew the consequences of his actions, that those actions were wrong, and that he was not under a reasonable belief that a threat to his own life or to the lives of his loved ones or his charges was in progress), the jury learns that it must determine which intent was primary from among a number of possible intentions or motivations. Perhaps the defendant was driven to act because of the way he was raised. Perhaps the defendant came to believe his life was threatened, by earlier experiences he had, that may have made him paranoid, or unreasonable in his conviction of what was required of him when facing a particular threat.

What the jury quickly comes to see in determining what a person's intent is at any given time is a historical reconstruction. Why did the defendant order the bombing? Was he righteously angry, feeling desperate, sad, in the fog of war, with a memory ripe in his mind of what had happened to a close friend or loved one, or was he acting as a result of what he had been taught, despite perhaps not even remembering who had taught him or when. He may defend himself by saying he was acting instinctively, from the very code of his being – whether learned on the street, on the battlefield, in the mosque, or in the classroom. In so acting he was *foundationalist* in his ethics, believing he had no choice because to not so act would violate his sense of himself, or his identity.

The jury is told, nonetheless, to make a determination about what the actor's *main, sole, major purpose* or *intent* had been. And as counselors at law know, sometimes, when confronted with a set of events and circumstances, the actor may come to a realization of what his or her intent had really been. The actor may become all the more determined that he did not have criminal intent. On the other hand, some actors may have enough self-awareness to realize that they did have criminal intent and must take responsibility for their actions. We will return to this latter point in the chapter on Truth and Reconciliation and forgiveness.

In the court of international public opinion, the issues are basically the same. Historical facts can serve as a means to make a determination of what may have been going on in the actor's mind when they made the decisions they made.

My method then will be to list the facts on a timeline and then "mind the gaps." This method is familiar to litigators as it opens up the past events to possible competing narratives. It is in the process of examining the competing narratives, of comparing what we know and what we don't know, what is usually done, and what was done in this case, and what was not done, after the event in question, that one can come to a more nuanced understanding of events in question. The judgment of what it means is more informed. We start our case for what happened in Syria with the case for and against Assad, recognizing that, without a confession, our task is a reconstruction based on circumstantial evidence. Still our case may hold up in the court of history and public opinion.

The case against Assad

The whole situation seemingly could have been avoided if Assad and his regime had not made a series of repressive choices that would lead to international condemnation. The civil war seemed to start from an overreaction to a rather benign protest. In March 2011, protests erupted in the city of Daraa when a group of boys were accused of painting anti-government graffiti on the walls of their school. Assad's security forces chose to move in and detain the boys. The boys' release was sought by their parents, and they were joined in a demonstration on March 15, 2011, held in the capital. The protest took place in Damascus's Old City. On March 18, back in Daraa, security forces opened fire on a gathering of protesters, killing four people. It is easy to see how supporters of the democracy movement would use these killings to drum up support for more demonstrations. As the word spread so did the protests.

Rather than see these demonstrations as ways for protestors to make their voices heard, Bashar al-Assad instead chose to crack down on any demonstrations against the government.

To understand Bashar al-Assad (the son's) reaction to these events, one first needs to understand the history of Syria and then a history of his father.

Alawites and religious tension within Syria[4]

Many non-Muslims know that there is a religious divide between Shia and Sunnis. Fewer understand the long-standing distrust between Sunnis and Alawites in Syria. Alawites (once known as Nusayris) believe in the divinity of Ali, Mohammad's cousin and son-in-law, and so line up more with the Shia than the Sunni. They share in centuries of oppression by Sunnis who believe that such belief makes them infidels.[5]

After centuries of oppression, Alawites became an insular community. One custom in particular reinforced this isolation, namely that of endogamous marriage, according to which the children of unions between Alawites and non-Alawites cannot be initiated into the Alawite community. As one might imagine this causes two key characteristics: a sense of separateness and a disdain for the "Other."

The French, who administered Syria after the fall of the Ottoman Empire, initially provided Alawites with their own state. The French encountered hostility to their rule from the Sunni majority and so encouraged an integration of Alawites and Sunnis, especially through service in the military. The following map (Figure 1.1) shows where the Alawites were congregated during the 20s and 30s.

The division of Syria under French administration in the 1920s

Joshua Landis, a professor of Middle East studies at the University of Oklahoma, explained in a blog post about the Alawites in June 2011:

> There was considerable tension within the Alawi community over the notion of unity with Syria in 1936, which was mandated by the Franco-Syrian treaty of that year. Part of this tension was the fear that Sunnis would discriminate against Alawis in their courts, as had happened in the past. Under Ottoman law, Alawis were refused the right to give testimony in court because they were not considered to be Muslims or People of the Book.[6]

Evidence that this distrust of the Alawites for Sunnis in 1936 had an impact on how Syria would later be governed comes from a letter written by an Alawite to the then Jewish prime minister of France, Leon Blum. The letter emphasized an Alawite objection not just to Sunnis but to Islam generally, as well as the years of oppression the Alawite community has experienced as a minority community. The Alawites wanted guarantees from the French that they would be protected from oppression. Eventually this would lead to the Alawites being seen as a group that was more secular and more neutral than other Muslim groups in Syria. Still, as we will see later, in the emergence of ISIS Assad would see a Sunni backing. This attitude would also lump other rebel groups as associated with Sunnis (backed by Saudi Arabia) and see the terrorist threat as connected to an attempt by Sunnis to return to its repressive majority status. Alawites would see a threat in Sunnis should they ever lose their ruling status in Syria.[7]

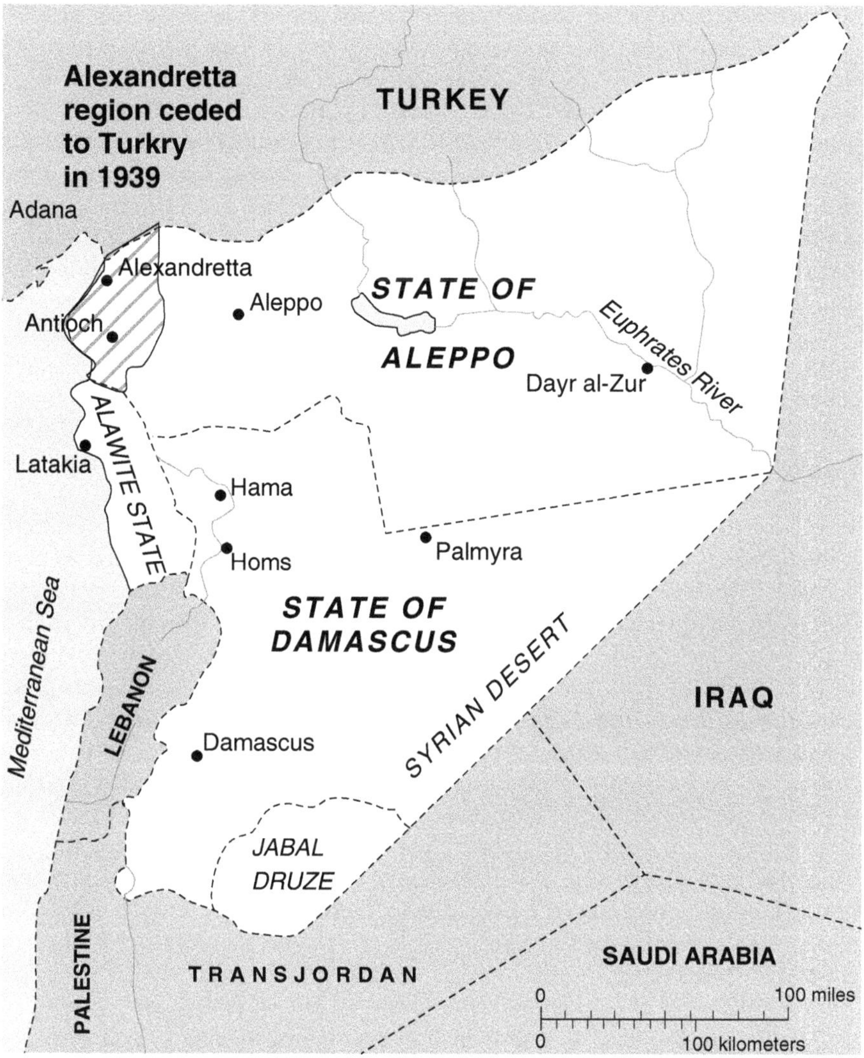

Figure 1.1 Syria Before World War II

In the lead-up to World War II, after their plea to the French prime minister failed to stop plans to integrate the Alawite state into Syria, some Alawites tried a new tactic. They urged assimilation with Shiites in order to gain the protections of a larger minority group. Alawite religious leaders published a number of tracts declaring that Alawites were Shiites and that any Alawite "who did not recognize Islam as his religion and the Koran as his holy book" would not be considered a member of the sect.

Next for our discussion is to place Israel into our understanding of Syria foreign policy. Part of Syria's understanding of itself is not only its colonialist past but also the rise in pan-Arabism in response to what it saw was the West's support of Israel. Key to this history is Syria's 1967 war with Israel. Before the start of the 1967 war, attacks conducted against Israel by fledgling Palestinian guerrilla groups were based in Syria, as well as Lebanon and Jordan. These attacks had increased, leading to a strong response from Israel. In November 1966 an Israeli strike on the village of Al-Samūʿ in the Jordanian West Bank left 18 dead and 54 wounded, and, during an air battle with Syria in April 1967, the Israeli air force shot down six Syrian MiG fighter jets. In addition, Soviet intelligence reports in May indicated that Israel was planning a campaign against Syria, and, although inaccurate, the information further heightened tensions between Israel and its Arab neighbors.

Syria had earlier criticized Egyptian president Gamal Abdel Nasser for Egypt's failure to aid Syria and Jordan against Israel. Syria also complained that Egypt was excusing its lack of involvement in relying on the United Nations Emergency Force (UNEF) stationed at Egypt's border with Israel in the Sinai. Already the UN was being portrayed as a tool of the US and its interests in Israel.

Perhaps, to show himself no tool of the UN, on May 14, 1967, Nasser mobilized Egyptian forces in the Sinai, and on May 18 he formally requested the removal of the UNEF stationed there. Four days later he instituted a blockade, closing the Gulf of Aqaba to Israeli shipping. The result was to endanger the port city of Elat in southern Israel. Jordan then escalated the situation when on 30 May 1967, King Ḥussein of Jordan went to Cairo to sign a mutual defense pact with Egypt, placing Jordanian forces under Egyptian command. Iraq, Syria, Egypt and Jordan all joined forces together.

Early on the morning of June 5, Israel responded. It staged a sudden preemptive air assault against Egypt that destroying more than 90 percent Egypt's air force before it could leave the runway. A similar air assault incapacitated the Syrian air force. Without cover from the air, the Egyptian army was left vulnerable to attack. Within three days the Israelis had achieved an overwhelming victory on the ground, capturing the Gaza Strip and all of the Sinai Peninsula up to the east bank of the Suez Canal.

Jordan honored its commitment to the alliance the same day, commencing an artillery barrage aimed at West Jerusalem. Israel responded with a counterattack – disregarding Israel's warning to King Ḥussein to keep Jordan out of the fight. Already by June 7, Israeli forces had driven Jordanian forces out of East Jerusalem and most of the West Bank.

The UN Security Council called for a ceasefire on June 7 that was immediately accepted by Israel and Jordan. Egypt accepted the following day. Syria held out, however, and continued to shell villages in northern Israel. On June 9 Israel launched an assault on the fortified Golan Heights, capturing it from Syrian forces after a day of heavy fighting. Syria accepted the ceasefire on June 10.

The Arab countries' losses were both humiliating and devastating. Egypt's casualties numbered more than 11,000, with 6,000 for Jordan and 1,000 for Syria, compared with only 700 for Israel. The Arab armies also suffered crippling losses of weaponry and equipment. The lopsidedness of the defeat demoralized both the Arab public and the political elite. Nasser announced his resignation on June 9 but quickly yielded to mass demonstrations calling for him to remain in office. In Israel, which had proved beyond question that it was the region's pre-eminent military power, there were celebrations. Some in Israel attributed its victory as a miracle, orchestrated by the hand of God. The Six-Day War also marked the start of a new phase in the conflict between Israel and the Palestinians, since the conflict created hundreds of thousands of refugees and brought more than 1 million Palestinians in the occupied territories under Israeli rule.

To understand Hafez al-Assad, the father of Bashar, who came to power in the mid-1970s we must understand that he was first and foremost an Alawite. From a small tribe in western Syria, Alawites were then directly aligned with neither Sunnis nor Shi'ites. They saw themselves as Arabs. They soon identified as a political movement called Socialist Ba'athists. As with Ba'athists in Egypt and Palestine they minimized differences between Muslim sects. What it also did for the Alawites was to give them flexibility in future alignments with partners, allowing it to align itself with various religious factions, depending on the respective political advantage. Hafez would form alliances with Christians, Hezbollah (Shi'ites), the Muslim Brotherhood (Sunnis), or whomever would promote Syrian positions. And whatever the source of internal opposition that challenged his governing, Hafez al-Assad would act with brutality to repress it.

Bashar al-Assad seemed haunted by his father's advice, gleaned from experiences from his father's early days in power. Hafez al-Assad had told his son that he was convinced the success of his leadership was dependent on his having acted swiftly and brutally to put down an uprising of the Muslim Brotherhood in the late 1970s and early 1980s. Even though Assad's son was away at school, and largely shielded from these events, their impact was still felt on his psyche.

The sins of the father. Hafez al-Assad. Syria, Lebanon, and the Palestinians

Hafez al-Assad took over the reins of power in the mid-1970s threatened by events both foreign and domestic. On its border, in Lebanon, warring parties had been at it since 1975. The spark that ignited the civil war in Lebanon occurred in Beirut with Phalangists, a Christian political party and militia, pitted against Palestinian militiamen (thought by some observers to be from the Popular Front for the Liberation of Palestine). The confessional layout of Beirut's various quarters facilitated random killing.

Lebanon's political structures became paralyzed that following summer. Lebanon's political system, resulting from its 1943 National Pact, proved inadequate for urgent conflict resolution. To some it seemed that the pact had placed too much faith in the workings of a liberal democracy. The Maronite Christian minority refused to trust the good faith and reasoned representatives of the Muslim majority to respond to violent attacks. It refused to share power, distrusting that the other party would adequately protect Christian liberties. The government could not act effectively because leaders were unable to agree on whether to use the army to stop the bloodletting.

Consequently, in May Prime Minister Rashid Solh and his cabinet resigned, and a new government was formed under Rashid Karami. Although there were many calls for his resignation, President Franjiyah steadfastly retained his office. As various other groups took sides, the fighting spread to other areas of the country, forcing residents in towns with mixed sectarian populations to seek safety in regions where their sect was dominant. Even so, the militias became embroiled in a pattern of attack followed by retaliation, including acts against uninvolved civilians.

Syria, on the immediate border, had various groups and militias aligned with Lebanese groups. Although the two warring factions were often characterized in the West as Christian versus Muslim, their individual composition was far more complex. Those in favor of maintaining the status quo came to be known as the Lebanese Front. The groups included primarily the Maronite militias of the Jumayyil, Shamun, and Franjiyah clans, often led by the sons of Zuama. Also in this camp were various militias of Maronite religious orders.

The side seeking change, usually referred to as the Lebanese National Movement, was far less cohesive and organized, though it had a vaguely associated Palestinian base. For the most part it was led by Kamal Jumblatt and included a variety of militias from leftist organizations and guerrillas from rejectionist Palestinian (non-mainstream Palestinian Liberation Organization [PLO]) organizations.

By the end of 1975, no side held a decisive military advantage, but it was generally acknowledged that the Lebanese Front had performed as well as expected against the disorganized Lebanese National Movement. The political hierarchy, composed of the old Zuama and politicians, still was incapable of maintaining peace except for occasional, short-lived ceasefires. Reform was discussed, but little headway was made toward any significant improvements. Syria, which was deeply concerned about the flow of events in Lebanon, also proved powerless to enforce calm through diplomatic means. And, most ominous of all, the Lebanese Army, which generally had stayed out of the strife, began to show signs of factionalizing and threatened to bring its heavy weaponry to bear on the conflict.

Syrian diplomatic involvement grew during 1976, but it had little success in restoring order in the first half of the year. In January it organized a ceasefire and set up the High Military Committee through which it negotiated with all sides. These negotiations, however, were complicated by other events, especially Lebanese Front-Palestinian confrontations. That month the Lebanese Front began a siege of Tall Zatar, a densely populated Palestinian refugee camp in East Beirut; the Lebanese Front also overran and leveled Karantina, a Muslim quarter in East Beirut. These actions finally brought the main forces of the PLO, the Palestine Liberation Army (PLA), into the battle. Together, the PLA and the Lebanese National Movement took the town of Ad Damur, a Shamun stronghold about 17 kilometers south of Beirut.

In spite of these setbacks, through Syria's diplomatic efforts, compromises were achieved. On February 14, 1976, in what was considered a political breakthrough, Syria helped negotiate a 17-point reform program known as the Constitutional Document. Yet by March this progress was derailed by the disintegration of the Lebanese Army. In that month dissident Muslim troops, led by Lieutenant Ahmad Khatib, mutinied, creating the Lebanese Arab Army. Joining the Lebanese National Movement, they made significant penetrations into Christian-held Beirut and launched an attack on the presidential palace, forcing Franjiyah to flee to Mount Lebanon. Continuing its search for a domestic political settlement to the war, in May the Chamber of Deputies elected Ilyas Sarkis to take over as president when Franjiyah's term expired in September. But Sarkis had strong backing from Syria and, as a consequence, was unacceptable to Jumblatt, who was known to be antipathetic to Syrian president Hafiz al-Assad and who insisted on a "military solution." Accordingly, the Lebanese National Movement (LNM) successfully pressed assaults on Mount Lebanon and other Christian-controlled areas.

As the Lebanese Front faltered, Hafez al-Assad faced two potential scenarios, neither of which was acceptable. One was the establishment in Lebanon of an independent Christian state, aligned with Israel or, two, if the Lebanese National Movement won the war, the creation of a radical, hostile state on Syria's western border. To prevent either scenario, at the end of May 1976 Syria took its own military action against the LNM. It hoped for a quick end to the fighting. Assad's decision, however, did not anticipate the realities in Lebanon. Its forces suffered many casualties. Its adversaries, protecting their homes, provided the kind of fierce resistance that is born of desperation.

It also placed Hafez al-Assad and his ruling Alawites, though supposedly neutral between Sunni and Shia, on the side of the Christians in Lebanon. In so doing Assad provoked outrage from much of the Arab world. Instead of backing away, Assad doubled down. He decided to launch a massive force to destroy the LNM. This time his forces were far more successful than they had been in earlier battles: in two weeks Assad had almost completely wiped out LNM. But then, in a move his son has not yet learned to make, Assad showed some restraint and entered into talks. Rather than crushing the resistance altogether, in October 1976 Syria chose to participate in an Arab peace conference held in Riyadh, Saudi Arabia. That conference was then followed that same month by an Arab League Meeting.

These conferences produced a formal end to the Lebanese civil war. Resolving the underlying causes was left for another day. There was no accountability for various atrocities. The fog of that war continues to hang over Lebanon to this day. However, Assad did legitimate Syria's presence in Lebanon. Syria was behind the establishment of an Arab Deterrent Force (ADF), technically formed by the Arab League. It would not take long for Syria to take it over. By January 1977 the ADF consisted of 30,000 men, of whom 27,000 were Syrian. Because of his difficulties in reforming the Lebanese Army, President Sarkis, the ADF's nominal commander, requested renewal of the ADF's mandate a number of times.

Thus, after more than one-and-a-half years of fighting, an uneasy truce was maintained in Lebanon. By some accounts total deaths from the war may have approached 44,000, with about 180,000 wounded. Thousands of others were displaced or left homeless or had migrated. Beirut was divided into Muslim and Christian sectors, separated by the so-called Green Line. Much of the proud and ancient city had once again, as from the time of the Crusades, been destroyed.

Perhaps Hafez al-Assad learned that the liberal democracy envisioned for Lebanon was not what it was cracked up to be. Instead of leading to power sharing and cooperation, these factions reverted to using religion to protect tribal structures. Christians made secret alliances with both Syria and Israel. The various Palestinian factions also made alliances with whoever could help their cause. The result was a dysfunctional and corrupt system and a divided government where every sector of the city was structured in a way to protect power and exact bribes. In any event, Hafez al-Assad most likely became less willing to see democracy as the political system that would inevitably govern in Syria. Better to rule like a dictator, enforcing your will on behalf of your tribe, Lion that you are for the Alawite, than to put any faith in democracy.

Hafez al-Assad faces a coup at home

A more threatening rebellion was brewing at home. The first hint of the impending attempt to overthrow the Ba'ath Party rule came in June 1979, when the Muslim Brotherhood massacred 50 Alawite cadets in the dining room of the military academy in Aleppo.

Then in June 1980, the fighting became personal. Extremists were able to get close enough to Assad to throw two grenades at him. Assad kicked one grenade away while a bodyguard flung himself on the second in an act of heroic self-sacrifice. In revenge, the military unit controlled by Mr. Assad's headstrong younger brother, Rifaat, descended on a desert prison near Palmyra and gunned down at least 250 religious dissidents in their cells.

With every action there is a counter-reaction. The Muslim extremists next rose up in 1982 in Hama. They killed Ba'ath Party officials and broadcasted appeals from mosques for a nationwide insurrection.

In pursuing the rebels, the Syrian military leveled half the city of Hama, killing at least 10,000 residents. The carnage brought widespread condemnation in the West, but it was the kind of act that ensured Mr. Assad's utter control. When the choice came down to spilling blood or preserving his hold on power, there was really no question.

"He wouldn't be apologetic," recalled Ambassador Christopher Ross, who served as American envoy to Damascus for most of the 1990s. "Assad would justify it entirely by saying it was the necessary price to end years and years of Muslim Brotherhood terrorism."[8] He was now using religion more explicitly, aligning himself with his tribe, the Alawites, and the years of oppression the tribe experienced at the hand of the Sunnis. The lesson learned by Hafez al-Assad and his Alawite security forces was that brutal repression was the only viable option to insurgent challenges. Part of his justification was the demonization of his opponents and the attribution of responsibility to their supporters, family, and civilians. He used religion to justify his oppression.

Bashar al-Assad

The international community is often puzzled when a son takes over for his father. Did the son learn anything from his father's mistakes? And what impact did any education outside the country play in shaping the son's thinking?

One might think that Bashar al-Assad had the opportunity to learn different lessons about how the world works, and in a context where he wasn't expected to someday become president of Syria. Born in September 1965, Bashar al-Assad was not the first son if succession were to be determined by monarchical pecking orders. By the time Bashar was 8, the original 1950s' constitution had been suspended and reinstated four times. In 1973 his father succeeded in enacting a new constitution that would serve Syria till 2012. It consolidated power in the president, head of the Ba'athist Party, and so controlled by Alawites. It had on paper a legislature, an independent judiciary, and a list of fully protected human rights.[9] Democracy appeared to be on the rise, despite the fact that Syria had aligned itself with the Soviets during the Cold War.

Not expected to follow his father, his initial interests were in the health care. At 14 he joined the Ba'ath Youth Movement, as did most of his fellow students at the Hurriya School in Damascus. He did not go abroad for his Medical education, graduating instead from the University of Damascus, College of Medicine in 1988. In the four years following graduation, he completed his residency in ophthalmology. He was no stranger to the horror of war, caring for soldiers at Tishrin military hospital in Damascus. He also went abroad for more medical training, studying in London at the Western Eye Hospital. Bashar al-Assad was a doctor whose boss recalled him as humble and whom nurses considered exemplary in reassuring anxious patients about to undergo anesthetic.[10]

It must have been somewhat unsettling to Hafez-al Assad, when the Soviet Union collapsed in March 1990. Who would have Syria's back in its dealings with Israel and the US? Perhaps it would be better for Syria to move more toward the West and gradually establish relations with Israel. But, as we will see, this was not to be, for by 2000, the Russian state and Syria would once more be closely aligned. In any event, one wonders how Bashar might have viewed the collapse. He may have asked himself what this meant for the future of Syria.

Then, in 1994, when his older brother Basil and the heir apparent to the presidency died in a high-speed car crash, Al-Bashir was called back to Syria and put on the fast track for grooming for leadership. He started military training. He matriculated in the military academy at Homs, north of Damascus. By 1999 he reached the rank of army colonel. In addition, he led an anti-corruption effort that reputedly led to the arrest of high-profile political figures for corruption. According to the government, some of these figures were even put on trial.

Little is known about the role that religious beliefs play in Bashar's thinking. Like his father, he appears to be predominately pragmatic, aligning with various religious groups for political support and ready to shift allegiances when it fits his purposes. Early on he appeared to support the Muslim Brotherhood, and they him. This has led him to align with Iran, as its militia has joined forces with Syrian troops in the fight against ISIS. At the same time, there is significant evidence that Assad was buying oil from ISIS, and thereby them, in its fight against other Sunni–Saudi-backed rebel groups in Syria. Some commentators feel that Assad saw ISIS as a straw man that he could use as an excuse for his fighting against other dissidents in Syria. In any event, Bashar's religious alignment with Shiite Islam appears to be primarily an alignment of convenience.

As to hints at a foreign policy doctrine or governing philosophy or set of principles that would provide a guide to his use of power, there is little to go on. His surprise rise to power and then need to act decisively in response to events, gave little time for developing a theory. What we come away with is that he continued, like his father before him, a sort of Syria first foreign policy, defining Syria in relationship to that which promoted his own ability to rule. In that regard, he is a representative of the dangers of a "country first"-driven foreign policy. Where the dictator is under threat, that policy can quickly turn to the forming of inconsistent and apparently arbitrary alliances if such alliances help the dictator survive and maintain personal power.

Early on, it was not clear Bashar would go in the direction of expanding his authoritarian powers. He initially cultivated a reputation that would appeal to the modern Syrian. He participated in projects to develop the internet and to provide internet access in Syria. He became president of the Syrian Computer Society. There were high hopes among many Syrians at that time that he would be more open and democratic, if he were ever to take over the presidency.

On June 10, 2000, in Damascus, his father died of a heart attack. Hafez al-Assad had ruled Syria for three decades. During his reign he had transformed Syria from a Middle East bit player into a major force in the Middle East. He was known most in the US for his intransigence with regard to Israel, refusing any peace without Syria getting back all of its land. He was 69. But had his secular pragmatism set up his son, Bashar, to be able to move to a more open and democratic society? The answer to that question was unclear.

Bashar al-Assad's turn

In his inaugural address, Bashar al-Assad promised wide-ranging reforms, including modernizing the economy, fighting corruption, and launching "our own democratic experience." This was not long before the authorities released hundreds of political prisoners and allowed the first independent newspapers for more than three decades to begin publishing. A group of intellectuals pressing for democratic reforms were even permitted to hold public political meetings and publish statements. The "Damascus Spring," as it became known, was short-lived.

By early 2001, the intellectuals' meetings began to be closed down or to be refused licenses, and several leading opposition figures were arrested. Limits on the freedom of the press were also soon put back in place.

For the rest of the decade, emergency rule remained in effect. The many security agencies continued to detain people without arrest warrants and to hold them incommunicado for lengthy periods. Islamists of various stripes and Kurdish activists were frequently sentenced to long prison terms. Any economic liberalization benefitted only the elite and Bashar's allies rather than creating opportunities for all.

Why, then, this sudden turn? Many analysts believe that reform under Bashar al-Assad has been inhibited by the "old guard," members of the leadership loyal to his late father and the ideals thereof. His family is also said to have played a role in encouraging him to suppress dissent, including his brother Maher, the head of the Republican Guard, and his first cousin, Rami Makhlouf, arguably the most powerful economic figure in Syria.

But what responsibility did Assad bear for the turn toward repression? I will turn to our timeline analysis to see what conclusions can be drawn.

Hardline diplomacy

In foreign policy, Bashar al-Assad continued his father's hardline policy towards Israel. He repeatedly said that there would be no peace unless occupied land was returned "in full," and continued to support militant groups opposed to Israel, including Hezbollah and Iran.

His vocal opposition to the 2003 US-led invasion of Iraq, and the Syrian authorities' tacit support of Iraqi insurgent groups, prompted anger in Washington, but these moves proved popular in Syria and in the wider region.

Syria's already tense ties with the US soured in the wake of the February 2005 assassination of Lebanon's former prime minister, Rafik Hariri. Political leaders in Lebanon suspected Bashar-al Assad. Lebanon had petitioned the UN and was able to get a Security Council Resolution (announced by a Russian Council member in 2006) to establish a special tribunal to investigate Hariri's death. Hariri had been killed in a car bomb. He had been threatened before his death by Assad. Suspicions immediately pointed at President Assad, his inner circle, and the Syrian security services, which dominated Lebanon. Despite their denials of involvement, international outrage at the killing forced Syrian troops to withdraw from Lebanon that April, ending a 29-year military presence.

Assad's involvement was suspected for three main reasons. First, let's look at evidence of the threat.

Chronology of events, mid-2004–September 2005[11]

August 26: Rafik Hariri meets in Damascus with Syrian president Bashar Assad to discuss the extension of the term of President Lahoud. (President Lahoud, of Armenian dissent, was commander in chief of the military before becoming president in 1999. The Lebanese constitution had to be amended to make this happen, and its amendment was supposedly orchestrated with the backing of Syria, who had troops stationed in the country. When Lahoud took over he took steps to expand his power, and Hariri, the past president and then prime minister, balked at his actions. Hariri was summoned to Syria for Assad for Assad to express his "support" for Lahoud, who was believed to be the key to Syria's control in Lebanon. Lahoud also had support from Hezbollah, affiliated with Iran. Harari had support from Druze, Christians, and Sunnis).[12]

September 2: The United Nations Security Council adopts Resolution 1559 concerning the situation in the Middle East, calling for the withdrawal of all foreign forces from Lebanon.

September 3: The Rafik Hariri bloc approves the extension law for President Lahoud.

September 3: The Lebanese parliament adopts the extension law for President Lahoud and forwards it to the Lebanese government for execution.

September 7: Economy Minister Marwan Hamadeh, Culture Minister Ghazi Aridi, Minister of Refugee Affairs Abdullah Farhat, and Environment Minister Fares Boueiz resigned from the cabinet in protest at the constitutional amendment.

September 9: Prime Minister Rafik Hariri indicates to journalists that he will resign.

October 1: Assassination attempt on Marwan Hamadeh (a Druze politician and journalist) in Beirut, Lebanon.

October 4: Rafik Hariri resigns as prime minister.

October 11: Syrian president Bashar Assad delivers a speech condemning his critics within Lebanon and the United Nations.

October 19: The UN Security Council expresses concern that Resolution 1559 has not been implemented.

October 20: President Lahoud accepts Hariri's resignation and names Omar Karame to form the new government.

February 14: Rafik Hariri and 22 other individuals are killed in a massive blast in a seafront area of central Beirut. (Shortly thereafter, on the same day the director of Al Jazeera TV in Beirut received a telephone call from a man who stated that the Nasra and Jihad Group in Greater Syria claimed responsibility for the assassination of Mr. Hariri. This message was broadcast shortly thereafter).

February 25: The United Nations Fact-Finding Mission arrives in Lebanon.

March 8: Hezbollah organizes a 1 million strong "pro-Syrian" march.

March 14: A Christian/Sunni-led counter-demonstration demands the withdrawal of Syrian troops and the arrest of the chief of the security and intelligence services.

March 19: A bomb explodes in Jdeideh, a northern suburb of Beirut, wounding 11 people.

March 23: Three people are killed and three others wounded in an explosion in the Kaslik shopping center, north of Beirut.

March 25: The UN Fact-Finding Mission issues its report in New York.

March 26: A suitcase bomb explodes in an industrial zone in northeast Beirut, injuring six.
April 1: Nine people are injured in an underground garage in an empty commercial and residential building in Brummana.
April 7: The Security Council forms the United Nations International Independent Investigation Commission into the assassination of Rafik Hariri and 22 others on February 14.
April 19: Lebanon's prime minister Najib Mikati announces that parliamentary elections will be held on 30 May 2005.
April 22: General Jamil Al-Sayyed, head of the Internal Security Forces and General Ali Al-Hajj, head of the Sûreté Générale, decide to put their functions at the disposal of Prime Minister Najib al Makati.
April 26: The last Syrian troops leave Lebanon ending a 29-year military presence.
April 26: The United Nations Verification Mission starts its mission to verify the complete withdrawal of Syrian military and intelligence agents from Lebanon and its full compliance with the Resolution 1559.
May 6: A bomb explodes in Jounieh north of Beirut, injuring 29 people.
May 7: Parliament convenes to adopt the proposed changes to the electoral law of 2000.
May 30: The first round of the elections was held. The Rafik Hariri Martyr List, a coalition of Saad Hariri's Future Movement, the Progressive Socialist Party, and the Qornet Shehwan Gathering, won the majority of the seats in Parliament.
June 2: Journalist Samir Kassir is killed when his car explodes in east Beirut.
June 21: Former Lebanese Communist Party leader George Hawi is killed when his car explodes close to his home in Wata Musaytbeh.
June 30: Fouad Siniora, former finance minister under Rafik Hariri, forms the new government composed of 23 ministers.
July 12: Defense minister Elias Murr is wounded, and two other people are killed in a car bomb attack in Beirut.
July 22: At least three people are wounded near Rue Monot when a bomb explodes in the Ashrafieh quarter.
August 22: Three persons are injured in an explosion in a garage near the Promenade Hotel in the Al-Zalqa area north of Beirut.
September 16: One person is killed and ten others wounded by a bomb near a bank in Ashrafieh.
September 19: One person is killed and two wounded in a small explosion at the Kuwaiti information office in Beirut.
September 25: A car bomb injures prominent news anchor May Chidiac in north Beirut.

The commission reached a number of conclusions. It found that the assassination was carried out by a well-organized and sophisticate organization with ties to Syria. It found that it was well known that Syrian Security forces were operating in Lebanon at the time. It was troubled that the Syrian government refused to cooperate with its requests for information. It recommended to the UN that a special tribunal be formed to continue prosecution and investigation.

As can be seen from the events in May 2005 and in the months following, the political situation changed in Lebanon, restoring power to a Harari back coalition. It created the environment for a formal request from Lebanon for a UN prosecution and establishment of a tribunal. With the Syrian troop presence removed, the work of UN slowed. Perhaps, as I will argue in Chapter 3, the UN started to confront that the role of the international criminal tribunal might affect peacemaking opportunities going forward. In any event, it would not be until 2016, that the tribunal would start trials of five individuals it found were directly involved in the assassination of Harari. The delay also coincided with the UN's move away from specialized tribunals to house its investigations in the permanent International Criminal Court (ICC) in The Hague.

Still, the court, indicting five different members of Hezbollah as having been involved in the murder, who potentially could point the finger at Assad, may have already forced Assad into a corner on other international matters. He has some relief from the fact that all are on the run, and so are being tried in absentia. Both Hezbollah and Syria deny any involvement, calling it all a plot by the US to undermine the Assad regime.

Bashar al-Assad and Russia

Starting in 2000 Syria aligned itself more and more with Russia, continuing to buy military jets, weapons, and equipment from Russia. Putin would establish a naval base in Syria, the only Russian naval base on the Mediterranean Sea. Even though Russia had initially joined in the investigation of Harari's assassination, it maybe that Russia was more focused on its own developments toward joining the West, than focused on extending its influence in the Middle East. Yet since 2005, when the assassination occurred, as Assad has felt he that he has been the true target of the international investigations, he may have also drawn more support from Russia. Perhaps, then these two forces are what is behind his hardening positions against dissent over the course of his term in office.

In any event, there were international diplomatic overtures made to him in starting in 2006, with some early success. Iraq's leadership, in the midst of the US war against Saddam Hussein and shortly between when Saddam was captured and killed, established diplomatic relations with Syria for the first time after nearly a quarter century. Then, in March 2007, the European Union opened a dialogue with Syria. Syria and Israel were also reportedly starting to talk. And in the following month US House of Representatives Speaker Nancy Pelosi traveled to Syria to meet with President Bashar al-Assad in Damascus. She was the highest-ranked US politician to visit Syria in recent years. Secretary of State Condoleezza Rice met Syrian foreign minister Walid Muallem the following month in the first contact at such a level for two years.

In May 2007, Mr. Assad won another referendum with 97 percent of the vote, extending his term for another seven years. He seemed to have enough popular support that he could have become more open and democratic, yet events soon took him in the opposite direction.

Mystery site and back and forth with the West

In September 2007, Israeli forces destroyed what they said was a nuclear facility under construction in Syria. The Syrian government claimed that it was an unused military facility. One can only imagine what impact this might have had on Assad. Having had recent discussions with Israel. Assad may have felt misled. Invasion of Syria's airspace and the destruction of property, if not the loss of life, must have been humiliating. Syria was unable to defend itself. As we will see, the Israeli air force continues to this day to make strikes in Syria. Beyond threatening to rain down SCUD missiles on Tel Aviv, there is little that Syria can do.

But it is not for want of trying. Between 2007 and 2010, the value of Russian arms deals with Syria more than doubled – to $4.7 billion from $2.1 billion US dollars – compared with 2003 to 2006. The ability of Syria to actually pay for the weapons has always been a bit iffy. One reason why Russia may be so devoted to Assad is that if he is deposed, the values of Russian loans to Syria might disappear.[13]

Still, some in Europe appeared to also be making overtures into Syria and Bashar seemed to be open to them. In July 2008 President Assad met with the French president Nicolas Sarkozy in Paris. This meeting was said to signal the end of the diplomatic isolation of Syria by the West that followed the assassination of former Lebanese prime minister Rafik Hariri in 2005. In October of the same year, Syria also established diplomatic relations with Lebanon for the first time since both countries gained their independence in the 1940s. Perhaps things were opening up? The US picked up on these signals. In March 2009, Jeffrey Feltman, acting assistant US secretary of state for the Near East, visits Damascus with White House national security aide Daniel Shapiro. It was the first high-level US diplomatic mission for nearly four years. Feltman met with Syrian foreign minister Walid Muallem. If one were looking for positive signs, that developments were under way toward a more market economy in Syria need to be noted. It set up a stock exchange. And by the end of March 2009, trading launched on its stock exchange in a gesture towards liberalizing the state-controlled economy.

It is important to remember that Assad sat in-country, caught among Israel, Lebanon, Iran, Iraq, and Jordan. Is it any wonder that he would make a number of alliances, some with apparently contradictory motivations? One of those alliances was with Hamas, who was obviously embroiled in a political and terrorist fight with Israel over Gaza and the West Bank. Unfortunately, then, Assad got caught playing both sides of the conflict between Israel and the Palestinians. In May 2010 the US would renew sanctions against Syria, citing alleged Syrian support of terrorist groups. The US had also found evidence that Syria was seeking to acquire weapons of mass destruction and had provided Hezbollah with SCUD missiles in violation of UN resolutions.

"External conspiracy"

When anti-government protests erupted in the southern city of Daraa in mid-March 2011, President Bashar al-Assad initially appeared to be unsure how to respond, but it was not long before force was used against the demonstrations. Protesters tear down a portrait of Bashar al-Hafez al-Assad in Deraa (March 2011).

Mr. Hafez al-Assad was quick to blame "a small number of troublemakers and saboteurs" for the unrest.[14]

In his first speech regarding the protests, two weeks after the first unrest, he insisted that questions of reform and economic grievances had been overshadowed by a small number of troublemakers and saboteurs who had sought to spread discontent and rebellion among Syrians, all as part of an alleged external conspiracy to undermine the country's stability and national unity.

In April, Mr. Assad dismissed the cabinet and officially lifted the hated Emergency Law, which had been in place since 1963 and under which security forces detained and tortured people with impunity. But days later, the crackdown against protesters was stepped up. Over the next month, soldiers supported by tanks were sent into restive towns and cities to combat "armed criminal gangs." Then, security forces raided a sit-in in Syria's third-largest city, Homs, where thousands of people tried to re-create the mood of Cairo's Tahrir Square, the epicenter of protests against Egypt's autocrat Hosni Mubarak. By mid-May, 2011, the death toll had already reached 1,000. Despite the security forces' concerted and ruthless efforts, along with pledges by President Assad to start a "national dialogue" on reform, the uprising continued unabated in almost every part of the country. Opposition supporters began to take up arms, first to defend themselves and then to oust loyalist forces from their respective areas. The president denied having ordered the military to kill or to be brutal in its crackdown on anti-government protesters, saying that only a "crazy person" would kill his own people.

Then, on August 18, 2011, President Barack Obama called on Assad to resign and orders Syrian government assets frozen. Until then, and even for a time following, some in the international community were hopeful that the US and the UN would find a way to bring Syria to the negotiating table. Perhaps, with the price of oil falling and budgets in Russia and Iran tight, the hope was that they would pressure Assad to compromise. And there was even "hope" that someone in Assad's inner circle would assassinate him. It seemed, however, that the more desperate the situation the more repressive Assad and his group became. Assad went to the media to give interviews to help explain what was going on in Syria. He played up the predictable themes, denying the accounts of atrocities, saying he would never use barrel bombs on his own people, and that these acts were either fabrications of the West or alternatively committed by terrorists. He then declared himself justified in acting with brutal force in the face of such terrorism.

Again let's look at the timeline to see what narrative emerges. This timeline of events is reported in Casten Wieland's book *Syria-A Decade of Lost Changes: Repression and Revolution from Damascus Spring to Arab Spring.*[15]

2011 January: Assad was in no mood to compromise. He promised in a public address to crush with an "iron fist" terrorism in Syria.

2011, April: Security forces raid a sit-in in Syria's third-largest city, Homs, where thousands of people are killed.

2011, Summer: Fighting spreads to Aleppo, Syria's largest city and its former commercial capital.

2011, August 9. Assad severed international relationships further isolating himself. One example is Turkey. Relations between Syria and Turkey strengthened from 2004 till 2011. The two countries 'abolished each other's' visas and established free trade across their borders" (57). Once the uprisings started, Turkey "opted for the side of human rights and democracy" (57). On August 9, 2011, Turkey's foreign minister Ahmed Davutoğlu traveled to Damascus to deliver a message from Erdogan "that called for an end to the violence, and on the acceptance of a Turkish-sponsored peace plan" (57). Assad responded, "If you came for a compromise, then we reject it. If you want to have war, then you can have it-in the entire region" (Original quote source: "Unruhen in Syrien 'Wenn Sie Krieg wollen, können Sie ihn haben'," in *Süddeutsche Zeitung*, August 9, 2011, translated from German by the Wieland).

2011, September: "The Arab League presented two peace initiative in September and November 2011. Reportedly, several Arab states and Russia offered asylum to Assad to defuse the political situation. The mediation attempts included a call to halt all violence against civilians and to withdraw Syrian troops from the cities. The League urged Syrians to avoid sectarianism and-entirely in line with the Syrian government-strongly recommended not to create a pretext for any kind of foreign intervention. . . . The initiative moreover called on Assad to commit to the political reforms he had announced, including a multi-party system. Assad chose not to benefit from either of the initiatives, although he (58) formally accepted to the second one (59)."[16] After these proposals, however, the killings continued (59). In November 2011, the Arab League suspended Syria's membership (59).

March 2012: General Secretary Kofi Annan was "selected to act as a mediator" (60). "But Assad's forces chose to ignore Annan's peace plan, too, and continued shelling Syrian cities" (60).

> The report presented at the UN Human Rights Council found evidence of hundreds of summary executions; the use of live ammunition against demonstrations; the widespread deployment of snipers during protests; the detention and torture of people of all ages; the blockading of towns and cities by the security forces and the destruction of water supplies. Security forces were found guilty of systematic human rights violations. Soldiers were ordered to 'shoot to kill' unarmed demonstrators. Patterns existed of arbitrary arrests and enforced disappearances. Torture was pervasive, which suggested that it was state-sanctioned policy. Men and boys were sexually abused at military facilities.

2012 August 20: Obama says the use of chemical weapons would be a "red line" that would change his calculus on intervening in the civil war and have "enormous consequences."

2013 March 19: The Syrian government and opposition trade accusations over a gas attack that killed some 26 people, including more than a dozen government soldiers, in the town of Khan al-Assal in northern Syria. A UN investigation later finds that sarin nerve gas was used, but does not identify a culprit.

2013 August 21: Hundreds of people suffocate in rebel-held suburbs of the Syrian capital, with many suffering from convulsions, pinpoint pupils, and foaming at the mouth. UN investigators visit the sites and determine that ground-to-ground missiles loaded with sarin were fired on civilian areas while residents slept. The US and others blame the Syrian government, the only party to the conflict known to have sarin gas.

2013 August 31: Obama says he will go to Congress for authorization to carry out punitive strikes against the Syrian government but appears to lack the necessary support in the legislature.

2013 September 27: The UN Security Council orders Syria to account for and destroy its chemical weapons stockpile, following a surprise agreement between Washington and Moscow, averting US strikes. The Security Council threatens to authorize the use of force in the event of non-compliance.

2013 October 14: Syria becomes a signatory to the Chemical Weapons Convention, prohibiting it from producing, stockpiling or using chemical weapons.

2014 June 23: The Organization for the Prohibition of Chemical Weapons says it has removed the last of the Syrian government's chemical weapons. Syrian opposition officials maintain that the government's stocks were not fully accounted for and that it retained supplies.

Russian involvement

2015 September: Russia was invited by Syria to help it fight terrorist opposition groups in Syria. From then on Russia jets have provided air support to Syrian government troops as they have retaken land previously held by ISIS and other opposition groups. Since then Assad as returned to hardline positions in negotiations with the UN and opposition groups.

2017 January: Russia, Iran, and Turkey agree to enforce a ceasefire between the government and non-Islamist rebels, after talks between the two sides in Kazakhstan.

2017 February 28: Russia, a stalwart ally of the Syrian government, and China veto a UN Security Council resolution authorizing sanctions against the Syrian government for chemical weapons use.[17]

2017 April 4: At least 58 people are killed in what doctors say could be a nerve gas attack on the town of Khan Sheikhoun in the rebel-held Idlib Province. Victims show signs of suffocation, convulsions, foaming at the mouth, and pupil constriction. Witnesses say the attack was carried out by either Russian or Syrian Sukhoi jets. Moscow and Damascus deny responsibility.

2017 April 4: President Donald Trump issues a statement saying that the "heinous" actions of Assad's government are the direct result of Obama administration's "weakness and irresolution."

2017 April 5: Trump says Assad's government has "crossed a lot of lines" with the suspected chemical attack in Syria.

2017 April 6: The US fired a barrage of cruise missiles into Syria Thursday night in retaliation for this week's gruesome chemical weapons attack against civilians, US officials said. It was the first direct American assault on the Syrian government and Trump's most dramatic military order since becoming president. Trump said the strike on Syria was in the "vital national security interest" of the US.

2017 May: US decides to arm the Peoples Protection Unit, (YPG), otherwise known as the Kurdish Popular Protection Units. These fight alongside the main opposition Syrian Democratic Forces, which captures the important Tabqa dam from Islamic State.

2017 June: The US shoots down a Syrian government jet.

2017 July: The Trump administration announces that it is discontinuing its covert military support for moderate rebel groups in Syria.

Assad might now feel that he is on his way to winning the war. And this may change things dramatically for peacemakers. For now Assad can participate in the shaping of the narrative against him. Evidence of that is already appearing in the press. Assad, with Russia backing, is blaming others for the use of chemical weapons on April 4.[18] Assad asks why would he need to resort to using chemical weapons if he is winning the war. (Of course, the answer is he was seeking to demoralize the opposition in order to win the war more quickly.) Second, he argues that others used them, perhaps with the permission of the US, to try to make Syria look bad and to undermine Assad's legitimacy. (Who else would have access to that kind of weapon and how would they get it?) Third, he argues that it was an accident that was the result of the bombing of a weapons dump held by other military groups? (How did the cloud of gas spread so far from the dump to the city?) In any event it shows the ability of Assad, with Russia backing to further cloud the issue.[19]

As one reviews the timeline of Assad's actions it is clear that he has been accused of a number of different things, that may evoke different responses. He is accused of assassinating Harari. He would say the allegations have not been proved and that even if his security forces had been involved in backing Hezbollah, it is no different than the time of backing the US had been giving rebel groups in Syria. It should prevent him from serving as president. He was pursuing Syrian foreign policy in Lebanon, and political forces there presented a real threat to Syria.

As to his use of force in combatting political uprisings, as we have seen, he has a number of excuses. This was strategy learned from his father. It is necessary against radical groups that themselves engage in terrorist activities and embed themselves in civilian populations. The rise of ISIS complicates the case against Assad, as many in the international community have joined forces to try to root it out. Civilian casualties have resulted from these attacks, from different sources.

Assad's systematic killing and torture of political opponents is perhaps his most difficult issue to be resolved. We will discuss this more in the next chapters, but for it to be truly resolved, there may need to be involvement of a judicial body to make findings of fact, and determinations of intent. The UN and various human rights groups may be well on their way to providing the proof needed to make this determination. Similarly, the refugee problem may be at its heart, a problem of intent, coupled with causation. Assad would argue that refugees chose to leave, and so were unintended consequences of violence used on both sides.

And so we return to where we started.

Use of Chemical Weapons

We must pause here in the story to assess Assad's responsibility for his use of chemical weapons. To extend we have seen his defenses in response to the earlier allegations. Why do sons repeat the sins of their fathers and respond brutally to civilian populations were terrorism resides? Or why did Assad, who, at 34, was making all the sounds of opening up and becoming democratic, choose the path of dictatorship, barrel bombs, and chemical weapons over democracy and rule of law? Some blame it on the power structure in place that pushes the "young kid" to prove his toughness. Perhaps young Assad is like a young John Kennedy, who may have even reached out through his brother Robert to the Russians during his transition only to later order the Bay of Pigs invasion, and the blockading of Cuba. Assad like Kennedy, might blame his hardline get-tough approach on the nature and determination of his opponents.

Depending on one's perspective, the US serves the role Soviets used to serve in other countries unlined with a superpower, as an excuse for the US and its allies to become fearful of a superpower's intention. As Bob Pastor (former president Carter's White House aide, member of his National Security Council, head of Latin America) has argued,[20] the US may have inadvertently served to radicalize Viet Cong, Osama bin Laden, and North Korean leader, Kim il Sun (and others have seen the US as doing the same with al Shabbat[21]). In each of these cases, the US missed an opportunity early on to befriend someone who seemed open to partnering with the US. These leaders and their followers seek help from others, including Russia. This was one story about how the Viet Cong moved from freedom fighter to communist terrorist in the days before the Vietnam War. Or, more recently it is the story that is told about how al Shabbat has become radicalized from a group providing services to the poor to radical fundamentalist Islamist when attacked by US-backed Ethiopians.[22] How come these opportunities are missed? An enemy of my friend is my enemy.

For Assad, the need to respond with brutality, followed by secret police and repression, were moves taken one step at a time. Rumors that he was going to be assassinated persisted into the summer of 2015 and may have exacerbated his fears and intransigence even further. Depletion of his military force and tenuous financial situation – caught between Iran (suffering under sanctions) and Russia (suffering from a declining price of oil) – likely led to his using chemical weapons and barrel bombs, last-ditch efforts till Russia intervened.

Bashar al-Assad and the role of religion

Did religion play any role in Bashar's decisions to use chemical weapons, barrel bombs, and other oppressive measures against those who expressed their disapproval of him and his regime? On one level it seems not: his excuses have been that he has a right to use whatever force necessary to fight terrorism from within. The memory of Sunni oppression of Alawites may have provided a further motivation for the use of extreme force in some areas. But the situation is, of course, more complicated. A number of officers promoted to senior ranks in the Syrian government are Sunni. Still, since 2011 Sunni influence has been weakened, and Assad's brother Maher controls key military units made up almost entirely of Alawite soldiers.

Perhaps Bashar and his brother share the worries of other Alawites: that Sunnis have not made clear what their plans would be for Alawites should they take power. Other than regime change, would Sunnis seek a religious revenge, based on beliefs that Alawites were infidels? In any event, without various rebel groups making explicit their plans for the Alawites, Bashar has a "religious justification."

Moreover, the connection between Shia religious leaders and the Alawite sect is tenuous and complicated. There are times when Alawites play up the Shia connection in fighting Sunnis that have Saudi backing. Assad lumps together all Sunnis with Al Qaeda terrorists, and in receiving support from Iran, he seems to be making the war a kind of religious war. In statements to the West, Assad makes few references to the Sunni faith but argues that the rebel groups are Saudi backed, and backed by the US, imperialist in its motives.

Alawite leaders distance themselves from Assad's use of Shia rebel groups. Recently, they argued that Alawites have never been motivated by Shia religious principles, instead claiming that they achieved their legitimacy through democratic principles.[23]

The tyranny of the majority that may result in "elected" rulers declaring emergencies and oppressing minorities haunts discussions of democracy in Syria and in other countries in the Middle East. Assad and Israel share the same concerns of a radicalized majority that may take over from a minority regime. Without a culture of *liberal* democracy – by which I mean an emphasis on human rights and the rule of law – majority rule going forward could very well create existential dangers to the existing ruling group. Some see this phenomenon as the vestiges of colonialism – that is those who take over in any independence movement know ways of ruling from those who last ruled and who acted with brutal intent at the end of their reigns. It is hard to look at the opposition leaders without seeing them as having learned lessons of how to rule from their oppressors. As a result, history teaches the existing rulers not to too readily give up power. How could democracy give them sufficient protections and guarantees? Making peace with a promise of democracy is akin to suicide for the Alawite ruling class. And, on the other side, the problem will be that to allow peace with impunity for those committing war crimes will only encourage others to act the same way in the future. In the end they will be excused from their war crimes in the name of peace.

Conclusion

What, then, can be said on behalf of President Bashar al-Assad to a jury of public, international opinion? He grew up Alawite, the son of the president of Syria. He likely was raised with an understanding that the Alawites had been subjected to oppression by Sunnis before gaining control of the government. They rose to power during the time of French colonialism, which was considered a statement of Alawite leadership, in order to provide the security necessary for Syrians of different faiths to live side by side. He learned from the example of his father that the responsibilities of leadership may require the use of brutal force when confronting religiously inspired terrorists.

After becoming president, Assad was accused by the international community of orchestrating the assassination of the former head of state of Lebanon, and a UN Special Tribunal was formed to prosecute those who had committed the killing. The special tribunal is still conducting its proceedings.

Bashar al-Assad had also inherited from his father the consequences of decisions Hafez al-Assad had made in the Middle East. Having lost the Golan Heights to the Israelis during the 1967 War, Hafez continued to act on Syria's behalf for the return of its land. With Syria's air force devastated in that war, Bashar's father had turned to the Soviet Union for military support. His father had authorized the establishment of a Russian military base in Syria, and Bashar felt it was necessary to continue to develop both military and economic relations with Russia. In 2010 Syria owed billions to Russia, 75 percent of which the Russians chose to forgive.

Demonstrations turned increasingly violent in 2011. Very quickly various opposition groups formed that sought support from Syria's enemies. The Saudis backed the Sunnis. ISIS gained support from other disaffected Sunnis inside Iraq. Assad therefore was drawn into courting support from Iran, in its proxy war with the Saudis. And, again, Sunnis were not willing to guarantee that Assad and the Alawites would survive their insurgencies. Assad saw all insurgencies as basically alike, as seeking to undermine Alawite leadership and eventually seek revenge. As the price of oil plunged Syria's situation became more and more desperate. Iran was under US sanctions and unable to continue economic support of the war. Russia, similarly, was strapped economically and proved unwilling to support Assad in the long run. That is, at least until it started to see Syria as vital to Russian interests, and stepped up its support in the war. But in the interim, Assad also knew that he was likely the target of assassination. When things looked darkest, Assad combatted insurgent groups through a security service that frequently relied on torture. In addition, Assad himself turned to barrel bombs and chemical weapons in a desperate attempt to terrorize its citizens into rejecting the insurgents.

To make matters worse, the Israelis yet again dropped bombs in Syria. Israel sent its jet to bomb what it said was an effort by Assad to provide arms to the Muslim Brotherhood (crossing the Sunni–Shia divide when it served his purposes, perhaps making it less likely that he was genuinely acting from a set of religious beliefs, but only to promote and protect his own power), who posed a threat to Israel from Lebanon. The impunity with which Israel struck then, like in September 2011, had to be maddening to Assad. The international community was essentially mute on the subject. As a result Assad may have been pushed into a corner by the need to react to attacks from within and without. In any event, he would use chemical weapons in April 2017, shortly after that most recent Israeli bombing.[24]

On the other hand, Assad missed a number of opportunities to negotiate a lasting peace with those Syrians he should have known were looking to create a

Syria that was more open and democratic. He chose to lump all who opposed him into the same camp. He chose to demonize whole communities. His use of barrel bombs and chemical weapons ignored the civilian casualties that he had to know would result from their use. He had given Obama plenty of reasons to see him as evidence of the real evil that existed it the world.

Assad had been warned. When caught, he agreed to work with the UN to remove the chemical weapons. But he did not remove them all. And then he used them again in April 2017. The proof is in the videos. He committed war crimes on his own people.

Maybe he would give excuses. Maybe he thought he had the green light from Putin to use whatever force necessary to ensure his own survival. But more importantly, maybe he misread the US's own commitment to human rights and democratic principles. Maybe he misread Trump in his admiration of Putin and his seeming willingness to combat terrorism through the use of torture and even nuclear force. But, despite having misread Trump, he still bears responsibility for his actions. And, as I will make the case in Chapter 3, Assad has put the UN in quite a dilemma. It has evidence of war crimes, and yet there may be no way out of the war without making peace with Assad. Before we turn to the UN's dilemma, we must first look more carefully at the US's role in Syria. In particular, we need to examine Obama's decision-making with respect to Syria in an effort to assess his responsibility for the war. Eleven million refugees and the existence of ISIS, together with the spread of terrorism throughout Europe, are, indeed, a high price to pay for the Obama Doctrine. Can the international community tolerate making peace with a brutal dictator? It may have to run out of options in how to stem the tide of refugees. Still the peace it helps make should be carefully made and fully incentivized; it should not to provide impunity in the short run and permission for totalitarianism in the long run.

Before we look at the peace process, we must also examine other causal factors in the Syrian conflict. So we turn next to the US's own responsibility for the Syrian war, looking first at its history toward Syria as part of its general policies in the Middle East. Then we will look at Obama, in particular, his rise to the presidency, his theoretical approach to peacemaking, the role his religious belief played in shaping his dilemma, and his individual decision-making in the lead-up to Assad's use of chemical weapons.

Notes

1 www.cnn.com/2017/05/09/middleeast/syria-chemical-attack-ward/index.html.
2 www.cnn.com/2017/05/09/middleeast/syria-chemical-attack-ward/index.html.
3 The figure for deaths in prisons comes from Bethan McKearnan, "Inside Assad's prisons: Horrors facing female inmates in Syrian jails revealed," *Independent*, Monday 28 August 2017, http://www.independent.co.uk/news/world/middle-east/assad-prisons-women-syria-female-inmate-treatment-conditions-exclusive-life-jails-a7899776.html.
4 Robert Mackey, "Syria's Ruling Alawite Sect," *NYT*, June 14, 2011, https://thelede.blogs.nytimes.com/2011/06/14/syrias-ruling-alawite-sect/?_r=1.
5 As Malise Ruthven explained in *The New York Review of Books*, the Alawites of Syria, "who make up only 12 percent of its population, split from the main branch

of Shiism more than a thousand years ago." He then traced the sect's evolution into a quite distinct community over the centuries:

> Before the twentieth century they were usually referred to as Nusayris, after their eponymous founder Ibn Nusayr, who lived in Iraq during the ninth century. Taking refuge in the mountains above the port of Latakia, on the coastal strip between modern Lebanon and Turkey, they evolved a highly secretive syncretistic theology containing an amalgam of Neoplatonic, Gnostic, Christian, Muslim, and Zoroastrian elements. Their leading theologian, Abdullah al-Khasibi, who died in 957, proclaimed the divinity of Ali, the Prophet Muhammad's cousin and son-in-law, whom other Shiites revere but do not worship. Like many Shiites influenced by ancient Gnostic teachings that predate Islam, they believe that the way to salvation and knowledge lies through a succession of divine emanations. Acknowledging a line of prophets or avatars beginning with Adam and culminating in Christ and Muhammad, they include several figures from classical antiquity in their list, such as Socrates, Plato, Galen, and some of the pre-Islamic Persian masters.
>
> Nusayrism could be described as a folk religion that absorbed many of the spiritual and intellectual currents of late antiquity and early Islam, packaged into a body of teachings that placed its followers beyond the boundaries of orthodoxy. Mainstream Muslims, both Sunni and Shia, regarded them as ghulta, "exaggerators." Like other sectarian groups they protected their tradition by a strategy known as taqiyya – the right to hide one's true beliefs from outsiders in order to avoid persecution. Taqiyya makes a perfect qualification for membership in the mukhabarat – the ubiquitous intelligence/security apparatus that has dominated Syria's government for more than four decades . . .
>
> Nusayris believe in metempsychosis or transmigration. The souls of the wicked pass into unclean animals such as dogs and pigs, while the souls of the righteous enter human bodies more perfect than their present ones. The howls of jackals that can be heard at night are the souls of Sunni Muslims calling their misguided co-religionists to prayer.

6 Robert Mackey, "Syria's Ruling Alawite Sect," *The New York Times*, June 14, 2011 5:16 PM quoting his blog and original source of map. https://thelede.blogs.nytimes.com/2011/06/14/syrias-ruling-alawite-sect/?mcubz=1&_r=0 The NYT times link is to http://www.joshualandis.com/blog/did-four-alawi-clans-dissociate-themselves-from-the-assads-as-the-opposition-claims-not-likely/

7 Fearing for their future in any Syrian state dominated by Sunni Muslims, in 1936 six leading Alawites, including Sulayman al-Assad, the grandfather of Syria's current president, wrote a letter to Léon Blum, France's first Jewish prime minister, explaining that their community would "refuse to be annexed to Muslim Syria because in Syria the official religion of the state is Islam, and according to Islam the Alawites are considered infidels."

The authors of the letter even appealed to Mr. Blum's presumed Zionist sympathies, arguing that the persecution of the Jews in Syria and Palestine would be the fate of all religious minorities if the majority Muslim population was allowed to rule. They wrote,

> The spirit of hatred and fanaticism embedded in the hearts of the Arab Muslims against everything that is non-Muslim has been perpetually nurtured by the Islamic religion. There is no hope that the situation will ever change. Therefore, the abolition of the Mandate will expose the minorities in Syria to the dangers of death and annihilation, irrespective of the fact that such abolition will annihilate the freedom of thought and belief . . . Ibid.

8 Neil Macfrquhar, "Hafez al-Assad, Who Turned Syria Into a Power in the Middle East, Dies at 69," *New York Times*, June 11, 2000, http://www.nytimes.com/2000/06/11/world/hafez-al-assad-who-turned-syria-into-a-power-in-the-middle-east-dies-at-69.html?mcubz=1
9 Constitutional History 1950–73.
10 *The Guardian*, "He Trained as a Doctor, How Did He Become a Mass Murderer," www.theguardian.com/commentisfree/2017/apr/18/bashar-al-assad-trained-as-a-doctor-how-did-he-become-a-mass-murderer.
11 This chronology is taken from Report of the International Independent Investigation Commission established pursuant to Security Council resolution 1595 (2005) Detlev Mehlis, Commissioner Beirut, 19 October 2005, (otherwise known as the McArthur Report). www.un.org/News/dh/docs/mehlisreport/.
12 The commission's report contained a summary of evidence that it had gathered concerning Assad's meeting with Harari and the threat:

> Relations between Mr. Hariri and Syria (p.) 25.
> The Commission's investigation has confirmed what many in Lebanon have long asserted, that senior Syrian intelligence officials had a powerful day-to-day and overall strategic influence on the governance of Lebanon. The apparent growing conflict between Mr. Hariri and senior Syrian officials, including Syrian President Bashar Assad, was a central aspect of the information provided to the Commission through interviews and documents. A meeting in Damascus between Mr. Hariri and President Assad on 26 August 2004 appeared to bring the conflict to a head. In that meeting, which allegedly lasted for 10–15 minutes, President Assad informed Mr. Hariri, who was then Prime Minister, that President Assad intended that Lebanon would extend the term in office of Lebanese President Emile Lahoud, which Mr. Hariri opposed. (p. 26). Lebanese and Syrian witnesses, and the transcript of a meeting between Mr. Hariri and Syrian Deputy Foreign Minister Walid Al-Moallem, provided the Commission with sharply differing versions of what was said in that meeting. A number of Lebanese witnesses – including then former ministers Marwan Hamadeh and Ghazi Areedi, Druze leader and head of the Progressive Socialist Party Walid Joumblat, parliament member Bassem Sabaa, and Mr. Hariri's son, Saad – reported that Mr. Hariri told them that President Assad brusquely informed him of the decision to extend President Lahoud's term and threatened to "break Lebanon over your [Mr. Hariri's] head and Walid Jumblat's" if Mr. Hariri (and presumably Mr. Jumblat) did not agree to support the extension of President Lahoud's term. Syrian officials characterized the meeting differently. Syrian Foreign Minister Farouk Sharaa and General Ghazali, head of Syrian 6 intelligence in Lebanon, described the meeting in positive terms. General Ghazali told the Commission that Mr. Hariri told him that President Assad referred to Mr. Hariri as a "friend," and described a cordial, respectful meeting in which President Assad consulted Mr. Hariri on the matter. 27. Following are excerpts of interviews conducted by the Commission regarding the 26 August 2005 meeting, relevant parts of a letter to the Commission from Mr. Sharaa, and a portion of the transcript of a taped conversation between Mr. Hariri and Mr. AlMoallem: Minister of Foreign Affairs of the Syrian Arab Republic, letter to the Commission of 17 August 2005: "A meeting took place between President Bashar Assad and late Prime Minister Rafik Al-Hariri in Damascus on August 26th, 2004 within the framework of the ongoing political consultation between the Syrian and Lebanese leaders. (. . .) A general review was made of the local and regional developments, including the possible extension of the mandate of Emile Lahoud, the President of Lebanon, in view of the troubled regional conditions and based

on the mutual interest in maintaining stability in Lebanon. Mr. AlHariri requested that in case a consensus regarding the mandate extension is reached in the Council of Ministers, Syria should make endeavors to get President Lahoud to better cooperate in the forthcoming period. The President requested Mr. Hariri to consult with his group and with whom he deems suitable and to take the appropriate position." Rustum Ghazali, undated written statement, submitted to the Commission by letter of 17 August 2005: "I had two meetings at Anjar on that date (26 August 2004) with Prime Minister Hariri. The first was in the morning of August 26th, 2004, on his way to Damascus to meet President Bashar Assad in Damascus, and the second was on his return trip from Damascus to Beirut after meeting with President Bashar Assad in Damascus. The latter meeting was also held in our office at Anjar." (. . .) "We discussed his meeting with President Bashar Assad. He (Hariri) looked relaxed. Prime Minister Hariri said that his meeting with President Bashar Assad was cordial and brief. According to Prime Minister Hariri, President Assad told him: Abu Bahaa, we in Syria have always been dealing with you as a friend and as the Prime Minister of Lebanon. Today, I am also dealing with you as a friend and as the Prime Minister of Lebanon. Under the difficult circumstances currently witnessed by this region, with Lebanon in the midst, we are of the view that it is in the interest of Lebanon to maintain the continuity of the regime by extending the term of office of President Lahoud. As a friend, we would like you to clarify your position regarding this matter. We are in no hurry to know the answer, and you may wish to think about it at your convenience." Marwan Hamadeh, witness statement of 27 June 2005: 7 "On Wednesday 24 or 25 August, Mr. Hariri, Mr. Jumblat and Mr. Berri were all invited to go to Damascus in order to be informed about the decision to extend Mr. Lahoud's mandate. Mr. Jumblat informed R. Ghazali that he would need to discuss it with President Assad. R. Ghazali insisted that the answer should be "yes" before setting up any appointment. He actually advised Mr. Jumblat to respond positively because this was a strategic matter for President Assad. Mr. Jumblat's answer was negative. One hour later, Mr. Jumblat called me and told me that the Syrian Intelligence had cancelled his appointment. In the evening, Mr. Jumblat and myself went to visit Mr. Hariri. He said that R. Ghazali insisted that as long as his answer was not positive, he would not confirm his appointment either. He was asked to go to Damascus, stay in his house (. . .) until further notice. The following day, he was called in for a short meeting." (. . .) "The day Mr. Hariri met with President Assad, I was meeting at Mr. Jumblat's residence in Beirut, with Bassem Sabaa and Ghazi Areedi. We saw that Mr. Hariri's motorcade was back by 1 PM which meant that the meeting in Damascus was pretty short. We saw Mr. Hariri who looked tired. He was sweating. He told the four of us that President Lahoud was to be reelected or "he will have to pay a high price." (. . .) He reported President Assad saying to him: I will break Lebanon on your head and Jumblat's head." Ghazi Areedi, witness statement of 1 July 2005: "Mr. Hariri reported to us that President Assad told him: "If Jacques Chirac puts me out of Lebanon, I will consider different options and will let you know. Either you are with us or against us. My choice is Emile Lahoud for President. I will make sure he is the President. I will wait for your answer. (. . .) Tell Walid Jumblat that if he has Druze people in Lebanon, I also have a Druze community in Syria. I am ready to do anything." Walid Joumblatt, witness statement of 28 June 2005: "According to Mr. Hariri, Assad told him:" Lahoud is me. I want to renew his mandate. (. . .) If Chirac wants me out of Lebanon, I will break Lebanon. (. . .) During his visit to my house, Mr. Hariri was extremely tense and disappointed. He was in a very bad position." Jubran Tueni, witness statement of 25 June 2005: "Later on, in 2004, when the issue of President Lahoud's extension came up, Mr. Hariri also told me, that President Assad had threatened him directly and told him, that voting against the extension would be considered as being directed against Syria. According to Mr. Hariri, President Assad added that in that case they, the Syrians, would "blow him up" and any of his family members and that they would find them anywhere in the world." Bassem Sabaa, witness statement of 30 June 2005: 8 "When Mr. Hariri came back from his meeting with President Assad, I met him at Walid Jumblat's house." (. . .) "He reported to us President Assad's words who has put it bluntly: "I am personally interested in this matter. It is not about Emile Lahoud but about Bashar Assad". We asked him if he had had a chance to discuss the matter with President Assad. He said that President Assad told him that the matter was not open for discussion, that it was bound to happen or else I will break Lebanon" (. . .). He was extremely aggravated. He told me that for the sake of Lebanon and its interests, he must think about what he will do, that we are dealing with a group of lunatics who could do anything." Saad Hariri, witness statement of July 9, 2005: "I discussed with my father, the late Rafik Hariri, the extension of President Lahoud's term. He told me that President Bashar Assad threatened him, telling him: "This is what I want. If you think that President Chirac and you are going to run Lebanon, you are mistaken. It is not going to happen. President Lahoud is me. Whatever I tell him, he follows suit. This extension is to happen or else I will break Lebanon over your head and Walid Jumblat's. (. . .) So, you either do as you are told or we will get you and your family wherever you are." Rafik Hariri, taped conversation with Walid Al-Moallem on February 1, 2005: "In connection with the extension episode, he (President Assad) sent for me and met me for 10 to 15 minutes." (. . .) "He sent for me and told me: "You always say that you are with Syria. Now the time has come for you to prove whether you meant what you said or otherwise." (. . .) He did not ask my opinion. He said: "I have decided." He did not address me as Prime Minister or as Rafik or anything of that kind. He just said: "I have decided." I was totally flustered, at a loss. That was the worst day of my life." (. . .) "He did not tell me that he wished to extend Lahoud's mandate. All he said was "I have decided to do this, don't answer me, think and come back to me."" (. . .) "I was not treated as a friend or an acquaintance. No. I was asked: "Are you with us or against us?" That was it. When I finished my meeting with him, I swear to you, my body guard looked at me and asked why I was pale-faced" 28. In the meeting with Mr. Al-Moallem, Mr. Hariri complained that he believed that President Assad was being deliberately misinformed by the Syrian security services and Mr. Sharaa about the actions of Mr. Hariri. Translated excerpts of the meeting include the following statements by Mr. Hariri: 9 *f* "I cannot live under a security regime that is specialized in interfering with Hariri and spreading disinformation about Rafik Hariri and writing reports to Bashar Assad." *f* "But Lebanon will never be ruled from Syria. This will no longer happen." 29. During this discussion, Mr. Al-Moallem told Mr Hariri that "we and the [security] services here have put you into a corner." He continued, "Please do not take things lightly." 30. The recorded interview clearly contradicts Mr. Al-Moallem's witness interview of 20 September 2005 in which he falsely described the 1 February meeting as "friendly and constructive" and avoided giving direct answers to the questions put to him. Syrian cooperation with the Commission 31.

13 Russia's ties to Syria are old and deep. A Russian naval station at Tartus, in northern Syria, is its only military installation outside of former Soviet territories.

There are numerous other economic and cultural bonds, including the presence of Russian companies working in oil and natural gas in Syria, as well as a proposal for the state-owned nuclear energy company, Rosatom, to build a power plant there. Other Russian companies have interests in agriculture, irrigation, and telecommunications in Syria.

Syria, however, has a checkered history when it comes to paying for its weapons.

Mr. Assad arrived in Moscow for his first state visit in 2005, with his country owing Russia about $13.5 billion (US dollars). Mr. Putin welcomed him warmly at a ceremony in St. George Hall of the Grand Kremlin Palace. Their wives met for tea.

At the time, the two leaders signed a "joint declaration on friendship and cooperation," and Russia agreed to write off nearly 75 percent of Syria's unpaid bills.

Many Syrian arms purchases are financed by loans, said Ruslan Aliev, an arms-trade specialist at the Center for Analysis of Strategies and Technologies, a Moscow research group. "They are old customers, but they are very poor," Mr. Aliev said of the Syrians. "They don't have enough money – not like Saudi Arabia or United Arab Emirates." See David M. Herszenhorn, "For Syria, Reliant on Russia for Weapons and Food, Old Bonds Run Deep," *NYT*, February 18, 2012, www.nytimes.com/2012/02/19/world/middleeast/for-russia-and-syria-bonds-are-old-and-deep.html.

14 See, BBC News, Syrian President Bashar al-Assad: Facing down rebellion, October 21, 2013, http://www.bbc.com/news/10338256.

15 Casten Wieland, *Syria-A Decade of Lost Changes: Repression and Revolution from Damascus Spring to Arab Spring* (Seattle, WA: Cune Press at Smashwords, Syria Crossroads Series, 2012).

16 Report of the International Independent Investigation Commission established pursuant to Security Council resolution 1595 (2005) Detlev Mehlis, Commissioner Beirut, 19 October 2005, www.un.org/News/dh/docs/mehlisreport/

17 March 2017 Interactive, at http://umap.openstreetmap.fr/fr/map/desyracuse-syria-civil-war-5-march-2017_131222#6/35.335/39.705.

What will happen when the Syrian Democratic front and Syrian government meet in Raqqa? In democracy, the rule of law and human rights don't seem to be guiding his strategy. What rights will the Kurds have gained from their involvement in the fighting?

18 Katiana Krawchenko, "Syria and Russia Seek to Confuse About Chemical Attack, Says White House," *CBS News*, April 11, 2017, www.cbsnews.com/news/syria-and-russia-seek-to-confuse-about-chemical-attack-says-white-house/.

19 Natasha Bertrand, "An 'Infantile Argument': Experts Pour Cold Water on Russia's 'Fanciful' Explanation for Syrian Gas Attack," *Business Insider, Politics*, April 5, 2017, www.businessinsider.com/russia-explanation-for-syria-chemical-weapons-attack-2017-4.

20 Robert Pastor, *Existing the Whirlpool: U.S. Foreign Policy Toward Latin America and the Caribbean* (New York: Avalon Press, 2001); See also, Robert Pastor, "There Are More Than Two Options for US Policy on Syria," *Atlantic Magazine*, September 4, 2013, www.theatlantic.com/international/archive/2013/09/syria-reader-part-3-robert-pastor/279339/.

21 Jeffrey Gettleman, *Love Africa: A Memoir of Romance, War and Survival* (New York: HarpersCollins, 2017), Chapter 7, Somalia, 2006.

22 Ibid.

23 Caroline Wyatt, "Syrian Alawites Distance Themselves from Assad," *BBC*, April 2016, www.bbc.com/news/world-middle-east-35941679. (reporting on an Alawite document designed to distance Alawites from Assad).

Those behind the text say Alawites are not members of a branch of Shia Islam – as they have been described in the past by Shia clerics – and that they are committed to "the fight against sectarian strife".

They also make clear that they adhere to "the values of equality, liberty and citizenship" and call for secularism to be the future of Syria and a system of governance in which Islam, Christianity, and all other religions are equal.

And despite Alawites having dominated Syria's government and security services under Mr Assad and his late father, Hafez, for more than four decades, they stress that the legitimacy of his regime "can only be considered according to the criteria of democracy and fundamental rights":

'Muslim quality'

The Alawites emerged in the 10th Century in neighboring Iraq.

Little has been confirmed about their beliefs and practices since then because, according to the leaders, they had to be hidden to avoid persecution.

However, most sources say the name "Alawite" refers to their veneration of the first Shia imam, Ali, the son-in-law and cousin of the Prophet Muhammad.

Alawites are said to share the belief of members of the main branches of Shia Islam, of which Ithna Asharis or Twelvers are the largest group, that Ali was the rightful successor to Muhammad as leader of the Muslim community following his death in 632.

The Alawites purportedly differ from Twelvers in holding that Ali was a manifestation of God – a notion that some members of Syria's Sunni majority consider heretical.

In the document published on Sunday, the Alawite leaders insist that their faith is "solely based on the idea of worshipping God". They add that "the Koran alone is our holy book and a clear reference to our Muslim quality".

While acknowledging that they share some formal religious sources, the leaders stress that Alawism is distinct from Shia Islam, and decline previous legal rulings, or fatwas, by leading Shia clerics that seek to "appropriate the Alawites and consider Alawism an integral part of Shiism or a branch of the latter".

The leaders also acknowledge that Alawites have incorporated elements of other monotheistic religions into their traditions, most notably Judaism and Christianity, but say they should "not be seen as marks of deviation from Islam but as elements that bear witness to our riches and universality".

24 Tyler Rogoway, "Has Israel Actually Sent the F-35 into Combat Already?," March 24, 2017, www.thedrive.com/the-war-zone/8444/israel-warns-it-will-destroy-syrias-air-defenses-without-thinking-twice (reporting that Russia has delivered a message to the Israel government on behalf of Syria's Assad regime stating that any more Israeli air force (IAF) strikes into Syrian territory will be answered with a barrage of Scud missiles. In particular, it describes what will be targeted and why. If an Israeli air strike hits civilian infrastructure, Syria will launch missiles aimed at Israel's port in Haifa, as well as its nearby petrochemical plant. If strikes hit Syrian military-related targets, the SCUD missiles will be targeted at Israel Defense Force bases. the head of the Israel's Ministry of Defense made it clear that the IAF would "destroy Syria's air defenses without thinking twice" if their jets were fired upon. . . . Over the last week, Israel has only ramped up its strikes in Syria, with multiple missions being carried out including the assassination of a militant leader with close ties to the Assad regime. Since the Syrian civil war began six years ago, Israeli air strikes in Syrian territory were far less frequent, and the Israeli government did not officially even admit that they had been occurring until Syria fired on the IAF's jets nearly two weeks ago . . . it doesn't take much creativity to see how such a course of action could spiral the already highly convoluted Syrian conflict into a much wider war. Russia's air defense systems at Tartus and at Russia's master airbase south of Latakia could prove to a be a major tactical and geopolitical hazard for Israel should Russia officially deny Israeli movement through the area. The US, with its very close ties to Israel, would also be put in a tight spot as the Pentagon wishes to solely focus on the campaign against ISIS, not be drawn into a larger geopolitical affair with Russia and the Assad regime. The Israeli government has been clear that it has no intentions of stopping its airstrikes on weapons shipments headed for Hezbollah. As such, the Assad regime's latest threat will likely be put to the test in the coming days).

2 The history of US relations with Syria

The role of Obama – and now Trump

It is the morning of September 1, 2013.[1] It is nearly a year after the president has drawn his famous "red line" in Syria: that if chemical weapons are used by Assad, the US would intervene militarily. It is now suspected that Assad has done just that. As of August 31, the US military is ready to go. Targets have been selected. There are even reports that the French military is standing by to send in troops on the ground. All that they are waiting for is an order from the president to intervene.

But President Obama is having second thoughts. The British Parliament has not given its support for military intervention in Syria. And Obama has also gotten word from his national security council that Syria's use of chemical weapons is not a "slam dunk." (These are words that were used by the Bush administration to describe their confidence that Saddam Hussein had weapons of mass destruction.) That morning he asks Denis McDonough, White House chief of staff, to take a walk with him. They circle round and round the White House grounds discussing Obama's idea that they announce the president's decision to intervene but to go to Congress for support. They convene a meeting that same morning and discuss their idea. Many are stunned and worried that if the Congress does not give its support, Obama's standing in the world will be diminished. He will look indecisive and weak.

But Obama does not back down and, instead, calls a Rose Garden press conference to announce his decision, to intervene but to first seek Congressional approval.

Of course, we know now that Congress did not give its approval. We also know that with the help of the Russians, the US, and the UN was able to negotiate with Assad for a verifiable removal of chemical weapons from Syria. (We also suspect that Assad did not destroy all the chemical weapons but kept Sarin gas on hand for its later use.) In not intervening, some argue that Obama "blinked." This is loaded language. It sounds like Obama lacked the "manliness" to commit troops to combat. Harkening back to Kennedy and his standing up to the Russians, they make foreign policy a matter of being tough. (They forget that Kennedy, in fact, did not use nuclear weapons but, instead, made a deal with the Russians in order to get them to not put nuclear weapons in Cuba.) They argue that Obama showed an unwillingness to commit troops on the ground and arguably opened the door to ISIS. In so doing Obama was responsible for the rise of ISIS and the refugee crisis that resulted thereafter.

Is it fair to attribute the rise of ISIS and the refugee crisis to Obama's failure to intervene militarily? Did the failure to intervene undermine the US's faith in the democracy movement in Syria and undermine its faith itself? Or did Obama's appeal to Congress do just the opposite? In order to make this judgment, I will take a closer look at the facts and events leading up to the decision.

Context of US and Syria

I will first look at the US to ask whether it and President Obama, in particular, have contributed to the radicalization of Bashar al-Assad and, thus, can be said to be in some way responsible for what has happened in Syria. Are there any lessons here for future US administrations for how to keep the conflicts in the Middle East from spiraling out of control? Are there implications in what Obama did for how the US deals with dictators? What, if anything, are the implications of Obama's decisions on the US's view of itself and, in particular, its own faith in democratic principles and the rule of law?

I will follow the same broad organization framework in looking at Obama's motivations and reasoning that I used in discussing Bashar al-Assad. I will start with a brief and broad historical discussion and then look at his decisions in a personal context, as a matter of his relationship with his father, then religion, then foreign policy doctrine, and then as a matter of understanding what decisions were made in relation to specific historical events. Finally I will end with a brief discussion of Trump's decisions on Syria in an attempt to set up the next chapter, the role of UN in peacemaking in Syria.

Broader context: Oren – Syria as part of the US in the Middle East

As Michael Oren had shown in his excellent book *Power, Faith, and Fantasy: America in the Middle East 1776 to the Present*, the US was largely motivated in its actions in the Middle East vis-à-vis its relationship with and obligations to Israel. In so doing, the US was initially not motivated by oil or some grand scheme of national security and national interest. That would naturally come later. Instead, its motives were largely religious, bearing an even missionary zeal (Oren, 327). Its focus was on Palestine, where Jesus spent his short time on earth. Prominent US policy makers viewed Palestine as the key to the second coming of Christ. It was not uncommon for some of the US's best and brightest young rising stars to be inspired by their faith and beliefs in the second coming of Christ, travelling to Palestine – largely to convert the Jews living there – in order to bring about the biblical prophecies of Christ's second coming. In the process since the 1850s until World War II, more than 400 religious organizations had built colleges and other institutions that served the various elites in Middle Eastern society. The Ottoman elites, in particular, sent their children to these US-affiliated religious schools.

That is not to say that the US had exclusively religious motives for its foreign policy in the area. US businesses saw the Ottoman Empire, and then its Turkish successor state, Turks, in particular, as economic partners. The US and its businesses conducted over 20 percent of all trade with the Turks. Istanbul was a profit center for US trade. And it was one reason why the US, under the leadership of Woodrow Wilson, was so slow to side with the British and French against the Germans and Ottomans at the start of World War I. Much to its shame, not acting more forcefully to prevent the Armenian genocide was one of the great failings of US foreign policy. Despite the strong efforts of then secretary of state Henry Morgenthau to try to get Wilson to take condemning measures against the Ottomans, the US maintained a distinct neutrality regarding the Armenian–Turkish conflict. In so doing it showed a naiveté that made it look foolish. In his chapter on the Armenian genocide, Oren concludes that

> [f]or all their attempts to detach themselves from the conflict and its consequences, America had been caught up in the worst waves of bloodshed ever to ravage the Middle East, witnessing acts of inhumanity that, even by Great War standards, were appalling. The enormity of those horrors was to some degree diminished by the unflagging efforts of relief workers and missionaries, but the ability of Americans to alleviate Middle Eastern suffering would remain limited as long as the United States stayed aloof from the war.[2]

Morgenthau was unable to move Wilson despite his friendship with the *New York Times*, which wrote more than 140 articles during this period describing the Armenian genocide. As a result the US was seen in the Middle East as being neutral. And to some extent, this same neutrality was maintained through the beginning of the Zionist movement and up through the end of World War II.

I note here that the prevention of genocide was starting to bubble up in the US and international consciousness as an important justification for the use of military force. Still caught between the imperialism of its neighbors and the African independence movement which was starting to gain momentum following the formation of the League of Nations, the US was incapable of acting on its principles in preventing genocide.[3] But then in the aftermath of World War II, the US and the world as a whole confronted the horrors of the Holocaust. Part of the deep-seated understanding of its actions in World War II would be that it was stopping Hitler from carrying out the "Final Solution."

In June 1945, only three weeks after V-E Day, Truman had a tough choice to make regarding Syria. Should he honor promises that had been made by the allies to Syria about its independence and entice Syria to declare war against the Axis powers, or should he back France as it attempted to reassert its imperial power? Complicating the matter was the obvious aggressive nature of the Soviet Union regarding Libya, Iran, and Turkey. Truman decided to urge de Gaulle to withdraw from Syria, and the US and British attempted to do the same in Libya and Iran, using the UN as the protectorate of Libya and as the guarantor of a process headed toward its independence.

In Iran, Stalin dragged his feet withdrawing. His technique was to support and encourage the communist Tudeh Party, reinforcing its influence there. Stalin had already used the technique effectively in Kurdistan and Azerbaijan, causing each of these two countries to join the Soviet Union (Oren, 479). Truman protested and instituted a foreign policy that came to be called "containment," or the Truman Doctrine. He argued for an iron-fisted approach of military force and tough diplomacy to bring about the removal of Soviet influence from the region. A young senator from Massachusetts, John Kennedy, fully supported Truman's containment policy.

Truman's motives were mixed. Oil was now seen as a necessary resource for both military and national economic purposes. He denied imperialist motives while at the same time recognizing the national interest in oil. His focus was on fighting a cold war. He sent an aircraft carrier to the region to show that he meant business. The Soviets backed down, and the independence movement in Syria was allowed to flourish.

The impact of George F. Kennan

One cannot understand the motivations of the US without understanding the impact of former secretary of state George F. Kennan on US foreign policy following the civil war. And we must start with the recognition that Kennan had his doubts about democracy as that which would prevent future World Wars. He urged the US to see its actions on the world stage as being motivated by fighting its enemies. He argued that the public rhetoric of "making the world safe for democracy" was a rallying cry to motivate the US to protect its own nationalistic interests. This motivating force was not to be used as a basis to pick sides in an international conflict between democracy or a dictator. So, on Kennan's urging, the US could very well make partnerships with other dictators and known violators of human rights if the establishment of that partnership meant containment of the Soviet Union and the spread of Communism within certain boundaries. Some blame national interest theories (Kennan and later Kissinger) for the US's backing of the corrupt Vietnamese government and Central Intelligence Agency (CIA) involvement in Latin America (e.g. backing Pinochet over Allende and supporting a series "banana republics" to the long-term detriment of US interests in Central and South America.[4]) Yet Kennan is also admired, as it was his thinking that led to Nixon's Open Door policy with China. Moreover, Kennan's hard-edged pragmatism would allow the US to justify backing the shah of Iran over Mossadegh in addition to pitting Sunnis against Shias throughout the Middle East – as long as the US could get its oil.

After World War II, US attention would shift from Syria to elsewhere in the Middle East. The story is well known about the eventual backing of the US in the establishment of the state of Israel.

What is less remembered is the US's involvement in the rise of the shah.[5] It would serve as a historical warning to the Obama administration of the risk of backing the wrong party in a country in the Middle East. John Foster Dulles, a Kennan devotee, was the secretary of state during the Eisenhower administration. (He also had the support of his brother Allen, who was then head of the CIA.) John Foster Dulles would famously say, "Whether it is in Indo-China or Siam or Morocco or Egypt or Arabia or Iran . . . the forces of unrest are captured by the Soviet Communists."[6] Acting on this belief he targeted the Iranian leader, Mohammad Mosaddegh. Mosaddegh was believed to be beholden to the communist Tudeh Party and so must have been in the pocket of the Soviets. As prime minister, Mosaddegh caused the shah, Mohammed Reza, to flee the country. The Dulles brothers would orchestrate a coup resulting in the return of the extremely unpopular shah. Oren describes Dulles's motivations during this time as a mixture of Wilsonian (father of the League of Nations following World War I) and Jacksonian in his determination to protect US interests abroad.

This widespread hatred of the shah, then, would be precisely the fuel for the successful carrying out of the Islamic Revolution a number of years later – the new government of Iran would not forget the US's support of Mohammed Reza Shah, a foreign policy move that generated much of the enmity and distrust between the US and Iran today. The US's experience with the Shah was formative of current policies toward Syria. Of course, there were other reasons for recent administrations to be reticent to about intervening in Syria militarily. The Vietnam War, the sending of troops to Grenada, US involvement in Iran, Nicaragua, Afghanistan, and Iraq: none of these situations had produced the results the US had been looking for. With Nixon and Kissinger, US foreign policy seemed to veer back towards Kennan and national interest-based decision-making. It was then that the US developed a policy that it would not invade militarily unless its own national security required it and unless it had a plan for an end game should it choose to intervene.

President Carter, blamed for backing the shah, tried to reinject human rights and the rule of law into the decision-making process for foreign invasions. His peacemaking efforts at Camp David showed to some the promise that negotiation and mediation rather than using military force, might be an effective strategy. Guided by Robert Pastor and his own insights into the harm done by the US in it engagements in Latin America, Carter took into consideration much more the long-term impact of any strategy that was employed.

And there were plenty of examples where repressive regimes had fallen without the direct military support of the US.

What was the US to make of what happened to the Soviet Union? Was this the result of the USSR's own ruthlessness during the Cold War, the result of Glasnost, or did the collapse come about out of a movement that from within the Soviet Union that evolved naturally out of a realization of the common people that democracy was a superior form of government? As a student of this history, Obama and his advisors had reason to be cautious in flexing any military muscles. Without the existence of a superpower competitor, the US's exercise of power had to become more transparent in its justifications for the use of that power. If it acted on economic interest, the world would see the US as an imperialist bully. If it acted on principle, then what principle? And, in particular, how would acting on principle limit its ability to protect itself and pursue its own interests? Perhaps doing nothing was an option that needed to be examined more carefully and prominently as the US attempted to sort out what its obligations were in intervening militarily.

In order to judge Obama's reasoning for acting or not acting in Syria, we are greatly benefited from four different sources: Bob Woodward's *Obama's War*, Jeffrey Goldberg's *Atlantic* article "The Obama Doctrine,"[7] and Obama's own books, *Dreams from My Father* and *The Audacity of Hope*.[8] What follows relies much on insights gained from these works.

So, in Russia, despite Reagan's tough talk about "doing whatever it took to make the world safe for democracy," the Soviet Union fell without direct military US interventions.[9] To Obama, attributing the Soviet Union's collapse to Reagan toughness was a political argument base on a myth.[10]

Obama thought there were plenty of examples of Reagan eschewing a military response, such as Reagan's decision to almost immediately pull US forces out of Lebanon after 241 servicemen were killed in a Hezbollah attack in 1983. Obama would, in fact, learn from Reagan, but what he learned was significantly more about diplomacy than using military power to achieve US goals. He thought Reagan acted masterfully toward Gorbachev by drawing him in, showing trust, and providing the room Russia then needed to move away from totalitarianism toward democracy. This was followed by a number of former Soviet Republics turning away from dictatorship and towards democracy and the rule of law. The US seemed to learn that democracy could ascend, as if on its own initiative, from popular uprisings of citizens looking for freedom, the end of corruption, and the rule of law.

Obama was, of course, aware of counter-examples from the Clinton era. Perhaps the US could attain its ends simply by using its air force and not putting any troops on the ground. Yet the conventional wisdom would doubt the predictions coming from the air force solutions. In Vietnam, the air force predicted that the Viet Cong would be defeated in short order, but bombing only drove them farther underground and made them more determined. From the "Shock and Awe" of Iraq, the US learned that troops were still necessary to effect a regime change. Once the regime was removed, the problem then became what to do with the old military, whether it should be disbanded entirely or integrated into the new regime. There were no easy blueprints for what would happen following an invasion or an overthrow. Would an embrace of democracy reminiscent to that which occurred in Europe after World War II emerge? Or would countries find themselves struggling more mightily with whether they wanted democratic reform or simply a new dictatorship?

Even in the Balkans, the US did not produce the long-term benefits it was hoping for in the breakup of former Yugoslavia. The Dayton Peace Accords were widely panned as being forced, without sufficient buy-in from the parties themselves. Still, Dayton was an example of the US using military force to end the genocide that was occurring on both sides. The wars in Yugoslavia, along with President Clinton's experience in Rwanda, framed for Obama the dilemmas he felt existed when he took over the presidency in 2008. He came to believe (as he writes in *Audacity of Hope*) that the US could do more for global democratic reform by not putting troops on the ground and providing only limited strategic support to internal groups and stakeholders who would build a new government. The US could engage its interests in democracy best if it provided humanitarian support for all the innocents and technical support for combatting the enemy, frequently branded terrorists. The theory seemed to be that whoever prevailed could form a government without the taint of US involvement or any imperial motives that might be ascribed.

But before we get too carried away, we need to quickly mention two additional US uses of military force and how they had an impact on Obama's thinking on Syria: the Iraq War and the war in Afghanistan. Like in examining Assad's motivations, we may be engaging in some reconstructions of memory, motivation, and motives. Still it is important to look at some of the available sources on Obama's reasoning and thought processes in order to understand why he neglected to take earlier steps to stop the situation in Syria before it escalated. In doing so, the hope is to examine what might be done in the future to avoid the pitfalls of imperialism and artificial nation building while still acting in a decisive way to avoid the dangers of genocide and war crimes. Setting aside the broad context of US foreign policy, I turn next, as I did with Bashar al-Assad, to look at Obama's personal history and how his relationship with his father has colored the decisions he made.[11]

Relationship with his father

In comparison with Bashar al-Assad, and his father, Hafez, we know a good deal more about Barack Obama's father's impact on him from his book, *Dreams from My Father*. Told when Obama was in his mid-30s, it contains chapters that describe his journey to Nairobi, Kenya, in search of an understanding of his father after he died, suddenly, in a car crash. Obama's father had abandoned him and his mother when Obama was two years old.

As one reviewer said, "[a]ll men live in the shadow of their fathers – the more distant the father, the deeper the shadow. Barack Obama describes the phenomenon of belonging to two different worlds [one white and one black], and thus belonging to neither."[12] The elder Obama met Barack's white mother when they both were students at the University of Hawaii. In the book Barack describes the period between his adolescence to his early 30s and a cacophony of strange relatives and friends hailing from Hawaii to Indonesia to Chicago to Kenya.

In trying to explain to his schoolmates in Hawaii where his father is, Obama falls back on his imagination. He tells them his father's tribe in Africa "is full of warriors." He also tells them that the name Obama, "means 'Burning Spear' The men in our tribe all want to be chief, so my father has to settle these feuds"[13] before the boy can go visit him.

Following education in California at a small college, followed by two years at Columbia, Obama leaves college inspired to be a community activist. He writes that he is attracted by the ideal of people united in community and purpose: "A promise of redemption." He is thrown into the heart of it at the Altgeld Gardens public housing project in Chicago. His idealistic fire is almost completely smothered by how these community activists seem to have manipulated the city budget meant for the poor for their own purposes.

His father's sudden death after the two had re-established contact prevents Mr. Obama from confronting anything but the man's legacy. He travels to Kenya, where he and his newly found siblings visit their father's Luo tribal lands.

What Obama takes away from his trip is not clear. He seems disappointed by what he learns about his father – that he seemed to have not lived up to his potential, from his education and reputation as a successful academic. He learned his father spent a lot of time drinking and pontificating, becoming an object of pity to those who knew him. His primary lesson was in examining his father's failings and committing himself not to waste what he had been given. He does remember that when his father visited him he urged him to be his very best and that he could be the best. In that encouragement, he felt his father's confidence and love. It gave him a sense of purpose and self-confidence to try to be the very best. He returns to the US to attend Harvard Law School. He becomes the first black editor of the *Harvard Law Review*.

I think Barack would have us learn a couple of things from his African visit. First, that people of mixed-race backgrounds do face some important challenges when they are looking to find their roots or the sense of self that will carry them forward in life. He also seems to be genuinely appreciative of the US's brand of liberal democracy: that it provides the room for all people, whatever race and background, to gain opportunities to grow and succeed. Whether and how his belief in democracy and his faith in reason would actually play out on both the national and international stage would come to be sorely tested. He will face racism, both subtle and explicit, from his political opponents. Still he seems to have faith in the ultimate rationality of the US electorate to choose what is right.[14]

Oren's criticism of Obama from *Dreams*

I want to note here one of Obama's critics and how tricky it can be for one to ascribe motives to a person or finding character flaws in what they write. In his book *Ally*, Oren offers a rather harsh assessment of Obama. Writing from the perspective of a historian of US foreign policy, yet also as the Israeli ambassador during whose tenure Israeli–US relations deteriorated, he criticizes Obama for not having enough faith in democracy. He saw Obama as not respecting Netanyahu's position as Israel's democratically elected leader. He attributes some of Obama's attitude towards Netanyahu as coming from his own lack of faith in US democracy. Where does Oren get that from?

He acknowledges that he "risks armchair psychoanalyzing" Obama, drawing his hypothesis from *Dreams from My Father*. In *Ally*, Oren says he scoured *Dreams from My Father* in vain "for some expression of reverence, even respect, for the country its author would someday lead." Instead, in Oren's reading, "the book criticizes Americans for their capitalism and consumer culture, for despoiling their environment and maintaining antiquated power structures." He writes that Obama accused Americans traveling abroad of exhibiting "ignorance and arrogance"[15] – the very same shortcomings, Oren notes dryly, that the president's critics assigned to him.

Of course, whether it is true that Americans traveling abroad are arrogant is beside the point to Oren, as he somehow sees in Obama's writing evidence of the former president's own arrogance. Instead of attributing Obama's empathy for the foreigner as growing out of his religious and community-building experiences in Chicago, Oren attributes it to a lack of love for the US. He ignores what Obama says: that he claims for motivation his hope arising from the US's track record of finding a way to be a place of opportunity for the immigrant. Oren understands Obama's appeals to the Muslim world to come from his attempts to reconcile with his father and that his motivation wasn't a love of democracy but to somehow reclaim the love of a dead father. There is little support for that. Whether Obama saw his father's background in the Muslim world as giving him some potential credence as a mediator or a peacemaker in Middle East would not make his actions there less admirable, showing only that he had a legitimate hope born out of his background. What can be said about Obama's faith in democracy is that it is pragmatic and realistic. Clearly, his experience with downtown Chicago taught him that democracy was not working all that well for the poor blacks who lived there. He saw that democratic politics was not above the corrupting influences of even the most well-intentioned actors. He also saw that city government could become an obstacle, and so was always a small-"***d***" democratic. To see his pragmatism one has to understand the role that his religious faith plays in his view of democracy and role of government.

What role did religion have on his thinking?

I return now for a moment to Obama's experiences in Chicago. Unlike with Bashar al-Assad, whose faith was basically tribal, growing out of a history of oppression by Sunnis against Shiites, and Alawites in particular, Obama's religious faith, his Christianity, was shaped by his life experiences and his relationships with those he worked with. It starts in Chicago through the organizers and activists there who seemed genuinely inspired by a progressive brand of Christian faith. These colleagues used and shared their faith to inspire other members of Chicago's black religious community to action. Their Christianity was progressive but not naïvely optimistic. They took sin seriously, subscribing to the doctrines of original sin and human imperfection. They worried about their own motivations and recognized how their own reason could become perverted into an elaborate and facile set of justifications wrapped in self-interest. They did not restrict their efforts to help others based on a litmus confession of faith. They did not require perfection and were willing to try second-best solutions over doing nothing. Adherents of this particular theology frequently refer to Matthew 25: "Whatever you neglected to do unto the least of these, you neglected to do unto me." Everyone, in other words, is in this salvation thing together.

As a result of living in such a community, Obama's faith became a matter of the heart as much as it was a matter of the head. In *Audacity* he writes the he "felt God's spirit beckoning me" and that "I submitted myself to His will, and dedicated myself to discovering his truth."

Some conservative Christians strongly opposed Obama's Christianity. They even question whether he was Christian at all. Instead of seeing in his exemplary life a strong devotion to his faith, they used a version of "proof texting," a simplistic and largely discredited way of using scripture that takes the passage out of context, ignores other teachings from scripture and other arguments that show that their interpretation can't have the meaning they ascribe to it. They chose to take his refusal to agree with their interpretation as giving rise to grounds for questioning whether he was a Christian at all. Not unlike how some radical Sunnis perceived Alawites as Shia (regardless of the complex relationship between Alawites and Shia), these conservative Christian commentators took a particular belief and turned it into grounds to declare a person no longer a member of their faith at all.

For example, Dr. James Dobson accused Obama of "deliberately distorting the traditional understanding of the Bible to fit his own world view, his own confused theology."[16] In addition, Franklin Graham asked Obama during the campaign how, as a Christian, he could reconcile New Testament claims that salvation was attainable only through Christ with a campaign that embraces pluralism and diversity.[17] Obama told a major newspaper that "[i]t is a precept of my Christian faith that my redemption comes through Christ, but I am also a big believer in the Golden Rule, which I think is an essential pillar not only of my faith but of my values and my ideals and my experience here on Earth. I've said this before, and I know this raises questions in the minds of some evangelicals. I do not believe that my mother, who never formally embraced Christianity as far as I know . . . I do not believe she went to hell."[18]

Unfortunately, during the campaign, there was little Obama could do to argue with Dobson's and Graham's misuse of scripture to create their claim that he was not Christian. That was left for other Christians to do later but only after the damage had already been done.

He did not take on Graham for taking Jesus's teaching of "I am the way" out of context. He did not show its inconsistency with Matthew 25. He could have argued, as many Christians do, that Jesus taught a different lesson for the story about the sheep and goats and about how who gets into heaven. Jesus's teachings contain no confessional litmus test from the sheep. Nor did he make the point that Christian theologians, at least from the time of the Reformation, have argued about the interpretation of a confession of faith in Christ as a precondition for salvation. Calvinists argue that such an interpretation of scripture would limit the "sovereignty of God" and make confession a necessary condition of salvation. What would that mean for everyone born before Christ lived? Were King David, Abraham, and Isaiah, not saved? What about those from countries whose people did not know Christ? What about infants who died before they confessed Christ? Obama's reference to his mother makes this case, but it did little to stop

Dobson and others from making their views a condition precedent for being Christian. And it didn't take a theologian to make the case. Under Graham's criteria, presidents such as Lincoln and Jefferson would not be Christians, and, according to a Pew Forum survey, 70 percent of Americans agree with the statement that "many religions can lead to eternal life."[19] One has to wonder, then, the true motivation behind their choice to make a religious claim as a basis for disapproval of Obama.[20]

The question for us here is how Obama's Christianity would impact his decisions in Syria. It is not apparent that it would make him align against Assad because of Assad's faith and the regime's complex relationship to Syrian Christians. Obama never urged removal of Assad because he had oppressed Syrian Christians when it had suited him, nor did he urge support for Assad because Assad would protect Christians against radical Sunnis. He did not urge a religious war.

President Trump would later do something akin to weaponizing his faith when he became president. In a cynical appeal to his base, he claimed that "we" Christians are under attack.[21] He urged his audience of Christian conservatives to see his travel ban and his positions on the use of military power, and even the Justice Department investigation of his ties to Russia, as proof that Christianity was under attack from Islam and liberals. He lumped progressive Christians, those concerned about climate change and being welcoming to refugees, in with terrorist and liberals.

Obama did not politically weaponize his brand of Christianity. Perhaps he saw that as disrespectful to another person's faith and counter-productive to any persuasive reasoning that actually produces democratic decision-making. Using religion this way is the sign of a dictator. It is a cheap trick that demonizes one's opponents and harnesses fear to increase power.

Nor is there any evidence that Obama did not consider the deaths of Muslims in Syria to be less important than deaths of Christians, thereby not warranting involvement. What is clear is that Obama did not and has not used religion in an undemocratic way. He did not use it to increase fear in order to justify his expansion of power. What we do need to examine is how his religious beliefs in human nature, and the existence of evil, has led him to be less impulsive and even slowed down in his thinking to the point of making him consider an even more democratic basis, making an appeal to Congress before committing military on the ground, for the use of power rather than acting like more of a strong man.[22]

To see how religious belief impacted Obama's decision-making I next take a close look at what others have described as Obama's attempt to thread the "Niebuhrian needle." To understand the Niebuhrian needle, or Obama's thinking regarding the use of military power, we start with his speech in accepting the Nobel Peace Prize, the text of which described the dilemma that he faced:

> And even as we strive to seek a world in which conflicts are resolved peacefully and prosperity is widely shared, we have to confront the world as we know it today. I am the commander in chief of a country that's responsible for ending a war and working in another theater to confront a ruthless adversary that directly threatens the American people and our allies.[23]

The speech itself contains evidence of a religious perspective. He seems inspired by the thinking an obscure Christian theologian, Reinhold Niebuhr. "I take away [from Niebuhr]," Obama answered in an interview with *New York Times* columnist David Brooks, "the compelling idea that there's serious evil in the world, and hardship and pain. And we should be humble and modest in our belief we can eliminate those things. But we shouldn't use that as an excuse for cynicism and inaction. I take away . . . the sense we have to make these efforts knowing they are hard, and not swinging from naïve idealism to bitter realism."

On one hand, Obama seems to despise, as Niebuhr certainly would have, the grand Bushian rhetoric about ridding the world of evil and tyranny and transforming the Middle East. But he also dislikes liberal muddle-headedness on power politics. In *The Audacity of Hope*, he says liberal objectives like withdrawing from Iraq, stopping AIDS and working more closely with our allies may be laudable, "but they hardly constitute a coherent national security policy."[24]

Brooks writes tellingly,

> If you ask him about the Middle East peace process, he will wax rhapsodic about the need to get energetically engaged. He'll talk about the shared interests all have in democracy and prosperity. But then when you ask him concretely if the U.S. should sit down and talk with Hamas, he says no. "There's no point in sitting down so long as Hamas says Israel doesn't have the right to exist."
>
> When you ask about ways to prevent Iran from developing nuclear weapons, he talks grandly about marshaling a global alliance. But when you ask specifically if an Iranian bomb would be deterrable, he says yes: "I think Iran is like North Korea. They see nuclear arms in defensive terms, as a way to prevent regime change."[25]

What Brooks is describing is the pragmatist dilemma. Principles only get one so far. Something can be evil, but that does not mean you will never talk with them, only that you won't talk with them if it won't do you any good. I think what goes without saying is that Obama does have opinions about the consequences of acting or not acting on principle. Those opinions need to be informed, and he does his best to be informed about those consequences. Still, he realizes that as president, he has been elected to exercise that judgment the best he can on behalf of the US. And so the dilemma is that he must make decisions, even without a full understanding of their consequences, informed by principles, both religious and secular.

Obama's view is that religious faith is best if it complements liberal democratic ideals, in that religious communities share many values with those who claim secular groundings for those values.[26] Otherwise, religion can create crisis, both internally and between nations. Look at the Middle East. For a time it looked like authoritarian governments there – Egypt, Tunisia, Libya – were all but set to collapse. The problem was there were no democratic traditions already in place to provide a means for post-authoritarian good governance. So, instead, existing or new, would-be dictators stood ready to stir old religious animosities and argue something to the effect of "see, you can't trust the religious extremists to compromise for the good of the whole." John Chandler, in his book *Faith-Based Policy: A Litmus Test for Understanding Contemporary America*, for me best captured Obama's thinking:

> He [Obama] talked about things that America can reasonably expect to accomplish, such as air strikes on ISIS targets and delivering humanitarian aid. He avoided the temptation to inflate the threat of terrorism, even as he pledged to keep America safe. And he refrained from the language of jingoism and belligerence to which such occasions lend themselves. And above all, he made a firm commitment that American troops would not fight a battle that, if it is to be won, must be fought by Arab armies. In short, the President more or less succeeded in balancing American assertiveness with the humility that Niebuhr prized as the essential – and usually the missing – ingredient of American foreign policy.
>
> And this too: Niebuhr was an enthusiastic champion of the checks and balances of the Constitution. He was reassured by the idea that each branch of government would ride herd on the others and thereby prevent abuses of power in pursuing foreign adventures. Here too the President got it right in calling for the full and robust engagement of the Congress in authorizing and shaping the campaign against ISIS.[27]

Obama, then, like US presidents before, used religious reasoning to align his thinking with core democratic beliefs – he did not behave like a dictator, using religion to shore up his base. In other words, not completely a secularist, he is pragmatic in his application of his faith on the world stage. He does not use Christianity to inflame the country into seeing ISIS and Syria as a religious war. He was careful never to say Islam was the problem but used radicals and terrorists as labels for ISIS, rather than reminding audiences of ISIS's relationship to Islam.

Contrast his approach to that used by Assad. In 2013, it appeared that Assad's rule was about to end. But he was able to enlist Hezbollah groups out of Lebanon, urging them to protect religious sites from attacks by Sunnis. Shia groups subsequently poured in from Lebanon and Iran. His regime seemed to stabilize.[28] In stark contrast, Obama's use of his religious belief slows down the passions. Did it slow him so much as to create a paralysis? Why would he draw a "red line" at the use chemical weapons and then do nothing militarily when Assad used them? Well, we will see that he didn't do nothing. He is, though, definitely more cautious than Assad, or Bush, in his use of force. He is more pragmatic and process-oriented than, say, Bush but is also still principled. And these principles are roughly the same as those he found in play between people of faith and the civil rights movement. He urged Assad to step down, and appealed to the international community for support, but worried that turning to violence would only make things worse. The complicating principle was that he felt a superior obligation to protect and defend the people of the US from all threats, foreign and domestic. In other words, he looked to national security interests first in making decisions on foreign policy and seems to be the first president to worry about the long-term harm to the US from appearing to take regime-changing sides against Shi'ite Muslims. As a result we have to see what national interest analysis is, according to Obama, and how it might be different from the US first policy of his successor, Donald Trump.

The facts on the ground and Obama's decisions

In the lead-up to the outbreak of violence in 2011, it may be that Syria was not the highest priority for the Obama administration, though events there had gradually begun drawing its attention. As we saw in Chapter 2, Assad likely came to Obama's attention based on allegations that he may have been behind the assassination attempt on the (former) president of Lebanon. The UN had, at the request of Lebanon, agreed to investigate the matter, and, with US backing, it had begun the process of setting up a special tribunal.

The International Atomic Energy Administration (IAEA), a nuclear watchdog, may have inadvertently contributed to the isolation of Syria. In June 2011, the IAEA reported Syria to the UN Security Council for alleging that Syria was undertaking a covert nuclear reactor program. The building that contained the alleged reactor was previously targeted in the 2007 Israeli air raid. The timing of the release of the report was likely seen by the US as implicit support for sanctions against Syria. On the other hand, Assad must have been under the impression that the international community was conspiring to bring about regime change in Syria.

Assad doubled down on his strategy of oppression

In July 2011, Assad fired the governor of the northern province of Hama after a mass demonstration there. He then sent in troops to restore order at the cost of scores of lives. The same month, internal and exiled opposition activists announced the informal creation of the Syrian National Council (SNC) in Turkey to coordinate political strategies to unite different political and religious groups against the regime. In October, the SNC announced a structure to become more united since more opposition groups sprung up during the beginning of the uprising. In such a move, the SNC was hoping for the world to see it as a government in exile.[29] In November even the Arab League turned against Assad. It voted to suspend Syrian membership, accusing it of failing to implement an Arab peace plan, and imposed sanctions. Perhaps it would be the Arab league that would take responsibility for setting things right in Syria.

By early 2012, the uprising against President Assad gradually turned into a full-scale civil war. In February, the government stepped up the bombardment of Homs and other cities. The sanctions did not seem to be working, instead making Assad only that much more desperate. The international community responded. In March the UN Security Council endorsed a non-binding peace plan drafted by UN envoy Kofi Annan. China and even Russia agreed to support the plan after an earlier, tougher draft was modified.

By June 2012 Turkey was pulled into the fighting. Turkey changed rules of engagement after Syria shot down a Turkish plane, declaring that if Syrian troops approach Turkey's borders they will be seen as a military threat.

By July, one group of rebels consolidated itself under the banner of the Free Syrian Army. It killed three senior-level members of Syrian security police in Damascus and seized Aleppo in the north. By August the Assad regime appeared to be coming apart. Syrian prime minister Riad Hijab defected. Here is an interesting moment in history that bears examining. What one wants from sanctions is pressure. But if the pressure is too much, the subject can take all the more desperate measures out of self-defense. One wonders if there could have been any way for Obama to reach out to Assad to relieve the pressure he was feeling? The problem is that once principles and rhetoric have been used to rally the sanctioning by allies, it could very well appear to those same allies that if you make a deal with the subject of those sanctions you are also rewarding the subject. Giving a golden parachute to someone who has done such harm to citizens and friends just doesn't seem right. Still, there were those in the non-governmental organization (NGO) community that wished Obama had shown some willingness to negotiate with Assad. At the same time, there were those who couldn't see how Assad could survive. Iran was making its own deal for the lifting of sanctions and was, and still is, capable of supporting a proxy war. Russia was not yet then fully in the picture, and with the falling price of oil and interventions in Crimea and Georgia, it was hard to see how Russia would want to get involved. In any event, Obama talked tough. He warned Assad that use of chemical weapons would tilt the US towards intervention.

In the next month, the Syrian government ratcheted up its attacks on the Free Syrian Army in Aleppo. The refugee crisis became exacerbated. Fire in Aleppo destroyed much of the historic market as fighting and bomb attacks continued in both Aleppo and various other cities. Other rebel groups seemed to start to coordinate with each other. The National Coalition for Syrian Revolutionary and Opposition Forces formed in Qatar. They attempted to exclude Islamist militias and Al Qaeda–affiliated groups, but those tracking these groups on the ground were skeptical that Al Qaeda could be effectively excluded. The Arab League stopped short of full recognition, perhaps fearing that it would appear to be picking Sunnis over Shi'ites in the civil war even though the Coalition reserved up to five seats for Alawites.[30]

By December, the US, Britain, France, Turkey, and the Gulf states formally recognized the National Coalition as "legitimate representative" of Syrian people. Each country who provide its own level of support. The US would provide humanitarian aid and start the process of providing training and logistical support.

The conflict in Syria displaced millions of people, many of whom sought refuge in camps in Jordan, Turkey, and Lebanon. An estimated 11 million Syrians have fled their homes since the outbreak of the civil war in March 2011. Now, in the sixth year of the war, 13.5 million are in need of humanitarian assistance within the country. Among those escaping the conflict, the majority have sought refuge in neighboring countries or within Syria itself. According to the United Nations High Commissioner for Refugees (UNHCR), 4.8 million have fled to Turkey,

Lebanon, Jordan, Egypt and Iraq, and 6.6 million are internally displaced within Syria. Meanwhile about 1 million have requested asylum to Europe. Germany, with more than 300,000 cumulated applications, and Sweden with 100,000, are the EU's top receiving countries.

Before getting ahead or the analysis of Obama's decisions we need to understand what he knew and when he knew it. A timeline will keep the analysis on track.

2013 January – Syria accuses Israel of bombing military base near Damascus where Hezbollah was suspected of assembling a convoy of anti-aircraft missiles bound for Lebanon.

Chemical arms claims

Government forces have faced – and denied – repeated allegations of chemical weapons use.

Rise of Islamists

2013 September – UN weapons inspectors conclude that chemical weapons were used in an attack on the Ghouta area of Damascus in August that killed about 300 people but do not allocate responsibility. The government allows UN to destroy chemical weapons stocks, process complete by June 2014.

2013 December – US and Britain suspend "non-lethal" support for rebels in northern Syria after reports that Islamist rebels seized bases of Western-backed Free Syrian Army.

2014 January–February – UN-brokered peace talks in Geneva fail, largely because Syrian authorities refuse to discuss a transitional government. (No threat made by the US to deal or face consequences.)

2014 March – The Syrian army and Hezbollah forces recapture Yabroud, the last rebel stronghold near the Lebanese border.

2014 June – Islamic State of Iraq and Syria militants declare "caliphate" in territory from Aleppo to eastern Iraqi province of Diyala.

2014 September – the US and five Arab countries launch air strikes against Islamic State around Aleppo and Raqqa.

2015 January – Kurdish forces push Islamic State out of Kobane on Turkish border after four months of fighting.

2015 May – Islamic State fighters seize the ancient city of Palmyra in central Syria and proceed to destroy many monuments at a pre-Islamic World Heritage Site.

The Jaish al-Fatah (Army of Conquest) Islamist rebel alliance takes control of Idlib Province, putting pressure on government's coastal stronghold of Latakia.

The case for and against Obama's failure to intervene with military force in Syria

I have attempted to use Obama's own words to determine if he acted consistently to his principles, I have tried to fairly present the facts on the ground in Syria as they unfolded to give context to the individual actions and failures to act for which he might be criticized.

There are three key issues that need to be assessed in determining whether Obama's foreign policy regarding Syria was effective. The first is whether he should have announced that Assad needs to step down from the presidency. The second is whether, having drawn a "red line" with regard to Assad's use of chemical weapons, Obama should have taken military action against Assad instead of negotiating a removal of those chemical weapons. The third issue is whether he should have backed one of the anti-Assad rebel groups early on in order to help stop and prevent the refugee crisis that has been destabilizing much of Europe.

What about his having announced that Assad must go on August 18, 2011?

Why did he make the threat in the first place? Should he have threatened Assad that he must step down despite knowing that Assad's back was against the wall? If you look back at the chronology, you can see that the US, through Assistant Secretary of State Hof, had been trying to negotiate a peace agreement between Syria and Israel. The US had opened an embassy in Damascus in January 2011, and there had already been a number of visits with Assad. On the other hand, Obama might have thought that Assad's character was showing through: it would have been easy for Obama to think that Assad's alleged involvement in the assassination in Lebanon, his support of Hezbollah in Lebanon, and his building of a nuclear weapons facility would make it highly unlikely that he would play well with others. And then he responded brutally to the demonstrators and ramped up the actions of his security force. Assad showed no interest in cooperating or negotiating with demonstrators.

Perhaps Obama was taking lessons from the Arab Spring uprising in Egypt. January 25, 2011, was the day of nationwide student protests in Egypt. President Mubarak had already announced his resignation on February 11, 2011. The US hadn't backed Mubarak, but neither had it announced support for any group in Egypt. In early 2011, Obama might have thought that the same process was underway in Syria. His announcement would only encourage the process and was perhaps not meant to foreclose later negotiations.

It was also not as if Obama was acting alone. His administration vetted the idea with European allies and on the same day that Obama delivered his statement on Assad's future, the leaders of France, Germany, Britain, and the EU also called on the Syrian leader to step aside. Obama also telephoned Turkish leader Recep Tayyip Erdogan about two weeks before issuing his statement, giving Erdogan advanced notice.

Additionally, Obama unveiled new economic sanctions that froze Syrian government assets within the US and prohibited US firms from buying, selling, or processing Syrian oil.

But why make the threat if you were not willing to actually do something about making it happen? Obama would have a number of responses to his. As we have seen, he may have felt the US had not been sufficiently supportive of regime change in Egypt and so lost an opportunity to partner with Egyptians in their first attempts at real democracy. In other words, if you don't say what side you are on, you lose the opportunity to be partners with the winners later. In addition, the US's position could be seen as an encouragement to the democratic forces on the ground. Obama would likely regret this later, as the adoption of such a position also runs the risk of giving the rebel groups a false hope that the US would intervene on their side. Such groups would later feel abandoned, and disrespected, when they were not joined in their fight by the US.

And then there was Libya, but the lessons there would not be learned for a number of months yet. What was learned in hindsight was that even where you are successful in fomenting a regime change, the new situation created may be worse than the one before. This lesson that you might better negotiate with the existing leader to avoid a Libyan-like power vacuum that would lead to disaster was a lesson the Obama administration, again, would regrettably learn only later on.[31]

Obama might say that in the end, none of these considerations mattered because Assad was set on a course of violent suppression of protests that would make him unacceptable to most Syrians regardless of what Obama said. "This is a guy whose portfolio of war crimes and crimes against humanity is very impressive," Hof said. "If you're looking for someone able to inspire confidence, this is the last guy you would look for to provide that."[32]

It would be interesting if in making his case for his actions and in actions regarding Syria, Obama would now argue that he was acting consistently with his religious beliefs. The least he should do in the face of evil would be to speak against and condemn it. The Nieburhean needle he was threading between combatting evil and trusting that, over the course of history, actors will do the right thing seemed to have left him feeling like he must at least say something. Obama was still at this point committed to using force, if, like in the case of Rwanda, the US could prevent a genocide. The problem was correctly determining whether Assad's brutal repression of his own people was turning into war crimes, and war crimes into mass exodus. Let's look at each of these in turn.

Should Obama have drawn a "red line" concerning Assad's use of chemical weapons, and then once Assad crossed it, should he have intervened?

Obama mistrusted his own instinct to use military force because he wondered seriously about the consequences that would actually follow from its use. Without more information about consequences, this reluctance left him timid to trust his feelings of outrage. He seemed to take to heart Michael Kahneman's advice in his book (one on Obama's reading list) *Thinking Fast, Thinking Slow*: that it was important to think through the hard complexities of a problem and not cheat by reverting to myths and traditions in substitute for careful calculation of consequences.

What were the US's real motives for intervening? Was it to prevent further harm to civilians? At least Obama did not need to worry as much that US intervention in Syria would be perceived by countries in the Middle East as being motivated by oil. Suspicions of the US's oil-related national security motivations for intervention had been assuaged by a number of factors. The US was not nearly as dependent as it had been on Middle East oil: it had by this point developed a robust gas industry at home as well as fracking techniques that turned the US into an exporter of natural gas. It had a burgeoning alternative power industry in the way of solar and wind energy that made it less dependent on oil, in the short run, and more responsible regarding the threat of climate change. And Syria, itself, was not a major market for oil and gas. This is not to say that the price of oil had fallen in 2011–2012. It was trading above $100 a barrel (US dollars). Still, there is no evidence that any intervention in Syria would have had oil as a motivating factor.

Note that in its form during George Walker Bush's presidency, neoconservatives shared Obama's skepticism about government interventions as being always a force for good. Conservatives are generally worried about creating dependencies or about doing more harm than good when some big government program attempts to make things right. Conservatives, generally, are clear about their skepticism regarding solving domestic conflicts but are much less clear concerning international conflicts. Neoconservatives would find agreement with Obama that such views were overly optimistic about the ability of actors, no matter how well intentioned, to be both successful in their interventions and to later be embraced by "those on the ground" for the intervention. But neoconservatives tended to take that argument in a different direction. They thought such skepticism about effectiveness should not foreclose intervention but rather reinforce it if one could find a national interest at stake in the given dispute. In other words, perhaps interventions based solely on promoting American values to and for others would not take seriously the existence of evil in the world. The priority was to be national interests, and then the need for the US to make proud and confident appeals to its principles that would promote the "buy-in" from the US electorate.

Following the exact meaning of "neoconservatism" as a matter of foreign policy is a matter of some complexity, as its meaning has evolved in response to the politics of those using it. The meaning initially was meant to convey resistance to the New Left policies of George McGovern. So while Paul Wolfowitz had initially learned his brand of neoconservatism from Henry "Scoop" Jackson, that is, as a reaction to the anti-war movement against the Vietnam War, during the late 1970s Wolfowitz wedded his ideas to the lessons learned from Ronald Reagan, the Republican who renewed Truman's promise to confront Soviet expansionism.[33]

Wolfowitz's brand of neoconservatism drew its ideas from the political science professor Leo Strauss. Strauss helped inspire at least one major group of neoconservatives. Strauss was a refugee from Nazi Germany who taught at the New School for Social Research in New York (1939–1949) and the University of

Chicago (1949–1958).[34] His thinking was a response to the slowness with which the US and the international community responded to the Holocaust. If the US had acted more quickly, might the Holocaust have to some degree been prevented? According to Strauss, "the crisis of the West consists in the West's having become uncertain of its purpose."[35] He proposed a restoration of the vital ideas and faith that in the past had sustained the moral purpose of the West. The US's Judeo-Christian heritage was essential to its view of itself and to its understanding of the "Great Tradition."[36]

Conservatives, then, are rejecting a post-Enlightenment and post-modern view of the US's role in the world. They, along with Strauss, are ready to repudiate the philosophy of John Locke. They see Locke not as having grounded human rights in the common dignity of what it means to be human, but as a major mistake in philosophy that would lead to a subjective epistemology: that of power and narrow self-interests. Locke and the liberals were on a path to 20th-century historicism and nihilism. Neoconservatives defended liberal democracy as being closer to the spirit of the classics and Judeo-Christian values than other modern regimes. Human beings could trust their natural instincts for distinguishing good from evil and right from wrong.[37] Instead of making neoconservatives lean against acting at all, they used Strauss to argue for trusting one's sense of self and ones' history. American awareness of ineradicable evil in human nature was not turned inward, to make one distrust, as Obama would, his own motivations and reasoning. The neoconservatives instead turned the American awareness of evil outward, allowing decision makers to see and condemn the evil of others. The evil in the world called for a response. American exceptionalism, and its success in World War I and World War II, proved that its motivations were unapologetically on the side of the good. The US uniquely fit the role of the world's police, filling a great need for a moral response to the existence of evil. It was conservative because it was returning to the Enlightenment thinking, with its faith in human reason as being able to judge good from evil and right from wrong.[38] Strauss's influence caused his students to reject historicism *and* positivism. Instead, they promoted a so-called Aristotelian perspective on America that produced a qualified defense of its liberal constitutionalism.[39]

In *Audacity of Hope*, Obama is critical of this thinking. He preferred the foreign policy decision-making of Bush I's secretary of state, Brent Scowcroft. He worries more about the ability of reason and intuition to lead him astray. He did not take the subjectivity of history as a justification to act out a positivistic reasoning, a reasoning that would grow out of power as president to declare emergencies and to define the conditions of self-interest. He was more post-modern in his thinking but not all the way to denying that evil existed in the world. He is quoted in a marvelous interview by Jeffrey Goldberg, in *Atlantic Magazine*, as follows:

> For all of our warts, the United States has clearly been a force for good in the world," he said. "If you compare us to previous superpowers, we act less on the basis of naked self-interest, and have been interested in establishing

> norms that benefit everyone. If it is possible to do good at a bearable cost, to save lives, we will do it.[40]

Goldberg goes on to unpack Obama's thinking here:

> If a crisis, or a humanitarian catastrophe, does not meet his stringent standard for what constitutes a direct national-security threat, Obama said, he doesn't believe that he should be forced into silence. He is not so much the realist, he suggested, that he won't pass judgment on other leaders. Though he has so far ruled out the use of direct American power to depose Assad, he was not wrong, he argued, to call on Assad to go. "Oftentimes when you get critics of our Syria policy, one of the things that they'll point out is 'You called for Assad to go, but you didn't force him to go. You did not invade.' And the notion is that if you weren't going to overthrow the regime, you shouldn't have said anything. That's a weird argument to me, the notion that if we use our moral authority to say, 'This is a brutal regime, and this is not how a leader should treat his people,' once you do that, you are obliged to invade the country and install a government you prefer."
>
> "I am very much the internationalist," Obama said in a later conversation. "And I am also an idealist insofar as I believe that we should be promoting values, like democracy and human rights and norms and values, because not only do they serve our interests the more people adopt values that we share – in the same way that, economically, if people adopt rule of law and property rights and so forth, that is to our advantage – but because it makes the world a better place. And I'm willing to say that in a very corny way, and in a way that probably Brent Scowcroft would not say.
>
> "Having said that," he continued, "I also believe that the world is a tough, complicated, messy, mean place, and full of hardship and tragedy. And in order to advance both our security interests and those ideals and values that we care about, we've got to be hardheaded at the same time as we're big-hearted, and pick and choose our spots, and recognize that there are going to be times where the best that we can do is to shine a spotlight on something that's terrible, but not believe that we can automatically solve it. There are going to be times where our security interests conflict with our concerns about human rights. There are going to be times where we can do something about innocent people being killed, but there are going to be times where we can't."

At least part of Obama's reasoning is that he was being pragmatic. Could US troops even win in light of their rotated service on battlefields of Afghanistan and Iraq? He argued that his policy was based on simple common sense. It part was a consideration of "growing the size of our armed forces to maintain reasonable rotation schedules"[41]

While Obama was a fan of Brent Scowcroft he did not use Jeane Kirkpatrick's name (Kilpatrick was a Democrat who became a Republican and served in

Ronald Reagan Security Council) in justifying his position of nonintervention. Kirkpatrick argued a difficult distinction between authoritarian regimes and the totalitarian regimes, such as the Soviet Union. Obama might have agreed with her suggestion that in some countries democracy was not tenable. In those situations the US had a choice between endorsing authoritarian governments, which might evolve into democracies, or Marxist-Leninist regimes, which she argued had never collapsed once they achieved totalitarian control.

Obama might see something similar to Kilpatrick's distinction in the choice he had in Syria but disagree that inaction was limited to Marxist-Leninist regimes. In my view, the distinction Kirkpatrick drew between endorsing authoritarian governments or dealing with Marxist-Leninist regimes turns out to be not as important as an assessment of whether the country was ready for democracy, or could move toward democracy with substantial involvement from the United States. Obama might argue that neither Assad nor any of the prominent rebel groups were likely to evolve into democracies. Obama and Kirkpatrick might see these situations the same way, as tragic but not as evoking a duty or obligation to intervene. Furthermore, the religious nature of the situation, which could easily pit Sunni and Shi'ite Muslims against each other, made a conversion to a democratic system particularly difficult.[42]

But, of course, by the time of Obama, neoconservatism no longer reacted against clarion calls for democracy. They saw events in the Soviet Union as an example of the kind of rapid and largely unexpected regime change that can occur, even in long-entrenched communist regimes. Emboldened by the fall of the Soviet Union, US foreign policy again became more principled, teaming up national-interest analysis with Churchillian calls for the advancement of democracy and human rights. The US should not be afraid to call evil "evil" and act accordingly.

In fact, the neoconservatives, after laying low during George H. W. Bush's administration, reemerged more willing to advocate for democracy and human rights as justifications for intervening. Reacting in particular to President Bill Clinton, neoconservatives now advocated for a more principled and muscular use of force, claiming such force as the reason the Soviet Union fell. Now, instead of worrying that interventions are fruitless, they argued that use of power was an important factor in making the world safe for democracy. By the time of Clinton, they were endorsing the ouster of Saddam Hussein.[43] Was this simply a rediscovery of Strauss, a perception of Clinton as overly "New Left," or a shift to claim a moral high ground in politics?

Importantly, this shift was cloaked in a religious claim of the Christian right. Reagan had boldly connected the religious right's fight against abortion, and scientism, with the fight against communism. The Christian right was espousing a claim that Darwin's theories of evolution were lacking in that they only explained changes in the genetic makeup the species, without being able to explain progress: Darwin's theories lacked in normative values. One could mark change but not whether the change was good or evil. Instead, these Christian right philosophers argued for an "intelligent design" in the universe.[44] One could have hope, or have faith, that God was acting in the world, revealing God's self in the creation. And one could trust one's intuition of right and wrong to help them determine what was evil in the world.

During the late 1990s, prominent writers in neoconservative magazines began touting anti-Darwinist views as an endorsement of "intelligent design." They tried to inspire the religious right to see the potential religious implications of using force: to protect Israel and perhaps bring in Christ's second coming. For some, democracy was again part of the religious appeal for making the world safe and expanding right thinking around the world.

Again, note that Obama's religious perspectives eschewed the tactical use of religion to gain political support for a war. He saw these as blatantly manipulative and dangerous. He tried to maintain a "go-slow" approach based on a belief that human nature had a tendency to play tricks on one's reasoning, even when confronting evil. He would describe his approach as more practical and based on common sense.

Having drawn the red line about Assad's use of chemical weapons what did he do when there was evidence that Assad crossed the line? He chose not to use military force – at least not without the approval of Congress. Congress refused the opportunity given it to weigh in. So no military action was taken at that time. This is not to say Obama did nothing. As we will see, he went to the UN and got the UN Security Council to pass a resolution condemning Assad's use of chemical weapons. Important to our discussion in the next chapter, Russia and China joined in on the resolution. He also got cooperation from the European Community for further sanctions. In fact, he did not stop there but would go on to help orchestrate UN negotiations with Assad that got him to agree to the UN's inspecting whether chemical weapons were used and then helping him destroy them.

In September 2013, UN weapons inspectors concluded that chemical weapons were used in an attack on the Ghouta area of Damascus in August that killed about 300 people. The UN did not allocate responsibility. Assad then allowed the UN to destroy chemical weapons stocks and that process was supposedly complete by June 2014. During this same time, UN involvement helped to set up peace talks in Geneva. While these would fail, the Obama administration might have thought that it needed to give these talks a chance to work. The international community applauded the negotiations.

Why then the criticism now over his failure to intervene militarily? Well, as we now know, the refugee crisis only got worse. The war against ISIS has dragged on, and the sense that a power vacuum in Syria had contributed to the rise of ISIS again raised the criticism that Obama should have intervened militarily. Moreover, Assad did not, in fact, destroy all of his chemical weapons. So, the deal, in the end, did not stop Assad from committing further war crimes. In addition, not acting in response to the use of chemical weapons allowed Russia to get more intimately involved, which involvement likely means that the chances for a successful transition to democracy in Syria have been seriously diminished. Of course, all these events had not yet happened, and it is unfair if the criticism is that Obama should have predicted their occurrence.

Russian intervention and all-out proxy war

In September 2015, at the invitation of Syria, Russia carried out its first air strikes in Syria claiming to target the Islamic State while the West and Syrian opposition claim the targets had overwhelmingly been anti-Assad rebels. Obama seems neutral about Russia's involvement, saying at one point, "[G]ood luck."[45] Obama reasoned that Russia would soon discover that backing Assad would align it with Iran and other Shi'ite militia that would have negative consequences with Sunnis and the Saudis, who overwhelming opposed Iran. Russia might fear that Sunnis and Sufis in Chechnya might be upset. It was the opposite of the reason that Obama did not back rebel groups: Obama was hopeful that he could yet draw Iran back into the international community by negotiating an end to sanctions against Iran in exchange for their halting development of nuclear capabilities.

In December 2015, the Syrian army would allow rebels to evacuate the remaining areas of Homs, returning Syria's third-largest city to government control after four years. Assad seemed to be taking back land for the Syrian regime. With assistance from the Russian air force, Syrian government forces regained Palmyra from ISIS. But then they were driven out again. In August 2016, Turkey got involved. In the last months of the Obama administration, it appeared that Turkey would also take a more active role in helping rebel groups combat ISIS. In August, on the eve of the election, Turkish troops crossed into Syria to help rebel groups push back so-called Islamic State militants and Kurdish-led rebels from a section of the two countries' border. But what was Turkey's motive? Were they afraid of the Kurds forming an independent state within Syria and on Turkey's on its border? Things in Syria seemed to be getting even more chaotic, and with the rise of terrorist strikes in Europe, many started to blame the US for failing to take more decisive action in Syria.

Finally, in December 2016, Syrian government troops, backed by Russian air power and Iranian-sponsored militias, recaptured Aleppo, the country's largest city, depriving the rebels of their last major urban stronghold. It looked like US attempts to get Assad to step aside had failed completely.

Let's stop here to examine Obama's decision to involve the US Congress. His decision appears to show that he ultimately was putting his faith in democratic principles as the best basis – morally, effectively, and pragmatically – for involving the US in a war when there was evidence of war crimes being committed by the country's leader. Perhaps Obama was ambivalent to take on the decision himself when there was no immediate threat to the US (although the Syrian war created a growing refugee crisis to US allies and served as an incubator for future terrorist groups). After all military action to be effective would likely mean committing troops on the ground to a situation with no clear end game. Yet if the US saw itself as the necessary promoter of democratic principles and prevented or war crimes, Congress could see a legitimate basis for the US getting involved. The constitution does dictate that it is up to Congress to declare war.

Instead of his decision to involve Congress being seen as a return to the rule of law, it has been viewed as a sign of US weakness, of a step back from US values and confidence in itself to act with moral authority to stamp out obvious evil where it exists in the world. Let's see what Obama himself said was his reasoning and what it might tell us going forward about the US' view of itself as a moral actor on the world stage.

From Jeffrey Goldberg's interview with Obama we learn the following:

He gave several reasons for not intervening in Syria

- The bombing might not do much and have unintended consequences. He worried about bombing when there were UN inspectors on the ground in Damascus and did not want to risk their lives. Additionally, bombing chemical weapons could cause plumes of deadly poison to be released in the air.
- David Cameron hadn't been able to get the British Parliament to authorize the use of force, and Angela Merkel had informed him that Germany would not be participating in the Syria campaign either. The US would be going at it alone.
- He worried that bombing would only strengthen Assad's hand. Without committing troops on the ground, bombing may not properly destroy the chemical weapons. Assad could then argue he had stood up to the US, allowing him to recruit Iran and an even greater number of Shi'ite militia to his side. The unintended consequence here would be strengthening Assad's hand. Look at ISIS. The more they are reviled, the greater number their recruits. His fourth reason relates to theory: he was worried about the scope of presidential power in making war. He argued that he wanted to set a precedent for returning that power to the place where the constitution designated it to be, with Congress.
- Later in the article, Obama would give a fifth reason for not bombing. It turns out that early during the week in which the decision was being made, director of national intelligence James Clapper made clear that the intelligence on Syria's use of sarin gas, while robust, was not a "slam dunk." (Remember that "slam dunk" was the term famously used by George Tenet in guaranteeing to George W. Bush that there were weapons of mass destruction in Iraq.)
- And six, he found himself recoiling from using force as a matter of international law. (Note, he had no problem with using drones in Pakistan and in Syria.)
- And seven, while committed to preventing genocide on the scale of what had occurred in Rwanda, Obama just did not see the situation in Syria the same way. Assad may have been at war with his own people and committing war crimes, but the US could not fight every battle everywhere in the world. Already involved in two wars (Iraq and Afghanistan), the US could simply not afford to be drawn into another war.
- Eight, the US had other priorities, including its policies in Asia and in relation to global warming.

But what about the argument that US credibility requires that it act once it has drawn the red line? Won't others around the world who are contemplating war crimes, or invading another state, be comforted by the US's failure to support its own stated principles and make good on its threats? American national-security credibility, as it is conventionally understood in the Pentagon and the State Department, is an important force – one that, when properly nurtured, keeps America's friends feeling secure and keeps the international order stable. When confronted with his having, in a sense, set up Kerry to look foolish, Obama responded that he did not think the credibility argument was very credible. Again, Goldberg:

> Obama generally believes that the Washington foreign-policy establishment, which he secretly disdains, makes a fetish of "credibility" – particularly the sort of credibility purchased with force. The preservation of credibility, he says, led to Vietnam. Within the White House, Obama would argue that "dropping bombs on someone to prove that you're willing to drop bombs on someone is just about the worst reason to use force."

Obama also had excuses for why he did not arm any of the "moderate" rebel groups in Syria, to be the US proxy on the ground to fight Assad. He worried that these groups had shifting alliances and had already taken aid for other terrorist organizations. How committed were they really to democratic ideals? Hilary Clinton seemed to take the opposite position when she ran for president: that this is the policy Obama should have taken and the one she would have taken in Syria.

Hilary Clinton's position does ignore a number of practical considerations. Which group of the close to 2,500 groups that formed in Syria since 2011 would Obama have backed? Each group had multiple and shifting alliances. Arming one might inadvertently end up arming an Al Qaeda group, or a group affiliated with Hezbollah, or the Muslim Brotherhood, or Iran, or Saudi Arabia, or ISIS, or groups with a history of atrocities themselves. For instance, initially Obama was concerned that arming and involving the Kurds would alienate Turkey, but Erdogan's becoming more and more authoritarian and militant caused offending him to become less important.

Practical difficulties and the fear of unintended consequences may have been the real reasons for non-intervention. But still worth noting is what was behind Obama's decision to go to Congress. What does it say about the US's foreign policy and its view of itself?

On one hand, Obama's appeal to Congress might be seen as cynical move and one that was designed to expose and embarrass the Congress as being unwilling and unable to show leadership on a world stage. Perhaps worn down by its inaction on immigration, health care, infrastructure rebuilding, and the commitment of Republicans to oppose anything that might come from his administration, he thought appealing to Congress would show its moral failures. After all, if neoconservatives would be believed, then the US Congress ought to readily authorize force as a statement of who it was, its moral authority in the world, its exceptionalism, and its Judeo-Christian values. Perhaps he just wanted to show up the Republicans.

On the other hand, Obama appeared to be acting consistently with his own religious beliefs, pragmatically disciplined by the situation on the ground. If the US was to commit troops, it would want international support and clear support from the American people. Through Congress the US could express how it saw Syria as vital to its national interest and sense of self and had faith that democracy was still ascendant. It would express itself against totalitarianism, hoping that others would see it in decline.

As it worked out, in Congress's review of whether to send in troops to Syria, the Congress rejected the opportunity to exercise its power. By rejecting its power, perhaps the Congress, and the electorate who elected them, have lost faith in democracy as a basis for justifying war. They would rather have a strong leader acting boldly and defining what needs to be done, even when committing US troops. In so doing, Congress seems to enable the president to act as other dictators might act. And so there is confusion to the world about how the US sees itself.

Assessing Obama's doctrine

Any potential condemnation of the US and Obama's decision-making not to intervene in Syria in 2013 should be more sanguine of his perspective. His intentions were pure, for the most part, but perhaps his judgment of the consequences is where he erred. Here is what we know now. He was able to negotiate an agreement for the removal of chemical weapons but that there is some evidence that the UN inspectors were misled by Assad that all chemical weapons had been removed or destroyed. Obama worked with the Russians to get Assad's cooperation in the hope that Russia will cooperate in ending the Syria conflict, but Russia now comes to his defense, both in providing air support for his attacks on ISIS and other rebel groups and in helping Assad deny his responsibility for the 2017 use of chemical weapons.

The benefits from intervention now are clearer to see. While it is unfair to say that Obama was solely responsible for created ISIS (ISIS was formed, in part, from an earlier failure on the part of the US and Iraq to see the disaffection caused by the US invasion of Iraq on former Sunni military leaders), still, if the US had intervened, perhaps it would have been more ready to act to prevent its rise in Syria. On the other hand, ISIS seems now to be on the brink of defeat in Syria, and the US has not lost soldiers in the fight against ISIS. Perhaps non-intervention is still the better course.

The second benefit to intervening is that perhaps the refugee crisis could have been averted. This is perhaps the most troubling consequence to the Obama Doctrine as applied in Syria. That cost is born more directly by Europe than the US, though it has a destabilizing effect on democracy in both places.

The bet behind the Obama Doctrine is a long-term bet, that any real change in Syria and the Middle East, needs to come from within, (some say at least initially this is where the change came from), as opposed to from without. The doctrine rests on the belief that if democracy is imposed, its benefits are fragile at best. Egypt is a good example of what is likely to follow. Iraq still struggles with its brand of democracy. Better for Syrians themselves to come together and put religious and tribal differences aside than for the US to intervene and enforce a new peace. The bet is that, where mediated by the UN, or through some other coalition, democracy has a better chance. In the next chapter I will look more closely at what the UN's role might be in this regard. We will see how the International Criminal Court will complicate its decision-making concerning peacemaking in Syria. We will also see how it has also developed its role as a mediator in an attempt to "finesse" the legal dilemmas in making peace with evil. And this will lead, in turn, to a better understanding of the vital role that transformative justice principles will have to play as a post-conflict Syria struggles between dictatorship and democracy.

Notes

1 *Front Line* documentary: www.pbs.org/wgbh/frontline/article/the-president-blinked-why-obama-changed-course-on-the-red-line-in-syria/.
2 Oren, Ally, *My Journey across the American-Israeli Divide* (New York: Random House, 2016), 327.
3 Martin Meredith, *The Fate of Africa: A History of Fifty Years of Independence* (New York: PublicAffairs, 2005), 1–12.
4 Robert Pastor, *Existing the Whirlpool: U.S. Foreign Policy toward Latin America and the Caribbean* (Boulder, CO: Westview Press, 2001), Chapter 12.
5 Stephen Kintzer, *The Brothers, John Foster Dulles, Allen Dulles, and Their Secret World War* (New York: Times Books, Henry Holt, 2013).

> Well, many would argue that that was a simple pretense – Mosaddegh, of course, nationalized the oil industry and seriously upset British Petroleum, which then called in the British foreign service, which then called in the Americans and the CIA.
>
> Also worth noting is that this containment business was really even less nuanced – it was very much a case of "with us or against us," and it is frequently cited that many foreign policy leaders (especially the Dulles brothers) felt a *neutral* country to be in some ways even more dangerous than a Soviet-aligned one.
>
> That was a big problem with Mossadegh and Iran (and Sukarno in Indonesia and so on): he wasn't formally aligned with either side, but his moves to nationalize oil and to begin to be friendly with the Soviets was very disconcerting for the Cold War theorists in D.C.

6 Oren, *Ally: My Journey across the American-Israeli Divide*, 510–511.
7 www.theatlantic.com/magazine/archive/2016/04/the-obama-doctrine/471525/.
8 Bob Woodward, *Obama's War*, (New York: Simon Shuster, 2010); Barack Obama, *Dreams from My Father: A Story of Race and Inheritance*, (New York: Three Rivers Press, 2004).
9 Some even saw the hand of God behind what happened in the Soviet Union. After all Reagan had invoked God to the religious right, in his reasoning for being tough on and standing up to Soviets. He declared communism to be godless, a faith in man, rather than a faith in God. Remarks at the Annual Convention of the National Association of Evangelicals in Orlando, Florida, March 8, 1983, http:Reagan.edu/archives/speeches/1983/30883b.htm:

> there is sin and evil in the world and we're enjoined by Scripture and the Lord Jesus to oppose it with all our might.
>
> Id.

10 See *Atlantic* article. "If you think about, let's say, the Iran hostage crisis, there is a narrative that has been promoted today by some of the Republican candidates that the day Reagan was elected, because he looked tough, the Iranians decided, 'We better turn over these hostages, . . .'

In fact what had happened was that there was a long negotiation with the Iranians and because they so disliked Carter – even though the negotiations had been completed – they held those hostages until the day Reagan got elected. Reagan's posture, his rhetoric, etc., had nothing to do with their release. When you think of the military actions that Reagan took, you have Grenada – which is hard to argue helped our ability to shape world events, although it was good politics for him back home. You have the Iran-Contra affair, in which we supported right-wing paramilitaries and did nothing to enhance our image in Central America, and it wasn't successful at all." He reminded me that Reagan's great foe, Daniel Ortega, is today the unrepentant president of Nicaragua.

11 During George W. Bush's presidency he referred to his reasoning for intervening in Iraq. It included a reference to Saddam's attack on his father. See John King, "Bush Calls Saddam, 'the Guy Who Tried to Kill My Dad'," *CNN*, Friday, September 27, 2002, http://edition.cnn.com/2002/ALLPOLITICS/09/27/bush.war.talk/.

12 Paul Watkins is the author of a memoir, "Stand Before Your God," and five novels. Paul Watkins, "A Promise of Redemption," *New York Times*, August 6, 1995, http://www.nytimes.com/1995/08/06/books/review/06obama-dreams.html

13 Obama, *Dreams from My Father*, 63.

14 Paul Watkins, "A Promise of Redemption," www.nytimes.com/1995/08/06/books/review/06obama-dreams.html.

15 Oren, *Ally: My Journey across the American-Israeli Divide*, 92–104.

16 Alexander Mooney, "Evangelist accuses Obama of distorting Bible," *CNN Politics*, http://www.cnn.com/2008/POLITICS/06/24/evangelical.vote/

17 Mary Bruce, "Franklin Graham Questions Obama's Faith," *ABC News*, February 21, 2012, http://abcnews.go.com/blogs/politics/2012/02/franklin-graham-questions-obamas-christian-faith/; Lisa Miller, "Cover Story: Barack Obama's Christian Journey," *US Newsweek*, April 11, 2008, http://www.newsweek.com/cover-story-barack-obamas-christian-journey-92611

18 Lisa Miller, "Religion and Politics of Division," *The Washington Post*, February 23, 2012, https://www.washingtonpost.com/national/on-faith/the-religion-and-politics-of-division/2012/02/22/gIQArmLVVR_story.html?utm_term=.6f51dce6c94c

19 Mary Bruce, "Franklin Graham Questions Obama's Faith," *ABC News*, February 21, 2012, http://abcnews.go.com/blogs/politics/2012/02/franklin-graham-questions-obamas-christian-faith/

20 Lisa Miller, "Cover Story: Barack Obama's Christian Journey," *US Newsweek*, July 11, 2008, www.newsweek.com/cover-story-barack-obamas-christian-journey-92611.

21 Lauren Markoe, "As Comey Testified, Trump Addressed Crowd of Conservative Christians: 'We're Under Siege'," *Religious News Service, Sojourners*, June 8, 2017, https://sojo.net/articles/comey-testified-trump-addressed-crowd-conservative-christians-we-re-under-siege

22 On the other hand, he also may have used the rhetoric of religion and of good and evil in a manner like Winston Churchill did to inspire the British during World War II. By condemning Assad as a threat to democracy and human rights, Obama also pushed Assad into the arms of the Russians.

23 The full speech on You Tube is at www.youtube.com/watch?v=AORo-YEXxNQ.

24 David Brooks, "Obama, Gospel and Verse," *NYT*, April 26, 2007, http://www.nytimes.com/2007/04/26/opinion/26brooks.html?mcubz=1

25 Ibid.
26 John Chandler, *Faith-Based Policy: A Litmus Test for Understanding Contemporary America* (England: Lexington Books, 2014).
27 *Faith-Based Policy: A Litmus Test for Understanding Contemporary America*, (Lanham, MD: Lexington Books, 2014), 115.
28 Daniel Burke, "Syria Explained, How It Became a Religious War," *CNN, Religion Blog* (http://religion.blogs.cnn.com/2013/09/04/syrian-wars-got-religion-and-that-aint-good/):

> In May, 2013, it appeared the rebels had the momentum and Assad's fall was just days away. Then Hezbollah, a Lebanese militant group, announced that it was joining the fray, and backing Assad. Within weeks, this fierce group, led by Hassan Nasrallah, had managed to wrestle key cities from rebel control, turning the war's tide. There aren't many Shiites in Syria, but the Assads courted them from neighboring Iran, Iraq and Lebanon, allowing them to build major shrines to the faith's founders in Syrian cities. The strategy seems to have worked. When Sunni rebels attacked those shrines, Shiites rushed in to defend them. Not that Sunnis and Shiites need many excuses to fight. They've been battling since the earliest days of Islam and continue to clash in Iraq and other countries. Nasrallah harkened back to those early clashes when Hezbollah entered the fray, calling the Syrian Sunni rebels "murderers of Hussein." Hussein ibn Ali was the Prophet Muhammad's grandson who refused to pledge allegiance to the ruling Muslim caliph in the 7th century. Shiites believe that he and his family were the rightful rulers of the Muslim community.
>
> **Sunnis**
>
> Sunni Muslims are by far the biggest Muslim sect, in the world and in Syria. It's estimated that Sunnis make up 75% of Syria's population of 22 million. But they've long been sidelined by the Assads. It's little surprise, then, that most of the Free Syrian Army, the largest rebel group, is Sunni. Within the Sunni coalition, there are remnants of the Muslim Brotherhood, who were brutally suppressed by the Assads; Salafists, who believe in a purified Islam based on its earliest days; and more secular-minded Sunnis. In recent months they've been joined – sometimes to their consternation – by fighters from al Qaeda-linked groups. Always eager to fight Shiites and sow discord, these jihadists are every bit as fierce and battle-tested as Hezbollah, their sworn enemy. It's unclear, however, how al Qaeda itself is involved in Syria.
>
> The Iraqi-branch commander reportedly overstepped his authority in June by **announcing a merger with Syria's al-Nusra Front**, earning a smackdown from Ayman al-Zawahiri, al-Qaeda's global leader.
>
> At the same time, some Syrian fighters say they **pretend to be al-Qaeda** just to annoy the Assad regime.
>
> Still, prominent Sunni Muslim cleric Sheikh Yusuf Qaradawi has called on all Sunnis to join the fight against the Shiites and Hezbollah, calling them *Hizb al-Shaytan*, the "Party of the Devil."
>
> Saudi Arabia and Qatar are backing that call with their wallets, **according to international reports**, hoping to prevent Shiites from gaining a stronghold in the region.

29 For a comprehensive analysis of the military side, see Brooking's Charles Lister: https://www.brookings.edu/wp-content/uploads/2016/11/iwr_20161123_free_syrian_army.pdf

30 Neil MacFarquar and Hala Broubi, With Eye on Aid, Syria Opposition Signs Unity Deal, Nov. 11, 2012, NYT, http://www.nytimes.com/2012/11/12/world/middleeast/syrian-opposition-groups-sign-unity-deal.html
31 Steve Mufson, in an article in *The Washington Post*, October 19, 2015, described the internal debate concerning Libya and Syria as follows:

> Two days after the statement was issued, (on Syria, that Assad must go), rebels launched an attack on Tripoli, Libya. Gaddafi fled before being captured and killed later that month. Four years later, however, Assad is still standing. Should Obama have been more restrained to avoid boxing himself into an untenable position?
>
> A former senior administration official, who was at the center of the debate over calling for Assad's removal, said that "initial decisions to *not* engage more were made against the backdrop of most analysts' belief that Assad would be gone in four to six months."
>
> However, he said, "after a while it was apparent that no matter what you did militarily you wouldn't be able to affect whether he was gone or not. We had been through instances in last 15 years where we didn't have a clear concept of where we were going and it was not in the interest of the United States."

32 Ibid.
33 Kubilay Yado Arin, *Think Tanks, the Brain Trusts of US Foreign Policy*, 81–93 (Wiesbaden: VS Springer, 2013).
34 Allan Bloom, "Leo Strauss: September 20, 1899 – October 18, 1973," *Political Theory*, Vol. 2, No. 4 (November 1974), pp. 372–92, an obituary and appreciation by one of his prominent students.
35 John P. East, "Leo Strauss and American Conservatism," *Modern Age*, Vol. 21, No. 1 (Winter, 1977), pp. 2–19 online.
36 Ibid.
37 Kenneth L. Deutsch and John Albert Murley, *Leo Strauss, the Straussians, and the American Regime* (Lanham, Toronto, Oxford, Boulder, CO and New York: Rowman & Littlefield, 1999), 63.
38 Thomas G. West, "Leo Strauss and the American Founding," *Review of Politics*, Vol. 53, No. 1 (Winter, 1991), pp. 157–72.
39 Johnathan O'Neill, "Straussian Constitutional History and the Straussian Political Project," *Rethinking History*, Vol. 13, No. 4 (December, 2009), pp. 459–78.
40 Jeffrey Goldberg, "The Obama Doctrine, the President Talks through His Toughest Decisions About America's in the World," *Atlantic*, April 2016, (hereinafter Obama Doctrine), www.theatlantic.com/magazine/archive/2016/04/the-obama-doctrine/471525/.
41 Michiko Kakutani, "Book Review of Audacity of Hope, *Obama's Foursquare Politics, with a Dab of Dijon*," *NYT*, October 17, 2006, www.nytimes.com/2006/10/17/books/17kaku.html.
42 Kirkpatrick argued that by demanding rapid liberalization in traditionally autocratic countries, the Carter administration had delivered those countries to Marxist-Leninists that were even more repressive. She further accused the Carter administration of a "double standard," of never having applied its rhetoric on the necessity of liberalization to communist governments.

> Jeane Kilpatrick, *The Economist*, December 19, 2006.

43 On February 19, 1998, an open letter to President Clinton was published, signed by dozens of pundits, many identified with neo-conservatism and, later, related groups such as the PNAC, urging decisive action to remove Saddam from power.

Stephen Solarz, et al., "Open Letter to the President," February 19, 1998, online at IraqWatch.org. (The following persons signed the letter, William Kristol, Gary Bauer, Jeffrey Bell, William J. Bennett, Jeffrey Bergner, Eliot Cohen, Seth Cropsey, Midge Decter, Thomas Donnelly, Aaron Friedberg, Hillel Fradkin, Francis Fukuyama, Frank Gaffney, Jeffrey Gedmin, Reuel Marc Gerecht, Charles Hill, Bruce P. Jackson, Eli S. Jacobs, Michael Joyce, Donald Kagan, Robert Kagan, Jeane Kirkpatrick, Charles Krauthammer, John Lehman, Clifford May, Richard Perle, Martin Peretz, Norman Podhoretz, Randy Scheunemann, Gary Schmitt, William Schneider, Jr., Richard H. Shultz, Henry Sokolski, Stephen J. Solarz, Vin Weber, Leon Wieseltier, and Marshall Wittmann.)

44 James Sennett, ed., "Chapter 13, Christian Philosophy at the End of the 20th Century," in *An Analytic Theist, An Alvin Plantinga Reader* (Grand Rapids, MI and Cambridge, UK: Eerdmans Publishing, 1998), 185.

45 Michael Crowder, "Obama to Putin, 'Good luck with that.'," *Political Podcasts*, *The Politico*, October 1, 2015, http://www.politico.com/story/2015/10/vladimir-putin-barack-obama-russia-syria-214344

3 UN and NGO peacemaking efforts

One can only the imagine the conversation between Ban Ki-moon and Antonio Gutiérrez concerning Syria in December 2016, when Ban Ki-moon turned over the reins of the UN secretary-general position to Mr. Gutiérrez. Ban Ki-moon held office from January 2007 to December 2016. What role had the UN played in the current Syrian conflict, and what assessment was made about whether decisions could have been made differently that would have made a difference in the way the conflict has played out? How has the UN seen itself in the context of peacemaking in the Middle East and Syria, in particular? In particular, did they discuss the continued dysfunction of the Security Council? Or perhaps that was just taken as a given. And how has its three-part role as potential peacekeeper, criminal prosecutor, and mediator played out in Syria? Looking at the developments of UN's three-part role gives us a chance to see how the religion of the secretary-general might impact the principles that the UN employs as a peacemaker. I also show how the emergence of first the international specialty criminal tribunal, and then the permanent court, puts the UN in a dilemma between the rule of law and peacemaking, with its peacekeeping role having been made particularly problematic. Finally I also discuss how the UN has evolved as a mediator, and what principles it employs as a force of liberal democracy in moving the nation beyond conflict and towards sustainable peace.

After all, the UN does have some peacekeeper assets at its disposal. During the time of the Syrian conflict the UN had a peacekeeping military force of close to 100,000. However, these resources were already stretched to their capacity as UN peacekeepers had already been sent to multiple peacekeeping missions. Stung by its failures in Rwanda, the UN had sought to clarify its principles for deploying its peacekeepers and its terms of engagement. Its two principles of engagement included the protection of human rights and adherence to humanitarian law and the prevention of war crimes. Even these two rather straightforward goals had been difficult to implement. Especially as peacekeeping missions dragged on, the peacekeepers themselves became embroiled in their own humanitarian disputes. The UN depended on armed forces contributed from UN nations, who ideally could be seen as neutral but, more pragmatically, may have been selected because of their experience in or willingness to deploy forces. In any event, too often these forces were themselves accused of having violated humanitarian law once they found themselves embedded in the conflict.

A quick primer on the history of the UN as a peacekeeping force puts the Syrian conflict in context

It is important, at the start, to see that the UN Peacekeeping role was born at a time when Cold War rivalries frequently paralyzed the Security Council. UN peacekeeping was primarily limited to maintaining ceasefires and stabilizing situations on the ground, providing crucial support for political efforts to resolve conflict by peaceful means.

The first *armed* peacekeeping operation was the First UN Emergency Force (UNEF I) deployed successfully in 1956 to address the Suez Crisis. That was soon followed by the UN Operation in the Congo (ONUC) in 1960. The ONUC was the UN's first large-scale mission, having nearly 20,000 military personnel at its peak. The force was deployed over objections from the Soviet Union, which argued that the UN was violating neutrality when it came to the governance structure of the Congo. The Soviets would argue for a UN with a single secretary-general and a three-part executive branch that would respectively represent socialist governments, democracies, and then independent governments. The ONUC demonstrated the risks involved in trying to bring stability to war-torn regions: 250 UN personnel died while serving on that mission, including Secretary-General Dag Hammarskjöld.

A quick word here about Dag Hammarskjöld. An Episcopal Lutheran, he was much loved and admired for his skills not only as an economist but also as a diplomat. He was also profoundly spiritual. His diary was published with the help of the poet Auden under the title *Markings*. It revealed how he struggled with his faith in the midst of the heart of darkness. As to the role of religious faith in his work at the UN he famously said, "The United Nations stands outside – necessarily outside – all confessions. But it is, nevertheless, an instrument of faith. As such, it is inspired by what unites and not by what divides the great religions of the world."[1]

The circumstances of Hammarskjöld's death show just how tricky UN peacekeeping can be. First, as with many conflicts today, part of the responsibility lies with the countries' colonial pasts. As Martin Meredith shows in his wonderful history of the post–World War II independence movement in Africa, there exists a cycle of violence inherited from the colonial power that often takes some time for the newly independent government to put behind it.[2] The colonial power often pits tribal groups against each other in a strategy of divide and conquer. As the colonialist's power wains, it elevates one group over the other, creating animosities that enable oppressed groups to see the new rulers as traitors, with elites unlikely to change much in regard to how the oppressed group will be treated. In support of the new ruling group is often the business and elite landowners who came to their position during the colonial period. They either find support in the new government or may lose not only their property but also their lives.

At the time of the negotiations Hammarskjöld's task was to try to maintain some sense of UN neutrality as between the US and the Soviets and, otherwise, encourage the independence movement to choose for itself how it wanted to be governed. Embedded in his peacekeeping role was the Belgians' history of oppression that led to Belgian businesses' ownership of most of the mines in the Katanga region.

At the heart of the UN's mission and responsibilities that often draws it into the conflict is its role in protecting refugees: its mission in the Congo was the UN's first experience with protecting refugees. During the fall of 1961, Swedish troops were assigned as peacekeepers in a refugee camp of approximately 40,000 refugees. The camp mainly emerged because of severe persecutions of the Baluba people in the Kasai area. Conditions in the camp were appalling: desperate refugees could murder each other in the crush around food distributions. A group of about 1,000 young men of uncertain origin called Baluba Jeunesse put fear in the camp, committing murder and rioting. The Swedes came to be in open conflict with the Baluba Jeunesse and on a number of occasions, the situation developed until the Swedish peacekeepers shot straight into the angry crowds, killing several people. No legal investigation was ever made into the shootings.

After Hammarskjöld's death, his replacement, U Thant, took a more aggressive approach. Ironically, U Thant was likely selected by the Soviets because of the neutrality and nonviolent reputation of his faith, Buddhism. U Thant is also an example of a leader motivated by his religious beliefs who would struggle with how to integrate his Buddhist faith into the UN decision-making concerning the Congo.

Removing Tshombe from Katanga became the primary military objective for the UN.[3] The "last resort criterion" was also very much on Thant's mind. Indeed, the first Security Council resolution, adopted during Hammarskjöld's tenure, urged the UN to prevent civil war using force "if necessary, in the last resort." But the last resort was demanded in the Congo. Thant learned from many experiences that Tshombe could not be trusted: he seemed to always go back on his promises. Therefore, Thant would take steps to blockade Katanga in order to prevent further exploitation of the region. Tshombe responded with an inflammatory speech in the Elizabethville stadium, declaring that

> U Thant will launch a war on our territory. . . . You cannot all have automatic weapons or rifles. But we still have our poisoned arrows, our spears, our axes . . . not one United Nations mercenary must feel safe in any place whatever.[4]

Tshombe's speech had the anticipated repercussions: a number of UN officials in Katanga, including (Sir Brian) Urquhart, were kidnapped and assaulted a few days later. Thant responded forcefully, declaring that indiscriminate arrest or molestation of UN civilians must be resisted by all possible means including the use of force, offensive and defensive, as necessary. The UN also had under its protection some 35,000 people who had been made refugees by the fighting. In order to protect them, the UN peacekeepers backed Lumumba and shut down the Katanga secession. UN troops from Sweden, Ireland, India, and Ethiopia were involved in heavy fighting for Katanga's capital, Elizabethville. UN forces defeated the Katangan gendarmes in the city and took Elizabethville. During the fighting, eleven Swedish soldiers were taken prisoner. These were released in exchange for UN-captured Katangan mercenaries.

The casualties suffered by the ONUC during its three rounds of action in 1961–1962 were 42 killed and 200 wounded. Several hundred Katangan forces and close to 50 civilians were also killed. Overall, the ONUC (1960–1964) suffered the most fatalities of any UN mission, even more than the post–Cold War missions in Bosnia and Somalia.

These events show how Thant was drawn into the use of violence. He negotiated continuously with Tshombe, but he soon realized that the Katangan leader was acting in bad faith. When a secret Katangan plan for a full-scale attack on ONUC was intercepted in early December 1961, Thant authorized a UN action In December 1961.

In taking over after the death of Hammarskjöld, Thant was providing a fighting leadership for his institution and for the Blue Helmets already on the ground. He proved to be a determined fighter. He rallied the international community, and he supported the troops in the field. Yet the UN found itself supporting Mobutu, who turned out to be a brutal dictator. Its intervention, from hindsight, would raise the question of whether interventions to keep peace would result in supporting winners who would most often be the existing ruling group. While in the case of the Congo a new group came to power that was interested in setting aside the exploitation that had preceded it, in other situations the ruling class might itself seek financial gain and exploitation. In most situations where the UN was invited to intervene, it would perpetuate existing business and colonialist property ownership.

What could justify Thant's resort to such force? The answer is provided not in the principles or writings of Buddhism but in the "just war theory" that arose out of the Christian tradition. Though he himself did not refer to it, a look at Thant's explanations at the time and in his memoir shows that all the elements for a just war existed in his thinking: just cause, right intention, right authority, last resort, proportionality, and minimum use of force. That is not to say that he found just war theory inconsistent with his Buddhist principles: in his Buddhism he took a broad view. Thant found inspiration in the works of great spiritual thinkers of other religious and cultural backgrounds. He deeply appreciated Albert Schweitzer and his ethic of "reverence for life," because, as Thant wrote, "I had trained all my life to regard human life as sacred."[5] Thant also embraced the concepts of Pierre Teilhard de Chardin, a Jesuit priest, which included the unifying power of love, an orderly universe, and the world community: "a common soul in the vast body."[6] In his memoir he would also even argue the compatibility between his Buddhism and the UN Charter.[7]

By 1988, UN had become more assured in its use of peacekeepers, and the world took notice. UN peacekeepers were awarded the Nobel Peace Prize. At that time, the Nobel Committee stated that "the Peacekeeping Forces through their efforts have made important contributions towards the realization of one of the fundamental tenets of the United Nations. Thus, the world organization has come to play a more central part in world affairs and has been invested with increasing trust."[8]

Post–Cold War surge – Kurt Waldheim (the enigma) and . . .

The UN shifted and dramatically expanded its field operations from "traditional" missions involving generally observational tasks performed by military personnel to complex "multidimensional" enterprises in the post–Cold War period. These multidimensional missions were designed to ensure the implementation of comprehensive peace agreements and to assist in laying the foundations for sustainable peace.

The nature of conflicts also changed over the years. UN peacekeeping, originally developed as a means of dealing with inter-state conflict, was increasingly being applied to intra-state conflicts and civil wars.

UN peacekeepers were now increasingly asked to undertake a wide variety of complex tasks, from helping to build sustainable institutions of governance to human rights monitoring to security sector reform and to the disarmament, demobilization, and reintegration of former combatants.

Although the military remained the backbone of most peacekeeping operations, there were now many faces to peacekeeping including administrators, economists, police officers, legal experts, electoral observers, human rights monitors, civil affairs and governance specialists, humanitarian workers, and communication and public information specialists. With the fall of the Soviet Union, the mission of nation building also started to take on the specific goal of building liberal democracies. As we will see, the UN never quite gave up its neutrality with regard to governance structures and tried to build in options that might even include dictatorships should that be the choice of the newly independent nation.

After the Cold War ended, there was a rapid increase in the number of UN peacekeeping operations. With a new consensus and a common sense of purpose, the Security Council authorized a total of 20 new operations between 1989 and 1994, raising the number of peacekeepers from 11,000 to 75,000.

Peacekeeping operations established in such countries as Angola, Cambodia, El Salvador, Mozambique, and Namibia. These were deployed to help implement complex peace agreements, stabilize the security situation, re-organize military and police, and elect new governments and build democratic institutions.

The mid-1990s: a period of reassessment-Kofi Annan

When Kofi Annan took over the secretary-general position in 1990, the UN went through a period of reassessment of its role as a peacekeeper. Annan was educated as an economist at McAlister College and was known for his calm demeanor and keen mind. He was fluent in five languages. His religious beliefs played a role but only at the highest and most abstract level. In a speech he gave at a conference on religious belief and international conflict, he would extol the potential good that religious faith could do in inspiring respect for others and a passion for dignity and due process for oppressed and minority groups, while also expressing worry about the evil religious faith could do if it leads to bigotry and intolerance.[9] His own faith formation came in school. From 1954 to 1957, Annan attended the elite school in Ghana, a Methodist boarding school in Cape Coast founded in the 1870s. Annan has said that the school taught him "that suffering anywhere concerns people everywhere."

During the mid-1990s, under Annan's leadership, the UN became more and more engaged in promoting human rights and democracy. Yet there were times that it could not act as quickly and easily as other NGO actors, who might also be engaged to mediate peace, when the parties sought mediation. President Carter was particularly skilled as a mediator during this period, especially regarding Haiti and then North Korea. The situation in Haiti, also predating the International Criminal Court, bears mentioning here. First President Carter's, and then President Reagan's, administration worked for "Papa Doc" Duvalier's removal. President Carter has since commented on how his negotiations to remove the dictator from power were made much easier by the absence of the ICC, as peacemakers had less concern for later indictments and did not worry as much about impunity for past atrocities. Duvalier could negotiate his absconding to a beautiful villa in France and die there, having never been made to answer for his past crimes.

Annan would be blamed for not acting strongly towards Rwanda, where he did little to prevent the genocide (there are still suspicions that the Hutus had the "permission" of the French for their orchestration of violence against the Tutus) and failed to galvanize the international community into taking stronger action once the genocide became known. Such criticism ignores the fact that the UN's ability to act was restricted by financial problems and by the very makeup of the Security Council. The general success of earlier missions raised expectations for UN peacekeeping beyond its capacity to deliver. This was especially true in the mid-1990s in situations when the Security Council was not able to authorize sufficiently robust mandates or provide adequate resources.

The UN had three major missions during Annan's tenure: the former Yugoslavia, Rwanda, and Somalia. In each of these situations the UN was put in the middle of active conflicts, where the parties had not yet agreed even to a ceasefire. There was no peace for the UN to keep. Annan came under criticism in each of these situations because despite the UN's best efforts the warring parties failed to adhere to peace agreements. Yet the peacekeepers themselves were not provided adequate resources or political support. As civilian casualties rose and hostilities continued, the reputation of UN peacekeeping suffered.

The setbacks of the early and mid-1990s led the Security Council to limit the number of new peacekeeping missions and begin a process of self-reflection to prevent such failures from happening again.[10] In the meantime, UN peacekeepers continued their long-term operations in the Middle East, Asia, and Cyprus.

After this reassessment the UN renewed its efforts. There was a new surge of UN peacekeeping missions after the fall of the Soviet Union. With the US now unopposed by the Soviets, as we have seen, it adopted a policy of not going into conflicts without international support. Interestingly enough, Russia and China would cooperate with the US during this period in authorizing UN missions abroad. In addition, Russia also signed onto key humanitarian declarations and seemed to cede ground to democratic principles as a foundation for the UN's long-term peacekeeping missions. The UN would often negotiate for elections, power-sharing arrangements, independent judiciaries, and a separation of powers in an attempt to reach sustainable peace agreements.

As we will see, and as the UN learned, the Achilles' heel of democracy is that the nation can itself choose to prefer the order over democracy and a dictatorship over taking the time to build capable and strong legislatures to balance its strong men. Once such a strong man is elected, he will almost inevitably take steps to secure his power: it becomes very difficult for the post-conflict nation to return to free and fair elections in the future. This is especially true in regions with long-standing animosity between religious groups. The dictator can easily inflame the religious passions of his own religious supporters or partners against the "terrorism" employed by their opponents. The UN, then, would be caught in the middle. Consider the UN's missions in Angola,[11] Bosnia and Herzegovina,[12] Croatia,[13] and the Former Yugoslav Republic of Macedonia,[14] and compare them to the relative success in Guatemala[15] and Haiti,[16] where religion played less of a role.

Towards the 21st century: new operations, new challenges

At the turn of the century, the UN undertook a major exercise to examine the challenges to peacekeeping in the 1990s and in introducing new reforms. The aim was to strengthen its capacity to effectively manage and sustain field operations. Armed with a greater understanding of the limits – and potentials – of UN peacekeeping, the UN was asked to perform even more complex tasks. It turned from peacekeeping (making sure the killing stopped) to peace maintaining (setting up security forces that acted as police and secured borders) to peace sustaining (setting up offices to act to provide services, gather data, and provide for elections). This started in 1999, when the UN served as the administrator of both Kosovo in the former Yugoslavia and in East Timor (now Timor-Leste), which was in the process of gaining independence from Indonesia.

Peacekeepers also returned to resume vital peacekeeping and peacebuilding operations where fragile peace had frayed, in Haiti–UN Stabilization Mission in Haiti (MINUSTAH) and the newly independent Timor-Leste–UN Integrated Mission in Timor-Leste (UNMIT). As we will see, the UN found itself not only providing security but also acting as a mediator to help involved parties during times of transition. The UN needed now to understand how to recruit and train police and how to best deal with former fighters, especially former child soldiers. While the UN primarily relied on other nongovernmental organizations, it was drawn into coordinating and measuring capacity building in all areas of governance.

One result of the UN's reassessment, led by Kofi Annan, was the development of the UN's *Responsibility to Protect* policy (R2P). Canada was a prime mover of its development. Canada convened the International Commission on Intervention and State Sovereignty to bring the top foreign policy thinkers together to help the UN work out its commitment to protect the individual sovereignty of nations, but also to live up to its obligations to prevent war crimes and genocide. Australian politician Gareth Evenas was the primary drafter of what the convention adopted as the UN's guidelines for humanitarian intervention. The panel's report, "The Responsibility to Protect," released in December 2001, puts the term *protect* on paper for the first time.

At its world summit in 2005, the UN unanimously adopted "responsibility to protect" as a guiding principle for the prevention of "atrocity crimes." "It cannot be right," Secretary-General Kofi Annan declared, "when the international community is faced with genocide or massive human rights abuses, for the United Nations to stand by and let them unfold to the end."[17]

The R2P was invoked only two times before its "use" by the international community to justify its support for an intervention in Libya in 2011. In the earlier situations the UN refused to invoke the doctrine and intervene. Security Council members, including China, were concerned that the doctrine gave the UN too much discretion to intervene. In 2008, R2P was invoked to try to generate support for UN intervention in the case of a natural disaster. When Cyclone Nargis struck Burma, French foreign minister Bernard Kouchner argued that the "responsibility to protect" obligated the UN as representative of the international community to step in. Archbishop Desmond Tutu similarly invoked the principle in calling for a nonmilitary intervention in Zimbabwe.

The UN's early attempts to use R2P set a precedent for President Obama when he took office in 2009 to invoke the R2P doctrine with regard to Libya. As we have seen in Chapter 2, President Obama's foreign policy team included special assistant Samantha Power, who reported on the Srebrenica massacre as a journalist and later wrote *A Problem from Hell*, an influential critique of the US government's response to genocide.

Powers found support within the Obama administration for invoking the R2P policy. UN Ambassador Susan Rice, who was haunted by US failure in Rwanda, would make the case that R2P needed to be invoked regarding both Libya and Syria. Unfortunately, the worsening of the situation in Libya as a result of NATO bombing made both Obama and the UN more reticent to use R2P, even when the Assad was acting like Kaddafi.

The situation in Kosovo presented a new problem for the UN. Kosovo is the disputed borderland between Serbia and Albania. About 90 percent of its 2 million inhabitants are Kosovo Albanians (Kosovars). The Serbs, however, refer to Kosovo as the "cradle of the Serb nation." It was after the medieval Serbian Orthodox Church had established a new see at Pec in Kosovo in 1297 that the medieval kingdom of Serbia – founded a century earlier – reached its apogee. Serbian nationalists hold that Kosovo's numerous Orthodox monasteries, and the blood and the relics of those who died defending them, have "eternally sanctified" Serbian claims to Kosovo.

Kosovo led the UN to consider a policy of backing breakaway states. Kosovo declared its independence from Serbia in 2008. It received recognition from many UN member states. In 2010, the International Court of Justice declared that Kosovo had not violated international law in its breaking away. Russia was appalled. While not in play in Syria, the UN showed that it understood that it might play a role where a minority community had long sought relief from oppression and appealed to the UN for recognition and the legitimating support of a breakaway movement. While it was a long way from intervening to force the independence of any state, it might give the new state recognition and membership in the UN. The Palestinians are now trying to use the UN's principles developed in response to Kosovo to make a move to independence from Israel.

This was the situation at the UN at the time of the start of the Syrian conflict. By May 2010, UN peacekeeping operations had more than 124,000 military, police, and civilian staff

So why, with all of its different missions around the world, has Syria, in particular, been so hard for the UN to get its hands around? Perhaps it is because UN peacekeeping in 2011 had found itself stretched like never before. As we have seen, it had been increasingly called on to deploy to remote, uncertain operating environments and into volatile political contexts. It may have initially looked at Syria the same way we have seen the Obama administration does, namely as a part of the larger Arab Spring. This might've led the UN to hope that things would resolve themselves quickly, as had happened in Egypt. Moreover, the UN certainly did not relish inserting itself in any long-term mission, especially where it lacked the political support of the Security Council. Let's next look at what the UN did, in fact, do in Syria and why it was so ineffective.

Peacekeeping faced a varied set of challenges, including challenges to deliver on its largest, most expensive, and increasingly complex missions; challenges to design and execute viable transition strategies for missions where a degree of stability has been attained; and challenges to prepare for an uncertain future and set of requirements. Peacekeeping missions were turning into peace maintenance missions, and would inevitably come to involve issues of transitional justice and nation building. As a part of nation building, the UN confronted the failures of fledgling democracies to act in a timely manner to ensure security and prosperity following a conflict. What appeared to be needed in post-conflict societies was strong leadership. Unfortunately, strong leadership would become entrenched, and a cycle of violence would again be initiated.

The UN peacekeeping choices and Syria

Quickly after its start in 2011, the Syrian conflict grew to compete with the size and scope of some of the UN's major past peacekeeping missions. For example, compare the Syrian conflict on a scale of atrocities to Rwanda and Sudan. The number killed in Rwanda still boggles the mind: the BBC reports that over 800,000 people were killed over the time of 100 days. In Darfur, the numbers were also staggering. The UN convention to prevent genocide reports that 400,000 people died because of the fighting in Darfur region as of 2004. It has been reported that over 250,000 people have lost their lives in Syria, with millions having fled the country. We need to stop here to examine the numbers of refugees due to the fighting in Syria. The UN reports that of the 20 million people who lived in Syria at the start of the conflict, close to half were made refugees as a result of the fighting. Here are some of the specific numbers. As 2016 drew to a bloody close in Syria, over 4.8 million Syrian refugees continued to seek safety and a means of living a dignified life throughout the rest of the Middle East. There are 2.8 million Syrians currently registered in Turkey, over 1 million in Lebanon, and about 656,000 in Jordan. To put this figure into context, in the so-called European "refugee crisis" a total of 884,461 Syrian refugees applied for asylum in Europe between April 2011 and October 2016.[18]

As we have seen, Bashar al-Assad is responsible for much of the civilian casualties in Syria, and his brutal responses were at least a substantial factor in causing the refugee crisis. The UN's own internal processes had come to this conclusion. By the end of 2014 the UN Human Rights Council's Commission of Inquiry (CoI) had published nine major reports documenting gross human rights abuses perpetrated in Syria. The CoI found that pro-government forces "continue to conduct widespread attacks on civilians, systematically committing murder, torture, rape and enforced disappearance as crimes against humanity" and have also committed extensive war crimes. The CoI also reported on war crimes committed by some armed opposition groups, including "murder, execution without due process, torture, hostage taking," as well as widespread violations of international humanitarian law" (Adams, 2015: 8).

From the UN's perspective it could have invoked its use of force consistent with its *Responsibility to Protect* (R2P) doctrine, as it had in Libya. It was consistent with the UN's call for states to protect their citizens. It had declared that when this state protection no longer exists (or when the state is the one committing the rights abuses), then the international community can supersede issues of state sovereignty and can enter a country as a humanitarian-driven action. In addition, Assad's forces were not the only ones committing mass rights violations; these have occurred with various opposition forces as well. Overall, this has led to a highly unstable situation in Syria, one that has desperately needed international support in order to protect civilians caught in the conflict.

Yet, the Security Council would balk. Some members turned out to share President Obama's misgivings as to whether UN involvement would actually help or simply make matters worse. Early in 2011, for example, non-permanent members of the United Nations – India, Brazil, and South Africa – questioned whether the UN's Security Council involvement would actually make matters worse in Syria with regard to a possible sectarian conflict in the country (Adams, 2015). While they did call for the conflict to stop as well as criticize the government for its actions against the population, "all three countries subsequently abstained on an October 2011 draft Security Council resolution."[19] This resolution was aimed at holding the Assad government accountable for atrocities that had already killed close to 2,000 people. By this point, these members of the council were worrying about whether invoking R2P would cause a power vacuum like had happened in Libya. What UN members had learned from NATO bombing in Libya was that without putting a force on the ground following the removal of a dictator, other insurgent groups, bent on revenge, would seek to grab power. Explaining South Africa's unwillingness to vote for the resolution, Ambassador Baso Sangqu argued that with regard to the Syrian conflict, "the templates for the solution were very clear, it was along similar lines to Libya" (Adams, 2015: 10). He said this before the situation in Libya deteriorated.

The secretary-general, Ban Ki-moon, tried to use R2P to intervene in Syria. It is the Security Council, and, in particular, Russia's and China's (together with India's, Brazil's, and South Africa's) abstentions, that refused UN endorsement for the use of force. Was this perhaps because Russia was already looking for a way into the conflict? Russia had a military base in Syria and a port access that it didn't want to be taken over by an unfriendly government. In any event, the UN Security Council failed to take the needed action to intervene in Syria.[20]

Actions taken by the UN and UN states related to Syria

Despite the failures of the United Nations Security Council, the United Nations (and some UN states) did take individual actions against the Syrian regime. Consider the following examples:

- The League of Arab States (Arab League), the EU, Turkey and a range of other states publicly censured the Syrian government for its actions and diplomatically isolated the regime.
- By March 2012, one year after the conflict began, at least 49 countries had imposed bilateral targeted sanctions while at least 14 had closed their embassies in Damascus (Adams, 2015).
- In addition, there were also actions by the Human Rights Council, such as the following:
  - The Human Rights Council in Geneva passed 13 resolutions condemning mass atrocities in Syria between 2011 and September 2014 and established an independent Commission of Inquiry to document grave violations of human rights.
  - Similarly, the General Assembly passed seven resolutions condemning Syrian atrocities, with a February 2012 resolution drawing support from 137 states in the 193-member assembly.
  - While the number of abstentions fluctuated, no more than 13 states voted against any General Assembly resolution condemning atrocities in Syria.
  - The secretary-general and his Special Advisors for the Prevention of Genocide and the Responsibility to Protect also released numerous statements condemning mass atrocities in Syria and calling for the protection of civilians.

Still, the UN as a body was largely ineffective in stopping the fighting or in stemming the flow of refugees. Russia's eventual intervention would only further stymie, if not totally sabotage, the UN's own ability to intervene.

Russia's role in Syria

Given Russia's strategic alliance with Assad and its international relations and interests in maintaining an influence in the Middle East, it was no surprise to many to find out that Russia was directly supporting the Assad regime. As we have seen, in September 2015 Russia was invited by Assad to help fight terrorism in Syria. Russia sent in military support to target not only Islamic State forces but also other forces opposed to the Assad regime. Russia is not hiding its open support and interest in keeping the current Syrian regime in power. And thus, because of this strategic relationship, it has been in Russia's political interests to vote against any UN Security Council (UNSC) resolution that could potentially cause additional harm to Assad in Syria, and in turn, reduce Russian influence in the country. Yet, this clearly shows the problems with the UNSC: any of the five veto states have greatly unbalanced decision-making power and are able to make the UNSC completely inactive by using this veto power.

The UN's impartiality was taken advantage of by the Russian's actions, as the UN went to war with itself over it R2P doctrine. The UN's moral authority has been significantly undermined, and its leadership is increasingly being seen as all the more impotent. Once, the secretary-general of the UN might have been able to speak on behalf of the citizens of the world, not unlike a secular pope.[21] Now, the political structure of Security Council made that position impotent.

We turn next to the ICC.

Key to any long-term system of conflict resolution, whether local or international, is the rule of law

The rule of law provides deterrence, as it prescribes against war crimes and atrocities through a system of sanctions and punishments. It also provides precise definitions for these prescribed behaviors and so puts actors on the international stage on fair notice. The law satisfies moral philosophical objections towards the use of violence in the pursuit of peace, such as using military force to protect civilian lives violence in the form of punishment for actors who violate statutory provisions. The question then is whether the ICC can pursue its mission while, at the same time, the UN, as a whole, pursues its mission as peacekeeper and mediator?

International criminal law and its courts were initially based in common law and "natural law" theories of moral philosophy. The international community following World War II would form the first-ever international criminal tribunal at Nuremberg to try Nazi war criminals. The legal basis of the court was said to be based "just war" prescriptions. "Just war" did not make war illegal but prescribed against the unnecessary and out-of-proportion use of force in pursuit of an actors' otherwise legitimate exercise of power to maintain its own security. However, the international community would realize that an after-the-fact determination of war crimes was subject to criticisms of being a sort of "winner's" justice. The international community would come to prefer a more positivistic basis that would ground its criminal and humanitarian law in the twofold basis of consent of the governed and the existence of a founding (or grounding) document like a constitution. While in the situation with Nazi Germany, where moral philosophy (along with the Geneva Convention) was seen as the legitimate basis for the Nuremberg tribunals, the UN sought an additional legal basis for legitimizing its actions on an international stage, namely the Rome Statute, which would seek to prevent violence, to permit legitimate rule of law, and to answer some key objections to the UN's use of violence to prevent violence. Grounding the UN's actions in the cloak of law gives the international body its moral authority and legal legitimacy.

Peacekeeping and criminal prosecution grounded in the Rome Statute

Here are some key events that led to the creation of the ICC:

1946 October: Soon after the Nuremberg Judgment, an international congress meets in Paris and calls for the adoption of an international criminal code prohibiting crimes against humanity and for the prompt establishment of an international criminal court.

1948 December 9: The UN General Assembly (GA) adopts the *Convention on the Prevention and Punishment of the Crime of Genocide*. It calls for criminals to be tried "by such international penal tribunals as may have jurisdiction." Separately, member nations ask the International Law Commission (ILC) to study the possibility of establishing an ICC.

1948 December 10: The General Assembly adopts the *Universal Declaration of Human Rights*, detailing human rights and fundamental freedoms.

1949–1954: The International Law Committee (ILC) drafts statutes for an ICC, but opposition from powerful states on both sides of the Cold War stymies the effort, and the GA effectively abandons the effort pending agreement on a definition of the crime of aggression and an international *Code of Crimes*.

1974: The GA agrees on a definition of *aggression*.

1989: The end of the Cold War brings a dramatic increase in the number of UN peacekeeping operations and a world where the idea of establishing an ICC becomes more viable.

1989 June: Motivated in part by an effort to combat drug trafficking, Trinidad and Tobago resurrect the proposal for an ICC. The GA asks the ILC to prepare a draft statute.

1991–1992: Wars in Bosnia-Herzegovina and Croatia, which including clear violations of the *Genocide* and *Geneva Conventions*, lead the UN Security Council to establish a temporary *ad hoc* tribunal for the former Yugoslavia (in 1993) and strengthen discussions for a permanent court.

1994: The ILC submits a draft Statute for an ICC to the GA. The war in Rwanda leads the UN Security Council to establish a second *ad hoc* tribunal for Rwanda. The ILC presents a final draft statute on the ICC to the GA and recommends that a conference of plenipotentiaries be convened to negotiate a treaty to enact the Statute. The GA establishes an *ad hoc* committee on the ICC to review the draft Statute.

1995: The *ad hoc* committee holds two 2-week meetings at UN headquarters. In December 1995, the GA establishes a three-year Preparatory Committee (PrepCom) from March 1996 until April 1998 to finalize a text to be presented at a conference of plenipotentiaries.
1998 June 15–17: One hundred sixty countries participate in the UN Diplomatic Conference of Plenipotentiaries on the establishment of an International Criminal Court in Rome, Italy.
1998 July 17: Member states overwhelmingly vote in favor of the Rome Statute of the ICC, creating the treaty establishing the first permanent international court capable of trying individuals accused of genocide, war crimes, and crimes against humanity.
1999 February 2: Senegal becomes the first state party to ratify the Rome Statute.
2000, December 31: Deadline for signing the Rome Statute. The US joins Iran and Israel as the last states to sign the treaty, bringing the total number of signatures to 139.
2002 April 11: The 60th ratification necessary to trigger the entry into force of the Rome Statute is deposited during a special ceremony at UN headquarters. Countries to deposit their treaty instruments during this ceremony are Bosnia and Herzegovina, Bulgaria, Cambodia, Democratic Republic of Congo, Ireland, Jordan, Mongolia, Niger, Romania, and Slovakia.
2002 May 6: The US government under the Bush Administration formally announces to the UN its intention *not* to ratify the Rome Statute and its view that it is no longer bound by the terms of the treaty, implied by its signature under the Clinton administration in December 2001.
2002 July 1: Following the formula set out in the Rome Statute, the treaty enters into force, becoming binding for all countries to have ratified or acceded to the statute and for whom it had entered into force by that date.
2002 July 12: On this day, after intense US pressure and threats to shut down the UN peacekeeping mission in Bosnia-Herzegovina, the UN Security Council adopted Resolution 1422, granting U.N. peacekeepers immunity from the jurisdiction of the ICC, retroactively effective as of July 1, 2002, for a renewable one-year period.
2003 March 11: The first 18 judges of the ICC are sworn in during in a high-level ceremony in The Hague, the Netherlands.
2003 June 16: The first prosecutor, Mr. Luis Moreno-Ocampo, is sworn in in The Hague, the Netherlands.
2003 July 16: ICC prosecutor, Mr. Moreno-Ocampo, holds his first press briefing to discuss the nearly 500 communications to have been received by the court. He names the situation in the Democratic Republic of Congo as the most urgent situation that his office will "follow closely."

Jurisdiction of the court and then complications

The final implementation of the ICC created no panacea. It wrapped up the work of the specialty tribunals, the International Criminal Tribunal for the former Yugoslavia (ICTY), for Rawanda (ICTR), and ICT for Sierra Leone as its prosecutor stepped into the messy and political world of bringing to justice heads of state, many of whom would remain undeterred by the existence of the new court. What became apparent to peacemaking efforts on the ground was that the ICC's warrants made peacemaking more difficult. Why would a head of state step down only to become subject to criminal prosecution by the ICC? What happened to Liberian president Charles Taylor became an object lesson for future heads of state accused of war crimes? Taylor relinquished power and absconded with his entourage only to be later turned over to the court by Nigeria following the issuance of a warrant for his arrest. Slobodan Milošević similarly would face prosecution following his signing of the Dayton Peace Accords. Perhaps seduced by his role as the master negotiator[22] for his side against the US, he had such a warped view of the world that he felt justified in what he had done on behalf of the Serbs. So he would be blindsided when his fellow Serbs turned him in to the ICC. He would die while being tried for war crimes.

Whether future presidents accused of war crimes will similarly negotiate peace without negotiating immunity for similar crimes remains to be seen. Omar Basheer of Sudan faces continuing threats of extradition to the ICC whenever he travels in Rome Statute countries. The president of Kenya, Kenyatta, has successfully negotiated a tabling of his warrant for war crimes, or at least the ICC prosecutor has determined to table it because of a lack of support from the international community with his trial. As we will see, the situation with Assad is complicated by the ITCL's investigation into the murder of Rafiq al-Hariri.

International criminal courts

Impact of the Special Tribunal for Lebanon. The bomb that killed Rafiq al-Hariri weighed 2,200 pounds and left a crater 30 feet wide in the Corniche, Beirut's seaside promenade. In addition to Hariri, it killed 21 people and injured 220 more. It set dozens of cars on fire and knocked down several buildings; all the windows of the nearby 446-room InterContinental Phoenicia Hotel were blown out, and the hotel – a symbol of Beirut's post-war rebirth – was forced to close for months. Eight months later, a report to the UN about Hariri's assassination outlined a conspiracy of remarkable breadth and complexity. It revealed that three months before Hariri's death, his security detail had been mysteriously reduced from 40 to 8, that six anonymously purchased mobile phones were used on the day of the attack to keep the bomber informed of Hariri's movements and to provide intelligence on the three possible routes that Hariri could take from the parliament building to his home, that the suicide truck moved into position 1 minute 49 seconds before Hariri's convoy passed by, and that the truck itself had been stolen on October 12, 2004, in Sagamihara City, Japan. The killers appeared to be sophisticated, politically connected, and well funded: clearly this was not the work of a lone extremist or a fringe group. It bore the hallmarks of a government-sponsored assassination.

In sum, the situation is as follows: The UN prosecution of Assad has grave implications for the future peace in Syria. The Criminal Court, and its successor court, the ICC, is a great hope to any future UN roles in deterring war crimes. But the UN's Criminal Court can also create difficult dilemmas for peacemaking in Syria and elsewhere. First, why would Assad, or any leader subject to prosecution, make peace only to create the circumstances for his later arrest and conviction? Unless he is deluded, as Slobodan Milošević may have been or Charles Taylor, who was reportedly convinced that he didn't commit war crimes, Assad has no incentive but to keep fighting and make alliances with other rogue actors until he wins.

To avoid these difficulties in peacemaking, the UN tries to separate itself into a different role. It tries to present itself as a mediator, both for political reasons and for reasons of principle. In the process, as we will see, it opens up fundamental questions of the role that liberal democracy (elections, human rights, religious freedoms, and the rule of law) will play in Syria's future governance. In addition, a mediation process will allow for alternatives to formal justice principles to be employed in sustaining the peace. The UN as a mediator may help create the circumstances for the drafting of a new Syrian constitution. Truth and Reconciliation Commissions can come into play. Mediation can create room for forgiveness. At least, this is the hope UN mediation processes might create in Syria, for a future after the fighting stops. But what effects will such agreements have on the success of the ICC? Would they undermine the court's credibility? Would they make the indictment process superfluous?

Before we dive deeply into this mediation process, let's take a brief tour here into the UN's experience with mediation. What we will find is that its experience with post-conflict mediation has led it to start to question the necessity of democracy, at least in the beginning stages of nation building. Maybe a short-term dictator is a better vehicle for building security and starting the rebuilding process. Its experience has also made it more willing to compromise with the mission of the International Criminal Court, especially in exchange for making peace with current country leadership. What this may open up is how the UN can play a more nuanced role through its experience with Truth and Reconciliation processes as vehicles of particularized justice solutions and new openings for forgiveness and transformative justice.

Mediation as an alternative strategy

The world was spellbound by the results of the negotiation process in South Africa. When F. W. de Klerk reached out to Nelson Mandela in prison and opened up the negotiation process for a power transition, the international community was hoping that it was seeing a new blueprint for peace in difficult and intractable settings. Since then many see this experience as a "one-off." It was a peace unencumbered by other proxy fighters for the Cold War or by neighbors working out long-standing power struggles on the fields of another country. And both de Klerk and Mandela were truly uniquely equipped for their role in the negotiations. Mandela, by his strength of character, was able to forgive while also representing other victims in a manner that is hard to replicate. De Klerk was that rare president ready to share power and even concede it and resign, for the good of his country.

The parameters of their negotiations are well known. They instituted a transition process governed by an interim set of principles. The process was to take place over five years. Mandela and his party would take over the offices of president and vice president, and de Klerk would be third in line of power. The army would stay in place. A new constitution would be negotiated, guaranteeing the rights of all its citizens and due process of the laws. A Truth and Reconciliation commission was set up to provide a mechanism for dealing with past atrocities. The commission opened up the potential for forgiveness from victims to perpetrators of violence. It also opened up transformative hope that the sins of the past could be put aside, if not forgotten, in order to build for the future. Of course, South Africa is still struggling with its history of apartheid. It has severe capacity problems, including fighting corruption, systematic inequalities built into its educational system, and simmering racism existing in both the white and black communities.

Still, the UN thought that it was seeing for itself a new way that it could operate as a peacemaker. Perhaps it could help in intra-state conflicts, serving as a mediator to help the parties share a way forward. It took steps to put itself forward as a mediator.

The UN as mediator

Article 33 of the Charter of the United Nations provides that

> [t]he parties to any dispute, the continuance of which is likely to endanger the maintenance of international peace and security, shall, first of all, seek a solution by negotiation, enquiry, mediation, conciliation, arbitration, judicial settlement, resort to regional agencies or arrangements, or other peaceful means of their own choice.

The charter envisages roles for the secretary-general, the Security Council, and the General Assembly, among others, in the peaceful settlement of disputes, and UN resolutions and practice have further contributed to the development of its peacemaking functions.

As we have seen in the UN's peacekeeping role that developed in the context of the Cold War, its number one principle in any mission was to maintain neutrality on the ground so that the combatants, often in the context of gaining independence from a colonialist past, could choose for themselves between socialism and democracy. With the fall of the Soviet Union, maintaining this neutrality has become less and less important. In fact, the UN would announce that in its role of mediator, it was making some assumptions about what was necessary in any post-conflict society in order to reach a sustainable peace. Its mediation documents adopted principles that included promotion of human rights, free and fair elections of leaders, and institutions for ensuring the rule of law. We have seen before that it was also not shy in promoting rights for women, insisting that women's groups be at the table in any settlement negotiations.[23] In the case of disputes between African countries, it would also involve the African Union (AU) and invoke its principles.

Both the UN and the AU would become involved as mediators in numerous disputes. Each were drawn into "nation building" as parties moved from ceasefire to disarmament. Then they stay to help implement interim governance periods. Then they were partners to elections and then to Constitutional drafting to helping ensure the peace and security until the new government could take over for itself.

I want to briefly comment on three different conflicts where the UN was involved as a mediator, or at least as a keen observer of peacemaking dilemmas, to show how its experience in this role might have an impact on any mediation it may do in Syria. In particular, we need to see the rise and fall of democratic principles during these conflicts and their resolutions, as necessary elements of peacemaking and peace maintaining, as well as whether the UN will play a role in encouraging democracy over dictatorships.

Kenya is the first example worth some mention. In the follow-up to the post-election violence of the 2007 election, Kenya invited the UN to help it mediate between Mwai Kibaki and Raila Odinga, the two candidates whose supporters carried out acts of violence, and even genocide, in the aftermath of the election. Most observers feel that Kibaki had been caught rigging the election results. He held the vote total from an area of the country he controlled and then announced it to carry him over the top in the election. The problem was that the vote total was greater than the total number of people who lived in the region.

In an attempt at mediation, Kofi Annan negotiated a power-sharing arrangement in Kenya. Odinga was made premier, and the total number of seats in the cabinet were doubled so that Odinga supporters could have an equal number of governing positions as Kibaki supporters did. Annan put off the issues of war crimes by getting the parties to set up an investigative commission, the Committee for the Investigation of Post-Election Violence (CIPEV). Interestingly enough, one of the targets of that investigation Uhuru Kenyatta, who is now Kenya's president. He would come to be indicted by the ICC, but such an indictment would later be tabled, as the UN got caught between its principles. It simultaneously stood against leaders enjoying impunity for war crimes while also backing democratically elected leadership as the best way forward for sustainable governance (PZ, 327–28). In this case, the UN was putting forward democracy, and its institutions, as the best way forward in the post-conflict setting.

The rise of fall of democracy in Egypt must also have informed the UN in any peacemaking role it might have in Syria. Briefly, Egypt was subject to an Arab spring democracy movement in the beginning of 2011. Inspired by the events in Tunisia, Egyptians gathered to protest on January 25, the national "Police Day" holiday, calling for an end to corruption, injustice, poor economic conditions, and the 30-year-old regime of President Hosni Mubarak. Street demonstrations quickly grew into a national revolutionary movement that in 18 days removed Mubarak and his National Democratic Party (NDP) from power. In the beginning of the uprising, mass demonstrations in Cairo (most notably in Tahrir [Liberation] Square), Alexandria, and other cities were met with repression and violence by police and supporters of the ruling NDP. But Egyptians broke through the wall of fear and fought back in street battles. On January 27, the government shutdown the Internet, and mobile service providers complied with government requests to suspend cell phone services. Still, the uprising continued, and the army made the decision ultimately not to act against the protesters. Mubarak's weak concessions – appointing intelligence Omar Suleiman as vice president on January 29, installing a new cabinet on January 31, conceding that neither he nor his son Gamal wouldn't run again for president after he finished his term in September 2011 – failed to appease the Egyptian people's demands. On February 11, the day of the massive "Friday of Departure" demonstrations, Mubarak was finally forced to resign. The Supreme Council of Armed Forces (SCAF), headed by Field Marshal Mohamed Hussein Tantawi, took over control of Egypt and later dissolved the legislature and suspended the constitution.

There were elections, but the results were troubling. The elected leader, Mohamed Morsi, moved to consolidate his support, much of which was radical. Minority rights were jeopardized, and the tyranny of the majority asserted itself as a time of "taking back" what was believed to have been taken by the Mubarak regime. The Muslim Brotherhood swept the early elections. The Muslim Brotherhood put forward Mohamed Morsi as its candidate for president. It controlled the constitution-drafting process. Sharia law was instituted, to which minority and free speech rights took a back seat.

By 2012 there were more protests in the streets from various religious groups. General el-Sisi warned Morsi the military would reassert itself. Protests in the streets called for Morsi's removal. el-Sisi replaced the chief justice of the Supreme Court and declared a state of emergency. After removing Morsi from office, el-Sisi would suspend the constitution. By 2013 the country was ruled by a military junta. el-Sisi is now the duly elected president of Egypt. In a 2016 address to the UN, he asserted his support for human rights and fighting global warming and terrorism but made no mention of democracy or democratic principles.

Finally, as we have already mentioned in discussing Obama's hesitancy to intervene militarily in Syria, the Libyan experience has also informed the UN and its mediators about the potential risks of intervening too early in a conflict situation. The intervention that removes a leader like a Gaddafi or Mubarak might leave a power vacuum that can make matters worse, and it is not always clear that democratic principles will provide the way forward in all situations.

The UN became less sure that it possessed the best practices or blueprint for post-conflict peace building. It found itself too often lacking in the fundamental knowledge of the particular perspectives of the combatants. It became too quickly partial to one side or the other. It came off as arrogant to the parties, lacking fundamental empathy for and understanding of the losses that the parties had suffered. But what should the responsibility of the UN be to address inequalities and wealth disparities going back decades, some to colonialist times? The UN was often too hasty in its insistence that the parties successfully put aside past grievances. And then, as mediators, because they were there only as long as the parties wanted them there, the UN lacked any serious leverage over the parties to make them live up to the promises they made. What could they do if one the parties promised a ceasefire and then reneged the next day? The UN found that even its own representatives would have difficulty delivering on their promises.

In addition, it found that many conflicts are more complex than, say, South Africa, where there were no proxy players playing roles behind the scenes and fighting their own battles on foreign turf. Should such external forces have a seat at the table? Or what if there is no Mandela? What if the opposition is seriously fractured and seeking support from anyone who will give it? Changing alliances and missions can lead the UN to start to partner with terrorist organizations that risk the UN in its mission elsewhere in the world and in the general mission to fight terrorism.

Another complexity relates to the inability of party representatives to enforce the agreements that they reach. Because the leader may worry about the trustworthiness of the peacemaking setting (will he be arrested at the negotiations?), the combatants send representatives. They may get the approval of the leader to agree to certain provisions that later become unpopular when made public. Individuals in the group may decide to go off on their own, or the leader may change his or her mind. Proxy supporters may also balk at the agreement. The "square table" assumption behind negotiation theories often does not stand up to the realities on the ground.

The problem of the UN's role during any interim period is how quickly it can become stuck in a quagmire of continuing disputes, lacking the leverage to make the parties behave. The experience in Tunisia also informs the UN. Tunisia is an example, at least so far, of a country that came out of the Arab Spring as a democracy. One of the remarkable successes was the negotiation held between the various groups involved and their "commitment" to work out their differences. On the other hand, country experts point to the role that organized labor played in keeping the parties at the table. Any time the parties deadlocked, labor would organize a demonstration or a strike. The parties often faced the choice of either compromising or having the government shutdown. If labor had not played such a role in Tunisia, many worry that the parties would have resorted to violence to resolve their differences. It was as if the labor-organizing ability of Tunisia served as a proxy for public economic concerns in a way that overrode tribal and religious differences.

The UN has learned that it is very difficult to establish the trust necessary to engage in problem-solving negotiations. Problem-solving negotiations look to the underlying goals of each respective party to identify creative solutions to dividing issues. They often use "shared interests" (fighting diseases, fighting poverty, attracting foreign investment, protecting against future religious discrimination) to frame solutions that are "win–win" for all parties. The problem is that the parties' time horizons are often too short. Leadership of rebel factions is continually changing and shifting. From a negotiation standpoint it is hard for the parties to think about the long term, as they are far from certain they will even still exist the following year. So they look to adversarial bargaining to try to get the best deal they can get in their present situation. The problem then is that the present situation is itself continually shifting. The territory each party controls changes; the number of recruits changes; the resources they get from their supporters change. The ability of the mediator to appeal to some future five-year process for building institutions, having new elections, and implementing a new constitution is very limited. The parties demand real power right away and in an area that they can control. Trusting in some future "independent" judiciary and the rule of law is often seen as nothing more than a frail pipe dream.

Consequently, formal peace talks are all about stages. First, we need to decide who is at the table, who is a terrorist and should not be there, and how to provide the legitimate parties security. Then peacemakers must identify the issues.

With these lessons in hand, let's turn next to the UN mediation efforts in Syria

Syria and the United Nations I: Kofi Annan

Syria would come to the Security Council's attention in early 2012. Divisions at the Security Council were immediately drawn. The US, the UK, and France wanted to take decisive action, and the Arab League was in support of taking a tough stance against Assad. The Arab League, made up of mostly Sunni-majority Middle Eastern countries, stands opposed to Iran, which still sees itself as multi-ethnic, and Shia-affiliated countries. Russia and China, however, opposed any support, implicit or explicit, for regime change in Syria. When a draft resolution was put to a vote in February, it contained language unacceptable to Russia and China (that Assad must step down), leading them to exercise a veto.

The UN secretary-general, Ban Ki-moon, naturally turned to mediation as a potential peacekeeping effort that would avoid the political deadlock in the Security Council. Perhaps the secretary-general also saw it as a way to do an avoid making prominent whatever would be the implications of the Lebanon special tribunal – the one investigating whether Assad had played a role in the assassination of Hariri. And this was before the UN had evidence of Assad's use of chemical weapons, so the mission of the ICC would not be compromised by the UN's role as a mediator. Ban Ki-Moon appointed his predecessor, Kofi Annan, as the UN mediator in Syria. As we have seen before, Annan was coming off his success in Kenya, where he had followed the democracy-infused peacemaking assumptions originally drawn from the South Africa experience in negotiating the power-sharing arrangement between Kibaki and Odinga. Having been brought back from retirement, Annan soon engaged in a wide range of consultations, meeting state representatives at UN headquarters, visiting stakeholders in the Middle East, including Egypt, Qatar, and Turkey, and conferring with Bashar al-Assad in Damascus in March, as well as with representatives of the opposition. His strategy was to use external leverage to reach a ceasefire agreement, thereby opening up space for internal democratic political contestation and wider transformation of governance in Syria.

Annan had earlier been successful as a mediator in first drawing up a six-point plan as a way to set an agenda for any talks. He had this plan ready and then headed into a set of intense and quickly called meetings with Assad. He was able to put enough pressure on Assad to get him to agree to a ceasefire in April. The UN then sent a 300-member peacekeeping force to Damascus and six other sites throughout Syria. The peacekeepers were charged with engaging in observations, which seemed to have the desired effect: reports of hostilities were reduced in both number and intensity for about six to eight weeks.

As we saw in our early discussions of Assad's record during this period, Assad engaged in a number of military actions that created disproportionate civilian casualties. He repeatedly used indiscriminately aimed barrel bombs. There were also troubling and confirmed reports of security roundups and torture. In early June 2012, key parts of the opposition revoked their commitment to the ceasefire, and the UN monitors ceased operations.

Annan accelerated his efforts. He assembled a "contact group" of states with interests and influence in Syria. Meeting in Geneva, the group laid out a set of guidelines for a potential peace process that included the establishment of a transitional government. The outcome was summarized in the so-called Geneva Communiqué, which has remained a focal point for negotiations ever since. A six-point plan was agreed to, to commit to and implement a sustained ceasefire with UN supervision[24] For a moment, it appeared that the world powers were united behind a common approach, an approach that even included the democratic blueprint that had worked in other situations. This blueprint included a transitional government towards a newly elected leadership. Assad, however, was not ready to concede power. He interpreted the adopted text as to include his continued role as the Syria's president. He insisted that he was the duly elected president and that he had the right to exercise power in order to protect Syria in the face of terrorist threats. Assad's intransigence seemed to stem from having Russian support. Initially hoping that Russia would not have the resources for long-term funding of Assad's military efforts, especially considering the declining prices of oil, Annan instead soon learned that Russia was trying to protect both its existing bases in Syria and its access to the Mediterranean. Russia also seemed to be doubling down on its own aggressive tactics in Ukraine and Georgia. Russia seemed to believe that the US and its allies were unwilling to stand up to its use of military force to expand its power in Eastern Europe and so felt undeterred in militarily backing Syria.

In the summer of 2012, a clearly frustrated Annan resigned his mission, criticizing international and regional powers for failing to rally behind his efforts and to provide the kind of leverage that the execution of his plan required.

United Nations II: Lakhdar Brahimi

The UN then turned to Brahimi, who, while officially retired since 2005, had continually been involved as an international mediator for the UN. Mr. Brahimi, an Algerian who had been active in Algeria's independence movement from France in the 1950s, was best known from his work in Afghanistan, where he had been involved in negotiations that resulted in Afghanistan's post-Taliban constitution. He had similarly been involved in Iraq, after US-led forces ousted its government. As the UN special envoy in post-Saddam Iraq, he helped to establish the interim government that came to power in 2004. Brahimi's UN career also encompassed missions in South Africa, ahead of the 1994 election that brought Nelson Mandela to power, and in Haiti, where he was the senior UN envoy from 1994 to 1996. Mr. Brahimi has also represented the UN in Democratic Republic of (DR) Congo, Yemen, Liberia, Nigeria, and Sudan. The situation in Liberia, both for good and bad, likely had an impact on his approach in Syria. Also, between his stints in Afghanistan, Mr. Brahimi chaired an independent review of UN peacekeeping operations. His report was critical of the UN's failure to intervene to prevent atrocities in Rwanda in 1994 and in Srebrenica, Bosnia, in 1995. This report recommended a major overhaul of UN peacekeeping operations.

Much of his approach was thereafter a product of the experiences I have already mention in Liberia, Kenya, Libya, and Egypt. In a paper he wrote in 2013, he became hesitant to impose "square table" assumptions on current disputes.[25] For Brahimi, democratic solutions too quickly imposed in post-conflict settings could have destabilizing effects. Brahimi was willing to adopt a more cautious and consultative approach, at least initially, trying to convince the parties of the futility of continued war and repeatedly stressing the tremendous humanitarian costs that warfare had on the population. Still, the Geneva Communiqué, with its stipulations for regime change, remained a pillar of Brahimi's mediation, as did several components of Annan's plan, including a general ceasefire supported by international monitoring.

Assad saw Brahimi as a pawn of the US for his repeated references to the Geneva Communiqué. On the other hand, as Brahimi shifted in his strategies to try to lure in Assad to continue to be engaged, the other Arab states came to mistrust Brahimi because he no longer insisted that Assad had to go.

Under such inhospitable circumstances, it took a long time before the disputants could be brought back to the negotiation table in a process known as Geneva II that was carried out in January and February 2014. To a large extent, the parties' return to negotiations flowed from a temporary coming together of interests between the US and Russia, both of which had become more pragmatic after the rise of the Islamic state and the near intervention by the US following the usage of chemical weapons in Ghouta, near Damascus, in August 2013. After all, couldn't Russia agree that the use of chemical weapons was a war crime? It seemed the US and Russia shared an interest in preventing the use and spread of chemical weapons in the Middle East.

Geneva II generated little progress with the exception of some agreements for the international community to provide humanitarian aid. Assad and the rebels were deadlocked and equally inflexible on the question of whether Assad must go. While the regime continued to stress the importance of its fight against terrorism, the opposition conditioned further talks on guarantees that Assad play no role in a future Syrian government. This turned out to be to the advantage of Assad. While the US hoped Iran and Russia would lack the resources to continue to fund Assad's regime, and that other forces within the Alawite community would remove Assad from power (there were rumors to that effect among the Syrian expatriate community in Beirut), neither of these hopes came to fruition. With neither side budging from their positions, and with the government maintaining a slow military advance at the time, Russia became bolder in its support for the Assad regime. The UN process again faltered. Importantly, in conceding the potential continuation of Assad's presidency, the UN also seemed to shift its position on whether it insisted on a truly democratic form of government in any future Syria governmental structure. It also seemed willing to compromise on its own investigation of Assad's use of sarin gas. Impunity might be tolerated, with obvious consequences for the UN's emphasis on the rule of law, if peace could be made and refugees could return home. If there was a silver lining, it was that Geneva II represented the first instance of direct negotiations between the warring sides since the start of the war.

United Nations III: Staffan de Mistura

After Brahimi, who resigned as UN–Arab League envoy on May 31, 2014, the leadership of UN mediation efforts was taken up by Staffan de Mistura, an Italian-Swedish diplomat who previously headed the UN mission in Iraq. In light of the failure of his predecessors, de Mistura's initial strategy was to de-emphasize the search for a comprehensive, top-down ceasefire and to instead seek to facilitate limited truces in different places across the country. The pilot case for this confidence-building approach was the ceasefire for Aleppo, the country's largest city, divided among regime, opposition, and Kurdish forces since 2012. The "freeze" in Aleppo was framed in modest language: "It is only a test,' said De Mistura, but he raised hopes that it could contribute to 'building confidence in an incremental fashion amongst the warring parties."

De Mistura had a couple of things going for him. One was that the rise of ISIS (or ISIL or DAESH), gave the different sides a common enemy. The second was the nuclear agreement with Iran and the potential removal of sanctions creating the potential for Iran to seek membership in the international economic community, and its potential desire to lessen the tensions between it and the Arab League. Suffering from mounting war exhaustion, the parties seemed riper for negotiations than perhaps at any stage since 2011. But then Russia intervened, seeming to take the position that Assad should at least be allowed to defend his regime from all sorts of violent opposition. Matters of negotiating any governance change were to be worked out after armed opposition stopped. But would Russia also be willing to put pressure on Assad once the fighting stopped, to make a move toward power sharing?

These developments paved the way for a re-energized and concerted diplomatic push starting in October 2015. Meetings in Vienna brought together a group of twenty states and international organizations, labelled the International Syria Support Group (ISSG), for the negotiation of a new peace plan, again based on the Geneva Communiqué. The new plan was formalized in a Security Council resolution (2254) adopted in December 2015. It requested de Mistura to convene formal UN-led negotiations toward a political process that would prepare the way for a ceasefire and, ultimately, a system of "credible, inclusive, and non-sectarian governance." Thus, Resolution 2254 provided the strategic vision that would underpin the UN's work in Syria from the start of 2016.

The provision contained in 2268 that was either its genius or that which would simply postpone till later, the real intractable issue of Assad's continued leadership, was that Syria would decide for itself who would lead it and how it would be governed. From Assad's side of this agreement, he could take comfort in the fact that a truly free and fair election for Syria would only take place years in the future. After all, millions of refugees and displaced people, some of whom will now choose to stay in their new environments, could create major impediments to democracy. For instance, who will vote, and when? Who will *return* and vote, and for whom? With Assad able to declare future emergencies and control the message and circumstances of future voting, it is unlikely that he would be unseated. For opposition groups, they may see that what they have to gain is a principle: that of free elections as a democratic determinant for the future of Syria. Or they may be more pragmatic and simply express a willingness to live in a dictatorship, albeit one with stronger guarantees for free speech, human rights and protections for religious minorities. Some refugees may see this option as a "ship that has already sailed." Having given their names at the border, they may worry that any attempt to return will result in their "disappearance," if border security is so directed by Assad.

Based on Resolution 2254, talks re-commenced in February 2016 but were immediately suspended on account of enmity between uncompromising opposition delegates, especially between the Islamist organization Jaish al-Islam and regime representatives. The parties remained, de Mistura's said, "locked in fixed positions and a zero-sum game."[26] It is here where an official UN role in the mediations was sidelined. What would happen instead is that a new group has now formed to give a new framework for the continuing negotiations? What role the UN will then play in the future of Syria is yet to be seen. De Mistura has been hesitant to convene new talks if progress can now be made.

The ISSG was organized to provide a new framework for peace. It was initially made up of 19 countries and was co-chaired by the US and Russia. It has since been expanded to include countries in the Arab League, Australia, Canada, Netherlands, Japan, members of the Organisation Islamic Cooperation, and Spain.

Meeting in Munich in February 2016, the ISSG presented a proposal for a nationwide "cessation of hostilities," further outlined in a joint statement by Russia and the US on February 22, 2016, and endorsed by the Security Council in Resolution 2268.

Signatories of the agreement agreed to participate in political negotiations, cease military attacks, allow humanitarian access, and refrain from grabbing territory from other signatories. A monitoring mechanism, co-managed by Russia and the US, was set up to gather, evaluate, and disseminate reports of noncompliance, with the understanding that violators may be militarily punished.

The ceasefire of February 27, 2016, had an immediate and significant effect as guns went silent across large portions of Syria. According to the Syrian Observatory for Human Rights, the death toll in the month following the ceasefire was the lowest since November 2011. Given the pessimism that has prevailed for a long time, the tentative success of the February ceasefire came as a surprise to many. Optimism was further bolstered when meetings in Geneva in March 2016 resulted in a document listing "Points of Commonalities" between the parties, which included references to the political transition envisioned in the Geneva Communiqué and Resolution 2254.

Meanwhile, the war against the Salafi-Jihadist opposition, who were excluded from the ceasefire, continued unabated. Russian airstrikes were instrumental in the recapture of the oasis city of Palmyra from the Islamic State, an important symbolic victory for the regime. In and around Aleppo, where groups not covered by the ceasefire operated alongside groups that were, the ceasefire proved vulnerable, as the intermixing of groups made it difficult to contain hostilities.

Against a backdrop of resurging violence in Aleppo, the ISSG met again in mid-May 2016, seeking to reinforce the fragile ceasefire and reinvigorate the mediation process. The group elaborated on the principles for ceasefire implementation, but talks again stumbled on the question of the fate of al-Assad, leaving both the survival of the ceasefire and the envisioned political transition in uncertainty.

On August 1, 2016, a key deadline has come and gone.

What do the changes in intervention strategies mean?

Starting as it did with Annan's Geneva Communiqué, the UN found itself in the same position as the US in calling for Assad's removal from power. It did so for many of the same reasons the US did, namely to encourage the democratic movement on the ground in Syria that had originally come out of the Arab Spring. This democracy movement seemed to be some evidence on the part of some Syrians that they were ready for more freedom. This movement did not seem to be motivated by tribalism or by a rising up of a repressed minority group looking for a chance to take power. These groups will emerge later. Initially, the democracy movement seemed to express the genuine will of Syrian young people, through their courageous acts of demonstration and protest, that it was now time for democracy to be established in Syria. Syria was expressing itself much like Egypt and Tunisia. Some Syrians saw dictatorship and oppression as getting in the way of a chance for freedom and economic opportunity.

Yet the UN, having committed itself to democracy, then had to come to face with its loss of neutrality in subsequent attempts to act as a mediator between Assad and his opponents. Russian involvement in the Security Council and its intervention on behalf of the Assad regime could not wash from Assad's mind the initial positions Annan had taken. He would not trust Annan, or Brahimi, or de Mistura: the suspicion was always present for Assad that they were all plotting his removal.

As the UN shifted in its strategies and sought to work for cessation of hostilities, it de-emphasized its role as protecting against future impunity for war crimes. Its strategy became less a problem-solving one that would encourage each party to take positions that would maximize its own gain. So far these strategies have led to deadlock. Position-bargaining strategies face great difficulties with questions of sovereignty versus freedom and of security versus free speech, religious freedoms, freedom of travel, and freedom of association.

The UN's shift to adversarial bargaining (where parties make demands and concessions are in the form of trades rather than in attempts to find common ground where both groups thrive) on local and regional issues also further divides the various groups into a zero-sum game with each other. Already impossibly fragmented, the opposition groups have little in common to give them leverage against Assad. It is at least in part, in their shared and uncertain minority status that they can start to see common interests in the protection of minority rights and freedoms. It is often from not knowing whether one's group will ever be in control, or stay in control, that the need to protect minority status emerges.[27] Discussion of liberal democracy leads to discussions of shared interests and to problem-solving solutions that remain hidden from adversarial and position-bargaining strategies.

The UN, in its shift towards narrower hostility-control strategies, can also lose its role in guiding the parties to transformative justice mechanisms. It is hard to see the need for a truth and reconciliation process if one is given the chance of control over one's narrow region. Other informal dispute resolution methods that the parties might employ to build toward a new national identity also go by the wayside. By becoming more pragmatic, the UN loses its principled basis for its role in the conflict resolution process. This has particular ramifications when one considers the religious issues embedded in the dispute.

The religious dimension was present from the first days of the Syrian uprising, and in a country with a structurally weak civil society, these religious dimensions provided part of the narrative around which the Sunni opposition could coalesce. Assad could rally most Alawites and other Shia, given their common fear of oppression from Sunni groups. The arrival of fighters who viewed the war as just one battleground in the larger rivalry between Sunni and Shia accentuated religious fault lines, fortifying essentialist convictions that commonly make disputants less willing to entertain negotiations. One wonders whether, without the UN in the role of a secular pope, the parties who have internalized part of the religious narratives can find their way through the religious legacies of their dispute.

Indeed, in the absence of institutional organization and common ideological narratives, the opposition has largely been kept together by its uniform demand that "Assad must go." Because this demand provided the opposition with its main coordinating device, it could prove very hard for it to be set aside in the long run. It also is a dangerous point of unity, for common loyalty will cease if and when Assad goes. What will be the glue that holds the various groups together once and if Assad goes? Consequently, most opposition representatives never wavered from stipulating Assad's departure as a precondition for further talks. Given that the government has no incentive to be flexible on this point, the fate of al-Assad has essentially turned into an "indivisibility" – a good that cannot be efficiently partitioned – which the parties lacked both creativity and willpower to dissolve.

It would take a new group, the ISSG, to reopen a forum for new negotiations. What was lost in the new forum was a progression of peacemaking that would provide for democratic principles to be employed as the parties seek to build for a new Syria. The focus now is in conflict mitigation over conflict resolution. The parties are stuck at the point of ceasefires and humanitarian aid unless a way can be made for the principles of governance to become the new focus of negotiations. Left unresolved are the following issues for the long-term sustainable governance of Syria: (1) What rights will be given to minority groups in future of Syria? (2) How will the Kurds be treated in reward for their help in fighting ISIS? and (3) What protections will be given for freedom of speech, freedom of religion, freedom of association, right to contract, travel, or to own private property?

Conclusion

What can be learned from our review of the UN as peacekeeper is its conflicting role as the seat of the ICC and its role a mediator. I have tried to show, that in its role as peacekeeper, it confronts many of the same issues as the US confronts when trying to decide whether to intervene and put its troops on the ground. It must weigh whether it has enough evidence that it can do so without setting up the precedent that it violates the sovereignty of a nation too lightly and loses all opportunity to later make peace. Even though its motivations may be pure, it has to move carefully or it can contribute to making things worse. It can create a power vacuum that will either involve it in a quagmire or align itself too quickly with unsavory actors with no intentions except for revenge.

As a mediator, its role has evolved but then may have returned to where it has started. At first, it needed to maintain strong appearances of neutrality, if it was to ever get the cooperation of Russia. Then it increased its role, guiding failed states to compromise, using democratic principles, and a combination of rule of law strategies and Truth and Reconciliation Commissions to try to create the stability needed to move the country forward. Its secretary-generals showed an ability to use their individualized religious perspectives in a progressive and unifying way, taking on the role of a "secular pope" as it tried to do justice and insist on peace.

But then Libya and Egypt took dramatically different turns following their "Arab Springs." Libya turned into a playground for radical groups, and Egypt showed the flaw of democracy, that elections, without habits of democracy in place, can turn into tyrannies.

The Syrian conflict, the refugee crisis, and Assad's apparent violations of humanitarian law made the situation increasingly difficult to manage. Despite its best efforts it could do little, once Russia sided with Assad. Russia points out the dysfunction of the Security Council, where one of the parties is insensitive humanitarian law issues and violations of human rights. As a result, the UN as a mediator has had to try for peace, where the parties are interested in power and security. They look to settle for less democracy and less rule of law. The UN's ability to guide the parties toward democratic institutions has become so compromised that it has become irrelevant to the process.

Unfortunately, for the UN going forward, until the makeup of the Security Council changes even playing a mediator's role has made even more difficult. It takes a request from a member country for the SG to intervene without a Security Council resolution. This is unlikely in situations where the current executive is acting to repress opposition within the country.

Interestingly enough, it is the Russians who have opened the door for discussion of these issues. They have offered negotiations over Syria's new constitution as an important mechanism for making a lasting peace. And so, it is in the context lacking the UN's direct involvement that the negotiations proceed. Political options and the constitution, then, are the next topics I address in the next chapter.

Notes

1 Kent J. Kille, ed., *The UN Secretary General and Moral Authority: Ethics and Religion in International Leadership* (Washington, DC: Georgetown University Press, 2007); See also, Monica Bouman, "Dag Hammarskjöld and the politics of hope," in *Peace Diplomacy, Global Justice and International Agency: Rethinking Human Security and Ethics in the Spirit of Dag Hammarskjöld*, ed. Carsten Stahn & Henning Melber, (Cambridge: Cambridge University Press, 2014), 77–105. doi:10.1017/CBO9781139583855.009

2 Martin Meredith, *The Fate of Africa: A History of Fifty Years of Independence* (New York: Public Affairs, 2005).

3 My source over the next paragraphs regarding Thant's thinking comes from, Kent J. Kille, ed., *The UN Secretary General and Moral Authority: Ethics and Religion in International Leadership* (Washington, DC: Georgetown University Press, 2007), *Chapter 5, U Thant: Buddhism in Action.* (hereinafter, Moral Authority).

4 Moral Authority, *supra*, note 2, at 166.

5 Ibid, chapter 5.

6 Walter A. Dorn, "Chapter 5, UTHANT, Buddhism in Action," in *The UN Secretary General and Moral Authority: Ethics and Religion in International Leadership*, ed. Kent J. Kille (Washington, DC: Georgetown University Press, 2007), 143 (see footnote 62).

7 Ibid.

8 Ibid.

9 Annan addresses summit for Religious Leader and International Peacemaking, August 29, 2000. For many of us, the axiom could well be: "We pray, therefore, we are.

Of course, the practice of religion differs widely. But at heart we are dealing in universal values. To be merciful; to be tolerant; to love thy neighbor; no religion can claim a monopoly on such teachings.

There is no mystery here. Such values are deeply ingrained in the human spirit itself. It is little wonder that the same values animate the Charter of the United Nations, and lie at the root of our search for world peace.

. . .

So I humbly suggest that today's meeting is also an opportunity for religious, spiritual and political leaders, as well as their followers, to look within, and to consider what they can do to promote justice, equality, reconciliation and peace. Men and women of faith are a strong influence on group and individual conduct. As teachers and guides, you can be powerful agents of change. You can inspire people to new levels of commitment and public service. You can help bridge the chasms of ignorance, fear and misunderstanding. You can set an example of interfaith dialogue and cooperation.

Dag Hammarskjöld once said, "The United Nations stands outside – necessarily outside – all confessions. But it is, nevertheless, an instrument of faith. As such, it is inspired by what unites and not by what divides the great religions of the world."

As the world's religious and spiritual leaders, you embody humanity's deepest yearnings. You have travelled many paths to this time and place. Some of you have been imprisoned for your beliefs. Some have survived the Holocaust, or seen your people targeted for genocide. Still others have lived through other tribulations and indignities. Whatever your past, whatever your calling, and whatever the differences among you, your presence here at the United Nations signifies your commitment to our global mission of tolerance, development and peace. For that, we must all be profoundly grateful.

10 The secretary-general commissioned an independent inquiry [S/1999/1257] into the actions of the United Nations during the 1994 genocide in Rwanda and, at the request of the General Assembly, provided a comprehensive assessment [A/54/549] on the 1993–1995 events in Srebrenica in the former Yugoslavia. The circumstances that led to the UN withdrawal from Somalia were also carefully examined [S/1995/231].

11 Angola – UN Angola Verification Mission III (UNAVEM III) and UN Observer Mission in Angola (MONUA).

12 Bosnia and Herzegovina – UN Mission in Bosnia and Herzegovina (UNMIBH).

13 Croatia – UN Confidence Restoration Operation in Croatia (UNCRO), UN Transitional Administration for Eastern Slavonia, Baranja and Western Sirmium (UNTAES) and UN Civilian Police Support Group (UNPSG).

14 Yugoslav Republic of Macedonia – UN Preventive Deployment Force (UNPREDEP).

15 Guatemala – UN Verification Mission in Guatemala (MINUGUA).

16 Haiti – UN Support Mission in Haiti (UNSMIH) UN Transition Mission in Haiti (UNTMIH) and UN Civilian Police Mission in Haiti (MIPONUH).

17 "In Larger Freedom: Towards Development, Security and Human Rights for All", Report of the Secretary General, March 21, 2005, 59th Session, United Nations General Assembly, p. 35.

18 UNHCR on Sudan, convention to prevent genocide. UNHCR, United Nations Refugee Agency, Syria, http://www.un.org/en/sections/issues-depth/refugees/

19 Taken from UN Human Rights Council's Commission of Inquiry (CoI) (Adams, 2015). https://documents-dds-ny.un.org/doc/UNDOC/GEN/G15/019/37/PDF/G1501937.pdf?OpenElement

20 However, further statements against intervention in Syria were made in UN deliberations that show the depth of the feelings that nonintervention by the UN was a mistake. As Adams (2015) explains,

> Three years ago in February 2012, for the second time since the conflict began, Russia and China vetoed a United Nations (UN) Security Council

> draft resolution aimed at holding the Syrian government accountable for crimes against humanity. Watching the discussion in the chamber after the vote, the depth of un-diplomatic emotion was palpable. In particular, Susan Rice, then United States Ambassador to the UN and now President Barack Obama's National Security Advisor, said her government was "disgusted" by the veto of a resolution intended to help protect civilians and halt atrocities. Although the resolution had been supported by 13 of the 15 members of the Council, diplomats and human rights advocates in New York were despondent.
>
> (5)

21 Kent J. Kille, ed., *The UN Secretary General and Moral Authority: Ethics and Religion in International Leadership* (Washington, DC: Georgetown University Press, 2007)

22 Association for Diplomatic Training and History, "Moments in U.S. Diplomatic History: The Dayton Peace Accords," http://adst.org/2014/11/the-dayton-peace-accords/.

23 See Report of the Secretary-General, Strengthening the role of mediation in the peaceful settlement of disputes, conflict prevention and resolution, A/66/811, June 25, 2012. In its resolution 65/283, the General Assembly requested the secretary-general to submit a report on the implementation of the resolution titled "Strengthening the Role of Mediation in the Peaceful Settlement of Disputes, Conflict Prevention and Resolution." The present report outlines progress made in implementing the resolution, in the context of key trends in the field of mediation. Also submitted as annexes to the present report are the Guidance for Effective Mediation and the views of member states.

24 The six-point plan bears a quick glance. It provided as follows:

1 commit to work with the Envoy in an inclusive Syrian-led political process to address the legitimate aspirations and concerns of the Syrian people, and, to this end, commit to appoint an empowered interlocutor when invited to do so by the Envoy;

2 commit to stop the fighting and achieve urgently an effective United Nations supervised cessation of armed violence in all its forms by all parties to protect civilians and stabilise the country.

To this end, the Syrian government should immediately cease troop movements towards, and end the use of heavy weapons in, population centres, and begin pull-back of military concentrations in and around population centres.

As these actions are being taken on the ground, the Syrian government should work with the Envoy to bring about a sustained cessation of armed violence in all its forms by all parties with an effective United Nations supervision mechanism.

Similar commitments would be sought by the Envoy from the opposition and all relevant elements to stop the fighting and work with him to bring about a sustained cessation of armed violence in all its forms by all parties with an effective United Nations supervision mechanism;

3 ensure timely provision of humanitarian assistance to all areas affected by the fighting, and to this end, as immediate steps, to accept and implement a daily two-hour humanitarian pause and to coordinate exact time and modalities of the daily pause through an efficient mechanism, including at local level;

4 intensify the pace and scale of release of arbitrarily detained persons, including especially vulnerable categories of persons, and persons involved in peaceful political activities, provide without delay through appropriate channels

a list of all places in which such persons are being detained, immediately begin organizing access to such locations and through appropriate channels respond promptly to all written requests for information, access or release regarding such persons;

5 ensure freedom of movement throughout the country for journalists and a non-discriminatory visa policy for them;

6 respect freedom of association and the right to demonstrate peacefully as legally guaranteed.

25 United Nations, Report of the Secretary-General on peacebuilding in the immediate aftermath of conflict, A/63/881– S/2009/304, 11 June, 2009. "A New Partnership Agenda: Charting a New Horizon for UN Peacekeeping" (New York: UN DPKO/DFS, July 2009).

26 Colum Lynch, Exclusive "U.N. Envoy Signals That Riyadh Is Obstructing Syria Peace Talks," *Foreign Policy*, January 20, 2016, http://foreignpolicy.com/2016/01/20/u-n-envoy-signals-that-riyadh-is-obstructing-syria-peace-talks/

27 Perhaps recognition of these shared minority interests that crossed state boundaries is what is behind not only the state's rights structure of the US constitution but also behind its Bill of Rights! Once its citizens want not only autonomy and religious freedom, but also liberty to travel and start over, without having to give up these aspects of their identity, that the need for a national bill of rights and legal institutions to protect them suggest themselves.

4 Options for a constitution-based transition in Syria

The Russian draft and a problem-solving approach

Preliminary perspectives

Imagine that you are a mediator, charged with mediating a discussion between representatives of Syrian rebel[1] groups at a first meeting where Russian representatives are involved. Assume that representatives from the Kremlin have agreed to meet unofficially with the Syrians to open a dialogue on the future of Syria. Further, assume that neither Assad nor his representatives are present. What might go right and what might go wrong?

In some ways, you might think that the Syrian opposition figures have been preparing for this meeting for quite some time. Similar groups have been meeting almost since the war began in 2011. The issues have changed with the occurrence of the UN processes, Geneva I, and Geneva II. As we've discussed, Annan's Geneva protocol had continued to haunt the meetings. Will the Syrian group insist on the removal of Assad and on the institution of a transition to a more democratic system of governance? If so, what should serve as the governance document during the transition period? One option is the 1950s Constitution, first adopted at Syrian independence, as it eventually became amended in 1973 by the senior al-Assad. A second option is the 2012 Constitution as amended and adopted with Bashar Assad's participation. Or should the group advocate for an interim Constitution based on a set of principles that would only be meant to guide the parties during the interim period? This option might give the parties more flexibility to both deal with lingering security issues and build to work towards establishing nation-wide elections of the national assembly. During this interim period, the parties negotiating with Assad might alternatively adopt the Brahimi approach, focusing more on regional cease fires and ending hostilities; this would leave for later any agreements concerning governance of the future state of Syria to see if there are forces keeping the country together. Or perhaps some meaningful persuasion will occur between the parties that would move Russia, thereby also moving Assad. With the Russians at the table, Russia might see firsthand the group's commitment to a new Syria. As a result Russia might put pressure on Assad to reform Syria's governance structures and/or put the idea in Russia's mind that after saving face and insuring its interests, Russia can gradually move Assad to the dust bin of history.

Before getting to any of these alternatives, you, as the mediator, might give some thought to the strategies and processes that might be in play during the mediation. For example, will you follow conventional procedures and provide the groups with an opportunity for an opening statement? After all, if the Russia delegate gives an opening statement it might set off quite a reaction amongst the Syria delegation: Syrians might leap to their feet and scream in defiance. Midway through the opening statement they might walk out of the meeting. What might set the Syrians off is likely to be the apparent arrogance of Russian's position. It is likely to sound to the Syrians like a series of demands. Russia demands a secular Syria, it wants its military bases to remain where they are, and it wants Assad to stay in power for another 17 years.

What gives the Russians the right to make such demands about the very identity of Syria? The secular state demand will be a nonstarter. Many in the opposition will dig in on positions that will be very difficult for them to back away from. "Syria was and always will be an Islamic state, and nothing gives the Russians the right to alter its identity."

The mediator in our imagining, will then face two difficult tasks. First, the mediator will need to convince the Syrians that the Russians were merely stating an opening position, and expected that the meeting would proceed through a set of adversarial position bargaining exchanges. Problem solving strategies would later be employed after the parties understood each other's opening positions. If the Syrians could stay at the table they could eventually discuss the need for Muslims to be able to practice their religion according to each individual group's understanding of the faith. The mediator would urge them to consider that there were legitimate concerns about the future emergence of ISIS-like groups. On the table should be a discussion of how to be Islamist while also restricting extremist practices that impose one version of Islam on others, like ISIS had done. The Syrian contingent should stay at the table so it could discuss how Russia's main interest in assuring the presence of its military bases could be accomplished by other methods than through assuring Assad's continued role as President of Syria. The Syrian opposition delegates would likely remain skeptical. Would they agree to return to the table if it was clear that Russia was merely stating a set of opening statements and was in no position to make demands?

In addition the Russians would need to be persuaded to soften their rhetoric. Could they say these were merely ideas they were putting forward without claiming that these represented Putin's bottom line demands? Or, would the Russians think that conceding on rhetoric would be a sign of weakness? Of course they were setting forth opening positions, some of which were deal breakers. That is the way they were used to negotiating with the West. Putin had taken a strong public stand that Assad had a right to use military force to put down terrorist extremists within the country. Putin had expressed elsewhere his understanding that Yeltsin's and Gorbechev's weaknesses in responding to the Perestroika movement in Russia had led to the fall of the Soviet Union. Putin seemed to believe that brutal force was a necessary response to demonstrations for democracy. Perhaps, though, his statements did not mean that he was totally opposed to democracy in Syria.[2] And he has a point. Democracy demonstrations like those that occurred in the Arab Spring might lead to anarchy, like it did in Libya. A power vacuum, like what occurred in Libya could lead the rise of even more extremist state. Extremist Islamist governments can pose risks to Russia. In this, Russia is different in its interests and positions from those of its ally, Iran, and the various Shia groups operating in Syria. And so there may be room for compromise.

In the end, the Russian representative might tone down his rhetoric and put forward the ideas as only coming from him, personally, but there are no guarantees. Perhaps the best that could be hoped for is to keep the delegation together for a few more days. No agreements would be reached, but the parties would likely at least agree to keep talking. And so the issues are on the table along with different negotiating strategies. One role for peacemaking advisors that would be made clearer is that to be successful, part of what the parties may need is advice about how to integrate each group's different strategies and styles into one cohesive framework.

Our hypothetical is instructive of the pitfalls of mediating a transition in Syria. It shows that position bargaining strategies can easily lead to deadlock. Again, demands over the continued role of Assad can deadlock the negotiations. Opposition parties and their allies can take great umbrage over Assad's demands, as can Assad in return. The opposition can argue about the injustice imbedded in negotiating with a person who uses a security police to torture and kill those who oppose him, who uses chemical weapons and barrel bombs against civilians, and who is responsible for the refugee crisis that is tearing Syria apart. How will past atrocities be dealt with? Will there be impunity for past war crimes? On the other hand, Assad can claim his sovereign right, backed by his legislature, to make decisions for the security and protection of Syrian citizens. Foreign interference is illegal and immoral. He can form alliances with whomever he wills.

What right does the international community have to step into and interfere with Syria's governance structure?

Between these two positions there is little room for compromise. If the issues are framed this way then the bargaining is zero sum. Who is "right" is a function of force, elections, or a court, assuming such a court has jurisdiction. Assuming that the parties see no room to compromise yet also acknowledge the necessity of making peace, how can this deadlock be resolved? There are some important unresolved questions and issues that the parties will have to face during the interim period. What legal institutions will make these decisions? Syrian? International? A hybrid? Or will the Syrians agree to a Truth and Reconciliation Commission?

As part of the discussion of Assad continuation in power, or perhaps has a separate issue, will Syria be a dictatorship or a democracy? Should this question even be on the table, or should it wait till the Syrians have a chance to hold new elections? If Syria wants to be an Islamic state like Iran, shouldn't it be allowed to do so? Of course, for the delegation assembled, many of whom are Sunni affiliated and have been driven out by Assad, this alternative has little, if any, appeal. Some in the opposition may prefer a state like Saudi Arabia, where Sunnis prevail. Still, regardless of which kind of religious state takes precedence, should a short-term dictatorship even be an option in these negotiations?

In addition, our discussion of negotiating strategy shows how tricky the question of religion is to the question of the future of Syria. Syria needs to consider what role the state will play in furthering Islam. It will need to confront the question of whether Syria will be governed by Sharia law. Which version of Islam will take precedence over the others? Will the Sunnis be allowed to practice their religion? What role will religious freedom play in the future of Syria?

At the heart of these discussions is the role that Syria's constitution might play in both resolving these issues and holding Syria together. The hope of the international community is that Syria, like Tunisia, can come together in its constitutional negotiations to decide for itself how it will be governed. Interestingly enough, it is the Russians who have put forward a draft constitution as an important vehicle of Syria going forward. It has offered its draft as both key to Syria's future and a discussion starter in resolving these critical issues for Syria's future. Such discussions have the potential to break the mediation out of its position-bargaining strategies to engage the Syrians in a genuine problem-solving strategy that is necessary to keep it from breaking apart. Like with Iraq, if it wants to go forward as a state that contains both Sunnis and Shias, and other religious minorities, it must figure out a way to get at some foundational principles that can make that happen. Let's look next at the transitional options for Syria, and in particular take a deep dive into the Russian draft to see what problem-solving possibilities emerge.

As we've discussed, the UN has led multiple efforts with Syrian partners (including Geneva I and Geneva II) where options for political transition have been discussed and debated. Included in those discussions and discussions led by other NGOs were debates about whether to use the 1950 Syrian constitution, with its repeated repeals and reinstatements leading to the 1973 constitution;[3] the 2012 constitution; or an interim constitution (or statement of principles for use during a transition period). This last option was designed to provide a mechanism for power sharing in order to help end the conflict and to deal with the military and security forces. It was also designed to better deal with issues of impunity and to create the best circumstances for Syrians to adopt a constitution in the first place.[4] Until the Russia draft, the Syrian opposition groups and the NGO community seemed to favor an interim constitution or agreement over the 1950, 1973, or 2012 version. Let's see why this might be.

Early constitutional history[5]

There is no doubt that over the course of its history, what is now Syria has been ruled by dictators. The Ottoman Empire ruled Syria from 1516 until the end of World War I. Yet even the Ottoman period felt some pressure towards democracy. In 1876, the Ottomans allowed Syria to have a written constitution for the first time. The constitution gave Syria an administrative council of elected and appointed officials, as well as municipal councils whose members were chosen by religious leaders.

For some historians, the seeds for the breakup of the Ottoman Empire were sowed by its unwillingness to maintain its strong authoritarian control. Others saw the dissolution of the Ottoman Empire as having little to do with the rise of democracy, but more with the Ottoman alliance with Germany, the eventual loser in World War I.[6] It was natural for the Ottomans to ally with Germany, since the British, Italians, and French were in full imperialist mode in the early 1910s, with the British in Egypt, the Italians' brutality in Libya, and both the British and the French in Syria. Germany was also exercising its colonialist impulses and asserting itself in the Middle East but seemed to take for granted that the Ottomans would rule in the Middle East.

During the First World War, Allied forces overran the entire Middle East, leading to a partition of Syria between the British and the French in 1920 at the San Remo Conference, hastily convened and attended by the prime ministers of Great Britain, France, and Italy and representatives from Japan, Greece, and Belgium.

Several issues were addressed there: a peace treaty with Turkey, League of Nation mandates in the Middle East, Germany's obligations under the Versailles Peace Treaty of 1919, and the Allies' position on Soviet Russia.

Great Britain and France agreed to recognize the provisional independence of Syria and Mesopotamia while claiming mandates for their administration. Palestine was then composed of the Ottoman administrative districts of southern Syria. Under international law, premature recognition of Palestinian independence would be a gross affront to the government of the newly declared parent state. It could have been construed as a belligerent act of intervention without any League of Nations sanction.[7]

This is all well and good for the Europeans, but the Ottomans were not at the San Remo Conference, and neither were the Syrians.[8] Even under the stipulations of the San Remo Conference, the European powers exercised only "spheres of influence," not direct control over regions. The French mandate over Syria conflicted with a Syrian national congress action, which had already declared the sovereignty of the Kingdom of Syria under the rule of Sherif Hussein. This congress even approved a constitution on July 3, 1920 (one day before US Independence Day) and ignored a French demand to accept the San Remo decision.

The French then took a page from the British during US colonial times and forcibly occupied the capital of Damascus on July 25, 1920. This was followed by an almost 50-year period of constitutional instability characterized by the constant adoption, suspension, and restoration of different constitutional charters. Still, it is an error to say that Syria had never thought of itself as a constitutional democracy before 1950. The main issue of contention was the election of the president and whether such an election would be done by members of Parliament, or would be the result of the direct will of the people.

In 1930, the French drafted a constitution modelled on that of the French Third Republic. The charter, which provided for a president and a unicameral legislature, was, however, suspended two months later when the parliament was also dissolved. In 1943, the charter was restored and remained the basic law even on Syrian independence from France in 1946. Three years later, in 1949, the constitution was again suspended and replaced with a new one that was promulgated in 1950. This constitution expanded the Bill of Rights and included articles relating to land and education. However, this document was dissolved in 1951 following a military coup which resulted in yet another charter. The 1953 constitution mandated that instead of the president being elected by the parliament, he would be elected by a direct popular vote.

Pan-Arabism was the next force that would threaten Syria's constitutional democracy. Syria's attempt in 1958 to join the United Arab Republic, with Egypt effectively suspended the existing constitutional framework. When an army coup ended this experiment in 1961, the 1950 constitution was again restored. In 1964, a constitutional referendum approved a provisional charter, which was immediately suspended when a new group of military leaders from the Ba'ath Arab Socialist Party staged another coup, suspended the 1964 constitution, and established a regional command in which all the executive and legislative powers were concentrated. In 1966, the party was taken over by its more radical wing, which produced a new constitution in 1969. The party split in 1970 when a group of more moderate party members under General Hafiz al-Assad seized power. As we discussed earlier, Assad was elected as the new president in 1971, and in 1973, he promulgated a new constitution, which, but for few periodic amendments, remained in place until 2012.

1973 constitution[9]

Unity with the Arab world continued to be a major motivating force behind the Syrian constitution of 1973. It was drafted under the strong hand of the senior Assad. The Cold War was in full swing. As a result, with the US backing Israel in the 1967 war, Syria sought an alliance with the Soviets. The 1973 constitution was the first Arab constitution to adopt socialist-nationalist principles. It stated five principles in its preamble that stressed the unity of the Arab world. The first states that the Syrian revolution was part of a larger Arab revolution. The second states that any threats to any individual Arab nation are threats to the entire Arab world. The third commits Syria to the fight against Zionism and imperialism, reflecting the nation's religious and historical heritage. The fourth principle reasserts Syria's view that the fall of the Ottoman Empire was a good thing. In that regard it stated that freedom is a sacred right and that democracy is the ideal form of government. The fifth and final principle likewise states that the Arab revolution is part of a worldwide liberation movement, not an isolated phenomenon. The constitution then continues to state that Islam is the official religion of the president and the republic and that legislation is to be governed by Islamic law. It then divides power among the president, the prime minister, the legislature, and the courts.

Executive branch

Under the 1973 Constitution, the Executive is given strong presidential powers:

- The president is the head of state.
- Like under the Soviet model, he is also the leader of the one and only political party in Syria, the Ba'ath Party.
- He is commander-in-chief of the armed forces.

This makes him the single most powerful actor in the Syrian government. The president is elected to a seven-year term. The candidates for president must be presented by the People's Council from among their ranks at the suggestion of the regional leadership of the Ba'athist Party. The candidacy is then submitted to the people by referendum.

The president's executive powers include upholding the constitution, overseeing the functioning of government authorities, and developing national policy. In overseeing the functioning of the government, the president is to ensure efficiency by being given the power to call the legislative body to work and to disband it. He also *promulgates* laws passed by the legislature. Moreover, the president

- declares war,
- appoints and receive ambassadors,
- concludes international treaties,
- grant pardons, and
- promotes civil and military officials.

The president can also directly submit issues for a referendum to the people.

The president is assisted in his task by a prime minister and a cabinet, all of whom are appointed by the president himself. The prime minister is the supervisor in chief, as opposed to the promulgator. He is a bureaucrat, tasked with leading the cabinet, supervising the enforcement of laws and policies, and overseeing the general functioning of the government.

Legislative branch

Under the 1950 and 1973 constitutions, the parliament is a unicameral body. It is called the People's Council. Its 250 members are elected to four-year terms by direct vote, though the term of parliament may be extended during war. At least one half of the seats in the People's Council are reserved for *peasants* and workers by law. The term for peasant is an anachronism, harkening back to the Soviet Union or the agrarian proletariat as per Mao. The council has the power to pass laws, question ministers, nominate the president, approve development plans and the budget, ratify treaties, and pass a no-confidence vote in the Council of Ministers or any minister. Members of the People's Council have immunity from criminal and civil proceedings while in office with one important exception: if they are caught in the criminal act, the president can refer the accused to a judicial proceeding. Additionally, the Speaker or a majority vote of the council can suspend this immunity. The council may also accept or reject any member's resignation.

Judicial branch

The Syrian judicial system under the 1950 and 1973 constitutions is a complex system of uncertain independence. It is divided between secular and religious courts, as well as many specialized courts established by law. The secular courts have jurisdiction over criminal and civil matters. There are also separate courts of appeals and a court of assizes for major crimes. The highest of these courts is the Court of Cassation, which hears appeals regarding law and procedure, with sections devoted to criminal, civil, military, commercial, religious, and real estate matters. The Court of Cassation is made up of members appointed by the president. Its independence, as with all courts, including the Constitutional Court, religious courts, and administrative courts, is maintained by the president and Legislative Council.

Important at the time, provision was made for religious courts. The concept of religious courts for "personal" matters was important for two reasons. First, it was a recognition that local imam possessed the authority, whether for Sunnis or Shia, over matters involving the interpretations of the Quran and Sharia. Second, in providing an area of religious power, the constitution limited it both by the jurisdiction given to such courts and by the religious perspectives of the disputants. In other words, there was a voluntary nature to Syria's view of religious courts. This intent was made clear in the second aspect of constitutional rights for "religious courts" as defined by the constitution. Religious courts were not just Islamic courts. There were separate courts for Christians, Jews, and non-Muslims with jurisdiction over cases concerning personal matters. The constitutional assumption made was that personal relationship conflicts are usually inter-religious rather than intra-religious. Still, it also belied the requirements for a unified religious approach under one branch of Islam. It also carved out for the national court system all matters determined to be personal.

A Council of State has jurisdiction over administrative cases. The highest court of Syria is the Constitutional Court. Its five members are appointed by the president and they have the authority to decide on the constitutionality of laws before promulgation if requested to do so by the president or by one-fourth of the members of the People's Council. It may not challenge the constitutionality of laws passed by referendum, but it does have the power to oversee the constitutionality of elections.

It is easy to see why today's opposition is skeptical of the 1973 constitution. Criticisms of this constitution can be summarized as follows:

- The 1973 constitution does not contain any formula for a transitional government or transitional executive body, for the scope of the transitional

government's executive and legislative powers or for the event of a constitutional or governmental vacuum, as is anticipated with the fall of the regime.
- Moreover, reinstating the constitution of 1950 after suspending the constitution of 2012 will not have significant value or a positive practical effect on governance during the transitional period. Instead, it will merely be a cosmetic step that does not address the dilemma of actual constitutional legitimacy.
- It was initially drafted 67 years ago amid a sociopolitical situation that was extremely different from that of today.
- In the meantime, Syria has signed UN documents that better promote human rights and protections, especially the International Covenant on Economic, Social, and Cultural Rights that Syria ratified in 1968.

In addition, it has been widely seen as unworkable by the opposition groups. They are particularly skeptical that a parliamentary system of government, one based on a unicameral legislative body enacting the necessary legislation to respond in the interim period to the scope and varying range of legislative needs, is likely to be too slow and cumbersome. A parliamentary system would present too many legitimate arguments to any executive that something needs to be done, causing the executive to likely step in and take over. Better have the strong presidential model already in place during the interim period. If, as is discussed with the interim constitutional option, the emergency powers of the executive can be defined and the executive's discretion curtailed by separation of powers in both the judiciary and legislative branches, then a strong presidential model is preferable. And its limited power and duration will provide its own mechanism for limiting illegitimate power.

Political challenges[10]

As we have discussed in Chapter 1, Assad's father was part of the Alawite community, which was seen at times as a compromise community between the more radical Shias and more radical Sunnis. The Alawites operated as a political force through the Socialist Ba'athist party, exercising a monopoly on power in that it was only the Ba'athist Party that could nominate members of the executive and legislative branch. This caused Syria significant challenges, as there was no way for the opposition to mount meaningful challenges to the single party power structure. Between the two Assads, the Ba'athists have led the country for more than three decades. While in the early days of his presidency, Bashar al-Assad demonstrated tendencies towards reform by releasing political prisoners, easing press restrictions, and allowing political groupings to assemble, the political elite of the army and the Ba'ath party felt threatened by these reforms. They have tried to block the reform process whenever possible, and may have initially forced Bashar to tighten the reigns, as he, in fact, did. These tensions revealed a major flaw in the 1950 and 1973 constitutions and its emergency powers provisions. The opposition is fearful that unless there are multiple amendments, Assad will too easily set aside minority rights and rule-of-law protections.

One aspect of this constitution that might be brought forward and retained is its view of religious courts. These could help Syria avoid the political fights that might otherwise occur between Sunnis and Shias. It could serve as precedent for a certain amount of local control. Or it might further "Balkanize" Syria into its various constituent parts and never allow it to really come together to have the conversations necessary to sustain a unified state.

The 2012 constitution

In the wake of the Arab Spring that swept the Middle East in early 2011, the entire Syrian political establishment again came under increasing fire from protesters demanding political reform. As we have seen, a major demand of the protest movement was the repeal of the Emergency Law that has been a basis for restricting freedoms for over three decades. Protestors also wanted a real democratic legislative body and constitutional reforms. Specifically, there was a demand to repeal Article 8, which secures the Ba'ath Party's control of power. For a time, President Bashar al-Assad seemed to respond somewhat positively to the protests. He repealed the Emergency Law, removing certain corrupt officials, and releasing some political prisoners. He also instituted a legislative process for a new Syrian constitution.

The 2012 constitution was drafted by the Syrian government and put to the Syrian legislature for its approval. In the meantime, though, Assad had acted strongly to put down the protests. The new constitution's timing made the new intent clear: rather than to reform, the idea was to shore up the powers of Assad in the face of threats coming from the civil war. Its preamble stated its motivation:

> **Preamble**[11]
>
> The Arab nation managed to perform a great role in building human civilization when it was a unified nation. When the ties of its national cohesion weakened, its civilizing role receded and the waves of colonial conquest shattered the Arab nation's unity, occupied its territory, and plundered its resources. Our Arab nation has withstood these challenges and rejected the reality of division, exploitation, and backwardness out of its faith in its ability to surmount this reality and return to the arena of history in order to play, together with the other liberated nations, its distinctive role in the construction of civilization and progress. With the close of the first half of this century, the Arab people's struggle has been expanding and assuming greater importance in various countries to achieve liberation from direct colonialism.
>
> The Arab masses did not regard independence as their goal and the end of their sacrifices, but as a means to consolidate their struggle, and as an advanced phase in their continuing battle against the forces of imperialism, Zionism, and exploitation under the leadership of their patriotic and progressive forces in order to achieve the Arab nation's goals of unity, freedom, and socialism.
>
> In the Syrian Arab region, the masses of our people continued their struggle after independence. Through their progressive march they were able to achieve their big victory by setting off the revolution of March 8, 1963, under the leadership of the Socialist Arab Ba'ath Party, which has made

authority an instrument to serve the struggle for the construction of the United Socialist Arab society.

The Socialist Arab Ba'ath Party is the first movement in the Arab homeland which gives Arab unity its sound revolutionary meaning, connects the nationalist with the socialist struggle, and represents the Arab nation's will and aspirations for a future that will bind the Arab nation with its glorious past and will enable it to carry out its role in achieving victory for the cause of freedom of all the peoples.

Through the party's militant struggle, the November 16, 1970, corrective movement responded to our people's demands and aspirations. This corrective movement was an important qualitative development and a faithful reflection of the party's spirit, principles, and objectives. It created the appropriate atmosphere for the fulfillment of a number of significant projects in the interest of our large masses, primarily the emergence of the state of the Confederation of Arab Republics in response to the call for unity, which figures prominently in the Arab conscience, which was buttressed by the joint Arab struggle against imperialism and Zionism, regionalist disputes, and separatist movements, and which was confirmed by the contemporary Arab revolution against domination and exploitation.

Under the aegis of the corrective movement, an important stop was taken on the road leading to the consolidation of national unity for our popular masses. Under the leadership of the socialist Arab Ba'ath Party, a national and progressive front with developed conceptions emerged in such a manner as to meet our people's needs and interests and proceed toward unifying the instrument of the Arab revolution in a unified political organization.

The completion of this constitution crowns our people's struggle on the road of the principle of popular democracy, is a clear guide for the people's march toward the future and a regulator of the movement of the state and its various institutions, and is a source of its legislation.

The constitution is based on the following major principles:

1 The comprehensive Arab revolution is an existing and continuing necessity to achieve the Arab nation's aspirations for unity, freedom, and socialism. The revolution in the Syrian Arab region is part of the comprehensive Arab revolution. Its policy in all areas stems from the general strategy of the Arab revolution.
2 Under the reality of division, all the achievements by any Arab country will fail to fully achieve their scope and will remain subject to distortion and setback unless these achievements are buttressed and preserved by Arab unity. Likewise, any danger to which any Arab country may be exposed on the part of imperialism and Zionism is at the same time a danger threatening the whole Arab nation.
3 The march toward the establishment of a socialist order besides being a necessity stemming from the Arab society's needs, is also a fundamental

necessity for mobilizing the potentialities of the Arab masses in their battle with Zionism and imperialism.

4 Freedom is a sacred right and popular democracy is the ideal formulation which insures for the citizen the exercise of his freedom which makes him a dignified human being capable of giving and building, defending the homeland in which he lives, and making sacrifices for the sake of the nation to which he belongs. The homeland's freedom can only be preserved by its free citizens. The citizen's freedom can be completed only by his economic and social liberation.

5 The Arab revolution movement is a fundamental part of the world liberation movement. Our Arab people's struggle forms a part of the struggle of the peoples for their freedom, independence, and progress.

> This constitution serves as a guide for action to our people's masses so that they will continue the battle for liberation and construction guided by its principles and provisions in order to strengthen the positions of our people's struggle and to drive their march toward the aspired future.

Despite the 2012 preamble's mention of democracy in its fourth principle, the emphasis was overwhelmingly on Arab unity, the need for governance structured as socialism with Ba'athist party control, and a strong executive bent on fighting imperialism and Zionism. Its main flaw was the unchecked power of the president. The constitution provided no meaningful checks and balances on this power, and even the description of the legislative and judiciary branches was formulated with broad and vague words, filled with ambiguity.

For example, the president could dissolve the legislature, dismiss its members, and take over legislative power whenever the president determined that "absolute necessity requires" that he do so (Article 97 and 111 in conjunction 113). The president was given absolute authority over the armed forces. He could refer the prime minister and ministers and their deputies to court on criminal charges whenever he so chose, at which time they were immediately relieved of their duties. Impeachment required a two-thirds vote of the legislature, but with removal powers, the president could ensure the outcome.

Most troubling is the way the president can control the judiciary. The president is given the power to assure its independence and is assisted by the Supreme Judicial Council (SJC), also controlled by the president. The SJC was to be constituted by the parliament, which could impeach members of the court without reference to any constitutional protections for the court (Article 144). The context of the drafting of these articles (133 and 136) is not one that engenders trust in the parliament. After all, it was the parliament that came up with the 2012 constitution that had given such broad powers to the president. No provision was made for "religious courts." The independence of the judiciary was provided only by a provision that judges were to make their judgments solely by "law."

On the bright side, Chapter 1 enumerated a wide range of provisions for the protection of human rights, but these rights are curtailed through other provisions.

For instance, Article 53 allows for the government to detain individuals without proper cause. Its provisions and enumerated freedoms (speech, association, due process) were also undermined by the continuing existence of a state of emergency in Syria that set aside these rights.

Despite the fact that under the existing constitution, Assad's term would expire by the end of 2014 (limited to two 7-year terms, or 14 years), Assad also was given the right to stand for election in 2014 for a third and final term of seven years (Article 155). We will return to this point in our discussion of the possibility of compromise in the Russian draft of the Syrian constitution. The president must be Muslim, an Arab-Syrian over the age of 40 (Article 84), and nominated by the Arab Socialist Ba'ath Party (Article 85).

If the 2012 constitution were to serve as an interim legal document, it would need to be amended, at least if it were to conform to the principles agreed to and set out in the Geneva Communiqué.

Of course, for the interim period it could be amended to make it more workable. The president and the prime minister could share power (amend Article 83), and the president could be denied the ability to dismiss the prime minister (amend Article 97), formulate general policies (amend Article 98), or dissolve the parliament (111). Limitations could also be placed on the president's ability to convene cabinet meetings and receive reports, issue decrees, declare war, declare states of emergency (Article 103), exercise absolute authority over the armed forces (105–106), refer to the court ministers for criminal prosecution (Article 124), and control the Supreme Judicial Council (Article 132–33) and Supreme Constitutional Court (Article 141, 146, and 147).

As an interim document, then, the last provisions relating to the independence of the judiciary raise significant concerns about impunity and the rule of law. How will past and future atrocities be dealt with under its provisions? Will Assad, or whoever was responsible for the use of barrel bombs and chemical weapons, avoid having to answer for these decisions? Will security forces have to answer for their systematic torture and killing of their opponents? These issues are papered over by the window dressing about human rights, which can and will be set aside at the will of the president.

In addition, without serious reforms for free speech and free press legislation and an independent judiciary to enforce them, little will likely change. The monopoly that the Socialist Ba'athist Party has on the political process likely infect the institutions the way that the Communist Party does in communist countries. Assad will exercise too much control over the media, social and otherwise. Without reforms, he will control too much information to bring about a truly transparent election monitored by a truly independent and impartial electoral body. Free and fair elections are a necessary component for Syria to constitute a meaningful legislative body. Such elections would be a radical change for Syria and will be vital Syria's future.[12] This is why most NGOs and their Syrian partners have been advocating against using either of the existing constitutional options, instead favoring instituting a new transitional governing body.

An interim constitution–transitional governing body

One option that the NGO community and its Syrian partners have discussed is whether it would be better to have a transitional government during the interim period which would be governed by an interim "constitution-like" document. Such a document would be "constitutionalized" by amending the existing 2012 constitution to give permission for that document to govern during the interim period.[13]

Drawing in part on the UN's experience in Kenya and the international community's experiences in South Africa, Tunisia, Sudan, Egypt, Libya, and Yemen, this option could set out a set of principles that would guide the government's decision-making. South Africa operated relatively successfully during its interim period using principles that guided Mandela and de Klerk's decisions. Key to South Africa's success was its power-sharing arrangements that also gave to Mandela the ultimate power to resolve disputes in a way that honored the principles of the interim agreement.

The NGO community and its Syria partners discussed a number of principles that might guide the transitional period. These include the Principle of Healing (acknowledge the injury caused, stop further injury, prevent the resumption or continuation of injury, repair the relationships between various groups in the best means possible, and a quickly as possible), the Principle of Respect (acknowledge the existence and dignity of all faiths, acknowledge the legitimate fears that many have for their faith, and protect all faiths), the Principle of Peace (acknowledge the violence and search for mechanisms for the nonviolent resolution of issues of competition and dispute resolution, and build progressively a culture of peace), the Principle of Participation (acknowledge that authority stems from the people, ensure that citizens are reasonably informed, and establish practical mechanisms to ensure access to and participation in governance), the Principle of Gender Equality (adopt a gender perspective that includes the special needs of women and children and involve women in all implementation mechanisms), the Principle of Freedom (acknowledge the dignity of everyone and acknowledge that gross injustice has occurred and continues to occur and implement effective means to ensure security from violations of freedoms of everyone and exercise responsibility for balancing various aspects of protecting and balancing freedom and dignity for all of its peoples and communities), the Principle of Change (acknowledge core principles and develop new open and respectful relationships between peoples and groups, implement transitional arrangements, and either build on or modify existing structures consistent with core principles and give effect to decisions from institutions' legislative bodies and courts in this regard), the Principle of Accountability (accept that public revenue is raised from the citizens and that there needs to be accountability and transparency for how money is spent and carry out official duties properly and implement effective mechanism so that accountability can be maintained and ensure checks and balances between governance structures and implement new laws and systems in the furtherance of an independent judiciary), and the Principle of Effectiveness (acknowledge the need to compromise and agree and implement practices to build a culture of respect and recognize that the need to implement processes may require the instituting of fair ways to carry out the processes, and establish mechanism for fair implementation of laws and practices).

The principled approach met with a different and unfortunate result in Egypt. Some observers feel like the transitional agreement was rushed through, without "buy-in" from the Muslim Brotherhood, on one side, and the military elite, on the other side. It was an elites' agreement that failed to hold when democracy's major flaw was revealed; that is, it became captured by the tyranny of the majority led by Morsi. If the voting public does not understand or anticipate the tyranny that can be imposed on it by the public's own votes, the resulting leaders can very quickly move to consolidate power and limit the freedoms of the minority. While no constitution is bulletproof in this regard, unless the new leaders understand the norms, or principles embedded in the constitutional framework, a situation like that which played out in Egypt can occur. The principles are designed to try and teach these norms of behavior. Unfortunately, as principles, they have uncertain status and impact in actual practice.

In Egypt, when opposition groups protested, the military elite stepped in and took over control of the government. Some feel that Egypt is now in a more repressive state than what had existed under Mubarak. Morsi was no Mandela and quickly abandoned the principled approach that was contemplated by the interim agreement. The question for Egypt is whether its current leaders will be motivated to move it from an oligarchy, or dictatorship, to a liberal democracy with protections and due process. When will the threat from radical groups dissipate? When this happens it is also an open question whether the leaders will give up their powers voluntarily.

Indeed, who will serve as Syria's Mandela? And would Assad ever agree to share power with anyone else? Yemen's transitional agreement might be the best option here, if Assad would agree to it; such an agreement would provide that the president would step down during the interim period with immunity, leaving for another day whether he could stand for election at the end of the interim period.

Or some other executive body could be instituted that could govern during the interim period. Getting its power right to keep the process moving and provide for security so that refugees could return, but ensuring that it not take over too much the governance process is tricky, to say the least. For example, Tunisia seems to be an example of a Transnational National Assembly that has held together in the face of extremist forces that have sought to pull it apart or grind it to a halt. It has weathered for now these storms but has also been kept together by a military that does not want to take over and a labor movement that insists that the nation not be pulled into extremism or deadlock. Yet, it currently seems bogged down in a stalemate, and many worry that it needs stronger leadership to break out to the next level. (Is it turning into Lebanon, where the resolution of religious difference was in its turning over of governance to regional and local structures? The result was each regional group consolidated power to itself within the region, which may further have paralyzed the country to act effectively in pursuit of its national interests.)

Perhaps the parties could agree to a strong executive council. Who would serve in such a council?[14] How would its member's commitment to the principles be ensured? One option is to check its executive power through an assembled Transnational National Assembly, and Transnational Constitutional Court. These bodies would make decisions based on the principles previously agreed to, keeping the country together and secure, protecting minority rights, and advancing the processes of mediation of the various issues toward resolution in a free and fair election process and a new constitution. Such a National Assembly could be representative of the many factions making up Syrian society.

Whether Syrian opposition groups are ready for such an assembly is highly doubtful. On the other hand, once constituted, it may foster non-violent approaches to resolving disputes. It may develop the coalitions of shared interest that might provide for meaningful protections of minority interests. Another option is to populate the executive council with at least one international neutral and trusted figure who could keep the council on track. Mandela has served this role in the past, as President Jimmy Carter did in the case of Nicaragua. A UN special envoy of the secretary-general has also served this role in Cambodia.

Or Syria could take advantage of a judicial body to serve as the main arbiter of its interim principles. Under this option there would be a special opportunity for the design of a Supreme Islamic Constitutional Court to also provide checks and balances on the executive council. However, there are important issues with the use a religious court in Syria. It could provide Syria with a way for it to underscore its Islamist character. Instead of merely stating as much, as the 2012 constitution does, the transition court could be made up of lawyers and judges drawn from the various Islamic groups. It might start the process of defining a common understanding of Sharia for both Sunnis and Shia. Or it could decide that Sharia is religious law, meant to be adhered to voluntarily and administered by separate religious community leaders, for its religious adherents only.

Sunnis and Shias could make up the court, and a legal dialogue could take place in light of the principles previously articulated. Would this lead to real inter-religious dialogue? Would it result in protections of minority rights and provide for religious freedom? And what about Christians and Jews? How would such a court operate to protect religious freedom for everyone without also opening up the possibility for extremist groups, like ISIS or al-Shabat, to take over?

The question for Syria will be whether the various religiously affiliated groups will be willing to turn over power to such a court to resolve, from the top down, issue of religious significance. The regional and local interests held by various strong leaders are already leading toward a use of violence to protect their power, belying the ability of such a court to meaningfully exercise power.

In addition, judicial power depends on competent police willing to enforce its provisions and lower local judicial bodies willing to dutifully follow its decisions. The real-world effectiveness of such a body remains substantially untested. How will cases be brought to the court? How will decisions be disseminated? What processes will be used for the gathering of evidence, and what law will have precedence in guiding court decisions?

A transitional period and governance structure also opens up the possibility of discussion of impunity, more broadly than just for Assad. After all, there have been atrocities committed by ISIS, Al Qaeda–affiliated groups, and others in addition to just the Syrian government. In the next chapter we will look more closely at the use of transformative justice strategies during the interim period. Suffice it to say that if such strategies are to be implemented, they need to be constituted during the interim period.

Perhaps the main attraction of the interim solution is that it is temporary, with a fixed time frame during which the parties agree not to resort to violence. The period needs to be long enough for the parties to get used to the benefits of non-violence and to learn to understand the shared needs that keep them together. It needs to be long enough that the legitimacy of the electoral process can be sufficiently ensured. But it can't be so long that the parties get frustrated and fracture into regional and local governance structures that will resist any later attempts at unification and minority protection. The experience in Zimbabwe is telling in this regard. While in Kenya the parties were able to stay together, in Zimbabwe, the implementation decisions reached by the National Assembly were resisted locally.

Current drafts of interim documents do not make any mention of the religious nature of the conflict.[15] They also don't provide for jurisdiction of local religious courts and imams. It presumes that these issues will be settled in a process of national dialogue, which will be organized during the transitional period. Again, like with Tunisia, this process can lead to the forming of a transitional body that can itself lead the constitutional process. The problem is that if there is deadlock, parties may return to violence if forces are not in place (in the case of Tunisia, the labor movement) to insist that members return to the negotiating table and work out their differences.

Russian draft as a new opportunity to negotiate

The arrival on the scene of a Russian draft for a Syrian constitution in early February 2017 may provide new energy to discussions between Assad and the opposition. Occurring as it does ahead of any official ending of the conflict, but at a time when ISIS appears to be dissolving, it provides a head start on discussing what the eventual constitution will look like. As such it may serve as a "pre-transition process" that can potentially provide the same benefits that a full interim process may provide. It may allow the various parties – Shia, Sunni, Alawite, Druze, Kurd, and Christian, as well as those divided by region and groups supported primarily by loyalties to various local figures – to discuss what they may have in common. As we discussed in the last chapter, the opportunity is much greater in discussions of a draft of a national constitution to get at problem-solving solutions to long-standing problems. The apparent conflicts between freedoms and powers can be identified, and the underlying goals of each provision can serve as means for discussing institutions and creative solutions. If each party is allowed to negotiate for separate respective agreements with Assad, the groups will see themselves in a zero-sum game complicated by competition with other groups. In looking to negotiate individual peace agreements, the need to discuss shared goals, including minority and human rights and the importance of the rule of law through a national court that is independent from sectarian controls, is less prominently before the parties. But in the context of discussing the Russian draft, the parties might decide to take up discussions of the Syrian constitution in earnest, believing that there may be strength in numbers. Instead of seeing their diverse interests as a reason to divide and limit their issues to a set of predetermined bottom lines, the parties might instead unite in a shared need to bring about a Syria that is secure for all its disparate groups. It also finesses to a great extent the makeup of the interim institutions. The opposition groups who have been working with their NGO partners constitute the opposition side of the negotiations. The fact that Assad continues to exercise power also keeps these negotiations from being subjected to the "Liberia" problem: that whatever agreement is reached has simply been forced on the Syrians by the international community.

Setting aside the strategic concerns of whether Syria should jump straight to a new constitution rather than provide for an interim period, the draft proposed by Russia on its surface has much to commend it for. Its preamble declares the constitution's authority to govern as arising from the people. It goes on to specify the Syrian people as consisting of a multicultural, multi-religious, and pluralistic people. The constitution draft endeavors to protect free speech and freedom of conscience, and it prohibits discrimination on the basis of gender, creed, or ethnicity. It prohibits torture. It divides power between three branches of government, a bicameral legislature, a judiciary, and an executive. It provides for a secret ballot election of the president. It provides for impeachment of the president for grave crimes dependent on the vote of the legislative bodies. It also gives the legislature the power to override the president's power to declare an emergency. In addition, it provides for the amendment of the constitution through the legislative process. In so doing it seems to ground the legitimacy of the state in the flourishing of its citizens. It endeavors for the peaceful sustainability of the state. It seems to embrace the concept of free elections, the rule of law and independence of the judiciary. It recognizes a need for government reform through amendments to the constitution.

Russian history and translation of Russian words reveal what may be intended in the draft and its non-liberal/strong statist/strong presidential origins.[16] Russia, perhaps having been reminded about the perils of writing another country's constitution,[17] has made it clear that the draft is only meant to serve as a framework.[18] There are reports that Syrian opposition groups have been at least initially skeptical of the draft.[19] On the other hand, it may present some unique opportunities to sort out some difficult issues that might otherwise have to wait till the Assad question is settled.

I will offer an analysis of the draft and suggest some problem-solving solutions.[20] These solutions take the goals of the parties seriously. My approach is based on the idea that in taking underlying needs seriously, one can see in these needs which ones are shared amongst the various interested parties and where they are in conflict. Multiple creative options may emerge as a result. This approach might also allow for the draft to serve as a bridge between the goals of security through a strong state capable of combatting terrorism and the need for both legitimacy and sustainable government structures that are able to combat abuses of power. It is impossible to know whether the best tactic for Syria to take is to reject the Russian draft out of hand or to attempt to work with it. For the sake of discussion, we will assume the latter option, which assumes that the Russian draft is offered in a good-faith attempt to provide for framework for Syrian security, the separation of powers, and democratic processes.

Russian history and Syria's draft constitution

Russia's constitutional history likely informs Russia's intent in authoring the draft and its openness to a hybrid model of governance: one with a strong president but with a local flavor.[21] Kazakhstan, the host of the peace negotiations, is a prime example. Kazakhstan's language is Russian, and it was a member of the former Soviet Union. Moreover, it was also part of Russia under the Tsarist Empire. It stands in a region of similar shared Soviet and Russia tsarist history. Countries in this region, including Azerbaijan and Kyrgyzstan, share a constitutional history that is telling.[22]

In the 1990s these countries adopted what might be thought of as *hybrid* constitutions, each with their own distinctive traditions.[23] Coming out of the era of Soviet dominance, they combined liberal and non-liberal ideas within the same document. Still, they were based on a Russian mind-set that sees Russian history as an evolutionary process. From an initial state of anarchy, according to the Russian view, will evolve or emerge a strong state, with power centered in the executive. The executive will be charged with the ultimate duty of uniting both the people and the state. What emerges is a strong "statist school,"[24] as opposed to a "minarchist school,"[25] providing a theoretical basis for constitutional discourse. *Strong Statism* argues that constitutions should create a strong leader that can maintain the integrated state in the face of terrorism, incompetence, external threats, and corruption. Scholars find evidence of statism in Eurasian constitutions.[26] Frequent textual references to statehood (*gosudarstvennost'*) and state integrity (*tselostnost'*) are telling because they are consistent with a Russian perspective of the need for the emergence of a strong state.[27]

An examination of the recent draft shows that the same reference to statehood and state integrity is present in other Eurasian constitutions with historical connections to Russia. The draft's preamble leaves out any reference to Syria as an Islamic state. It also leaves out any reference to Sharia law. References to an Islamic state and to Sharia were both contained in the 2012 Syrian constitution. This new draft emphasizes that the constitution derives its power from a multicultural people. Yet it now also contains an emphasis on the importance of "continuing" Syria's progression toward "statehood (*gosudarstvennost'*)."

Remember, as we have seen earlier in our discussions of the Syrian working group's reaction to Russia's initial demands, declaring Syria as a secular state may invoke a strong reaction from the various religious sects at the table. The draft's approach confronts the issue and looks to whether it can be met with a problem-solving response instead of a deadlock, allowing the parties to create meaningful solutions. After all, there is precedent in the Middle East for trying a secular approach to politics. Some see this as the approach used by the Socialist Ba'ath Party in Iraq and Syria, united as Arabs against colonialist and Zionist enemies than as being united under Islamic doctrines. Fights about what is true Islamic belief are avoided by using the secular paradigm. On the other hand, Islam might be defined in a way that provides room for various groups and sects of Islam to coexist under one nation. And so Islam might be defined as itself being tolerant of minority religious views, providing room for freedom of conscience and tolerant of other religious faiths. In any event, the provision of a secular state should not be a deal breaker in light of Syria's need to not repeat the mistakes of the past. Yet embedded in the need for a secular state is the concept of *statism*. This concept needs to be examined to see where it might create problem solving opportunities.

The evidence of statism in the draft comes from its repeated indications of the necessity of preserving state unity. There were far fewer of these in the 2012 Syrian constitution. Article 1 of the Russian draft explicitly states that it is the duty of the people and government to protect both national unity and territorial integrity (*tselostnost'*).[28] A provision that all political parties must "respect" the "territorial integrity" (*tselostnost'*) of the state is contained in Article 5.[29] Again, protecting the integrity of the state is not a deal breaker if handled from a problem-solving perspective. Of course, the state needs to be able to defend itself from enemies bent on its destruction, both from within and without. The question is how to define enemies as distinct from opposition political groups who seek to compete for power through democratic process. ISIS seems a clear example of a group that is an enemy of the state. Yet it is hard to determine whether an opposition group's religious affiliation will end up causing the oppression of minority groups once they gain power. If it is left to the president to make the call, the president may see a greater danger in political opposition, especially to Alawites affiliated with Shia, who have been persecuted in the past by Sunnis for not being true Muslims. Standing alone, then, statism can stand as a justification for the president to impose his will, ensuring the protection of his party, seeing the opposition as bent on destroying the state as it presently exists.

Early evidence for Russian acceptance of *etat de droit*

At the same time, what emerge from an analysis of the constitutions of these countries with a shared Russia history, are important pieces of evidence for the overwhelming success of the doctrine of "etat de droit.[30] "Etat de droit" means the *legal* state, or the state established and operating according to the rule of law. The concepts of constitutionalism and "etat de droit" have mutually enhanced each other. Prominent Russia historian and constitutional scholar Rett Ludwikowski describes their relationship as follows:

> The doctrine of constitutionalism grew out of the idea of limited government protecting individual rights and freedoms. The doctrine of the legal state stemmed from the concept that appropriate judicial mechanisms must be provided to ensure that individuals act within the framework of the law and that hierarchically organized organs of power not only observe law but operate exclusively on the basis of law. The constitution, recognized as the apex of hierarchically structured laws, was to provide a clear background for the assessment of legality of governmental and individual activities. The acknowledgement of the complementary character of the ideas of "tat de droit" and constitutional government accelerated the development of constitutional engineering. The consciousness that every mature state, well-organized according to the rule of law, should clearly determine in one act or a series of basic acts the principles of the political, social and economic organization of the state, the powers and duties of state organs, and certain rights of the people contributed to the recent rapid emission of new constitutions.[31]

The strong evidence of "etat de droit" is evidence of the underlying need that there be limits on the potential abuses of power by the sovereign. The underlying recognition and need for a well-organized state, organized according to the rule of law for the protection of the rights of the people, is also an important goal for a sustainable state. A problem-solving approach would look to make clear that statism, as properly understood through the lens of the rule of law, along with other provisions of the constitution, is not a deal breaker. It merely increases the need to ensure that there are legal limits on the president's exercise of state power. But the constitution needs to provide checks and balances on the president's power, with special emphasis on an independent judiciary and the rule of law.

Religion and rights in the Russian draft

The simultaneous statist/"etat de droit" approach is also reflected in the Russian draft's approach to religion. As we have noted, the draft constitution removes references to Islam as the state religion. Syria's official name is also changed from the Syrian Arab Republic to the Syrian Republic. Second, it makes significant changes to Article 3 of the constitution. In the 2012 Syrian constitution, Article 3 states that the president must be Muslim and that Islamic jurisprudence is a major source of legislation. In its place, a new Article 3 declares the state to "respect all religions and religious organizations" and that "religious organizations shall be equal before the law." This provision might provide an opening if it is interpreted as a reflection of the wide religious autonomy that Eurasian constitutions have long recognized.

On the other hand, strong statism seems to predominate. The strong language providing for a government duty to protect the integrity of the state seems to take precedence over the rule of law – perhaps rightfully so since what must be juxtaposed against its desire for pluralism is Syria's history with ISIS, or DAESH. Some might argue that for a strong state given the power to restrict proselytizing and separatist teachings, in order to be able to protect itself from religions with separatist or monopolistic tendencies. Yet what lacks definition in the draft is the "etat de droit." The rule of law limitations might need clearer definitions if the need to protect against sovereign abuse towards individuals is to be provided for.

For example, what does Article 20, (5), mean by prohibiting *propaganda*? Does that mean political speech that is critical of the position of the president on any issue? Maybe this article should be dropped. However, prohibiting propaganda might mean restricting *proselytization* by ISIS for the recruitment of members. Here, a more nuanced prohibition could be used. A particular religion, or a religion that campaigns for the end of the state as such, might be made the target of the prohibition against proselytizing. Or the constitution could provide, for example, that limitations on freedom of conscience, or on religious freedom, must be prescribed by law instead of being subject to the whim of the executive. Any such law might also be necessary for the protection of an important governmental interest, proportionate to that government's interest.[32] Moreover, any challenges to these laws could be made by individuals whose speech has been limited, and the jurisdiction of the Constitutional Court could be invoked. As a result, there could be more rule of law restrictions for certain types of speech in an effort to more effectively balance the various parties' respective needs.

Another amendment option would be to give more definition to certain terms to ensure they do not become veto rights, or coercive exercises of power that should rightfully be the prerogative of the legislature. The parties might agree to share the belief that a strong state is needed to deal forcefully with terrorist groups, while also acknowledging that such force has little place in the midst of a legislative process. The power to review alleged state abuses might be given to the courts.

Like most post-Soviet strong statist constitutions in the region, the draft contains a long list of rights, including both negative rights (i.e., freedom of speech) and positive rights (social security and right to health care). Again, when these provisions are considered in light of the broader goals of protecting the integrity and unity of the state (*gosudarstvennost'*), the rule of law is lost. What is missing from these provisions of rights is a clause providing for a limitation of these freedoms when the interests or integrity of the state is not in jeopardy.

A problem-solving approach would see an opening for amendment here as evidenced by statements of Russian officials that this draft is only offering "a basis for discussion." Thus, the key provisions that the drafters wanted to introduce into the discussions were not rights provisions, but instead, institutional arrangements that they thought could help rebuild the integrity and unity of the Syrian state. It is for Syria to work out its own limitations on the rule of law.

Again, the parties might suggest amendments that will provide for the better protection of civil rights. After all, Syria is a signatory nation of the 1948 UN Declaration of Human Rights (UNDHR) and as such seems to have long accepted the importance of human rights. The UNDHR's Article 30 provides that the declaration itself does not provide the right of any state to abridge these rights.[33] The Syrian constitution does not describe any limitations on the state's intrusion on these rights. Some amendment might be in order here if abuse of power is to be protected against. It might use the approach of the Egyptian constitution, which limits governmental abuse by providing due process rights to individuals. When the state attempts to take property or otherwise restrict liberties, due process rights are invoked.[34] The constitution might make clear that a government's use of classifications based on religious affiliations that don't call for an overthrow of the state are suspect and where property or liberty interests are curtailed on the basis of a suspect class, the court will set the actions aside.

Presidency

Perhaps the Russia draft contains ambivalence about whether Russia wants to be seen as the cause for Assad's continuation in power.[35] Again, this might be the intent behind the protestations from the Russian delegation that the draft only serves as a *model* for Syrian discussion. However, the text, itself, suggests otherwise. The Syrian president generally follows models of post-Soviet strong statist countries that have emerged from under Russian control, with a few exceptions. First, it keeps in place the long seven-year presidential terms from the 2012 constitution. The draft constitution creates a definite upper limit, stating that one individual can only serve two terms as president. This is more restrictive than many other post-Soviet constitutions. It is also inconsistent with the Russian constitution, which limits the president to two terms "in a row."[36] But inconsistencies run both ways: Tajikistan has recently amended its law to provide for a president for life.[37] The transitional provisions in Articles 81 through 84 provide that the "existing" Syrian president (Bashar al-Assad) will get what will amount to an 18-year possible extension. His current term ends on July 16, 2021, and allows him two additional seven-year terms till 2038.

Can the constitution then both provide for the need for a strong leader to combat enemies of the state without also giving the president free license for personal power and oppression? As a matter of adversarial bargaining, the parties are miles apart, even if they could set aside Assad's potential commission of war crimes. The opposition wants Assad to immediately step down. Assad wants to serve as president till 2038, betting that some of the worst memories of the civil war will have long faded. On the other hand, the needs behind the positions may open up room for creative solutions. The opposition wants to move from the civil war to a Syria where each group, regardless of religion, can live in peace. They want to be free from the oppressive policies of the past that restricted their property rights, discriminated against them, and repressed their religious freedom. Assad wants a Syria free from violent terrorism that protects himself, his family, and his community from revenge and violence and that allows for the possibility and understanding that his actions were motivated by a genuine effort to protect Syria from anarchy. And he wants the chance to stay in power should Syrians choose him as their leader. Options abound. One starting place is to negotiate for an amendment for a quicker end to his term. Another alternative is to offer the Egyptian constitutional structure that provides for two consecutive four-year terms.[38]

He might step down with immunity, agree to stay out of government for a time, agree to stay out forever, agree to power share, agree to a more limited term, agree to step down after two years to seven years, and so on. He might agree to be tried by an appropriate tribunal or to submit to a reconciliation process. Again, the Russian draft can get the process started in both articulating the underlying needs and in creating win–win solutions for the parties.

There is a range of possible creative solutions that might be explored. It is important to note that the draft constitution departs from the strong statist model by placing the Syrian president in the executive branch. Perhaps this suggests a willingness by Assad to consider other amendments in other chapters in order to better ensure the office doesn't abuse its power against individual Syrians. Other provisions in the draft go in the opposite direction and expand executive power. The president is given the power to *supervise* and *unify* all branches of power in the state. In addition, the president plays a "guarantor" role, ensuring national independence, unity, and the territorial integrity (*tselostnost'*) of the country (Article 55, Section 1). The president also is given a "coordinating" role, ensuring the permanence of the functioning of state power (Article 55, Section 2). Finally, the president serves as "mediator" between institutions of government as well as between the government and society (in order to ensure its unity; Article 55, Section 3). In this coordinating role, the president has power to establish "conciliation procedures" (Article 55, Section 3).

One option is to move these powers into the hands of the prime minister, who is the administrative head of the government. In the alternative, the constitution could provide at some certain date for the transfer of more power to the prime minister. The prime minister might also be elected. Moreover, the power to use conciliatory methods and mediate between legislative bodies might be taken from the president and given to the prime minister.

Compromise might come from more clarity that would limit the president's ability to issue decrees, edicts, and laws (Article 57) or his right to use *conciliatory procedures* to resolve legislative disputes, Article 55 (3).

Two legislative bodies[39]

It is hard to know what to make of the draft with regard to legislative power. It seems hopelessly vague in that it does not even specify how the "Constituent Assembly" is to be determined: Is it to be elected or are members appointed by someone, and if so, who does the appointing?

The draft Syrian constitution includes a Eurasian-style strong statist upper house. Article 40 creates a "Constituent Assembly" as the upper house of the Syrian parliament. This upper house is apparently to be drawn from Syria's regions, and it does not appear to be elected. The draft does explicitly describe the role of the Territorial Assembly as one allowing representatives of regional units the ability to "participate in the adoption of legislation and the administration of the state." The upper house in the hands of a strong president who appoints its members might serve as a method for strengthening sovereign presidential power over the regions.

Here there is much room for compromise. First, the assembly might be elected, as it is in Japan and Australia. Again, the parties share a goal of ensuring that the legislature doesn't devolve into pockets of dysfunction and corruption. Lebanon's constitution has come under criticism in this regard. Yet, again, there is a need to hold a future president accountable. Perhaps the Syrians can choose a more corporatist model or one that provides specific representation for business interests. This is the model chosen by the Chinese in its governance of Hong Kong.[40] Local business interests could help moderate the power of the president, fight corruption, protect private property, and provide for freedom of contract.

Or amendments might be offered to provide a clearer understanding of who these constituent groups might be.[41] There might be more constitutional clarity regarding which regions, districts, and constituent groups are intended to have representation in the Territorial/Constituent Assembly. There is some evidence that the exact terms of the constitution are less important to what actually happens (how well it functions to limit presidential power) than the determination of particular stakeholders to take ownership of whatever is provided by the constitution.[42]

This is an important point for our discussion. In Lithuania, Poland, Hungary, East Germany, and the Czech Republic, after the fall of the Soviet Union the institution of democracy seemed to take hold rather quickly, setting aside single-party systems and instituting separation of powers and elected legislative bodies exercising real power. Compare this with the "Stans," Afghanistan, Kazakhstan, Kyrgyzstan, Pakistan, Tajikistan, Turkmenistan, and Uzbekistan. For the "Stans," the shift to democracy has been more difficult. Tajikistan has even done away with its requirement of electing the president, making its president "president for life." The legislative bodies are largely rubberstamps on the decrees of the executive. There is little tradition or habit of filling these bodies with members who understand or act as representatives of their regions or, more important, purport to act for the good of the country as a whole. What seems to be crucial to these governments is not whether they are bicameral or unicameral but, rather, the political will of the organizing bodies to populate themselves with strong and independent members who "get" both the legislative and representative responsibilities required of them.

Having said that, Poland is an example of a conservative government rethinking even the independence of the nation's judiciary. In remarkable simultaneity with the rise of Trump, the Polish government is sensitive to the criticism that the courts might be serving the interests of the elites at the expense of the good of the common people. Better for the government to be slightly corrupt and get things done than to be inefficient but to stand on principle. Again, as we've seen in the case of the US, itself, one wonders whether faith in democracy and the rule of law has been significantly threatened by events in the Middle East, the economic crisis in the European Union, and the rise of China, now raising questions about the very effectiveness of liberal democracy itself. Maybe its institutions are an elaborate hoax through which elites can impose a stifling sameness on the rest of the country. Perhaps a good dose of corrupt nationalism, even mixing in a little dictatorship, is better for Poland than being made to pay for sins and failings of a democratic Italy, Greece, or Spain. But we digress.

The Kurdish question

Another area of interest is how the constitution will deal with the Kurds,[43] which may serve as an indicator of how it will generally handle questions of minority nationality and religion. Will it grant Kurds independence? As currently written, the draft only guarantees wide cultural, religious, and educational autonomy, but again, it does so in the context of a strong state system. The draft does nothing to limit the president as the single source of sovereign will.[44] Article 4 of the draft constitution provides that Syrian citizens have the right to "educate their children in their native language." It also provides that government agencies and institutions of Kurdish cultural autonomy shall employ both Kurdish and Arabic. In addition, Article 15 states that the organization of regional authorities is to be based on "the principles of decentralization and the separation of powers." There are no words to suggest granting autonomy to the Kurds. Again, this might be made clearer if that is the intention. Article 15 invokes "the law" as the means to determine either the appointment or the election of regional representatives. If more autonomy is to be the goal, the election of these representatives might be in order.

Interim provisions in articles – Articles 81–84

A final opening for discussion and compromise is provided for in Articles 81 through 84, which provide for some interim provisions. Areas not dealt with are the continued control of the military and state police. How will the rule of law intersect with these bodies? Compare the Tunisian approach with the approach of Egypt: as we've discussed, in Egypt, the military can step in to ensure country stability.[45]

This interim period raises in itself all the issues that we've discussed in the previous section. Its success would depend on the good faith implementation of the constitutional provisions that a National Assembly be constituted of truly representative and authentically elected members. Perhaps the parties would agree to the principles that we've previously discussed as guiding those implementing the assemblies. Otherwise, the temptation is for Assad, with backing from Shia rebel groups, to retake the Assemblies and the court to ensure his own control over them. Without a process of reconciliation with other Syrian groups, including Sunni groups, the Sunnis may fear revenge and repression from Assad and his supporters.

Would, then, that there could be some time taken for the development of truly democratic principles with minority protections and human rights to become the norm. How to avoid the situation in Egypt with Morsi from occurring is the question the international community must help the Syrians face. Or, instead of the Muslim Brotherhood, as in Egypt, what is happening in Iraq might spread to Syria. Iraq seems to be struggling with the rising influence of Iranian backed Shia militia taking over sections of the country and setting up a corridor for rebel fighters to then enter Syria. Having been recruited in Iraq (mainly for economic reasons[46]), these fighters are now operating in Syria. Will they leave, or will they stay and help Iran extend its influence in the region? And will the Saudis see the Iranian threat as a reason to continue to back Sunni rebels in Syria? Democracy has little chance to succeed in Syria unless either the proxy war between Iran and Saudi Arabia is addressed. And implicit in resolving the Iranian-Saudi dispute is the religious question of whether Sunnis and Shias can reconcile. Can Sunnis and Shias learn to live in a democracy together, or will Syria continue the cycle of violence, tracing the ebb and flow of the majority and minority status of the groups and the rise and fall of their backers? This is our question for the next chapter.

Other opportunities for problem solving

Drawing on a tradition of strong statism, this draft constitution views Syria's main problem as combatting its own existential enemies, and further sees these enemies as coming from outside itself. To combat this disintegration, it makes the unity of the state its highest priority. The constitution does this through provisions and institutions that will strengthen Syrian *gosudarstvennost'* (statehood) and *tselostnost'* (state integrity). Specifically, it places on the president duties to keep the state unified. It gives the president the power to legislate, make decrees, and issue edicts, bypassing an upper house of Parliament should the need arise. It currently provides for a list of rights drawn from the need for a cultural autonomy, but always within a structure that puts the state's integrity above all else. In other words, as presently constituted, the president's power is put first and foremost.

On the other hand, the framework does provide for separation of powers and checks and balances on the presidential powers, and it does provide openings for "etat de droit." With some negotiating of amendments, legitimate representative government and a real balance of a strong state with the rule of law, as designed for creating presidential accountability and combatting potential abuses of executive power, can be achieved. Perhaps, then, the parties might see the interim period as an opportunity to really engage in the process of building institutions that will work for the good of all Syrians, regardless of their cultural status. Democracy might be placed on hold for the short run but not forgotten. The hope for what may emerge during the transition is two fold. The first is that these constituents realize that to be effective, there will need to develop some shared interests in the ends of the political process (democracy and rule of law). In addition the hope is that these parties develop the normative behavior, or shared sense of duty, for those given the responsibility to implement the political structures, that they put peace ahead of personal power.

Notes

1 The term rebel, to describe the various opposition groups in Syria, is purposefully vague. During the negotiations with Assad and the Russians it will mean those groups who have opposed Assad who have seat at the table of the negotiations. At other times it will mean any group who opposes Assad, including ISIS, or other al Queda, Hamas, Moslim Brotherhood, or Hezzbolah affiliated groups. Membership in among these groups is continually shifting.
2 While most are skeptical of Putin's belief in democracy, he has made noises in the past that democracy is what legitimizes government in the long run. He manipulates the Duma and controls the selection process of prime minister and president. He steps down, and then steps back in. Putin has also made statements that he believes that democracy is part of Russia's future. In any event, he is not negotiating Russia's form of government. He is helping stabilize Syria's so that he can continue to exercise influence in the region. If these are Russia's real goals, then whether Syria eventually moves toward democracy is beside the point. What it needs are guarantees that its military base and interests in the region are secure.
3 Constitutional History 1950–1973.
4 The interim constitution option had the advantage of providing a time frame for the habits of war to dissipate and create the room for the parties to sign on to UN declarations and human rights conventions and allow for a more sustainable peace. It was also thought to also provide for greater sustainable peace results through the adoption of a constitution chosen by Syrians for their particular values and priorities.
5 See DIWAN, "Middle East Insights from Carnegie, Syria in Crisis: The Syrian Constitution–1973–2012," December 12, 2012, http://carnegie-mec.org/diwan/50255?lang=en.
6 Marion Kent, ed., *The Great Powers and the End of the Ottoman Empire* (London: George Allen and Unwin, 1984), 237.
7 International Law, Papers of Hersch Lauterpacht, ed. Elihu Lauterpacht, CUP Archive, 1970, ISBN 0-521-21207-3, p. 116 and Statehood and the Law of Self-determination, D. Raič, Martinus Nijhoff Publishers, 2002, ISBN 90-411-1890-X, p. 95.
8 The Ottoman Empire kept some of its power following World War I and did not disband until 1924.
9 Ibid. Much of this analysis also relies on a report on the constitutional options done by The Carter Center, (TCC) in various versions, 2014, 2015, and 2016. (Copies on file with the author, and on TCC website, https://www.cartercenter.org/peace/conflict_resolution/syria-conflict-resolution.html).
10 *Parts of the rest of this chapter rely on reports, both published and unpublished, done for TCC and its NGO partners.* See, The Carter Center, Options for a Political Transition in Syria, 2015, https://www.cartercenter.org/resources/pdfs/peace/conflict_resolution/syria-conflict/options-for-political-transition-in-syria-jul-2015-en.pdf. *The opinions expressed are those of the author and do not reflect the views of any other organization.*
11 Translation provided for The Carter Center and its report. https://www.cartercenter.org/resources/pdfs/peace/conflict_resolution/syria-conflict/options-for-political-transition-in-syria-jul-2015-en.pdf.
12 Some point to Nicaragua in 1990 as an example of how the time a country spends post conflict on working up a system for fair elections is time well spent.
13 This option draws on the Liberian transition for some of its provisions. In the Liberian situation, criminal defendants charged during the interim period argued that without having set aside the existing Liberian constitution, the acts of the transitional government, including actions taken by its Truth and Reconciliation Commission (that allowed reference to the Criminal Courts for criminal prosecution should the

defendant's "confession" lack sufficient sincerity and contrition), were not legal. They have a point. Peacemakers need to be aware that the transitional governing agreement has uncertain constitutional status unless something is done to amend the existing constitution. To avoid these problems, Yemen amended its constitution in 2012 to accommodate a transitional governing agreement. The Carter Center report contains an excellent Appendix which details a potential way that the interim agreement could be framed to try to insure both efficient executive power, yet not be too easily abused. The Carter Center, Options for a Political Transition in Syria, 2015, https://www.cartercenter.org/resources/pdfs/peace/conflict_resolution/syria-conflict/options-for-political-transition-in-syria-jul-2015-en.pdf.

14 Appendix II and III, details a potential way that interim agreement could be framed to try to ensure both efficient executive power, yet not be too easily abused.

15 Appendices to The Carter Center, Options for a Political Transition in Syria, 2015, https://www.cartercenter.org/resources/pdfs/peace/conflict_resolution/syria-conflict/options-for-political-transition-in-syria-jul-2015-en.pdf.

16 See William Partlett, "Understanding the Origins of Russia's Constitutional Solution to the Syrian Conflict," *Constitution Net*, February 24, 2017, www.constitutionnet.org/news/understanding-origins-russias-constitutional-solution-syrian-conflict?utm_content=buffer075ce&utm_medium=social&utm_source=twitter.com&utm_campaign=buffer. (In the article Partlett, a Russian historian, sets out to analyze the original Russian-language version of this draft constitution, "to trace how it draws on uniquely Eurasian conceptions of public power. In so doing, we will correct some of the key misunderstandings about the draft while also seeking to get a deeper understanding of how this constitutional order understands – and seeks to solve – the Syrian conflict. Ibid. Partlett's analysis is "that Russia sees the solutions to Syria's problems not as a reflection of too much concentrated authority in President Assad, but instead as the opposite: A consequence of a system that does not protect state unity and integrity by concentrating enough power in a strong, centralized government." Ibid. Hereinafter Partlett).

See also Samer Abboud, "Russia's Draft Constitution: End of Syria's Baath Era? The Makeshift Constitution Is the Latest Effort to Model Post-Conflict Syria in the Russian Vision," *AlJazeera*, May 29, 2016. Abboud reported that this draft constitution apparently has Putin's approval, since President Vladimir Putin stated that a new constitution would be critical in finding a political solution to the crisis in Syria. Drafted by Russian constitutional law and Middle East experts, this document has already been the subject of much speculation and controversy. www.aljazeera.com/news/2016/05/russia-draft-constitution-syria-baath-era-160529064231915.html.

17 See Henry Meyer, "Syrian Opposition Rejects Draft of New Constitution," *The Sidney Morning Herald*, January 26, 2017, www.smh.com.au/world/syria-opposition-rejects-russian-draft-of-new-constitution-20170126-gtyzco.html.

18 Ibid. The Kremlin envoy to Syria, Alexander Lavrentiev, who led his country's delegation to the talks in Kazakhstan, said on Tuesday that Russia had presented the rebels with the draft text of the constitution "to help speed up this process and give it some more impetus." Ibid. "In no way do we want to interfere in the drafting and adopting of the basic law of the constitution of the country," he said. "We believe that the Syrian people must lead this process." Ibid.

19 Ibid.

20 This approach is more fully explained in Paul J. Zwier, *Principled Negotiation and Mediation in the International Arena: Talking with Evil* (New York: Cambridge University Press, 2013), 48–60.

21 Rett R. Ludwikowski, "Constitution Making in the Countries of Former Soviet Dominance: Current Development," *Georgia Journal of International & Comparative Law*, Vol. 23 (1993), p. 155 (hereinafter Ludwikowski).

22 Ibid., 187.
23 Ibid. See also, Martha Brill Olcott, "Central Asia's Catapult to Independence," *Foreign Affairs* (1992), pp. 108–130.
24 Hannah Arendt, *The Origins of Totalitarianism* (New York: Harcourt Brace & World, 1966). See also, Ayn Rand, "Introducing Objectivism," *The Objectivist Newsletter*, August, 1962, p. 35.
25 Minarchist is a political theory that sees a minimal role for the state. It sees the state as merely a guardian for the rights of the people. Richard A. Garner, "Minarchy Considered," *Libertarian Papers*, Vol. 1, No. 37 (2009), libertarianpapers.org.
26 Ludwiktowski, *supra*, note 18, at 187.
27 Partlett writes,

> For instance, every Eurasian preamble contains recitations of the importance of continuing and developing the statehood (*gosudarstvennost'*) of the nation. They also recur frequently in discussions of the presidency and provisions limiting rights. The repetition of these concepts demonstrates a persistent and powerful Eurasian obsession with the unity and cohesiveness of state power which was "often in peril due to Russia's size and state of backwardness." This fear has carried forward to the present day.

See Partlett, supra, note 2.
28 Ibid.
29 Ibid. Partlett also sees statism as evidenced by the use of the word *territorial integrity* (*tselostnost'*) – found in seven different places – that "suggest that the Russian drafters see the solution to Syria's civil war as one that concentrates state power in one strong central government, rather than dispersing it." Ibid.
30 Ludwikowski, *supra*, note 7, at 157. See, for example, the constitutions of Poland and Hungary, which have rule of law and court enforcement of civil and political rights. Ibid., 215–38.
31 Ludwikowski, "Constitution Making in the Countries of Former Soviet Dominance: Current Development," 155.
32 See Chapter 15, T. Jeremy Gunn, *Permissible Limitations on the Freedom of Religion or Belief, Religion & Human Rights: An Introduction*, ed. John Witte, Jr. and M. Christian Green (Oxford, England: Oxford University Press, 2012). On the problem of proselytism, see articles in Symposium, "Soul Wars: The Problem of Proselytism in Russia," *Emory International Law Review*, Vol. 12 (1998), pp. 1–738.
33 UNDHR Article 30.
Nothing in this Declaration may be interpreted as implying for any State, group or person any right to engage in any activity or to perform any act aimed at the destruction of any of the rights and freedoms set forth herein.
34 Article 55, Due Process. Egyptian Constitution, www.constituteproject.org/constitution/Egypt_2014.pdf. Does the individual have right to counsel, (including protections for confidential communications between an accused and counsel, presumptions of innocence, and or, trial by jury?) Persons could at least be given rights to notice, and notification to family when freedoms are abridged by the state. Individuals could be provided protections against unreasonable search and seizure.
35 See Karim el Bar, *News Deeply, Syria Deeply*, January 31, 2017, www.newsdeeply.com/syria/community/2017/01/30/analysis-russia-plans-syria-name-change-in-draft-constitution (who is wondering if Russia might be worried about its negative polling numbers for its role in Syria).
36 This has allowed Vladimir Putin to serve two terms from 2000 to 2008, step down for one term (when he was prime minister), and then return to the presidency in 2012 for possible two additional terms.

37 Cholpon Orozobekova, "Central Asia's Presidents-for-Life: Don't Hold Your Breath Waiting for Democratic Transitions in Central Asia," *The Diplomat*, February 5, 2016, http://thediplomat.com/2016/02/central-asias-presidents-for-life/.

38 One creative solution that might allow Assad to save face is to allow two terms, one as president and one as an honorary king (like the British monarchy but as a figure head, only, and immune from prosecution.

39 See Alexander Mercouris, "Russia's 'Constitution' for Syria (Full Text and Analysis)," *The Duran*, February 2, 2017, http://theduran.com/russias-constitution-for-syria-is-not-intended-seriously-and-is-just-a-diplomatic-play-full-text-and-analysis/.

40 Public Consultation on the Methods for Selecting the Chief Executive and for Forming the Legislative Council in 2012. Government of Hong Kong, 18 November 2009, p. 11, 2.04–2.06, giving 200 votes each to different constituent groups: business and financial sector, professions, religious groups and civil service organizations, and various district based organizations. www.cmab-cd2012.gov.hk/doc/consultation_document_en.pdf.

41 Ibid.

42 José Antonio Cheibub, Zachary Elkins and Tom Ginsburg, "Beyond Presidentialism and Parliamentarism," *British Journal of Political Science*, Vol. 44, No. 3 (2014), pp. 515–44. doi: 10.1017/S000712341300032X. The article abstract provides:

> The presidential-parliamentary distinction is foundational to comparative politics and at the center of a large theoretical and empirical literature. However, an examination of constitutional texts suggests a fair degree of heterogeneity within these categories with respect to important institutional attributes. These observations indicate that the classic presidential-parliamentary distinction, and the semi-presidential category, may not be systemic. This article investigates whether the defining attributes that separate presidential and parliamentary constitutions predict other attributes that are stereotypically associated with these institutional models. The results suggest the need for considerable skepticism of the 'systemic' nature of the classification. Indeed, the results imply that in order to predict the powers of a country's executive and legislature, it is more useful to know where and when the constitution was written than whether the country has a presidential or parliamentary system.

43 See "The Russian-Drafted Constitution for Syria Promises Kurds Greater Autonomy," *The New Arab*, January 26, 2017, www.alaraby.co.uk/english/news/2017/1/26/russia-drafted-new-constitution-for-syria-promises-kurds-greater-autonomy.

44 See Partlett, *supra*, note 2. A good example of this in the Russian constitution is the position of the Jewish Autonomous Oblast, which is afforded significant linguistic and religious autonomy but little political autonomy. Ibid.

45 In addition, what provisions will be made for past war crimes? How will they be prosecuted, if at all? Will there be a Truth and Reconciliation Commission? Will there be a role for the UN? How will the state's legitimacy be protected without some provisions preventing impunity, at the lease, for ongoing and future crimes? Will there be a role for an independent prosecutor?

46 Tim Arango, "Iran Dominates in Iraq after U.S. 'Handed the Country Over'," *NYT*, July 15, 2017, www.nytimes.com/2017/07/15/world/middleeast/iran-iraq-iranian-power.html.

Part II

A moral theory for peacemaking with justice

History, imagination, and forgiveness on an international stage

5 History and imagination

The hermeneutics of Paul Ricoeur

What has been happening in Iraq, in places like Ramadi and Tikrit, is now spreading to Syria. Shia-backed militia is taking its revenge on Sunnis. For example, there is Mahmoud Omar, a Sunni, who was forced to leave Ramadi. Ramadi, until recently, was a majority Sunni province in Anbar. He reports what it was like when the militia came through. They were as ruthless and indiscriminate in their violence against Sunnis as anything he had witnessed from Assad or Al Qaeda. Mahmoud is not alone in his observations. Many fled Ramadi when ISIS captured the city in May 2015. Now (2017) Ramadi is under assault by the military forces from the Shia-led government in Baghdad and supported by Shia/Iranian-led militia trying to recapture it. Some 1.4 million people from Anbar, a central province in Iraq where Ramadi sits, or 43 percent of its population, have been displaced, according to the International Organization for Migration.[1]

And now these Shia militia have reached Syria. They come into a setting where they will enjoy the backing of President Assad. These militias primarily characterize their opposition as Sunni and there is some truth to this characterization. The Sunni Arabs have been a major part of the uprising against President Bashar al-Assad since 2011. The Shia Iranian–led fighters joined by other Shia from Iraq will join other non-Sunni communities as supporters of Assad.

As discussed earlier, Assad can be said to have brought a fair amount of Sunni opposition on himself. He has since the beginning of the war been targeting specifically Sunni districts with his artillery and barrel bombs. Whole districts of Damascus and Homs once under rebel control are, as of 2017, a sea of ruins with every building shattered by explosives. Assad's earlier military actions started the devastation, and now the new militia groups are destroying what little has remained.

But the situation in Syria has, of course, been more complex than just a pitched battle between Shia and Sunnis. The Sunni community is divided, often along social lines, with the better-off and better educated siding with Assad against the poorer, more rural and tribal Sunnis. Many Syrian Sunnis do not support terrorism, including Saudi-backed Al Qaeda–affiliated groups. The Sunni elites have no sympathy for ISIS, and many feel threatened by the democracy movement, worrying that regime change will jeopardize their property and businesses.

Some of the attacks on ISIS in the north of Syria are also not about Sunnis versus Shia. These attacks come from the Kurds, who are far more interested in making room for an autonomous region for themselves than in fighting Shia. The Kurds by some estimates are 98 percent Sunni.[2] Yet these groups are helping Assad in his fight against ISIS. Sunni Arabs in northern Syria themselves feel a threat from the Kurds. The Sunni Arab tribes in Raqqa province in northern Syria issued a statement in 2016 accusing Kurdish forces, the People's Protection Units (YPG), of displacing Arabs from the town of Tal Abyad on the border crossing with Turkey. This statement says that "no YPG fighter can enter the Arab areas where our fighters are present." The YPG denies that it has forced Arabs to leave Tal Abyad, but Syrian Kurds often see Sunni Arabs as ISIS collaborators.

Some Christians in Iraq and Syria are also being subject to mass displacement. Like for the Sunnis, the attacks are not uniform. Christians are targets largely depending on how well they have aligned themselves with Assad. Once aligned with Assad, they draw the ire of ISIS. For example, in the village of Sadad, the attack by ISIS approaches genocide. Once a home to 5,000 Syriac Orthodox Christians off the highway linking Damascus and Homs, people are leaving because there are only a few hours of electricity a day and prices are very high but, above all, because villagers are terrified of being slaughtered by ISIS. Christians in Sadad have been attacked by different groups. Two years ago extremist Sunni jihadis, this time led by the Al Qaeda affiliate Jabhat al-Nusra, captured Sadad and held it for 10 days, killing 45 Christians and destroying or looting 14 churches before being driven out by the Syrian army. Figure 5.1 shows the distribution of the various sectarian groups in Syria.

The total count of refugees from Syria is staggering, and the cause for this mass displacement is variously Assad, ISIS, and different rebel groups, some of whom have switched their allegiances between different religiously affiliated backers. In Syria many of the estimated 5.3 million refugees and 6.5 million internally displaced people are likely to find that their houses and neighborhoods have been destroyed or permanently occupied by well-armed members of a hostile community.[3]

The mass flight and expulsion taking place in Syria and Iraq is on the same scale as that of India and Pakistan at the time of Partition in 1947 or of Germany at the end of the Second World War. In a study called "Ethnic Cleansing Threatens Syria's Unity," Professor Fabrice Balanche of the Washington Institute for Near East Policy reports that the different groups take their turns at ethnic cleansing. They try to terrorize their way to achieving control by indiscriminately killing the former leadership of a region and then picking collaborators to rule on their side. Each group then promises to return and slaughter those who remain, if they do not stay loyal to their causes. Of course, this loyalty is fragile. For ISIS what maintains any such loyalty is that it pays better than Assad. Still, the impact of these groups is devastating. Balanche's report includes a finding that "sectarian diversity is disappearing in many areas of the country."[4] The takeover of a whole area by a single sect, ethnic group, or political affiliation tends to be difficult to reverse because houses are redistributed to new owners who do not want to give them up.

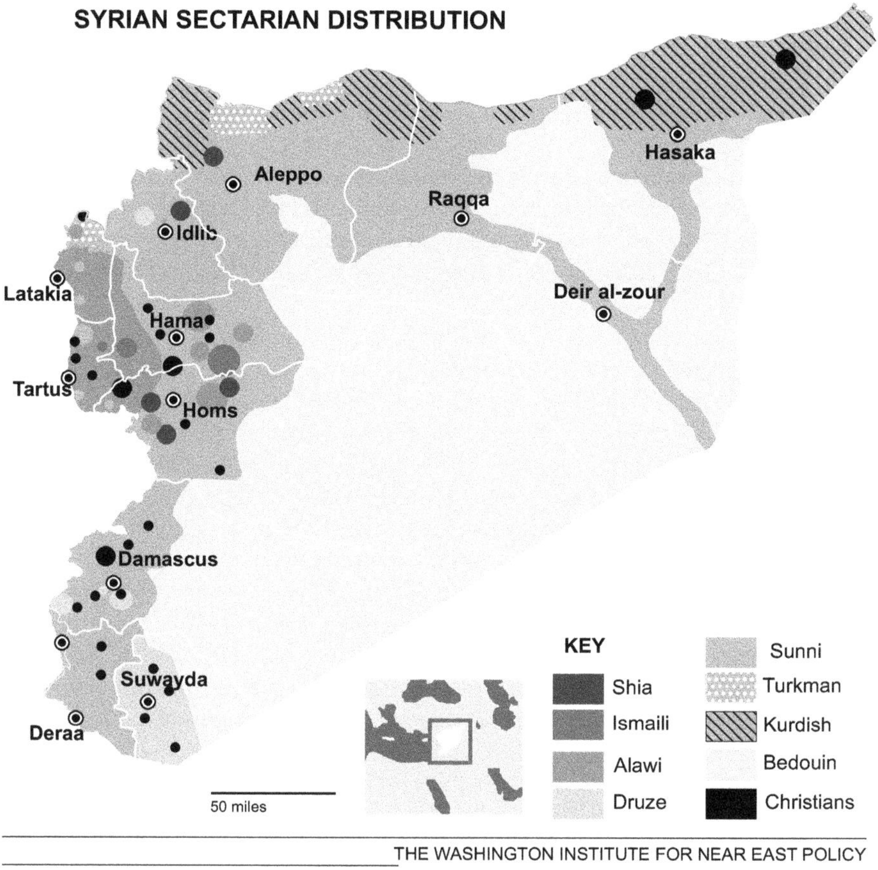

Figure 5.1 Sectarian Distribution in Syria

Mercy is scarce in the war in Syria and Iraq, especially with rebel groups receiving financial backing from contributors who have religious motives for offering their assistance. For example, Shia in Iraq say that since 2003 ISIS and its Al Qaeda–type predecessors have systematically targeted Shia mosques, marketplaces, bus queues, and pilgrimage sites, killing thousands of civilians. When ISIS took northern and western Iraq in 2014, its fighters filmed themselves executing 1,700 young Shia military recruits near Tikrit. In August of 2014, ISIS raped, murdered, and enslaved members of the Yazidi minority. Captured Syrian soldiers were ritually decapitated. In June an ISIS suicide squad killed 220 Syrian Kurdish men, women, and children in Kobani. Terror creates terror. Assad regime's tactics involved using other partners to do the terror, including enlisting Shabiha and the Hezbollah and Iranian-trained and led Jaysh al-Sha'bi. Religion motivates revenge. Terror and counter-terror created by these atrocities determine how different communities in Iraq and Syria perceive each other. Will it be possible for Sunnis, Shia, Christians, and Kurds to live together ever again?[5]

Yet with each atrocity, it is hard to sort out the true motivations of the fighters. As we have seen, in the case of Assad, he seems to have a mixed motive for his use of chemical weapons and barrel bombs. He seems to have demonized all who dare oppose him by reasoning that he is protecting Syria from all those who challenge his right to rule. He is protecting Syria, Alawites, and affiliated elites from outside forces designed to subvert the will of the Syrian people. At other times he seems to draw support by reminding supporters of a Sunni history of oppression. At other times he aligns with the Sunni elites who have entered his inner circles, and points to them, along with Christians and Jews, as evidence of his wide range of support among different Syrians.

Similarly, there are mixed motives among those who join ISIS. Many seemed to be motivated by the need to establish a pure caliphate for true Islam. Others are military leaders from the days of Saddam Hussein. They fought valiantly to stave off attacks from Iran, but their motivations then were more secular and nationalistic. These Sunnis appeared to use religion to recruit followers. Their motivation was more of a payback against the US for kicking them out of the Iraqi military and denying them their hard-earned prestige and position as professional soldiers. These Sunnis used the US invasion of Iraq as evidence of the West's war on Islam. Recruits came from around the world and from all branches of Islam. They were wildly successful in their ability to draw support from disenfranchised youth, as well as well-heeled donors.

What about the motivations of Shia militias? Many of these militias' members are similarly out for revenge for losses they suffered at the hands of Saddam Hussein in his war against Iran. Again, while often portrayed as Sunni versus Shia, these opposition groups also harbor tribal and nationalistic motivations. The Shia Iraqis the militias recruit have similarly mixed motives. Many are unemployed and simply want a job and paycheck.[6] Even in Iraq, where they are now the majority, they may not be employed in the Iraqi military. Iranian Shia recruit them, and as they fight they take inspiration from their leaders. After a while, religious ideology may creep in and give their fighting more substantial meaning and purpose.

As is clear, no formal justice system could take on the task of sorting out and proving all the potential criminal acts that took place and continue to take place over the course of the civil war in Syria. Overall, Syria's refugee situation approaches a Rwanda-sized need for reconciliation. If the country is to avoid splintering into small and isolated communities, there will need to be a huge effort at transformative justice. In particular, to imagine a future unified Syria, there would need to be a major effort at transformative justice. Mediation by skilled mediators will have to be at the heart of the transformation. Having taken a clear-eyed view of the scope of the problem during the transitional period, I next ask the question whether mediation may be up to the task.

There are at least two kinds of dispute resolution processes that would need to take place. One would be to understand and sort out the actions of Assad and his leadership group vis-à-vis Syrian citizens caught in his violent response to civil unrest. That kind of dispute resolution process is the focus of the next chapter and will need to include some considerations of formal justice mechanisms. The second kind dispute resolution process will likely take the form of community mediation. Under this type of dispute resolution process, I discuss the special and difficult forces blocking reconciliation between those who perpetrated violence motivated by a religious fervor. For example, how will community mediators deal with the following disputes if and when various refugee groups return to the places of their homes and families?

Where Shia militia drove out Sunnis, did some of them stay? Did Shia living there join in the violence? Or where Sunnis, including ISIS, killed and raped those that did not immediately join them, did some of them stay? Did other Sunnis join ISIS in their taking of land and in their oppression of Shia or Christians, or Yazidi, or Kurds? How will these groups return without a reconciliation? And how does a mediator deal with the issues of mediation across a range of motivations, including religious divides? These religious divides may be seen as motivated by revenge for the earlier oppression and disrespect of one's faith. How might mediation deal with these contemporary and historical religiously motivated acts of violence?

Mediation on any stage is, at its best, about transforming deadlocked negotiations into sustainable settlements. Three considerations are critical to achieving that goal. The first is history: What is the mediator's role in deconstructing and demystifying the parties' historical understanding of their dispute? The second is imagination: How does a mediator help the parties find the imaginative spark in their narratives that will facilitate a future-oriented approach to resolving their dispute, starting them on the road to reconciliation? Imagination is especially critical when the disputants' differences may be partly religious in nature or supported by on non-rational-faith-based differences between the parties. To help investigate these two considerations, I enlist here the ambitious and challenging philosophy of Paul Ricoeur.[7] In the process, the role that a mediator can play in transforming deadlock into more sustainable solutions can be better understood.

First let's start with a quick summary of the personal background of Paul Ricoeur. Like with Assad, Obama, and the leaders of the UN, it may shed some light on his motivations and his perspective on mediation. Ricoeur was French, the product of a regional university in Brittany rather than of the elite private university system. While raised Catholic, at some point in his youth he became a Protestant. Part of the French Resistance during World War II, he ended up in a German prisoner-of-war camp till the end of the war.

His first job was at the Protestant Collège Cévenol. Cévenol is in the city of Le Chambon-sur-Lignon, made famous for its having saved the lives of nearly 5,000 Jewish refugees at the end of the war. Whether shaped by the city's history or for other reasons Ricoeur was not the rigid Protestant fundamentalist like Franklin Graham. Ricoeur was very "ecumenical," or progressive. He felt it very important to look at sacred texts with a critical eye. He argued that theologians take up the "hermeneutics of suspicion." He directed his suspicions towards scripture. For nearly 50 years he argued that biblical criticism needed to take advantage of the tools of literary criticism. As I shall show later, he applied his theory not only to texts but to the meaning people give to historical events. This is the key to understanding how his philosophical theology impacted theories of mediation.

This does not mean that Ricoeur was a skeptic. He was at heart a phenomenologist, or one who believes that one's experience can be examined and that, through the process of examining that experience, one can experience transcendent meaning.[8] He was a humanist in that he argued that human had the capacity to know the good, the right, and the just. Humans share a capacity for love. Humans have ethics.

Ricoeur refined and improved the German sociologist Max Weber's well-known distinction between the *ethics of conviction* and the *ethics of responsibility* to make the point. Weber argued for striving for an ideal, regardless of the cost to oneself or others. Ricoeur insisted that, when necessary, ideals must cede to our fundamental duties toward fellow human beings. In that respect he was practical but would not give up on trying to reconcile convictions with responsibilities. He saw an internal conversation – a test, not a contest. In one sense he was anticipating the advice of Michael Kahneman: not to think fast but to think slow. For Ricoeur these dialogues between our convictions and circumstances oblige us to consider what is, at that moment and in that place, most important, and ask us to make the best choices we can with what we know. If we react too quickly, out of conviction, we are likely to get it wrong, to substitute a personal passion for a more careful account of what we know and don't know. Better to first be clear about the situation's tragic complexity than to act out of adherence to historical doctrines we too readily adopt as an ethical imperative. His ethics was in line with Aristotle's concept of practical wisdom. Practical wisdom that not only pays attention to duty but also counts and values known and unknown consequences will more likely lead to the better decision. Our experience informs our moral code, refines it, and transcends it, taking us to a new and more creative place.

In *Oneself as Another* (1992), Ricoeur prefers ethics over morality. He argues that ethics is grounded in aiming our actions toward what is good and what liberates. We have the freedom to choose what is new even if we are mistaken. Our lack of knowledge and understanding of the consequences of our actions unavoidably create risks. Part of this process is to see the other as fundamentally equivalent with ourselves. In opening ourselves to the equal dignity of others we open ourselves to new relationships. If we see in the other shared needs and goals – for security and growth and for meaning – we open ourselves up to the ideas of "flourishing." We become more vulnerable to the suffering of others. Ricoeur sees that in our ability to sympathize we open ourselves to a new understanding of the way that suffering deprives us of our ability to function. Suffering limits our ability to be human. To end our suffering we do horrible things. In sympathy with the suffering of others we open a new window to understanding the other. We see our common need for dignity and that our dignity precedes suffering. Once suffering is removed, there are new opportunities for dignity to reappear.

Ricoeur, then, has influenced the fields of legal and psychoanalytic theory. Paul Ricoeur is one of the giants of contemporary continental philosophy and one of the most enduring and wide-ranging thinkers in the 20th century, publishing major works on subjects from existentialism and phenomenology to psychoanalysis, politics, religion, and the theory of language.[9] His hermeneutics concerns not only the interpretation of sacred texts but also the study and interpretation of human behavior and social institutions.[10] One of his more powerful works includes a careful and beautiful remembrance of the Holocaust victims. As a part of this work, he writes about forgiveness. As such, his thought has direct and powerful applicability to resolution of disputes.

Ricoeur's hermeneutic philosophy emerges from and critiques the European philosophical tradition of phenomenology.[11] Phenomenology is grounded on the premise that consciousness is always conscious of something, or that the subject cannot be conscious without being conscious of an object – this concept is often referred to as intentionality.[12] Thus, phenomenology concerns itself with an examination of experience "as it in fact immediately presents itself, that is, as a structure of *meanings*, of intentional relations of subject engaged in a 'world.' "[13] For Ricoeur, however, phenomenology requires a hermeneutic turn. Whereas for Husserl meaning is "located in the subject's intuition of the 'things themselves,' " for Ricoeur, "intuition is always a matter of interpretation."[14]

Thus, for Ricoeur, experience is both a finding and a forming, a creating and a giving meaning to.[15] For Ricoeur, a hermeneutical phenomenology elucidates how humans make meaning in relation to sacred texts and to their shared history.[16] Specifically, it informs the meaning that can be given to their past behavior, to their institutional actors, and to their past narratives.[17]

Paul Ricoeur and the hermeneutics of history and imagination[18]

As I have shown, for Ricoeur, experience is both a finding and a forming, creating, and giving meaning to.[19] For Ricoeur, a hermeneutical phenomenology elucidates how humans make meaning in relation to sacred texts and to their shared history.[20] Specifically, it informs the meaning that can be given to past behavior, to institutional actors, and to their past narratives.[21]

Ricoeur interprets texts by using history in a particular way. He uses the process of historical analysis to discover the imaginative possibilities that arise anew from the search for meaning *in the present of the past* narrative.[22] To show how this works we need to first look at two related ideas, history and myth. Then we will need to turn to what is meant by two additional concepts, the role of language and the relationship of language to imagination.

Paul Ricoeur was taken by the role that *tradition* and *myth* play in the hermeneutic process, or the problem of understanding a dispute as both a product of the past and an imaginary projection into the future. Ricoeur subscribes to a quasi-Kantian idealist project, expressed by Ricoeur as "a civil society administering universal rights" to be a guide in our efforts to give practical shape to utopian expectations.[23] Growing out of this project, tradition should be properly understood as "an ongoing dialectic between (a) our being-affected-by-the past and (b) our imaginary projection of history yet-to-be-made (*la visée de l'histoire à faire*)."[24]

Ricoeur distinguishes at least three categories of historical memory. First there is *traditionality*: formally a dialectical process by virtue of which the "past is thus opened up as a-historical horizon which is at once detached from our contemporary horizon and included in it."[25] Expressed otherwise, traditionality is a "temporalizing of history by means of the dialectic between the effects of history upon us (which we passively suffer) and our response to history (which we actively operate)."[26] Ricoeur's insight is vital to a mediator. It provides the impetus for the mediator not only to ask about what happened in the past but also to ask what such experiences mean for the future.[27]

Second, there are *traditions*. Materially, traditions are essentially linguistic transmissions of acquired meanings which precede us[28] but which operate through what can be called *mutual questioning*: "the past interrogates and responds to us to the degree that we interrogate and respond to it."[29] Traditions, according to Ricoeur, are involved in every proposal of meaning; they are claims to truth that are posited before one is called to respond. There is a paradox in one's understanding of one's traditions: a person's understanding of his or her traditions both makes a truth claim (the inevitability of claiming the legitimacy of authority for the meaning of the history as preceding one's existence) and recognizes that traditions are subject to criticism. Practically stated, prejudice is inevitable and necessary to understand the world, but one's prejudices are subject to critical analysis as well. Pre-judgment involves expectations of behavior that are subject to challenge but without which we could not get along in the world.[30]

Third, there is *a tradition*, a particular acquired meaning that tells us one particular way to respond to our environment. It follows that there is a relationship between traditions and an individual tradition. For example, those who seek to hear the word of God in Holy Scripture both critically examine a particular text or historical event *and* open themselves to call into question who they are and what they may be called to be, even as they critically examine a particular text or historical event. The same opening is potentially available to anyone attempting to describe his or her cultural identity related to any one formative part of history: a battle, a law, a case, or other formative event.[31]

Ricoeur's analysis of imagination and language emerges from his unique approach to phenomenology: we know not only because of what is internal to us but also because there are phenomena that occur independent of us that impact us, or that we see, and are therefore grounded in facts outside our minds. Ricoeur's move from a descriptive phenomenology oriented to perception/vision to a hermeneutic phenomenology oriented to interpretation/understanding led him to rethink imagination in terms of language. *Imagination acts as an agent in the creation of meaning in and through language.*[32]

To Ricoeur, images are spoken before they are seen, and, paradigmatically, they are spoken in the form of poetic metaphor through which new meaning is created by the metaphorical reconciliation of pre-existing opposing meanings.[33] Interpreted ontologically, a poetic imagination "creates meaning by responding to the desire of being to be expressed."[34] Imagination works by revealing new possibilities of being in the world through semantic innovation, which points toward social transformation.[35] "Without imagination, there can be no action [or reconciliation or just peace]."[36]

Ricoeur speaks in a context describing how imagination and language work to make possible the interpretation of sacred texts. The language of the text is necessarily read to contain symbols. A symbol is a sign insofar as it stands for something, but a symbol is not merely a sign; rather, a symbol can aim at two or more meanings simultaneously. A symbol points to more than one meaning by way of enigmatic suggestion or evocation in contrast to allegory (which simply relates one meaning to another, without residue or ambiguity).[37] Ricoeur's argument (and hope) is that contemporary language can be restored to its poetic and symbolic power, recovering language in its symbolic fullness. This requires demythologizing myth as a false explanation of reality and embracing myth's capacity to describe a state of affairs that is yet to be fully realized.

Ricoeur sees two different types of symbols operating when one reads a text or seeks to interpret the past: cosmic symbols and poetic symbols.[38] Cosmic symbols read the sacred onto history. "[T]he imagination reads the things of the world as signs, and signs as things of the world."[39] So, the rainbow is a sign of God's promise not to destroy the world with a flood. Israel's victory in the Six-Day War is God's sign of approval for Jews in fighting their Arab neighbors. Assad's father's rise to power is a sign of divine approval to the Alawites to rule modern Syria. Opposition tenacity in the face of overwhelming force is a sign of divine approval for their efforts to bring down Assad.

Poetic symbols, on the other hand, are images that reveal "language in a state of emergence."[40] To understand Ricoeur's meaning of the poetic one must understand his definitions of the related concepts of metaphor and narrative. Metaphors operate at the level of sentences, in contrast to symbols, which operate at the level of words.[41] Narratives operate at the level of texts.[42] Metaphoric imagination as developed by Ricoeur combines elements of Aristotle's philosophy with that of Kant. The metaphoric function of imagination involves a verbal aspect by virtue of which it involves grasping identity with differences, and it does so with a sensible element or aspect which is intuitive. *By intuitive, Ricoeur means "'seeing-as' quite precisely plays the role of the schema that unites the* empty *concept with the* blind *impression."*[43] In this combination a new meaning can be confronted. The literal confronts the figurative sense: seeing one thing as another.[44]

Poetical language reveals a capacity for non-descriptive "reference to those ontological aspects of our being-in-the-world that cannot be spoken of *directly. Seeing-as* . . . not only implies a *saying-as* but also a *being-as.*"[45] Narrative works (both historical and fictional) function in their referential capacity as ultimately poetic symbols. The important point for our purpose is that history, thus understood, requires imagination for its reconstruction. Narratives properly understood rest on the "pre-narrative capacity of human imagination to act in the world in a symbolically significant manner."[46] One way to express it more simply is "human beings are continually transforming a sequence of life events into a story, creating a plot for a life."[47]

Ricoeur sees a role for poetry in moving from speculative theory to the ethical, because poetry is oriented to action:

> It is the function of poetry in its narrative and dramatic form, to propose to the imagination *and to its mediation* various figures that constitute some many *thought experiments* by which we learn to link together the ethical aspects of human conduct and happiness and misfortune.[48]

The implication for mediation of a dispute is quite interesting: Should a mediator ask the parties to express their cases in poetic narrative? As we will see later, the parties may already do so by way of their opening statements. Perhaps the real lesson from Ricoeur is that the mediator should be highly attuned to the parties' use of the poetic in their expressions of their cases or narratives of their histories. The mediator might help identify the party's use of themes, poetry, analogy, and metaphor to express their cases against each other. Inevitably the parties will express the evil they are suffering as a deviation from the way things are supposed to be. The evil they experience will be expressed not only in terms of blame but also as part of a narrative looking to the future where such acts are not the end of the story but where the parties may play a part in changing the situation. In a mediation, the mediator might try to see a poetic narrative, or help the parties to discover the values and common suffering and shared evil that can help them step outside of the currency of exchange into a future of forgiveness and new possibilities. Discussing the possible responses to such evil may include memorials, remembrances, while reparations may open up the possibility of a letting go, release, and forgiveness.[49] The mediator might then see four central tasks of narratives.

First, narratives help the parties realize their debt to the historical past. They see the heroic role played by their predecessors who often were victims of oppression and did not stand idly by but choose to try to change and respond to injustice. This teaches the parties the continued responsibility or debt that they owe to the dead.

Second, narratives help parties respect the rival claims of memory and forgetfulness. As we will see, forgiveness does not require forgetting, which is anathema to the representatives of innocent victims. Narrative involves a making present what is absent by retrieving pasts and projecting futures. Oral history involves the paradoxical task of imaginatively representing the past as it really was, subject to continuing reinterpretation, by both giving the past presence through analogizing representation and respecting the *otherness* of the past by refusing a reduction of the other (the past) to the self (the present of the historian).[50] In other words, narrative keeps the mediator humble in making any findings involving past events. Narrative history intrinsically involves literary elements: plot, composition, character, and point of view. The very uniqueness of individual historical events constitutes the anchor of reference to the real. Narration and explanation go together inasmuch as narrative's evocation of feeling with regard to singular concrete historical events provoke a striving to understand these events which ultimately is conducive to explaining them.

Third, narratives can cultivate a notion of *enlightened self-identity* that can help even in the face of religious differences operating on a non-rational plane. For example, certain events, such as the Holocaust, call for evocation of the *horror of victimization*.[51] Such suffering "reveals the scandal of every theodicy" which "no cunning of reason can ever justify."[52] Still, it reveals the same about any idea of God, in that suffering is the universal human condition. So while suffering is individual and unique – part of any given individual's identity – it is also shared.

Finally, narrative histories can lead the parties to recast them in ways that help the parties identify the shared sufferings that each has encountered and evaluate actions in order to see a new possible way of being. If human identity is narrative in character, where memory and imagination are commingled such that they are necessarily reinvented and reconstructed, a couple lessons follow. First, fundamentalism is a form of forgetting: it is a literalization of a story. Second, by virtue of reimagining the other in an empathetic process (remembering oneself-as-another) the possibility of pardon (a kind of forgetting after remembering) and a different freer future emerges. Ethical memory, as a process involving both illumination and illustration (e.g., of the horrors of the Holocaust), seeks to establish a proper balance between the dual fidelities of memory to the uniqueness and communicability of past events. In other words, narratives "are able to make sorrows *bearable*" and are thus part of the "work of mourning understood as the acceptance of the irreparable."[53]

Understanding the role that narrative plays in forming one's identity can help the mediator to make each individual more persuasive and, thereby, more imaginative at evoking the uniqueness of his or her experience that is also wrapped in the shared of human experience. While the imaginary knows no censorship, as might be suggested by a morality based on abstract rules, narratives do involve an element of ethical solicitation based on an ethics of experience (concerned with cultural paradigms of suffering and action, happiness, and dignity).[54] The mediator can turn the representative narrator to these concerns and propose a variety of ethical possibilities from which the parties are free to choose.

As a result of the foregoing, a mediator can help the parties rehabilitate their notion of self, whose substantial construction as essence or ego has rightly been shattered, by basing identity on the story of a life. Identity includes mutability and change within the cohesion of one lifetime subject to continual reinterpretation in light of new and old stories we tell about ourselves. The notion of one's identity can be clarified through critical narrative processes, which apply equally to societies and to individuals. The mediator can help the parties see that for their identity to be ethically responsible, *self-constancy* must be informed by self-questioning. It is in the moment of ethical decision that authentic self-constancy, a critical self-understanding open to the other, is manifest.[55] By acting, the actor transcends narrative through a responsiveness to the other who is irreducible to any or all narratives.[56]

Ricoeur's hermeneutics provides theoretical support for how some problem-solving mediators currently practice but often with those mediators not knowing why such practices work. These mediators get the parties to first focus on and then change the language they use to negotiate with each other. Called problem solving by facilitative mediators, these mediator/practitioners try to break the deadlock between parties by asking the parties to reframe their negotiations away from position bargaining. They suggest using a language of *interest-based*[57] negotiation, or of *problem-solving*.[58] Transitioning to a language of problem solving[59] from position bargaining by asking about underlying needs and goals helps teach Ricoeur's hermeneutics. It situates the parties' view of a dispute as resting both in the past and in a story that is yet to be, helping the parties value the past while also demythologizing it in order to reclaim a more authentic new myth that will give meaning to the group's narrative.

The language of problem solving asks the parties to state their continuing goals and needs going into the future. As a result, the parties are urged to see joint problems that need to be solved, including needs for mutual security and economic prosperity. They are urged to identify obstacles to resolving these joint needs, including psychological obstacles raised by the prospect of living and working side by side with individuals who are responsible for committing atrocities against innocent members of society. It follows that any ability to overcome such obstacles would require acts of forgiveness of heroic proportions. Imagining a future "utopia" where the parties live with each other in peace and prosperity may be the only incentive for the parties that can overcome the existing cycle of violence and mutual destruction.

Still, troubling questions remain. Ricoeur seems to sidestep binary alternatives and suggest instead that perhaps it is in the realm of the traditional – narratives of founding events publicly commemorated – that authority is grounded.[60] In ancient times the very antiquity of authority was considered its legitimation: "Authority relied on memory."[61] As a result the parties may attribute their beliefs to Allah that Allah will punish them if they do not continue to try to rid the land of infidels, when the real authority is ancient, natural historical memory. Or the belief that God will drive *us* into the sea, if we do not establish a holy nation, determined to follow God's laws, may be attributing a belief about God's will in the past as authority for God's will today.

For Ricoeur it is absolutely essential for traditional narratives to be reviewed and renewed in order that the creative imagination can rediscover the essential liberating narrative embedded in the traditional narrative.[62] For example, Israel's escape from Egypt is a narrative that resonates with the freedom and liberation experienced by any group that has once been enslaved and then set free. So reviewing the founding narrative can serve religious Jews as a narrative rediscovering the human suffering experienced by other groups longing for freedom, whether they be minorities of race, religion, or gender.[63]

The "process of *temporalization* which makes our present actions meaningful [operates] by interpreting them in terms of a recollected past and a projected future."[64] Authentic tradition and genuine innovation belong together. Tradition works as the living transmission of an innovation always capable of being reactivated by a return to the most creative moments of poetic activity. Reciprocally, innovation remains a form of behavior governed by precedents for behavior derived from history and culture.

Ricoeur's hermeneutics may give mediators a philosophical approach that helps them better respond to narratives that contain descriptions of past injustices. As a starting point a mediator can inquire about what meaning the party ascribes to its interpretation of a past event. The mediator should listen to see if the party has given divine or cosmic importance to the event, and inquire into the symbolism that their description entails. Insight into these meanings can be signaled by the language used by the party to describe what has happened in the past.

Ricoeur's hermeneutics must yet deal with the phenomenon of evil.[65] In the face of legitimate claims by the evil done to one party by the other and vice-versa, the mediator will face a significant challenge to making peace. Each group has a case to call the other evil. In particular, the mediator will have to look at the injustice described above to examine what the narrator may mean by the very word *evil*. Two responses to evil seem possible. One is to see evil as suffering and to lament that suffering. The other is to see evil as wrongdoing that needs to be blamed and punished.[66] Again, Ricoeur's hermeneutics provides valuable insights. The problem with myth is that it incorporates evil into origin stories that link human moral choice to cosmological cycles of fate, destiny, or predestination. The evil figure is an alienated figure determined by some force beyond itself to do what it does: the devil made him do it.

On the other hand, understanding the concept of evil will help the mediator understand the mythological character of the narrative and help the parties imagine the good that can come out of the evil. To facilitate this "seeing" the parties need a renewed awareness that they have a tendency to see the evil that has befallen them as either the doing of God, to punish them for their failures in the past, or, in the alternative, to see evil as something brought about by the devil, in the form of the actions of their enemies. In this latter way the logic leads one to see one's opponents as the devil and so to demonize one's opponents.[67]

Ricoeur's practical understanding of evil can help the parties view evil as distinct from speculative theory and as oriented to action. Mediators can help the parties see evil as enigmatic, contingent, and singular. Evil ought not to exist and should be struggled against.[68] As a result evil is something suffered, but also calls for both an individual and collective response. It must be "worked through" via a narrative of mourning, which turns passive lament into the possibility of active complaint or protest to make future evil resistible. As a result the parties may be led to ask, "Do we have a responsibility to try to end this evil?" Such a question is particularly appropriate where the dispute involves religious identity. It is at the heart of any group identity question, whether Sunni, Shia, Christian, or Jew. One can ask, "Is this continued fighting really what God/Allah intends for his people? How is it that the divine wants them to live?" In other words, evil can be seen as a problem that needs solving. Options for dealing with evil will often include the need for peace, the prevention of future evil, and a response to past evil that refers the parties to concepts of justice including responses of retribution and or punishment.[69] In other words, the parties, regardless of their religious differences, are bound in a common history that assumes that each is living out of a relationship with a God that created all that there is. Their histories share a hermeneutic circle.[70]

The power of the possible

Ricoeur's *hermeneutic circle* is that of *historical intersubjectivity*: we enter an ongoing conversation which does not come to a totalizing end (the process is circular, not linear) and to which we must familiarize ourselves by recognizing the distance we in our situation have from others we seek to encounter, thereby overcoming that distance to a degree.[71] Or, as Kearney would have it, "hermeneutics endeavors to render near what is far – temporally, geographically, scientifically, culturally – by reappropriating those meanings that have been 'distantiated' from our consciousness."[72] Texts bring about *semantic innovation* through symbols, metaphors, and configurations (plots).[73] Innovation is in a dialectical relation with *tradition*: "Tradition needs innovation in order to sustain itself as a living transmission of meaning capable of being reactivated in its inaugural moments, while innovation needs tradition in order to make sense as a form of expression governed by rules."[74]

Ricoeur transposes his analysis of the relation between tradition and innovation to the sociopolitical sphere – the *social imaginary* (the body of collective stories, histories, and ideologies which inform our modes of sociopolitical action). The social imagination serves an *ideological* role of grounding a social *identity* and a *utopian* role of the *disruptive* projection of alternatives to the present.[75] For Ricoeur a poetics of creation is linked to an ethics of just action.[76] In this regard he mirrors Aristotle, who sought "a good life with and for others in just institutions."[77]

Ricoeur's hermeneutic philosophy can be construed as centering on the relationship between poetics and ethics. He details how a process that focuses on demythologizing one's historical narrative and then reimagining and projecting that narrative into the future can lead to looking at one's life as if it were more than a *zero-sum game*. Such a process can use the analogy of seeing to promote a vision for the future. Such use of narrative invites ethical judgment to submit itself to the imaginative variations proper to fiction to uncover the essential connections between our actions and their consequences as good or evil.[78] Vision promotes initiative. Ricoeur argues that through stories we learn to plot our own lives and to project possibilities for our societies, with ethical intervention in history occurring in responsible *decisions* that themselves come up in the tension between the horizon of expectation (future/utopia) and the space of [current] experience.[79] Using narrative can also develop empathy, and narratives enable us to identify imaginatively with others, thereby extending the circle of selfhood.[80]

Mediators must note how the role of the poetic is more explicit in religious belief systems that have a Creator God.[81] In other words, understanding how humans know that God makes Himself known as a Creator God itself creates a human epistemology that is ultimately story making. Linking human imagination with a belief in a Creator God enables Ricoeur to transcend the sterile 19th-century debates over whether all our behavior is self-interested, as a Utilitarian would argue, or whether acts of disinterested generosity can and do occur. A Creator God's call for humanity to continually express its better nature makes such "better being" part of the human story.[82]

Ricoeur is, at bottom, a phenomenologist and so is making an appeal here to the shared experience of those committed to belief in a Creator God. He suggests or implies that inherent in the nature of a Creator God is such a god's demand for expressing better nature. He finds evidence for an experience of a God with those characteristics, in the sacred texts of Abrahamic religions: in the Bible, the Torah, and Quran. But he has not fully explained why that link is there and so strong as to be essentially a necessary implication. He leaves that for others to do, or to any opening created by the mediator who asks whether a party's members' belief in their God includes a call to forgive.

As a result, Ricoeur's hermeneutics provides a mechanism for disputing parties to realize the shared nature of their knowing, even where the disputes are in part religious. Mediators can use Ricoeur's philosophy as a practical way of getting the parties to think poetically. In thinking poetically, acting poetically, dwelling poetically, the parties can discover that all poetic modalities create possibilities for imagining poetically. As Kearney has said of Ricoeur's poetics, "[t]hey are ways of realizing the fundamental *possibilities* of what we are. For as the poet Emily Dickinson wrote, 'possibility is the fuse lit by the spark of imagination.' "[83]

In sum, Ricoeur provides a theory of mediation that sets up a process. That process will allow reason and faith to be in dialogue with each other. Because it sets up a dialogue where important questions can be raised about the power and potentiality derived from one's shared narrative with one's fellow person, a renewed understanding can arise of who the parties are and where they have been and to imagine a better future moving forward. At least one practical outcome of such a process is that it can raise the possibility of forgiveness as one of the autonomous choices that frees peacemaking from being a zero-sum game with justice.

Notes

1 International Organization for Migration, "3.4 Million Displaced from Iraq," https://www.iom.int/news/displacement-iraq-exceeds-34-million-iom

2 Besheer Mohamed, "Who are the Iraqi Kurds?," 2014, www.pewresearch.org/fact-tank/2014/08/20/who-are-the-iraqi-kurds/.

3 UNHCR (United Nations Refugee Agency), http://www.unhcr.org/en-us/figures-at-a-glance.html

4 Fabrice Blanche, "Ethnic Cleansing Threatens Syria's Unity, Washington Institute Improving the Quality of US Middle East Policy," http://www.washingtoninstitute.org/policy-analysis/view/ethnic-cleansing-threatens-syrias-unity

5 One wonders whether the Syrian civil war amounted to a radical *caesura*? A break so severe and so beyond the pale that these communities will never be able to reconcile with one another? Kind of like the *caesura* of the Holocaust, which created such lines as "there can be no more poetry after the Holocaust" and so on.

6 Tim Arango, "Iran Dominates in Iraq after U.S. 'Handed the Country Over'," *NYT*, July 15, 2017. www.nytimes.com/2017/07/15/world/middleeast/iran-iraq-iranian-power.html.

7 See especially Paul Ricoeur, *Figuring the Sacred: Religion, Narrative, and Imagination*, trans. David Pellauer, ed. Mark I. Wallace (Minneapolis: Fortress Press, 1995); see also Richard Kearney, *On Paul Ricoeur: The Owl of Minerva* (Burlington, VT: Ashgate, 2004). Not everyone is a fan. Some have found it hard to find a common thread in Ricoeur's work. See, for example, David M. Kaplan, introduction to *Reading Ricoeur*, ed. David M. Kaplan (New York: State University of New York Press, 2008), 4. Kaplan sees in Ricoeur's work more of a *response* to a set of

philosophical problems than an *answer* to them. He does find a unity in Ricoeur's work that describes a "thin but continuous thread" about the capability of humans. Kaplan, introduction to *Reading Ricoeur*, 4 (internal quotation marks omitted). He quotes from Ricoeur himself concerning the thread:

> The man capable . . . of speaking, acting, narrative and narrative himself, taking responsibility for his actions . . . but also remembering and forgetting, making history and writing it, judging and being judged, understanding his human condition, through the painstaking work of interpretation and translation, which is a way to say something again but differently. And capable also, at the end of a long lifetime journey, or realizing, through the difficult experience of forgiving, that humans are worth more than their actions and their faults and that the climax of wisdom is the capacity to be amazed by the splendor of the simple fact of being alive as human beings . . . as we are taught by those simple masters, the lilies of the fields and the birds in the sky.

Paul Ricoeur, *Memory, History, Forgetting*, trans. Kathleen Blamey and David Pellauer (Chicago: Chicago University Press, 2004), 505–6, quoted in Kaplan, introduction to *Reading Ricoeur*, 4.

8 Though he never achieved the same celebrity or notoriety in the United States as did Michel Foucault or Jacques Derrida, Paul Ricoeur was, ironically, the most "American" of his generation of French intellectuals. Not only did he teach for several years at the University of Chicago, but his works are also exceptional – at least among French philosophers – for their knowledge and engagement with Anglo-American thinkers ranging from P. F. Strawson and Alasdair MacIntyre through John Rawls and Michael Walzer to Frank Kermode and Wayne Booth. (In a typically self-effacing remark, Ricoeur once told an interviewer that he held a chair at Chicago "with a schizophrenic title; it was called 'theological philosophy' or 'philosophical theology,' I don't remember which.")

9 Kearney, *On Paul Ricoeur*, 1.

10 See ibid.

11 See ibid., 13–15. Ricoeur's early philosophical work heavily indebted to the phenomenological philosophers of the early twentieth century, and he established himself as a leading authority on phenomenology with his translation and commentary on Edmund Husserl's *Ideen I*. John B. Thompson, editor's introduction to *Hermeneutics and the Human Sciences*, by Paul Ricoeur, trans. and ed. John B. Thompson (Cambridge: Cambridge University Press, 1981), 2. Ricoeur's engagement with and critique of Husserl (who is generally considered the founder of phenomenology) can be seen in the introduction to his early work, *Freedom and Nature: The Voluntary and the Involuntary*, trans. Erazim V. Kohák (Chicago: Northwestern University Press, 2006), 3–34.

12 Kohák, translator's introduction to *Freedom and Nature*, xiii.

13 Ibid.

14 Kearney, *On Paul Ricoeur*, 2.

15 Paul Ricoeur, *The Conflict of Interpretation: Essays in Hermeneutics*, ed. Don Ihde (Evanston, IL: Northwestern University Press, 1974), 11. To at least one commentator, this is more than an insight about phenomenology, and constitutes an epistemological insight, or one about knowing. See Maria Villela Petit, "Thinking History: Methodology and Epistemology in Paul Ricoeur's Reflections on History," *Sage Journals*, http://psc.sagepub.com/content/14/2/147. Professor Petit derives Ricoeur's epistemology by integrating his works *History and Truth*, (Paul Ricoeur, *History and Truth*, trans. with an Introduction by Charles A. Kelbley, [Evanston, IL: Northwestern University Press, 1965 [1955]], p. 26.) with *Time and Narrative*, Paul Ricoeur, *Time and Narrative*, trans. Kathleen M.

McLaughlin and David Pellauer, Vol. 1 (Chicago: University of Chicago Press, 1984), ix. Petit sums up the connection as follows:

> The foregoing is a very succinct survey of Ricoeur's approach to the methodology and the epistemology of history in the first volume of Time and Narrative. But "thinking history" for Ricoeur means going far beyond these levels of reflection. As the third volume of Time and Narrative demonstrates, the epistemology is itself an essential though subordinate step in a project whose ultimate aim is a hermeneutics of the historical consciousness. Within this horizon, the historical and the fictional narratives assembled are considered as essential contributions to the refiguration of the field of human action and suffering, in other words, to the refiguration of our historical condition. This refiguration has necessarily an ethico-political dimension, a dimension which has always been the telos of Ricoeur's thinking on history.

16 Ibid., 11–12, 27–29. It is worth noting that Ricoeur's hermeneutic approach has its origins in approaches to resolving the problems of multiple meaning that emerged in biblical exegesis. Ibid., 11; see also Kearney, *On Paul Ricoeur*, 20.

17 Ibid.; see also Thompson, editor's introduction to *Hermeneutics and the Human Sciences*, 15–17.

18 In the next part I unpack Ricoeur's hermeneutic theory and analyze the challenges to its use in helping the parties understand their individual and collective histories. That is followed by a discussion of the role that meaningful forgiveness might play in resolving disputes by drawing on insights from the disciplines of moral philosophy, religion, and jurisprudence. Finally I discuss the practical procedural considerations and psychological paradoxes of mediating disputes in the Syria context. In particular, in this final section I ask whether we can draw any practical lessons for either ongoing or future international dispute resolution mediation processes that are considering forgiveness as a pathway to peace. In addition, in this last part I suggest some important possibilities for the design of future Truth and Reconciliation Commissions.

19 Ricoeur, *The Conflict of Interpretation*, 11. To at least one commentator, this is more than an insight about phenomenology and constitutes an epistemological insight, or one about knowing. See Petit, "Thinking History." Professor Petit derives Ricoeur's epistemology by integrating his works *History and Truth* (Paul Ricoeur, *History and Truth*, trans. with an Introduction by Charles A. Kelbley, p. 26.) with *Time and Narrative*, Ricoeur, *Time and Narrative*, ix. Petit sums up the connection as follows:

> The foregoing is a very succinct survey of Ricoeur's approach to the methodology and the epistemology of history in the first volume of Time and Narrative. But "thinking history" for Ricoeur means going far beyond these levels of reflection. As the third volume of Time and Narrative demonstrates, the epistemology is itself an essential though subordinate step in a project whose ultimate aim is a hermeneutics of the historical consciousness. Within this horizon, the historical and the fictional narratives assembled are considered as essential contributions to the refiguration of the field of human action and suffering, in other words, to the refiguration of our historical condition. This refiguration has necessarily an ethico-political dimension, a dimension which has always been the telos of Ricoeur's thinking on history.

20 Ibid., 11–12, 27–29. It is worth noting that Ricoeur's hermeneutic approach has its origins in approaches to resolving the problems of multiple meaning that emerged in biblical exegesis. Ibid., 11; see also Kearney, *On Paul Ricoeur*, 20.

21 Ibid.; see also Thompson, editor's introduction to *Hermeneutics and the Human Sciences*, 15–17.

22 Ibid, 28–29.

23 Paul Ricoeur, *Temps et récit III: Le Temps raconté* (Paris: Editions du Seuil, 1985), 311 (hereafter cited as *TR*), cited in Kearney, *On Paul Ricoeur*, 60. I am relying on Richard Kearney's translation of Ricoeur's *Temps et récit III: Le Temps raconté* found in Kearney on Ricoeur. Kearney cites to his own translation of Ricoeur's work as Ricoeur, *TR*.

24 Kearney, *On Paul Ricoeur*, 60. To the extent that modernism seeks to cut the ties to the past it loses its ability to formulate a path to its ideals: suppressing the notion of progress for a utopia cut off from reality. Ibid.

25 Ricoeur, *TR*, 313, quoted in Kearney, *On Paul Ricoeur*, 60.

26 Ibid., 62.

27 As an example, a family counselor dealing with children who are in conflict might ask, "What do you think your parent would want you to do about this problem in the future?" or "Do you think your parent would want you to go on fighting about this?"

28 Kearney, *On Paul Ricoeur*, 63.

29 Ibid., 64.

30 See Paul Ricoeur, "Hermeneutics and the Critique of Ideology," in *Hermeneutics and the Human Sciences*, ed. John B. Thompson (Cambridge: Cambridge University Press, 1981), 63–100. Ricoeur seeks to mediate between Gadamer's *backward look* of inherited pre-understanding and Habermas's *forward look* of communicative action, with a view to finding norms of validation as operative both within historical dialogue and as a *limit-idea*, which also serves as a regulative ideal. Kearney, *On Ricoeur*, 65.

Again, in a family counseling setting, a mediator might see Ricoeur's point to prompt the following: "I know you feel like your parent wanted you to have the property because you were the oldest boy, but do you think that was fair to your younger sister?"

31 For example, a sacred text seems to describe a historical event and attribute to God not only a victory against an enemy, but also an act of genocide against the civilian population of that enemy. How ought God's favor toward a person in that tradition interpret that tradition today?

32 Ricoeur, *TR*, 228–58, cited in Kearney, *On Paul Ricoeur*, 66. Ricoeur finds support for this move in the Philosophy of Kant, Heidegger, and Gadamer. See Martin Heidegger, *Kant and the Problem of Metaphysics*, ed. James S. Churchill (Bloomington: Indiana University Press, 1962); see also Hans-Georg Gadamer, *Truth and Method*, ed. and trans. Joel Weinsheimer and Donald G. Marshall, 2nd rev. ed. (New York: Continuum, 1993). Ricoeur's insight helps explain why the language of problem solving or interest based bargaining can have such a transformative effect. The language shifts the parties from winning and beating their opponent into thinking about a future that they may share. Instead of thinking about a zero-sum game they think about a future of possibilities, where each lives in a community within their group and with others.

33 Paul Ricoeur, *The Symbolism of Evil*, trans. Emerson Buchanan (Boston: Beacon Press, 1969), 12–14.

34 Kearney, *On Paul Ricoeur*, 40–1.

35 Ibid., 42.

36 Paul Ricoeur, *From Text to Action: Essays in Hermeneutics, II*, trans. Kathleen Blamey and John B. Thompson (Chicago: Northwestern University Press, 1991), 177.

37 Ricoeur, *Symbolism of Evil*, 15; see also Kearney, *On Paul Ricoeur*, 45n25.

38 See Ricoeur, *Symbolism of Evil*, 12–14. Ricoeur also discusses what he calls oneiric symbols. Oneiric symbols are like the meaning that individuals ascribe to dreams.

They remember and interpret the dream as containing messages from God, or of cosmic importance, or of subconscious meaning that caused the dream "facts" to occur. In other words, oneiric symbols interpret dream images as manifesting the sacred in the psyche. People act on oneiric symbols. For example, the three wise men of scripture were moved in a dream to seek the "Christ Child."

Oneiric imagination works by seeing dream images as concealing and revealing meaning, deforming and disclosing intentions, or expressing a sign through a *saying desire*, to be understood as a passion for possibilities not yet realized. A hermeneutics of suspicion encouraged by psychoanalysis can help us to discriminate between those images that are merely a return of the repressed and those which serve as symbols of an eschatological horizon of possibility. So understood, dreams provoke rational interpretation, but such interpretation never exhausts their surplus of meaning. Still we are to recognize the formalized, transparent, and technical language of the contemporary era and distinguish it from the hidden, sedimented traces of meaning embodied in and seeking to emerge from language. Kearney, *On Paul Ricoeur*, 48.

39 Kearney, *On Paul Ricoeur*, 43, citing Ricoeur's *Freud and Philosophy: An Essay on Interpretation*, trans. Denis Savage (New Haven: Yale University Press, 1970).
40 Ricoeur, *Symbolism of Evil*, 14 (quoting Gaston Bachelard, *La Poétique de l'Espace* (Paris, 1957)).
41 Paul Ricoeur, *The Rule of Metaphor* (London: Routledge, 1978), 199–200; Kearney, *On Paul Ricoeur*, 51.
42 Ricoeur, *Time and Narrative*, Vol. 1, 80–2; Kearney, *On Paul Ricoeur*, 54–5.
43 Ricoeur, *The Rule of Metaphor*, 207–8; Ricoeur, *Time and Narrative*, Vol. 1, 80–2.
44 Ibid.
45 Kearney, *On Paul Ricoeur*, 53.
46 Ibid., 54.
47 Kearney, *On Paul Ricoeur*, 55; Ricoeur, *Time and Narrative*, Vol. 1, 80–2; Paul Ricoeur, *Time and Narrative*, 80–2; Kearney on Ricoeur, *supra*, note 1 at 55.
48 Paul Ricoeur, "Life in Quest of Narrative," in *On Paul Ricoeur: Narrative and Interpretation*, ed. David Wood (London: Routledge, 1991), 23, quoted in Richard Kearney, "On the Hermeneutics of Evil," in *Reading Ricoeur*, ed. David M. Kaplan (New York: State University of New York Press, 2008), 84 (emphasis added in first instance).
49 These are parts of discussion between some Palestinians and Israelis concerning negotiations over the right of return for Palestinian refugees. Hrair Balian, The Carter Center, discussions with the author, Atlanta, GA.
50 Kearney, *On Paul Ricoeur*, 100–1. This anchor distinguishes Ricoeur's understanding of the historian's task from other (especially French) philosophers of his time. Ibid., 103.
51 Ricoeur, *Figuring the Sacred*, 289–92.
52 Ricoeur, *Time and Narrative*, Vol. 3, 187.
53 Paul Ricoeur, "Dialogue 5: On Life Stories (2003)," in Richard Kearney, *On Paul Ricoeur: The Owl of Minerva* (Burlington, VT: Ashgate, 2004), 160. Kearney interviews Ricoeur in a number of Dialogues that he includes in his book *On Paul Ricoeur: The Owl of Minerva*.
54 Ibid.
55 Ricoeur, *Figuring the Sacred*, 111; see also Emmanuel Levinas, *Otherwise Than Being or beyond Essence*, trans. Alphonso Lingis (The Hague: Martinus Nijhoff Publishers, 1978), 115.
56 Levinas, *Otherwise Than Being*, 112, 128–9. The creation of meaning in language comes from the specific human production of new ways of expressing the objective paradigms and codes made available by language.

57 Interest based negotiation is the language first used by Roger Fisher and William Ury, *Getting to Yes* (New York: Penguin Books, 1983) and then adopted by the Harvard Negotiation project as the heart of a new language for negotiating.

58 Carrie Menkel-Meadow, "Toward another View of Legal Negotiation: Toward a Structure of Problem Solving," *UCLA Law Review*, Vol. 31, No. 4 (1984), 755–821, (hereinafter "Problem Solving").

59 Ibid., 768.

60 Ricoeur, "Dialogue 5," 165.

61 Ibid., 161.

62 Ibid., 165.

63 See ibid., 166. Yet conflicting traditional narratives within a single tradition might be used as reasons for continued conflict; thus, Ricoeur still needs to describe how to select narratives of liberation and equality over narratives of conquering and destroying.

Ricoeur scholar Richard Kearney locates Ricoeur's philosophy in the context of other philosopher theologians. Ricoeur rejects philosopher Karl Barth's anti-metaphysical Protestant lineage in favor of a recovery or retrieval of an Aristotelian metaphysics of *possibility and actuality* (not metaphysics of substance) as a way to an ontology of the many meanings of being, coupled with a biblical and un-Greek understanding of being as being-with, being-faithful, being-with-one's people, as exemplified in Exodus 3:14. Ibid. Ricoeur's *phenomenology of being able* seeks to develop an *ethical ontology* beyond Heidegger's *ontology without ethics* and Levinas' *ethics without ontology*, Ibid., 167, playing itself out in a differentiated "phenomenology of 'I can speak', 'I can act', 'I can narrate' and 'I can designate myself as imputable' (*imputabilite*)." Ibid., 168.

Beginning with Aristotle but thinking along with Spinoza's and Leibniz's different sense of "possibility," Ricoeur ends this dialogue with a sense of "*possibility as a dynamic tendency or inclination.*" Ibid., 168 (emphasis added). Ricoeur suggests the viability of a certain retrieval of medieval thought in its attempt to think God and being in terms of each other. Perhaps the God of the Bible or the Allah of the Quran and the God of Being are not absolutely irreconcilable. Ibid., 169. Ricoeur's work with history specifically and with narrative in general lead him to transcend the historical hermeneutic bias in favor of understanding over explanation, as is captured in his maxim: "*To explain more is to understand better.*" Quoted in Kearney, *On Paul Ricoeur*, 3. This includes explaining alien meanings to understand ourselves better. Kearney, *On Paul Ricoeur*, 5. "Meaning . . . involves *someone saying something to someone about something.*" Kearney, *On Paul Ricoeur*, 4. Ricoeur complicates this dialogical model by noting how intersubjective relations are mediated by social institutions, groups, nations, and cultural histories, forming contexts for both the texts and the meanings given to fundamental beliefs.

Texts as written incorporate meaning which becomes autonomous: not constrained by original intention, original reception, or initial situation referred to. Kearney, *On Paul Ricoeur*, 5.

64 Kearney, *On Paul Ricoeur*, 54.

65 See generally Ricoeur, *The Symbolism of Evil*; see also Paul Ricoeur, *Evil: A Challenge to Philosophy and Theology*, trans. John Bowden (New York: Continuum, 2007).

66 Kearney, *On Paul Ricoeur*, 91.

67 Ibid., 93–4. Philosophers have struggled with how to reconcile the existence of evil with an all-powerful, omniscient, wholly good god. To Augustine evil entered the world through human action alone. To Leibniz, the principle of Sufficient Reason accounts for the judicious balancing of good with evil in this the best of all possible worlds. To Hegel, ultimately all that is real is rational. It is the real and rational response to what has happened before. Jung argued for a residual

inscrutability of evil. Ricoeur finds Kant's move away from a speculative to a practical discourse on evil the appropriate response to both speculative excess and an irrationalism of the "dark side of God." Ibid., 93.

68 Ibid., 94.

69 Paul Zwier, *Principled Negotiation and Mediation in the International Arena: Talking with Evil* (New York: Cambridge University Press, 2013), chapter 1.

70 Kearney, *On Paul Ricoeur*, 5.

71 Ibid.

72 Ibid.

73 Ibid., 6.

74 Ibid. To Ricoeur writing is in a dialectical relation with *reading* which eventuates in action in a world.

75 Ibid., 7–8. Ricoeur's *hermeneutics of suspicion* (a critique of false *consciousness*) exemplified by Marx, Nietzsche, and Freud is balanced with a *hermeneutics of affirmation*, which admits and explores an irreducible surplus of meaning grounded in the fundamental human *desire to be*, which to be opened up requires deciphering the masked workings of desire, will, and interest. Ibid.

76 Ibid., 8.

77 Bernard Dauenahauer and David Pellauer, "Paul Ricoeur," in *The Stanford Encyclopedia of Philosophy*, ed. Edward N. Zalta (Summer 2014), http://plato.stanford.edu/archives/sum2014/entries/ricoeur/.

78 Kearney, *On Paul Ricoeur*, 171.

79 Ibid., 172.

80 Ibid., 173.

81 Discussion by Ricoeur of the way that belief in a Creator God impacts on narrative and ultimately creates the space for the work of the imagination toward the ends of love and liberation runs all through his book *Figuring the Sacred*. See, for example, pages 31, 94–9, 102, 121, 131–5, 217–30, 236–48.

82 Ibid. Note that Ricoeur also describes a philosophical basis for the creative imagination that underlies the hermeneutics of religion in the thinking of Kant, Rosenzweig, Heidegger, Husserl, and Levinas. Ibid., 75–126. As such the key for a mediator to unlock the imagination in a conflict involving non-monotheistic disputants lies in the philosophical ideas of the "other," the mind, and memory. See Alvin Plantinga, *God and Other Minds: A Study of the Rational Justification of Belief in God* (Ithaca, NY: Cornell University Press, 1967).

83 Kearney, *On Paul Ricoeur*, 175.

6 Justice and forgiveness

It is a cool evening in the fall of 2015. After a long day of discussing with Syrians the experience of Tunisia and South Africa during the transitional period, the group heads out for dinner at a restaurant near the conference hotel. A couple of the Syrians are discussing the role that Mandela played in what happened in South Africa. They are marveling at Mandela's ability to negotiate with those who put him in jail. They both ask whether the other could forgive Assad enough to talk with him, much less make a peace with him that would include sharing power with him for a period of time.

One of the Syrians doesn't think he could be in the same room with Assad without flying into a rage and trying to kill him. He explains why. Assad's police arrested him at the start of the demonstrations on suspicion of supporting the democracy opposition. "I was a human rights lawyer, so of course, was meeting with detainees trying to secure their release. That was enough for them. They threw me in prison. It may sound trivial compared to what we know others have suffered but I was in prison for six months. But I was stripped, made to stand on one leg till I collapsed, and subjected to various kinds of torture, including having cigarettes put out on the soles of my feet. My wife, who was pregnant at the time, was not told where I was. She thought I was dead. Same with my family.

"When I got out, I immediately made arrangements to flee the country. I left my home and my practice and my parents, and bribed my way to safe passage to Beirut.

"My wife lost our baby. She continues to blame me for that.

"Things have been hard. My wife misses her family. She says, 'Why couldn't you have been a transactional lawyer instead of a human rights lawyer?' Sometimes I wonder whether maybe she is right. Then, I get angry. I know that I was right to choose what I chose to do. And I blame Assad for what he did to me and my family. What gave him the right to decide for Syria what Syria is and what it stands for. If I was in the same room I'd try to kill him. No, I am not ready to talk about forgiveness."

As important, then, as mediation that stresses historical scientism is to transformative justice, a second subject will need to be high on the dispute resolution agenda if peace in Syria can be sustained. That subject is forgiveness. As with the last chapter, I start our discussion with Ricoeur.

Forgiveness is particularly important for helping the parties design the appropriate Truth and Reconciliation process. Where the parties have perpetrated atrocities on each other, it will be necessary to also examine the topic most often raised in the imaginative spark of the renewed understanding of a group's identity narrative: that of the possibility that the parties offer forgiveness as part of a path to sustainable peace. On the topic of forgiveness, this chapter proposes that Ricoeur's philosophy highlights the essential features of forgiveness: that it is outside the exchange or bargaining that typically drives peaceful settlements but nonetheless gives a future to the disputants' past in dealing with each other.

In this regard, this chapter examines the necessary implications of forgiveness: that victims will most likely have to be engaged directly in the peace process, or immediately thereafter, in order for them to freely choose to forgive the perpetrators for atrocities that have been committed against them. Building on these contributions from Ricoeur, it will be necessary for the mediator to better understand what impact the victim's choice to forgive may have on whether any settlement that is reached is ultimately just. Because meaningful forgiveness can only be voluntarily given by individual victims, a process that provides as much will need to be agreed to by party representatives. As previously mentioned, such a process will insert fragility into the peace settlement.

This chapter then examines whether a mediated peace process that relies on forgiveness can overcome the objection that forgiveness is incompatible with justice. It shows that these objections can be overcome but only if the parties understand the hard trade-offs they are making in choosing to forgive and if those making the peace ensure that any peace processes will involve victims in the final resolutions. In addition, it shows that, as a matter of moral philosophy, such a process will have to involve a certain amount of fact-finding about the nature of the alleged atrocities and provide meaningful protections like those in play in formal legal processes to ensure that any victim's or group of victims' choice to forgive will be meaningful.

The challenge to mediating disputes: between justice and forgiveness

Importantly for peace and reconciliation, after taking the parties through a process that shows the historical complexity of their myths and creates space for the role of vision and the imagination, the mediator can put on the table one response that is always possible: to forgive and be reconciled to the opposing party. The parties may never have contemplated such a possibility because the conditions for forgiveness did not seem possible: that the other side would admit responsibility and sincerely commit to ending the atrocities. Asking what a party to a conflict might need to see in order to think seriously about forgiveness might prompt a first-ever consideration of the prospects of forgiveness on behalf of both parties. So we turn next to an examination of what might be involved in mediation where forgiveness is an option for one or both of the parties.

What exactly is this thing called forgiveness?

Ricoeur only takes us so far in his understanding of forgiveness, but still he makes an important contribution. To Ricoeur, pardon or forgiveness is intrinsically gratuitous, surpassing the limits of rational calculation and explanation.[1] Ricoeur's important insight is that forgiveness occurs only *outside* a currency of exchange; it stands outside the rational and bargaining process of justice and exists, if at all, in the creative imagination of one or both of the parties.

Before being carried away by Ricoeur's hermeneutics we must look at the apparent contradiction between justice and forgiveness. Here a renewed understanding of mediation in comparison to formal legal process is particularly helpful. Our examination will need to first give definition to what forgiveness may require. In this regard, we will explore the traditional religious roots of forgiveness and then see whether a secular understanding can be developed. Second, we will explore how human justice, as opposed to divine justice, seems to require a legal analysis in that it requires not only clarity about what law has been violated but also a fact-finding aspect (that the alleged wrongdoer actually did the illegal act). We will see that some aspects of what justice requires will need to be provided to the actual victims of the atrocities before meaningful forgiveness can occur. This is so because, as a corollary to the legal understanding of justice, the victims need to know *what* they are forgiving in order for their forgiveness to be truly informed and truly voluntary. The perpetrators may also need "due process" in order for them to receive forgiveness, since the forgiving party needs to understand that whatever guilt has been confessed has not been coerced. Finally, then, we will look at whether the process of forgiveness in a mediation can sufficiently replicate or make substitutions for the requirements of legal justice in order to bring about a moral peace and reconciliation.

First, what do we mean by forgiveness? To understand the role that forgiveness plays in reconciliation between disputants involved in past injustices we need to first see what it means in a religious context, as a way a person reconciles with her god. Then, after understanding forgiveness' religious history, the task will be to examine its meaning in a context where humans offer forgiveness to one other, either from within a religious context or towards those outside a given religious group.

The origin of forgiveness is commonly thought of as growing out of a religious context: as a dynamic between a human and her Savior or Creator.[2] Whether Muslim, Jewish, or Christian (Catholic or Reformed or Orthodox), the story of a religious people is in relationship to their Creator. As Ricoeur shows, it is through an understanding of human history in relationship to a Creator that one gets meaning out of asking, "Because of your history, tradition, or traditions, what action do you think is now required of you?" In the face of human responsibility for failing to live up to the Creator's law, the religious human seeks forgiveness and reconciliation with his or her Creator.

God's forgiveness is outside of what is required of God for his creation. God can do what God wants with his creation. On the other hand, common to most religious faiths is a belief that God's forgiveness teaches something about God: that God can put aside past wrongs against him and treat his creatures as if they had not committed those wrongs. Common to the monotheistic religions is the view that God's forgiveness requires two critical features: (1) the person seeking forgiveness must truly confess his or her wrongs to God, and (2) the seeker commits him- or herself not to do those same acts again in the future. This narrative of forgiveness leads to a common question: Once forgiven, how does God want you to live and be true to what God has created in you?

Despite the religious origins of forgiveness, moral philosophy has shown that forgiveness can be given a meaning apart from an act or command of God.[3] By treating God's forgiveness as something that humans are required to give to one another, forgiveness has meaning apart from the divine. There are five aspects of the forgiveness that might be granted to other human beings that must be understood in order to see how forgiveness and transformative justice might work. First, there is a distinction between the conditions for forgiving and forgiveness itself. Second, forgiveness teaches us about the human condition. Third, human forgiveness does not require forgetting.[4] Fourth, forgiveness does not require that one treats the act that caused the harm as never having occurred, only that the victim will choose to treat the wrongdoer as if that wrongdoer did not do the act. Finally, the act of forgiving may involve the victim agreeing to a deterrence theory of punishment rather than a retributive theory of punishment. Let's take each of these in turn.[5] Some say forgiveness is simply a matter of harboring feelings. Jeffrie Murphy is a proponent of this view. Thus, I may forgive you in my heart of hearts or even after you are dead.[6] To Richard Swinburne, on the contrary, forgiveness is an action one performs: you choose to treat me as not being responsible for or the originator of an act by which I wronged you. Feelings need not be involved.[7]

The key point of either view is that real understanding of the historical context of the violence is essential to forgiveness. For someone to choose to forgive another for the harm done to that person, the perpetrator needs to have actually done the act that caused the harm or be responsible in some way for doing the act that caused the harm. Otherwise, how a person chooses to treat someone is independent of what he or she has actually done. If the person is not to blame, then forgiveness is not the appropriate word for what a victim grants to the actor.

It may be the law that defines the blameworthy act, or it may be a matter of morals. In either case, the actor must be "blameworthy" if forgiveness is to take place. The third feature of the context where forgiveness may occur is that the victim remembers the deed and who did it and continues to condemn it.[8] Feelings are involved, in that the victim feels both resentment and anger for what has been done to the victim, but they are not determinative.

In the light of this context then, the forgiving party chooses not to act on these feelings of anger and resentment, but treat the actor as if the actor is not blameworthy for the actions done. There are a number of things to note here. First, forgiveness does not require forgetting. This is crucial for a victim to acknowledge about any decision to forgive the other. After all, if it were otherwise, the victim is right to say that forgiveness is impossible. The denial of the *dinge-an sich* – the thing that happened and its effect on one's memory, in its essential respects, is simply not possible. But forgetting is not necessary, and it then becomes a choice whether to act in spite of the memory in order that forgetting not be a precondition for forgiveness to occur.

In addition, treating the actor as not being blameworthy does not mean that the (victim) condone the act itself. The deed can continue to be condemned, while the actor may not be held responsible. The law (and the state) is comfortable with such notions. For example, murder can be both justified and excused. Murder is justified if it is done for protection (self-defense or defense of others), is coerced (duress), or is performed against the will of the actor. Murder is excused if the actor lacked the requisite capacity to form the specific intent to cause the harm specified by the law (insanity, incapacity, or incompetency) or was coerced by fear or by threats made to loved ones.[9] As in the domestic legal context, war and acts of violence in the context of mediation may be justified by the defense of others or excused because the acts were coerced or lacked the requisite blameworthy intent. The victims could choose to see these mixed motives – use of violence to protect oneself and loved ones – as, at a minimum, a complicating factor that may mitigate the blameworthiness of the act committed.

That may not be how the victims in a dispute see what has happened to them and their families.[10] Where the victims are truly innocent, or not even a member of the targeted group, killings may be rightfully and unconditionally understood as murder. Furthermore, victims' worth and dignity are impugned as a collateral effect of the intended act.[11] To the victims and their representatives, the actor treated the innocent victims unjustly. They see in the actor's defense an attempt to demonize the victim as if he or she was somehow to blame or simply chose not to recognize the dignity or human worth of the persons killed.[12] Whatever harm has been done was of lesser importance to the actors' own survival or power. To the victims, they have been treated as less than human or like collateral damage in selfish attempts to maintain or gain power.

The harm done by a decision to put others at risk may not be blameworthy as a matter of law and yet be blameworthy as a matter of morality. International law may not be sufficiently formed to make specific acts of war illegal, yet general principles of *just war* theory predominate the laws of nations.[13] Decisions to use deadly force may be made without regard to the exact proportionality of the harm they cause or mistakes concerning the "collateral" damage that occur to innocent civilians during the use of that force.[14] A certain indeterminacy results where the law of nations commingles intentional acts with negligent acts. Indeterminacy results when acts during war involve mistaken understandings of the amount of the threat the actor was facing or the dangers that were involved.[15]

Other complications that mediators will have to manage involve whether the moral law forbids acts of violence in the name of self-defense where too large a number of innocent victims are caused harm in the process. What victims may experience as an act of evil and lack of respect for fundamental human dignity – the indiscriminate killing of civilians – is experienced by the actor as part of a narrative where they are the hero: they are justified; their acts protected their wives and children; their very identity as a people was threatened, so their acts were motivated by self-defense or survival. In addition, an actor may be "justified" because his or her acts were necessary to deter future acts of terrorism. To not respond with sufficient force and brutality would encourage others to commit acts of terror. The actors may believe that no negotiations with terrorists are necessary because they would only encourage other terrorists. While victims of previous acts of violence may perceive a callousness towards innocent victims, the actors may be content that allegations of personal vengeance or grabs for personal power ignore the actual tortured nature of the decision to use violence to prevent future acts of violence.

Regardless of whether the violation is a matter of moral or international law, it is important to see how human forgiveness tries to make up for the lack of omniscience about by whom, why, or how harm was committed. Human forgiveness recognizes a moral hazard in granting amnesty before a clear understanding of the circumstances has taken place. Otherwise, forgiveness will be granted too easily, without sufficient reparations, or sincerity, or honesty regarding how or what was done. True forgiveness, forgiveness that freely makes the trade between what might be required in payment and the nature of the harm done, seems to involve at least a "finding" of facts, and a judgment of relative blameworthiness of the actors. One does not ask a governor for a pardon without the governor getting a careful and clear understanding of what was done and why it was done.

Yet even in these situations, it is common for the adjudicative process to see these matters as involving the framing of narratives and a certain deconstruction of these narratives as a choice between a winner and a loser. Forgiveness is an option but only after these findings have been made. In a mediation, forgiveness is imagined *first*, and then a process is created to work out whether forgiveness will be granted by the victims. It is done before the individual perpetrator's motives have been adjudicated. It is done in the hope that the individual victims will be led into a process where they, too, can see that the conditions for forgiveness are possible: (1) their act of forgiving is voluntary, (2) it does not involve forgetting, (3) their forgiveness involves some judgment that the actor has indeed committed the blameworthy act, (4) that perpetrators have sincerely asked for forgiveness and shown expressed contrition through the payment that is exacted, and (5) the victims will choose to treat the perpetrator as not having been responsible.

In other words, mediation must help the parties see what forgiveness will involve on the part of the forgiver. At a minimum, it will require a reframing of the narrative victims tell about the harm that has been caused, treating the actor as not being responsible/blameworthy, even if the actor is causally responsible for the harm done.[16] But to reach that point, another process needs to be provided for. Processes are needed for determining the truth about what happened and then judging the contrition on the part of the actors commensurate with the act committed and the harm done.

In the adjudication of these matters the distinction between levels of blameworthiness are extensively examined in order that findings can be made about what happened, and in order that punishments can be determined that truly fit the crime that occurred. The decision is not left to the parties themselves to sort out because they are likely to get it wrong. A person's own perspectives and experiences are thought to inevitably bias any fair, factual determination of what has happened in the past.[17] Mediators are said to be involved in a different sort of process: they are trying to facilitate the parties themselves to make the tricky trade-offs between not knowing the exact nature of the actors' responsibility or blameworthiness for the harm that has been caused, yet also asking whether they want truth in trade for justice, or will grant forgiveness before knowing the level of blameworthiness that can be attributed to the actors.

While Ricoeur's hermeneutics point to a process other than adjudication, they must deal finally and transparently with its non-rational limitations.[18] After all, a formal legal framework is based on a rational decision-making system that is agreed to either explicitly or implicitly through theories of universal rights or fictions derived from consent in a state of nature. When one chooses to forgive, the victim does so outside the logic of the law, a logic that claims that when one commits certain acts he or she "agrees" to be made to take responsibility for his or her actions. Appeals for forgiveness, especially because it is one's duty to forgive, are non-rational, religious arguments based on faith. As such, they are choices that are made "off the table" of rationality.[19] Claims based in the non-rationality of faith share in a certain human humility: that humans are not God. This gives each human a certain moral equivalence with each other. That equivalence is a humility that comes from a recognition that human knowledge is based in part on faith, or a non-rational basis.

I am not claiming here that we will be able to find in pluralism a common belief in the dignity of humans, but there is enough here in Ricoeur to find a foundation to argue that humans will always be dealing with each other out of this dual aspect of their natures, that they are not God, and so their knowing occurs through a combination of logic and reasoning that is based both on rational arguments and non-rational arguments, or faith statements. This common understanding of our *being* and *knowing* gives impetus for the creation of law – *or rules to live by*. Since a lot of what we say we know is ultimately non-rational, we must deal with each other according to universal principles: to do unto others as we would have them do to us. In other words, we deal with each other in humility and create processes that will try to factor out the most extreme forces of irrationality, hate, anger, and fear.

As a result, there is a word of caution here for mediators. Societies have evolved legal processes to try to contain these non-rational forces when managing disputes. The law prescribes what a crime is and what will be recognized as a defense. Some societies give to juries the job of "finding" the facts. Ranges of punishments are prescribed that are preset legislatively in order that they be based on theories of consent and notice. These pre-agreed systems of finding facts and making law help ensure equal treatment of one other in the light of that law, both substantively and procedurally. By choosing to empower different bodies with these powers, we conceal the non-rational nature of fact-finding. We set up politically authorized processes for determining facts in order to mitigate the non-rational bases of our knowing and ensure some measure of equal treatment under the law.

When parties engage in a mediation process, they are choosing to deal with each other without the protections otherwise provided by the legal process. The question remains whether parties to mediation can then deal with each other without providing the guarantees of moral equality that can be better maintained by a formal legal environment. Yet they may share the non-rational belief that they can collectively rise above the cycle of hate and violence that has enveloped the two sides of a dispute. They may not agree on the common dignity of all humans, but they may believe that they have the freedom to rise above their circumstances and choose a better future. In the shared humility with which they approach the non-rational nature of their gamble to choose to forgive, they may share a common vulnerability. In their common vulnerability, they may then choose to forgive rather than to destroy, choose to cooperate rather than to conquer, and choose to make peace rather than to perpetuate violence.

Still, what Ricoeur has shown is that while mediation may facilitate a discussion of forgiveness, ultimately the mediator will only be able to raise mediation as a possibility for the parties to choose as a means to peace. This is because forgiveness stands outside of the logic of exchange, and forgiveness can seldom be implemented on behalf of other victims. Moreover, even the kind of forgiveness that *can* be implemented on behalf of *other* victims is not meaningful because a mediation process itself stands outside the rationality of the law. As a result, forgiveness chosen in a mediative process will always be contingent and, at the very least, fragile. While it is tempting then to prescribe a Truth and Reconciliation processes, as a matter of moral philosophy, the final forgiveness stage will be left unresolved.

We have yet to apply these Ricoeurian tools in the real world of disputes. We turn next to present day international conflicts to see what the implication of Ricoeur's theory may be for an international dispute where atrocities have occurred on both sides.

Ricoeur's theory of mediating meets reality in Syria

As we have seen, Ricoeur's poetic imagining of a utopia can spark the imagination to consider the possibilities of forgiveness. We need yet examine how Ricoeur's theory will have to do more than work on a theoretical level to overcome the very real psychological and practical inhibitors the disputants experience during mediation.[20] While Ricoeur's theory does the work of helping the parties to empathize with the "other's" perspectives and inspire the energy necessary to imaginative problem solving,[21] woven throughout this discussion has been the interplay between Ricoeur's philosophy and the psychology of victim forgiveness. For a mediation process to help the parties generate empathy and then inspire energy to be creative, it will need to be teamed with practical techniques drawn from social psychology.[22] These will be important to employ for maximizing the benefits that can be gained from problem-solving mediations.

These practical difficulties will include the psychological and moral capacities of the individuals involved, the difficulty in finding representatives with the gravitas to negotiate on behalf of disputants, the agency problem that arises from both a multiplicity of atrocities and the multiparty nature of most disputes over the course of the dispute's history, the time that a hermeneutical process can take to develop the poetic imagination in the exigent circumstances of violence, and finally, the ability of the post-conflict peace process to be able to match the alleged perpetrators of violence with their victims and victims' families.[23]

Will Ricoeur's theory overcome victim incapacities and agency problems?

First, then, to be effective, the mediator must be fully cognizant of the therapeutic nature of the mediator's efforts and understand the limitations inherent in the therapeutic model, which depends finally not only on the individual autonomous choices of the disputing parties but also on the autonomous choices of the parties' representatives. If either the victims or their representatives' feel coerced or tricked into their choice to forgive, then the moral conditions for actual forgiveness are likely to be sorely lacking.[24] To some extent, then, any sustainable peace will depend not only on the strength of character of the actual representatives to the settlement talks, and the representative's moral courage to withstand the political fallout that is bound to occur in their agreeing to use forgiveness as part of any dispute settlement, but also finally on the moral courage of the actual victims to choose to forgive and live as if those responsible were not responsible for the harm that was done to them. Any agreements reached by these representatives can offer forgiveness on behalf of victims of past atrocities only in very rare circumstances, and perhaps only where the representative themselves have suffered great harm and are willing to forgive. Otherwise, the ultimate reconciliation will arrive only if and when the victims themselves choose forgiveness through a process designed for that forgiveness to truly occur.[25]

Both who counts as a victim and the choice of how to reconcile the different psychological factors between victims and victim types will also be crucial to the outcome of any mediation process.[26] Victims can be categorized as those who were physically harmed; those that were force to leave their homes; those whose family members were killed, "disappeared," raped, or suffered other physical harmed; those whose extended family was harmed; and those who suffered insult and humiliation from either being subjected to demeaning conduct or from the knowledge of general physical harm or suffering to a group, tribe, or sect to which they belong. Their particular age and life experiences preceding the trauma can also effect the type of intervention that is most likely to cause healing and reconciliation.

Psychologists will be quick to point out the special hazards of mediating between victims who personally suffered harm. Post-traumatic stress can be caused from a reliving of the initial trauma. With children, this can be particularly damaging to their psyche. It is almost better that the memory remains repressed or dormant than for it to be relived. For older, more experienced adults a group mediation that has some of the components of a Ricoeurian hermeneutical process, namely a focus during the mediation of the conflict on the *common ground* – the humanity or vulnerability of disputants that can *rationalize* the conflict – would have a high chance of effectiveness. Such group mediation can lead participants to *manage* their anger, to *expand their egocentric view*, and to spend *the time to acknowledge the history and complexity* of the conflict and *empathize* with the others feelings. Moreover, this kind of mediation can show participants how to treat all views with respect, enabling them to *air their grief without dominating* the process, accepting some responsibility *at a local level for how to live together* in the future.[27]

In addition, the agency problems are likely to be great. The agents at any mediation are likely themselves part of the decision-making team tasked with negotiating amnesty for those who have been engaged in the violence. Their principles will demand that any peace be contingent on an understanding that the principles will not be tried for past wrongdoing. The problem is that such amnesty is not something the representatives of the other side can give, except in precisely a *representative capacity*.[28] Yet the demands of peace placed on the parties can create strategies that will hold off on deciding the exact nature of the forum in which an individual's justice and opportunity for forgiveness will be decided.[29] At a minimum, the parties are given mixed messages about the justice constraints that will likely arise after the conflict has ended if these issues are not attended to. The representatives are placed in the untenable position of either blocking an agreement that would make peace with justice, or face the wrath of their principals for agreeing to peace without getting adequate assurances about the end game of the agreement.[30]

Will parties' representatives agree to take the risks of a just, forgiving process?

This chapter has shown that the paradigm of forgiveness requires peacemakers to take a fresh look at the distinctions between adjudication and mediation as methods of dispute resolution.[31] Ricoeur's hermeneutics have been employed to help peacemakers understand how attempts to design hybrid dispute resolution processes, like Truth and Reconciliation Commissions (TRCs), will often fail if they do not involve the parties in a clear understanding of their agreements. Party representatives will often lack either the moral capacity or the moral standing to effectuate meaningful forgiveness. Again, taking the conflict in Syria as an example: Will Assad choose to act more like Peter Botha, the president of South Africa who refused to negotiate an end to apartheid, or like F. W. de Klerk, the Nobel laureate who eventually agreed to share power with Mandela? De Klerk had the virtue to compromise, born out of an understanding that apartheid could not survive. De Klerk opened up the negotiation process with Mandela that led to the end of apartheid.[32] Will a person or persons in the Syrian opposition communities be willing and able to put aside the desire for vengeance born of personal and tribal animosities and speak like Mandela or Tutu to open the way for truth and forgiveness as a tradeoff for retribution? While history teaches us that these figures were "made" of their circumstances and were not born into these roles,[33] whether a person of such character will emerge in any given conflict is always an open question. Such a role cannot be forced on the leadership of any party. While Ricoeur's hermeneutics open up the possibility that a de Klerk or Mandela will emerge, they do not ensure that one or both sides will see it in their capacity to create the circumstances where forgiveness can take place.

In addition, parties will often have conflicting interests in trying to avoid responsibility they may have for their own actions. The best result that might be possible in the immediate situation of ending a conflict may be necessarily limited to the mediation of an end to hostilities, prisoner exchanges, and an agreement to later work out the conditions of a meaningful reconciliation.

Finding the time for a Ricoeurian hermeneutical mediation

As Ricoeur himself discusses, the ability for any victim to reach the decision to grant forgiveness takes time and reflection to develop, requiring a process of understanding the nature of narrative and of their individual and collective story, and then the energy to imagine a new course that may include forgiveness.[34] One frustration of the international community watching cycles of violence unfold again and again – whether in Israel and Gaza, Syria, Sudan, or Ukraine – is the seemingly mediable, and therefore preventable, nature of such violence if the various parties could have been brought together.[35] One particularly fruitful time for the use of Ricoeurian mediation is before the violence starts and before the atrocities occur. Making the space and time for leaders to meet and discuss the dispute before it happens provides the best chance of reaching a peaceful and just result. Yet history shows that the need for leaders to appear responsive and strong in the face of threats often overwhelms the decision-making process. Yet once the atrocities occur, and the number and their extent grow, the time that it will take to mediate will grow commensurate with the number of victims and the number of atrocities.

Are there any examples of Sunni Shia reconciliations that might open consideration of forgiveness?

Mark A. Gabriel, professor of Islamic history at Al-Azhar University in Cairo, in his book *Journey Into the Mind of an Islamic Terrorist: Why They Hate us and How We Can Change Their Minds*,[36] shows how difficult the argument for forgiveness might be for some of the more radical Islamists. He details the passages that radicals quote for waging "jihad" to the death against infidels.[37] One of the most chilling passages he quotes from the prophet is that killing a Muslim who does not follow the commands of the prophet does not violate Islamic law, which prohibits Muslims from killing each other, because if he does not follow the commands of the Prophet that person is no longer a Muslim.[38] Gabriel then details the best arguments for changing a terrorist's mind including making appeals to the teachings of the "Prophets," a group of three otherwise radical teachers, who, while writing from an Egyptian prison, argued for a new understanding of jihad. Karam

Zohdy, Assim Abdul Maghed, and Abod Zoummar, who had written the Constitution of Al-Jihad (1986), had also argued for ending the violence and a peaceful resolution to the conflict with the government in Egypt. Gabriel notes that many thought their statements were coerced by concern for the colleagues who were being rounded up and killed by the Egyptian police. Still others found support in earlier teachings of the Prophet, who taught that jihad had to be tempered if the situation required it: where saving other Muslims would require making peace. He quotes Hamdi Abdul Rahman for the teaching that Islamic law itself gives Muslims the right to change legal opinions according to the circumstances (170). Gabriel makes the argument from history that except for the 7th century, the great majority of time, including during the Ottoman Empire, Muslim's lived together in harmony. Sufism, a more pacifist version, was a major segment of the Sunni population. It has only been in and through the fundamentalist teachings since the 1970s, that various political leaders (Saudis, in the case of Sunnis, and Iranians in the case of Shia) have promoted jihad against other Muslims (169–173).

Absent in Gabriel's analysis is a discussion of forgiveness. Others, however, are starting to collect stories of forgiveness: some dealing between Christians and Muslims and others between Muslims. For example, Diana Darke, in her marvelous book *My House in Damascus: An Inside View of the Syrian Crisis*,[39] she details the stories of "Rashid the Lawyer, Marwan the shopkeeper, Maryam the bank manager and Abu Ashraf the caretaker," of kindness and human decency in the face of extreme violence. She shows us the possibilities are there, and the stories she tells appeal to the human decency in us all. She writes, "The overwhelming majority of Syrians have a strong sense of solidarity and sympathy with their fellow victims and suffers. How else could they have survived 4 decades of the Assad regime and the Ba'ath Party as remarkably as they have?" (195). Her book leads off with following widely known Arab proverb that says if Allah did not forgive, who would be in Heaven.

Post-conflict complications come from the fact that in many conflicts the rebels refuse to mediate on the broader issues because they demand justice for multiple past atrocities.[40] The first step in opening up forgiveness would be to find a way to get them in the same place.

Matching victims and perpetrators?

The practical difficulties of setting up a mediation, either by the UN or with the help of an NGO (like The Carter Center [TCC]), are familiar to mediators, whether they are involved in an international or a domestic mediation process. However, while familiar, these difficulties must be carefully considered and dealt with strategically. Ideally, the parties would need to agree to send representatives to talk together. The more legitimate these representatives are, either because of the selection process that identified them or because they have earned the respect of their parties, the better they will be able to enter into lasting agreements.

These representatives would need to be assured that any agreements reached would be subject to their individual consent and will be ideally subjected to a process that will ensure legitimacy and transparency to guard against being bribed or otherwise bought off by outside influences. During the mediation itself, the representatives would be urged to be respectful to each other and listen to each side's positions. The expectation of the parties would be that each would make its case against the other and then see if there was room for the parties to find a process for resolving their dispute and taking steps toward making peace.[41]

In many cases there would be a number of challenges arising out of either a clash of religions and clash of historical perspectives, but also from the psychological forces at work when enemies sit down to make peace. Heads of state demand the continued right to protect the state (and the elites in their group) and to rule. These demands are often made preconditions to any agreement. One side might insist that the settlement insures that the state will be secular and that guarantees need to be provided in the constitution that no religious group impose its religious views on the others. Another group might insist that the state be constituted as a religious state: either a Jewish state or an Islamist state subject to Sharia. Right away there might be a clash that involves questions of religion and fundamental democratic principles.

Moreover, there would be conflicting stories to tell. Innocent victims of past violence will want justice. From rebel perspectives, innocent victims of a state's security forces will have grievances that will need to be addressed. A state's failure to protect minority groups, failure to provide for religious freedom, and failure to institute democratic changes causes a loss of legitimacy. Heads of state will want recognition that they have a right of self-defense to protect the government from acts of violence by insurgent groups who have not been acting through the structures provided in the government. Furthermore, the fear that religious rulers will institute greater religious oppression on the dissident groups left in the state will need to be addressed.[42]

It should not be surprising in this context if a party ascribes motives to the actors and characterizes or demonizes the actors and their actions as evil.[43] At a minimum the parties interpret their experience as being perpetrated by an unjust and evil opponent. Of course, the rebels will point to the government's indiscriminate use of violence against minority groups as justification for its own use of violence in opposition. The various opposition groups will likely import a collective righteous motive to justify their conduct. This motive will soon become part of the *myth* of origin that explains the history of their movement's identity.

Issues of justice become intertwined with the psychology of the mediation processes for addressing the dispute. Whose story is "right"? Who has more rights violated and more victims that need redress? Does retelling the disputing party's story lead to empathy or only to stronger commitment to redress the harms done to and by the opposing party? These are some of the practical challenges any mediator would face.[44]

Many mediators remain uncertain about what role they are expected to play during the presentation of these case statements.[45] The mediator may be troubled that past atrocities committed against innocents show a level of hate and a lack of respect that will not bode well for the groups living side by side in the future. Also, on an international stage, the mediator may be expected to play a role in helping the parties break out of tired cycles of making demands on each other and setting up preconditions to moving forward that then mean loss of face should any party back away from such demands.[46] In the real world, however, international mediators report that there are times, perhaps in most cases, where the case statements seem to result in a different effect.[47] Instead of building trust, the parties seem to become more passionate about the wrongs they experienced in the past. Their demands for justice seem to become more hardened. Instead of moving easily into a conversation about creative problem solving, they stay fixed on their demands and positions. Instead of talking in terms of shared needs and goals, each party seems only interested in getting the maximum they can from the mediation process.

Diplomacy teaches that making peace is hard work. Mediators are often tempted to try to get the parties to forgo opening statements altogether and move straight into bargaining, especially where they see identity issues in play.[48] Identity mediations often end in deadlock because the meaning the parties ascribe to compromising is that a compromise constitutes a denial of who they are. In other words, to compromise without redress will not only dishonor and disrespect the value of the person previously harmed but also cause the party representative to lose identity. In addition, if the opponents' history is left unexamined, it will be only that much harder for the parties to discuss forgiveness and reconciliation.

How can the rebels make peace with a head of state after he is seen to have starved or gassed his own citizens? A mediator's suggestion to forgo opening statements may present the parties with a difficult choice. They may feel that the mediator is not sufficiently cognizant of the harm that has been done to the victims on each side. On the other hand, each side may be unwilling to hear and confront their own wrongdoings and instead want to move to problem solving, hoping they will not have to own up to their responsibilities. They may either feel coerced into giving up on the rights of victims or feel relieved that the process of mediation will help them avoid having to address their own wrongdoings. The mediator is caught in a desire to put the past aside in order to focus on making peace but is unsure whether in doing so, the parties will only be delaying the inevitable discussion of the atrocities that each side has committed against the other.

Mediation of international conflict provides examples of the problems in this regard. It doesn't take long for there to develop in any dispute opposing narratives about who is responsible for starting the dispute, who was the initial wrongdoer, and why the parties continue in conflict. It is tempting for mediators to see that the parties are not now ready or that will they may never be ready to put such grievances behind them. The disputes are labeled intractable. The parties are said to be not ready to make peace, or, the time is not *ripe* for them to make peace.[49]

Is there nothing to do but wait for one party to "win" or to wait for the parties to wear themselves out in the killing game, all at the cost of the lives of future innocent victims? Whether it is long-standing disputes like those between the Protestants and Catholics in Northern Ireland, or Israel and Palestine, or more recent disputes like Syria, rehashing who was at fault seems an exercise in futility. Often, even disputes seen as recent disputes may have roots in history. Yet by seeing the disputes as being rooted in history, Ricoeur finds a key to a transformative process.

For example, Syria's recent civil war might be seen as arising out of the Arab Spring. Or, it could be seen as a result of the long-simmering animosity between the ruling Ba'ath Party, and various Sunni tribes. Or it could be seen as the result of the artificial Sikes–Picot division of the Middle East between the French and the British after World War II, where tribes were split up into different states, secular ruling governments were formed, and these ruling groups stole the countries' resources and repressed the various tribes now trapped in the state's borders. In any case, it takes little time for the different sides to develop very different versions of the dispute's history and genesis. Such narratives become part of their traditions, or myths, that are said to define who they are. And even recent disputes have narratives subject to the many different formulations and demystifications. A trip through these different potential stories and causes can help demythologize each party's view of the dispute.[50] Again, such a demythologizing process will take time.

In any event, the hermeneutics of Paul Ricoeur can help the mediator use the parties' histories in a way that can both make peace and provide the pathway toward a more sustainable settlement that will more likely address the justice issues that remain. The shift is subtle but nonetheless transformative. In the right hands, the parties ought to be led to a deeper understanding of the complexity of their histories by examining what may be myth, what may be tradition, and what traditions they may be relying on in the retelling of their stories. Only then will there be a chance that they will be brought to the questions of whether the way things are is the way things need to be and whether the parties themselves bear any responsibility to end suffering and live into a better future. Again, though, the need for forgiveness and the requirements of forgiveness will likely present significant challenges for the parties to reach a lasting peace.[51] Ricoeur's hermeneutics provides a better understanding of why the language shift from position bargaining to problem solving can be transformative. Second, it provides support that exploring the identity narratives of the parties is vital to helping them imagine into the future a being that can be liberating. It facilitates the raising up of an examination of creative problem-solving solutions as a way of stimulating the imagination to explore new possibilities. Finally, it helps put on the table the possibility of forgiveness that is incentivized by possible gains that can come about by choosing to treat the other as not being fully responsible for the harm that has been done to victims of their actions.

Problem-solving mediators often urge the parties to use the language of problem solving, or interest-based negotiation, without really understanding what such a shift in language may bring about. The parties to disputes are most often naturally interest-based bargainers. They see the dispute – who rules Syria – as a zero-sum game. They bargain over ways for one to rule Syria in order to ensure each side's power to rule and exercise control over the country.[52]

What is clear is that Ricoeur's hermeneutics calls for the mediator to play a more active role in examining each side's narrative. The neutrality, moral character, and international standing of the mediator also become important. It is important to note here that Ricoeur's hermeneutics were developed from within religious communities where disputes had arisen over the interpretation of sacred texts.[53] Perhaps implicit in its efficacy was the moral standing of the mediator in this religious community. Perhaps peaceful resolution of such disputes often resulted after the mediator demonstrated the requisite empathy, respect, and staying power with the disputants such that that everyone could develop the safe spaces needed to engage his or her poetic imaginations.

What emerges is a renewed understanding of the dialogic nature of narrative. As discussed earlier, to Ricoeur, the crisis of modernity is the movement toward a schism between a calcified tradition and an a-historical utopia.[54] It is a mediator's ethical duty to engage in the strategic praxis sensitive to the concrete steps that need to be taken toward realizing what is "desirable and reasonable."[55] Most important, it is a mediator's ethical duty to seek to liberate the untapped potentialities of inherited meaning.[56] As a practical matter, how might the mediator help facilitate this effect?

We can see how developments in modern mediation theory correspond to Ricoeur's emphasis on language and imagination. Ever since Fisher and Ury's *Getting to Yes*[57] and Carrie Menkel-Meadow's description of ***problem solving***,[58] or ***interest-based bargaining***,[59] alternatives to position bargaining have been widely seen as a viable method for negotiations and mediation that can help break deadlocks in intractable disputes. Yet little care has been taken about why or how shifts in the language bargainers' use transform the negotiations from being adversarial bargaining between opponents towards a creative and trusting relationship between partners set on solving the problem. Paul Ricoeur provides the philosophical support for this theory by describing the relationship between language and imagination.

Problem solvers want the parties to instead see that they have interests that could be served by taking a different approach to the language they use to negotiate with each other. The mediator asks parties to consider what obstacles may prevent the parties from reaching a lasting peace. The mediator identifies threats to the security of the disputants, to their freedom of religion, to their economic well-being, and to their rights to develop their human potential. Seeing conflict as a problem that needs solving, they will first see themselves in history first but also in the present with responsibilities towards the future. By expressing these obstacles, the parties necessarily will learn that each side is seeking the same thing for themselves. Their interests can be reframed as common interests, interests that any human being has a right to pursue, or "shared interests."[60] They also see the security concerns as shared rights and correlative duties to protect each other from common vulnerabilities. As Ricoeur might have predicted, in putting their stories forward, their language provides for insight into that which is common, essential, shared, and fundamental to the human identity. Yet that recognition of the common or shared interests they might have, or the common or shared vulnerabilities, only can occur if the parties listen and are open to hearing each other's narratives.

As seen through Ricoeur's lens, the parties are not tricked by the language shift into seeing the game as win–win but are rationally drawn to a consideration of the benefits of cooperation and problem solving as they review each side's poetic narratives of moving from oppression to liberation. They will demystify and explore with more care their common history while also seeing in their traditions the heroic character of past actors and the imagination to renew and reimagine a better future.

Bearing witness to the oppression each has experienced leads one to ask whether each story would have been different had the oppression not taken place. What if the parties choose not to repeat oppressive conduct and cycles of violence, but instead choose to cooperate with each other to ensure that each group was liberated in its essential aspects and that the vulnerabilities – a lack of shelter, contaminated food, disease, polluted water and air – each experienced were guarded against?

The hope that strategies of cooperation provide greater benefits than strategies of totalitarian rule by one party over another[61] can take on a new reality through a Ricoeur-inspired mediation process. What free will and courage raise as a possibility makes the possibility poetically thinkable, and in being in the world, it makes the poetic imaginable and then makes it the ethical thing to do. It becomes not only more rational to cooperate, but the time for peace is also made ripe in the consciousness of the negotiators.

Distinguishing between adjudication and mediation

But what about the *rationality* lost by the loss of deterrence that occurs if the parties let each other "off" for the harms done to others? For example, won't a political actor who "gets away with" his acts of murder, or using gas on his own citizens, inspire others to do the same? If he gets away with such acts and maintains power what will deter other national leaders from using chemical weapons to weaken their opponents and stay in power? Doesn't the rationality of justice overwhelm any possible choice to forgive?

As discussed earlier, the meaning of forgiveness requires that the choices made by the parties are made by understanding their consequences as far as they can be determined. In short, forgiveness can only be voluntarily given and even then with an understanding of its consequences. Even though forgiveness is outside the bargaining process, it still needs to be explored through a transparent process for it to work. Forgiveness for the harm done seems irrational, or, at least non-rational,[62] when such forgiveness is granted without redressing those violations of basic human rights and thereby possibly encouraging future actors to commit similar atrocities.

At first blush, a UN mediator like Brahimi has an advantage over the adjudicator. After all, peaceful resolution of disputes is often reached through a formal court process that can take a long time. There, the parties go through a process where they first gather evidence to make their case. Then they carefully advocate through publicly telling their stories. They challenge and question the intent and motivation of the actors, through cross-examination, and then submit to a judge or jury who will render a judgment. They also submit to the judge for a determination of the appropriate punishment. Adjudication provides the due process for the redress of grievances and for justice.

Perhaps the parties know going in that the main purpose of mediation is to explore with the parties the options raised by the ability to do something extrajudicial, even possibly non-rational, forgiving and becoming reconciled to each other. But how exactly is this possible? We must look finally, then, more closely at the relationship between justice and forgiveness. Only then can we see how the mediator might facilitate this exploration with the parties and help them see the possibilities and limitations raised by considerations of forgiveness and reconciliation.

It might be tempting here to try and rely on social science for answers about what types of Truth and Reconciliation processes will work in what types of circumstances.[63] Preliminary findings suggest that forgiveness may be possible in some settings.[64] Yet the studies do not control for a number of important variables. For example, two conditions seem predictive of the success of TRCs. The first is whether the dispute is internal to a nation, usually between the ruling class and the oppressed minority. This seems to be one characterization of the conflicts that occur with a state – like in South Africa, Syria, or Israel. The second is the representative moral standing of those deciding to adopt a TRC process. Especially where the forgiveness is from an individual like a Nelson Mandela – someone who has experienced the atrocities for him or herself, and can reflect on the complex motivations of the parties committing the act – who chooses to forgive the perpetrators in the face of individual personal stories, then forgiveness seems to be something that can be adopted on behalf of other victims similarly situated. Where such conditions do not pertain, as in Sierra Leone, Liberia, and Kenya, experience suggests a very uncertain outcome. In other words, representative forgiveness requires a very unique forgiveness. It will usually lack the conditions of justice that will be required for true forgiveness to occur.

Again, Ricoeur's hermeneutics might suggest an additional process for TRCs in conflicts that involve parties with religious differences. Ricoeur has shown how the religious perspectives of the victims might be enlisted in order to raise the possibilities of forgiveness. The implication of this theory is that the fact-finding powers of the ICC, or some other watchdog NGO that has mapped the conflict, might be employed to help match victims with perpetrators in order that potential justice objections can ultimately be overcome. Ricoeur's hermeneutics have then raised a moral critique that should serve to enlighten and provide necessary preconditions to the use of TRCs and other community dispute resolution processes that attempt to serve as a pathway to a lasting peace.

In the case of conflicts in Syria, or Israel/Palestine/Gaza, or Kenya, where the first criteria seems to be in play, the question will be whether a representative like Nelson Mandela or Desmond Tutu will arise who can speak with any moral authority about the people's willingness to forgive and to be persuasive to others about the need to forgive and reconcile. Perhaps such figures can arise during the peacemaking process and step forward to express the deep longings of those struggling in the midst of violence to bring about its end. Perhaps such heroic individuals are not born with the requisite character of a Mandela or a Tutu but are born out of the great need for someone or some group to step forward and exercise the leadership and courage it takes to make peace on behalf of the victims with those very people who committed the acts of violence, all in exchange for saving the lives of future victims.[65]

Even then Ricoeur's hermeneutics will caution against reliance on such a process for a meaningful and sustainable peace, instead arguing for the need for a more formal fact-finding process. Meaningful forgiveness, in the end, will only be able to occur with the input of victims and their families. As discussed earlier, for victims to grant forgiveness they will need to know what they are forgiving. Their choice to forgive will need to be made in light of an understanding of the level of "evil" committed by the perpetrators of these atrocities. While self-defense will likely be a part of the narrative of these actors, the proportionality of the use of force and the level of knowledge that innocents were the likely target of violence will need to be considered and the legal punishment contemplated before forgiveness can be granted. Without these moral conditions in place, any reliance on a TRC will likely be seen as mere manipulations by outside political actors.

In the case of many present-day conflicts, all is not lost, and a hybrid TRC process can yet create the conditions where meaningful forgiveness can occur. This is because modern investigative technologies can be enlisted to match victims with the alleged perpetrators of atrocities. Where the UN is involved, it can enlist the investigative arm of the International Criminal Court, or other authorized investigative group (like those UN officials investigating the use of chemical weapons) to gather the necessary information that can eventually match the perpetrators of war crimes with their victims. In the case of Syria, this is not a far-fetched proposition.[66] As a result, one can yet imagine a process that will provide for meaningful forgiveness to take place. Yet, again, the party representatives will need to understand that such a process will follow the making of peace. They will need to understand that if they are to have true peace and justice, they will need the courage to submit to the choices of victims as to how perpetrators are to be judged.

Conclusion

Ricoeur's philosophy has provided a number of useful lessons for international peacemakers. It reaffirms what hard work making peace will be for the parties, yet it also provides more direction to the mediator as to what role the mediator should play in helping the parties present their cases to each other. Its successful implementation will require careful listening and an understanding of the role that history, Tradition, and myth play in each party's narrative. It will require a gentle dialogic process that will seek to place each party as a responsible agent in his or her own history. It will seek to draw the parties into rediscovering the religious narrative that sees God the Creator as requiring that they seek to live in peace and shalom with their neighbor.

In addition, mediators must show the parties that while they may share the fundamental insight of the non-rational nature of their humanity and of their common vulnerabilities, whether in the uncertainty about their past narratives or the unknowability of what their God wills for them, they are taking very real risks. Yet they are called to live imaginatively into the future by seeing the role that courageous forgiveness might play. Finally, the mediator will lead the parties to a deeper understanding of what a just forgiveness might look like and help those making peace to design meaningful processes enabling victims to forgive.[67] To that end, the mediator will be better able to describe the important conditions under which reconciliation can take place. The mediator can finally involve the peacemakers in an informed discussion of the role of a TRC and the important place that victim forgiveness will play in the process.

Notes

1 Paul Ricoeur, *Figuring the Sacred: Religion, Narrative, and Imagination*, trans. David Pellauer, ed. Mark I. Wallace (Minneapolis: Fortress Press, 1995), 100–1.

2 In a well-known passage in her book *The Human Condition*, Hannah Arendt wrote, "the discoverer of the role of forgiveness in the realm of human affairs was Jesus of Nazareth." Hannah Arendt, *The Human Condition* (Garden City, NY: Doubleday Anchor Books, 1959), 212–19. Nicholas Wolterstorff defends Arendt's claim of Jesus's origination of the idea of forgiveness from the argument that pagan ethicists also wrote of forgiveness by showing that forgiveness has in it the idea of the "fallenness" or imperfection shared by all of humanity in relationship to a perfect God. Nicholas Wolterstorff, *Justice in Love* (Grand Rapids, MI: William B. Eerdmans, 2011), 162, 178–90, 251–6.

For Islam forgiveness is something Allah does after a person confesses or recognizes their sin to Allah, then dedicates themselves not to repeat it, and does whatever they can within reason to rectify the harm they have done to others. Qur'an, *Surah al-Zumar*, Surah 39:53, 54. Then Allah will forgive. Sheikh 'Abd Allah b. 'Umar al-Dumayjî, "Allah forgives all sins . . .," *Islam Today*, accessed October 5, 2014, http://en.islamtoday.net/artshow-299-3181.htm. Forgiveness is the same for Sunni and Shiite followers.

For Jews, reconciliation with God comes from adherence to God's law. Above all, contrition and compassion are the indispensable coefficients of all rituals of forgiveness, whether they be expiatory sacrifices, Leviticus 5:5–6, 16:21; Numbers 5:6–7, or litanies for fasting, Joel 2:12–14; I Samuel 7:5–6. The Day of Atonement is a day to make oneself right with God by sincere confessions of wrongdoing and making atonement for what has been done. Leviticus 16. Part of getting right with God is to be right with one another. See *Mishnah Yoma* 8:9 ("Yom Kippur atones for transgressions between a person and God, but for a transgression against one's neighbor, Yom Kippur cannot atone, until he appeases his neighbor"). So some believe it important to ask for and give forgiveness, especially around certain seasons of the year.

For Christians, God is said to forgive sin through the reconciliation that occurs through the death of God's son on a cross. Forgiveness is something that God does, or that God's son Jesus grants. In these situations since God is believed omniscient; God already knows a person's sins before it is confessed. Inherent in God's forgiveness is an understanding that God has made a fair determination of the circumstances or facts that constitute a person's sin. God then is willing to forgive when one sincerely confesses their sin and looks to commit him- or herself to make amends for what he or she has done. See Wolterstorff, *Justice in Love*, 161–3, 257–82.

Ultimately, then human forgiveness can be patterned to the religious in terms of God's will. It can be viewed as if it is called for or required by Allah, Yahweh, or by the command of Jesus, or out of the example of Jesus's death for the forgiveness of sins of the world.

3 Wolterstorff, *Justice in Love*, 165. Even a cursory review of twentieth-century philosophy shows us that there is no easy consensus on the idea of God containing in it that such a being would want you to live in peace, shalom, or harmony with each other. Ibid.; See also Nigel Biggar, "Forgiveness in the Twentieth Century: A Review of Literature, 1901–2001," ed. Alistair McFadyen and Marcel Sarot, *Forgiveness and Truth* (Edinburgh: T&T Clark, 2001).

4 Wolterstorff, *Justice in Love*, 169. Biblical passages do suggest that God forgets sins and removes them as far as the east is from the west. Psalm 103:12. On the other hand, biblical descriptions of God as omniscient suggest a contradiction or paradox in God's nature in this regard.

5 Here I borrow heavily from chapters 15 and 16 of Wolterstorff's *Justice in Love.*

6 Jeffrie G. Murphy and Jean Hampton, "Forgiveness and Resentment," in *Forgiveness and Mercy*, ed. Jeffrie G. Murphy and Jean Hampton (Cambridge: Cambridge University Press, 1990), 21, cited in Wolterstorff, *Justice in Love*, 165.

7 Richard Swinburne, *Responsibility and Atonement* (New York: Oxford University Press, 1989), 85, 87n8, cited in Wolterstorff in *Justice in Love*, 165. For our initial discussion I use Swinburne's definition of forgiveness but try to keep cognizant of the "feelings" aspect of forgiveness in making recommendations for mediators to help the parties see the need for monitoring of any settlements that depend on forgiveness. In fact, the feelings aspect of forgiveness may be why the sustainability and practical workability of peace that depends on Truth and Reconciliation Commissions are so difficult.

8 Here human forgiveness might be seen as being different from God's forgiveness, because God might choose to forget, or remove the transgression out of mind (as far as east is from west). Again this forgiveness may be God choosing to treat the person as if not responsible even though God, being omniscient, does not forget what was done.

9 Marcia Baron, "Justifications and Excuses," *Ohio State Journal of Criminal Law*, Vol. 2, No. 2 (2005), pp. 387–406.

10 Steven Pinker, *The Better Angels of Our Nature: Why Violence Has Declined* (London: Penguin, 2012), 488–9.

11 Ibid. Pinker calls this the Moralization Gap, that is the gap between what really happened and how the victim retells what happened. Ibid., 490.

12 See ibid., 491.

13 Simone Zurbuchen, "Vattel's Just War Theory and the Law of Nations," *History of European Ideas*, Vol. 35, No. 4 (2009), pp. 408–17.

14 Ibid.

15 Ibid.

16 The law contributes distinctions in this regard that may be helpful in providing the ability of the parties to do this reframing. Victimization may occur because of a mistake. It may occur as a result of negligence, or of gross negligence, or may be intentionally done on the mistaken belief that it is the "only" way for the defense of other innocents to be secured. It may be truly evil, or indiscriminate. In that case it may be virtually impossible for the "reframing" to occur.

17 Pinker, *The Better Angels of Our Nature*, 488–96, 506–7.

18 I see it necessary to deal with this distinction between adjudication and mediation, in part, because of what might be embedded in human history and experience of the common law. If looking at chimpanzees for clues of how humans have evolved

to their resolution of disputes, then surely the common law also provides insights for the conditions of justice, and then forgiveness.

19 On this point I draw from arguments made by my colleague, Tim Terrell. Terrell argues in his article "Confronting the Legal Meaning of Religious Faith: Wringing Universal Values Out of Pluralism Itself," in "The Foundations of Law," supplement, *Emory Law Journal* Vol. 54, No. S1 (2005), pp. 337, 342–3, that human beings, as humans, must have limitations or they would be God. This argument may not work for Hindus, who believe they have reached the higher divine state. Still Hindus, too, believe that their divinity frees them from the body and liberates them to choose to rise above fear and even self-preservation. Sastri Shakuntala Rao, trans., *The Bhagavad Gita* (Bombay: Bharatiya Vidya Bhavan, 1959); Bhattacharyya Kalidas, "The Meaning and Significance of Social Revolution and of the Idea of Progress in Hegelian, Marxian and Indian Philosophies of History," in *Contemporary Indian Philosophies of History*, ed. Telliyavaram M. P. Mahadevan and Grace E. Cairns (Calcutta: The World Press, 1977), 61–92.

20 See Paul Ricoeur, "Critique of Religion," in *The Philosophy of Paul Ricoeur*, ed. Charles E. Reagan and David Stewart (Boston: Beacon Press, 1978), 213–23, cited in Kearney, *On Paul Ricoeur*, 29 ("The problem of false-consciousness could only appear by way of a critique of culture where consciousness appears in itself as a doubtful consciousness").

21 My argument does not rely just on moral philosophy but also on both psychology and theories from evolutionary biology that humans seem to be able to use ceremonies and rituals as part of a process that can lead to forgiveness. There seems to be some evidence from the fields of evolutionary biology and game theory that forgiveness is possible and may be helped along by rituals and ceremonies of forgiveness. Yet the exact conditions for the emergence of forgiveness have been left for further research and explanation. This paper seeks to unpack those further conditions using the mediation/adjudication paradigm, which seems to be important for peaceful resolution of disputes. Experience with mediation/adjudication in the domestic forum provides valuable insights in this regard. See, for example, William J. Long and Peter Brecke, *War and Reconciliation: Reason and Emotion in Conflict Resolution* (Boston: The MIT Press, 2003).

22 American Psychological Association, "Forgiveness: A Sampling of Research Results" (originally compiled for the occasion of the 59th Annual DPI/NGO Conference United Nations Headquarters Midday Workshop, Forgiveness: Partnering with the Enemy, 2006, Reprinted 2008), 31.

23 Ibid., 26–33.

24 Ibid., 31. See Eriwin Staub, "Constructive Rather Than Harmful Forgiveness, Reconciliation, and Ways to Promote Them after Genocide and Mass Killing," in *Handbook of Forgiveness*, ed. E.L. Worthington, Jr., (New York: Brunner-Routledge, 2005), pp. 443–60. See generally, Erwin Staub, *Overcoming Evil: Genocide, Violent Conflict and Terrorism* (New York: Oxford University Press, 2011).

25 Eriwin Stuab, "Healing Reconciliation, Forgiving and the Prevention of Violence after Genocide or Mass Killing: An Intervention and Experimental Evaluation in Rwanda," *Journal of Social and Clinical Psychology*, Vol. 24, No. 3 (2005), pp. 297–334. One such process could be a Truth and Reconciliation Commission. While not the focus of this book, our study may also provide some modest proposals for better ensuring the workings of Truth and Reconciliations Commissions as vehicles to a just peace.

26 Ibid.

27 Barbara Benedict Bunker, "Managing Conflict through Large-Group Methods," in *The Handbook of Conflict Resolution: Theory and Practice*, ed. Morton Deutsch and Peter T. Coleman (San Francisco: Jossey-Bass, 2000), 566.

28 Wolterstorff, *Justice in Love*, 55.
29 Ibid., 167. Wolterstorff describes the prerequisite context for forgiveness as follows: a victim can offer forgiveness only when that person did that victim wrong, the victim rightly believes that person was to blame, the victim continues to remember the deed and who did it, continues to condemn it, and feels resentment or some similar negative emotion for the act directed at the person who was to blame for committing it.
30 Recently the International Criminal Court has dropped charges against Uhuru Kenyatta, president of Kenya, after it decided that it did not have sufficient evidence to proceed against him for his actions in fomenting violence in the aftermath of Kenya's 2007 elections. Some see the ICC's failure to prosecute to be result of Kenyatta's refusal to cooperate and intimidation of witnesses testifying against him. Marlise Simons and Jeffrey Gettleman, "International Court Ends Case against Kenyan President in Election Unrest," *New York Times*, December 6, 2014, p. A7. As a result, perhaps the principal disputants could take the chance or gamble that the ICC would likely not have the interest from the international community, or the political will to follow through on their jurisdiction.
31 Here again, I draw on the wonderful insights provided by Wolterstroff's *Justice and Love*. Challenges to forgiveness from justice go to the heart of what it means to mediate peace as opposed to adjudicate the resolution of a dispute. In other words, the challenge to Ricoeur's theory is a jurisprudential philosophical challenge that comes out of the logic of the law, or "rights"-based theory. Especially, where what is required is either one or both of the parties "forgive" the other party and put the past behind them in exchange for the end of the conflict, there will emerge a tension between peace and justice. Experience suggests that making peace may be at the cost of doing justice, Wolterstorff, *Justice in Love*, 161; thus, making peace will seldom seriously redress the violation of rights that the parties have endured. In other words, we explore if a mediated settlement ever works out the tension between peace and justice and therefore enables the parties to make a lasting peace. In a way, Ricoeur's task is similar to that taken on by "process" theology in its attempt to resolve the tension between biblical interpretation and experience, or, as Ricoeur would say, between traditions and the future. Process theology is a derivative of John Whitehead's process philosophy. See generally, Bruce G. Epperl, *Process Theology: A Guide for the Perplexed* (New York: T&T Clark, 2011) (This is the best in-depth introduction to process theology available for non-specialists). I think Ricoeur does resolve this tension, but as Ricoeur explains, the connection is orchestrated only if the parties see the possibilities raised by the poetic symbols embedded in historical discourse and the demands of justice.
32 See Adam Habib, *South Africa's Suspended Revolution: Hopes and Prospects* (Johannesburg: Wits University Press, 2013).
33 Ibid. See also, http://myhero.com/hero.asp?hero=N_Mandela3_dnhs_US_2010.
34 See text, supra, Part II.
35 Take, for example, Syria. President Assad would not submit to the mediation process, and now the situation has been exacerbated by the possibility of his use of chemical weapons. Now that Syria's involvement in a peace process seems to have been coerced by the Russians, new opportunities to mediate a peaceful settlement may again be presented with the UN's involvement in dealing with Syria's chemical weapons. "Syria Says It 'Welcomes' Russian Proposal to Place Chemical Weapons under International Control," *CBS News*, September 9, 2014, www.cbsnews.com/news/syria-says-it-welcomes-russian-proposal-to-place-chemical-weapons-under-international-control/; cf. Michael Singh, "On Syria, Diplomacy and Coercion Are Not Mutually Exclusive," *The Washington Institute*, May

14,2013,www.washingtoninstitute.org/policy-analysis/view/on-syria-diplomacy-and-coercion-are-not-mutually-exclusive (opining Russia will only push so hard).

At the time of this writing a peace conference has been called by the UN, mediated by UN mediator Lakhdar Brahimi, to see if he can help the parties attain peace. At the time of this writing a peace conference has been scheduled between the parties in Geneva for January 2014. Nick Cumming-Bruce and Rick Gladstone, "Talks on Ending Syria's Civil War to Begin in January," *New York Times*, November 26, 2013, sec. A11. At the same time, the conditions (including whether Assad will be allowed to attend) for discussing peace are being negotiated among the US, Russia, and Syria, and no agreements have yet been reached. Nick Cumming-Bruce and Rick Gladstone, "Diplomats Fail to Agree on Details for Syria Peace Talks," *New York Times*, November 2013, sec. A6. But will any settlement be sustainable without forgiveness being a necessary part of the process, and will any agreements to forgive be truly just?

36 Mark A. Gabriel, *Into the Mind of an Islamic Terrorist: Why They Hate Us and How We Can Change Their Minds* (Lake Mary, FL: Front Line, A Strang Company, 2006) (hereinafter, Mind of Terrorist,

37 Ibid., 65–79.

38 Mind of a Terrorist, *infra*, note 238, at 65–6.

39 Diana Darke, *My House in Damascus: An Inside View of the Syrian Crisis* (London: Haus Publishing Ltd., 2014).

40 For example, Palestinians in Gaza have refused even a ceasefire because they demand some recognition that by refusing to adequately open its border, Israel has subjected Gazans to prison like conditions since Israel withdrew in 2003.

41 The author was an invited observer to several NGO convened groups working with various Syrian groups from 2011–2014.

42 In the case of the Syrian conflict the parties will need to see how each puts cosmic importance into the stories they tell about each party's past. Assad's representatives will likely describe how his father and his Arab Ba'ath Socialist party took power in an effort to fight a common enemy, Israel. See International Council on Security and Development, "Syria: A Way Forward" (2012), pp. 34–37, 43, www.ecoi.net/file_upload/1226_1362407083_icos-syria-a-way-forward-dec12.pdf.

The Sunni side is complex and evolving. The Sunnis make up large segments of the populations of Iraq and Egypt, and portray themselves as being unfairly oppressed by the military governments there. Disaffected Sunnis in these countries are drawn to join the rebels in Syria, where they see an opportunity to advance their cause. Sunnis opposition in Syria draws support from the Saudis and other Gulf states. Ibid., 82–3; see generally Line Khatib, *Islamic Revivalism in Syria: The Rise and Fall of Ba'thist Secularism* (London: Routledge, 2011).

43 "Syria Peace Talks Struggle in Switzerland," *Aljazeera*, January 28, 2014, www.aljazeera.com/news/middleeast/2014/01/syria-peace-talks-resume-switzerland-2014128113919556687.html.

44 Experienced mediators are often troubled about what to do with a party's opening statement of their positions about how they see the dispute, what their positions are about, and what they want in order to settle the dispute. These opening statements are sometimes called "clopenings" – a play on words used to describe the two times where a party representative addresses the decision-maker, whether judge or jury, in a common law trial, that is, the opening and closing statements. In an international mediation the parties' representatives often make one presentation that includes the parties' proof about what has happened to them in the past that includes their legal or moral arguments – including violations of their fundamental rights as individuals and groups – and what they are entitled to in the settlement of the dispute.

Some schools of thought suggest these "clopening" statements are counter-productive. All the talk about rights and justice sets up irreconcilable conflicts and a logic that can lead the parties to choose continuation of war to the hard work of making peace. Too often, representatives of the parties become stuck in the trap of identity politics. After making an impassioned plea for their side's victims they feel that if they make peace with their enemy, they have dishonored the innocent lives lost in the past, and in process they often feel that who they are as a group has been diminished by even a willingness to talk and listen to the other side's view. Give me liberty or give me death! "I would rather die than forgive and forget what has been done to innocent brothers, wives, children, and parents, caught in the violence of the past."

Thus, some argue that, it is better, instead, to avoid the psychological effects of making such statements and start with a *mapping* of the conflict, that is, to first identify all the parties or stakeholders in the dispute, then identify *shared needs* for cessation of conflict. These shared needs typically include security, economic development, food, education, health care, and justice for past wrongs. The next step in this "opening statement-less" approach would be to then identify obstacles to obtaining those shared needs. According to this approach it is better to never give the parties the chance to state grievances, as they only harden into positions and demands that run against building up of the relationships needed to engage in problem solving.

On the other hand, the practice of starting mediations with the parties giving an opening statement persists. This is because even with a mapping approach, the parties will eventually get around to discussing what obstacles stand in the way of reconciling differences. Inevitably the parties will discuss the justice of the matter: that making peace raises difficulties in addressing that which is due the victims and their families for what has been done to them. So, while not now an *opening statement*, there is still inevitably a need that at some point each side should make a statement of a demand for justice for what has been done to innocent victims by the opposing party in the past.

These statements of the case for justice are now believed to serve a number of conflicting purposes. On one hand, these statements can be useful as a way for each party to hear how the other side sees the dispute. Like in a classic adversarial process each can then challenge any part of the dispute that they think has been misrepresented or mistakenly communicated to the mediator. It sets the parties in an adversarial mode, challenging their opponent's case, and arguing that whatever was done was done with the intent to protect their own group from violence done to their innocents. On the other hand, the case statements may serve to help each side listen to the other side, and thereby show respect, and perhaps a little empathy, especially if they respond by restating the important facts the other side has presented, and expressing empathy, at least as far as recognizing the sincerity with which the other side may see the facts.

These latter purposes are all the more important in facilitative mediations, where the mediator is a neutral and does not make findings of fact or rulings of law. The facilitative mediator facilitates communication and helps the parties explore their options, rather than adjudicate the dispute. As a result of this facilitative role, it is less important for the mediator to learn all the relevant facts than for the parties to somehow be led into a process whereby they can start to work together to find resolutions to their problems. The psychological purpose of the case statements then seems to be of paramount importance. It gives the parties the sense of empowerment from having presented their cases, to have been listened to, and to have been heard, and so may legitimate the party from the status of terrorist or outsider, to victim, or person with rights that need vindication.

45 American Bar Association Section of Dispute Resolution, *Task Force on Improving Mediation Quality: Final Report* (2008), 8. https://www.americanbar.org/content/dam/aba/migrated/dispute/documents/FinalTaskForceMediation.authcheckdam.pdf
46 Seminar, Advanced International Negotiations, discussions with co-teachers.
47 Ibid.
48 Examples of Identity mediations include the mediations involving Northern Ireland, over a Palestinian State, and more recently, in Sudan.
49 Dean Pruitt and Paul Olczak, "Beyond Hope: Approaches to Resolving Seemingly Intractable Conflict," in *Cooperation, Conflict, and Justice: Essays Inspired By the Work of Morton Deutsch*, ed. B. B. Bunker and J. Z. Rubin (1995), 83.
50 Bunker, "Managing Conflict through Large-Group Methods," 566.
51 Imagine you are UN mediator Brahimi, President Jimmy Carter, President Bill Clinton, or some NGO mediator called to mediate between the parties in Syria. You need to be aware of how your instincts of where and how to start might lead you astray. You would also need to be aware of how using Ricoeur's concepts of tradition, traditions, and a tradition, might help you bring about a better process.

Your instincts might make you expect to start talking at the point of asking the parties what they are willing to do to make peace. Yet such a starting point places the parties into an adversarial posture. The question presupposes a game being played between the parties over the goods available to each side. Such a game is thought of as a zero-sum game. The mediator wants to eventually transform this game into a win–win game, where the parties see advantages to more goods if they can learn to be in relationship with each other.
52 Where the *game* is framed as each side trying to give up as little as possible and get as much as can be in return, the focus will be on protecting and posturing and survival. Assad wants to stay in power, and protect his group, and maintain their privileged positions in society. The insurgent groups want the same things; they want security for their group, as well as power, and freedoms in those areas that are keys to their identity. See also, Reinoud Leenders, "How the Syrian Regime Outsmarted Its Enemies," *Current History*, Vol. 112 (2013), 331–7. Therefore, while Assad argues for the role of the Alawites in maintaining a secular peace between Sunni and Shia religious groups, the religious groups represented in part by their most extreme members (who may feel they have earned a seat at the table because of the sacrifices they have made in the civil war) will argue that Assad has lost his right to rule and that they must control the new Syria.
53 Ricoeur, *Figuring the Sacred*, 68–72.
54 Kearney, *On Paul Ricoeur*, 67.
55 Ibid.
56 Ibid.
57 See *supra* note 52.
58 Carrie Menkel-Meadow, *Dispute Processing and Conflict Resolution: Theory, Practice, and Policy* (Burlington, VT: Ashgate, 2003).
59 Harvard Law School, Program on Negotiation, accessed on October 19, 2014, www.pon.harvard.edu/tag/interest-based-negotiation/.
60 Tal Y. Katz and Caryn J. Block, "Process and Outcome Goal Orientations in Conflict Situations: The Importance of Framing," in *The Handbook of Conflict Resolution: Theory and Practice*, ed. M. Deutsch and P. Coleman (San Francisco, CA: Jossey-Bass, 2000), 279.
61 The work of Acemoglu and Robinson gives authority for an argument that totalitarian regimes are a principal factor in creating cycles of violence that usually lead to the nation's failure. Daron Acemoglu and James A. Robinson, *Why Nations*

Fail: The Origins of Power, Prosperity and Poverty (New York: Crown Publishers, 2012), 398–402.

62 Terrell, "Confronting the Legal Meaning of Religious Faith," 337.

63 See Oskar N. T. Tomas, James Ron and Roland Paris, "The Effects of Transitional Justice Mechanisms: A Summary of Empirical Research Findings and Implications for Analysts and Practitioners," (University of Ottawa, Centre for International Policy Studies, CIPS Working Paper, 2008), http://aix1.uottawa.ca/~rparis/CIPS_Transitional_Justice_April2008.pdf; Long and Brecke, *War and Reconciliation.*

64 Thomas, Ron, and Paris, "The Effects of Transitional Justice Mechanisms," 12–13.

65 At a recent meeting of concerned Syrians sponsored by TCC, NOREF, Swiss Peace, and the Danish government, there was much discussion of whether victims of Assad's secret police could ever forgive.

66 United Nations Mission to Investigate Allegations of the Use of Chemical Weapons in the Syrian Arab Republic, *Final Report* (December 13, 2013), https://unoda-web.s3.amazonaws.com/wp-content/uploads/2013/12/report.pdf (reporting UN findings of Assad's use of chemical weapon outside of Damascus on August 21, 2013, on March 19, 2013, in Northern Syria, at Khan al-Assad and in the northwest town of Saraqeb on April 29, 2013); see also Somini Sengupta and Rick Glandstone, "U.N. Reports Attacks Using Chemicals in Syria," *New York Times*, December 13, 2013, p. A12. The report notes that Syrian governmental officials deny using chemical weapons in what they describe as a rescue operation in Khan al-Assad, after Al Qaeda took over in Khan al-Assad threatening civilians there. The UN report is based on its investigators' interviews with area doctors and various individuals involved in the area, as well as victims.

67 Peacemakers can provide for reconciliation in the following ways:

- Design adjudicatory processes to later sort out the justice issues.
- Rely on a Truth and Reconciliation Process but one that will have specific moral protections in place for victim forgiveness:

  1 Providing a separate mediator for mediating between specific actors and their victims.
  2 Increase forgiveness potentiality with mediation that employs Ricoeur's use of history that in turn taps into the creative imagination. (This is especially important for religious victims who may see their particular identity as being part of a Creation story where they are called to be responsible to God's creation)
  3 Providing victims a forum to judge the sincerity of these actors confessions of guilt.
  4 Providing victims the opportunity to make the decisions whether to forgive. Such decisions will nee.d to be reached by consensus of the victims after the full mediation process has been employed.

- Otherwise insure future access to an adjudicatory process for future grievances. This may be a community adjudicatory process but one that will make determinations on findings of fact and setting punishment according to victim/community decisions about the type of punishment. Forgiveness could be a feature of these forums and specifically suggested by the peacemaking process as an option that could promote long term integration.
- One option could also be to remove these actors from the community and separate them in a way to ensure that the victims will not ever need to live with them.
- Another could be to allow victims to opt for a community-based reconciliation process that is triggered by the perpetrator's willingness to confess guilt

and then provides for a process for assessing remorse and relies on a ceremony of forgiveness.

- Try Representative Forgiveness and Using Symbols of Confessions of Guilt.

Finally the peacemakers might be asked whether they are willing to give up on ever sorting out the justice issues in a gamble that people will forget about the past as they get focused on their future. Yet this option will need to be explored with a clear eye for the later violence that the parties will likely experience. Transitional Justice Institute at the University of Ulster, *Belfast Guidelines on Amnesty and Accountability* (Belfast, Northern Ireland: Transitional Justice Institute at the University of Ulster, 2013).

Part III

The potential impact of social media on peacemaking in Syria

7 Social media and conflict mapping in Syria

Implications for peacemaking, international criminal prosecutions, and for TRC processes[1]

It is the end of 2011, and David Crane, law professor at Syracuse University School of Law, is on to a new project. He is on the watch for evidence of war crimes being committed in Syria. He is experienced in such matters. He had been Chief Prosecutor of Charles Taylor at the International Special Tribunal for Sierra Leone. He knew the importance of gathering the right evidence if war criminals were ever to answer for their crimes. He decided to organize the Syria Accountability Project, (and the related, "Syria Deeply" group), to coordinate with various human rights organizations and researchers to help gather and preserve evidence

David and his team noticed earlier on that they were being assisted from the inside Syria through courageous postings of YouTube videos by witnesses on the ground. There were videos of many different sorts. Some were posted by victims or families recording evidence of Syrian government bombings. Some even showed unexploded barrel bombs and contained ordinance markings. Others, as we have seen, were of demonstrations, and then government responses. Others were of victims of chemical attacks.

Some were from various opposition groups. ISIS, and other groups, were posting recruiting videos that showed them committing beheadings and bragging of other atrocities. These were many and varied. These researchers started to categorize these videos according to their group identification. Some new groups tried to form and they also turned to the internet for recruiting purposes. Many videos contained horrific scenes designed to recruit young Muslims to their cause. Some showed images of weapons so clearly that one could even see the weapons' model numbers. Such information could be used to potentially track where the weapons had come from (US arms depots, Russians, Iranians, Saudis, Kurds). Researchers collected them all and would later learn that the videos could also be searchable using face recognition software.

Other humanitarian organizations were also noticing the postings. At first these researchers set out categorizing what they were seeing by groups and regions and religious or political allegiances. At Stanford a group started to map them to times and dates when the news reported violence occurring. One use of this mapping was that it allowed researchers to help advise humanitarian groups as to find safe passages to deliver aid. With the rise of ISIS, it also allowed for the tracking of messages, border crossings, and numbers in the group, to both raise concerns for how the internet was being used for recruiting and also in looking at the video to be able to track where it was being recorded (whether on location, or from a studio). Eventually it also led to the production by others of counter-videos to try and dampen the impact and effectiveness of recruiting messages.

Soon, David was leading a team of folks in tracking videos, whether posted on You Tube, Facebook, Twitter, or other social media. Soon, Syria stood out to the international community as the first conflict being tracked and recorded on social media. There are also reports that a group of Syrians, which calls itself the Syrian Institute for Justice, has also been collecting evidence.[2] The UN has also been involved in the evidence collecting business since it instituted a UN inquiry in 2011. In February of 2017 it intensified its efforts to collect evidence and coordinate potential prosecutions of those who may be now fleeing Syria.[3]

The use of social media presents some interesting challenges and dangers that will impact the peacemaking and transitional period in Syria. First, it will impact the choices that will be made as to whether there will be instituted formal or informal dispute resolution proceedings. I will argue that Syrians should adopt a mix of formal judicial proceeding for those to whom it does not grant amnesty in order to get a peace agreement and an informal – yet principled – mediation process during a transitional period for disputes that arise from actions from rebel group activities. These latter disputes should be followed by a process with a hybrid court for those who do not gain adequate resolution of their disputes through the informal mediation process. This option will best deal with the lessons learned in other Middle Eastern post-conflict transitions and, while presenting some risks, will best provide for the need for peace at the local level under a transition period that is relatively easy to execute, has a low cost, and avoids the glare of publicity. Applying both pragmatic and principled criteria (peace first, low cost, easy to execute) will best guide Syria as it seeks the stability needed to grow the peace process into its next stage of development.

Second, I will show how recent developments in the use of social media (with special emphasis on YouTube videos posted to Facebook, Twitter, and attached to e-mails) and the ability of various international monitoring groups, including the UN, to have mapped the conflict in Syria will greatly assist the efficacy of the hybrid option by not only providing the proof needed for assessing an individual's criminal responsibility but also making possible a more meaningful informal mediation process. Strategic use by the UN and its partners of these conflict-mapping capabilities presents new potentials for realistic reconciliation between individual victims and those who have committed criminal atrocities. Even if no peace transition is actually constituted in Syria, this section should be useful in providing an analysis of transitional options in similar countries in the Middle East that are in a process of transitioning from a dictatorship to a democratic form of government.

Part I

Much of what will end up dictating the final choice of which political option the Syrians end up with will be the result of the conditions for the ending of hostilities. For example, if the parties themselves meet and reach a settlement, without interference from the international community or regional powerbrokers, then the political transition will likely look much different than one brokered by the Russians or, in turn, one brokered by the UN. Still, it is important to understand the merits of each option so that the parties can be aware of the risks and trade-offs that are made under each one. After disposing of the first three options rather quickly, the chapter explores in more depth the options that are available if the international community, and the UN, in particular, becomes the broker of the eventual peace agreement between the Syrian government and the opposition groups. As I showed in earlier chapters, where the UN becomes involved the dilemmas between making peace and setting up the conditions for transitional justice become more acute. The UN as an institution must weigh the future deterrent impact on rogue states if it brokers a peace with impunity for past atrocities. It will help explain why the hybrid option will likely be the option that emerges where the UN is involved in the peace process.

What to do with the Syrian military and security forces during the transitional period: removing versus ignoring

Syrian decision-makers will be informed by recent events in Iraq, as well as the ongoing efforts in transitional governance processes taking place in Egypt, Libya, and Tunisia. Whatever power-sharing or transitional mechanisms the Syrians eventually employ during their transitional period, they will face the question of how to best ensure the long-term stability of the country while at the same time not repeating the mistakes of other transitions brought about by power-sharing arrangements with the military. In other words, Syria will have to find a way to avoid creating the circumstances that now threaten the stability of governance structures in Iraq, Egypt, and Libya if, indeed, Syrians choose to eventually adopt a democratic form of government.

Iraq, Egypt, Libya, and Tunisia present a wide spectrum of how to best set up a transition process after a conflict and a regime change. At one end of the spectrum is Iraq, which allegedly tried to clean house by removing much of Saddam Hussein's military personnel from the Iraqi military at the end of the war.[4] Some have made the argument that how the Iraqis dealt with Saddam Hussein's military and security forces in the aftermath of Iraq war has what led to the instability the Iraqis now face.[5] A number of former Sunni/Hussein military leader are now involved in ISIS, having been summarily initially dismissed by the coalition government[6] and then reintegrated into the Iraqi military, only to finally be once again cut out of the military during the Maliki presidency.[7] Many now criticize the Iraqi government (and the US) for not paying adequate attention to what should have been done with the more than 90,000 mostly Sunni military personnel during the post-conflict transition.[8] Some of the Sunni tribal leaders who had past Iraqi military experience were thereafter formed into a group called "the Awakening" to help the US and Iraq government fight Al Qaeda.[9] The Awakening forces were paid, trained, and armed by the US.[10] Thereafter some of these

Sunnis left the Awakening and eventually joined ISIS, having felt snubbed and excluded by Maliki's Shia government.[11] The lesson from the Iraqi experience for peacemaking in Syria may be that the Syrians should not take steps to exclude or remove or treat differently all of Assad's military and security forces, particularly considering how to integrate members of opposition military groups into the Syrian army; otherwise, they will potentially form a potent force for instability going forward.[12]

On the other end of the spectrum are the transitional structures used by Egypt, Libya, and Tunisia in the aftermath of their recent revolutions. In Egypt, the Muslim Brotherhood negotiated with Egypt's Supreme Military Council after many in the military had grown tired of Mubarak, and granted it immunity for any role it played in past atrocities.[13] Having granted amnesty, it did nothing to prevent the military from reasserting power. After a brief period of a Muslim Brotherhood–led government, the Egyptian military stepped in and took back control of the country.[14] The Military Council has, once again, taken control of the country and has recently taken a series of steps that suggest its desire to put stability ahead of democracy.[15] The lesson appears to be that without sufficient guarantees that the military leadership will not reassert itself, Syria will run the risk that the Assad military will return to power.

Make no provision for dealing with military or security leadership

In the case of Libya and Tunisia, no provision was made as to how the past military leadership was to fare during the transitional period. Kaddafi's military was destroyed, so there was no one left to restore order during the interim period.[16] The Libyan failure to try to resurrect or reform a new military may have created the sources of instability that have returned the various tribal groups to violence.[17] On the other hand, in Tunisia, not making express accommodations with the military seems to have worked out quite well.[18] In Tunisia, the existing military tacitly agreed to submit to the decisions of the "Constituent Assembly," confining itself to taking actions against jihadists and gasoline traffickers.[19] In the Tunisian case, the transitional period only provided for a legislative body to rule on any issues that arose during the transitional period, and its peace agreement never dealt explicitly with past criminal actions by the government.

Some look to Tunisia for an example of an Islamic state that has resisted the forces of radicalism and that has continued to hold together as a secular democracy that is committed to religious freedom, under the auspices of secular constitution. Again, there are important differences between Syria and Tunisia that must be factored into the situation in Syria. In Tunisia's case, the transitional period was supported by a strong labor movement capable of shutting down the government if the unions did not like the radical direction of some of its more extreme actors.[20] It was also supported, ironically, by a tradition of a more conservative use of military power in the hands of its previously ruling dictator, Ben Ali.[21] Tunisia's military and security services did not have the same tradition, capacity, and reputation for dealing ruthlessly and violently against its citizens as those of Syria.[22] The Syrians might wonder, then, whether the situation in Tunisia is likely to be predictive of the results of the kind of transitional structures used by the Tunisians or whether the mostly Alawite security forces in Syria would act more like the Egyptian military, should the leadership in a transition period start to turn against them. Without a strong labor influence, or other social-political movement, to counteract the Syrian military's involvement, not dealing directly with military leaders is likely to later derail the transition period.

The war crimes of Assad's military and security forces and the International Criminal Court

Should the transitional plan for Syria include an appeal to the International Criminal Court, as was done in Liberia and Kenya in the wake of conflicts there? The transitional government that might be negotiated in Syria could include a power sharing agreement that might contain provisions that commit the country to a number of UN resolutions.[23] In the case of Liberia, these included an agreement that past and potential ongoing human rights violations will be submitted during the transitional period to the ICC.[24] Its Comprehensive Peace Agreement (CPA) also included a provision that membership in opposition military groups would not exclude these from taking part in the political process.[25]

The capacity of an international criminal court (first the International Criminal Court for the former Yugoslavia [ICTY], the International Criminal Tribunal for Rwanda [ICTR], the International Criminal Tribunal [ICT] for Sierra Leone, and now the International Criminal Court [ICC]) to successfully prosecute past heads of state is mixed. By 2003, the time of the Liberia CPA, the ICTY had prosecuted a number of government leaders who engaged in war crimes under the Rome Statute, including Slobodan Milošević, and so Liberian peacemakers had precedent to expect an international prosecution of Charles Taylor.[26] After getting Kenya to turn Taylor over to the ICC, the ICC secured the conviction of Charles Taylor but did not successfully bring to judgment any other member of the military leadership in Liberia.[27] The ICC has since issued warrants for the arrest of Omar al-Bashir of Sudan[28] and Uhuru Kenyatta of Kenya.[29] This time, the ICC failed to produce convictions of these Presidents, though it spurred on successful Kenyan prosecutions of lesser political and military figures.[30] The ICC has announced it will no longer prosecute Uhuru Kenyatta and Omar al-Bashir because of a lack of cooperation from the international community.[31] Still, the ICC remains a major force in potentially bringing to justice at least some of the country's leadership for its promulgation of war crimes against its civilian population. What will be necessary in order to make this happen is either for the Security Council to back the ICC's efforts or for the Syrians themselves to decide to submit to the jurisdiction of the court.

Since the backing of Russia is unlikely,[32] the issue is whether the Syrian opposition forces can get the Assad regime to agree to a transitional government without giving at least some amnesty to some of its leaders. The ICC lacks jurisdiction (Syria is not a signature to the Rome Statute[33]), absent the transitional government making a request for its help (like in the case of Liberia or Kenya).

The situation for Syrian peacemakers will be made all the more difficult because the peacemakers will face enormous resistance to giving Assad these assurances. Such resistance will come from victims and the families of victims of Assad's government's war crimes. In addition, resistance will come from some members of the international community that will likely not be willing to support the Syrian transitional period if it appears that the Assad government will be granted impunity for any of its past war crimes.

The legal case against Assad seems pretty strong should the ICC be granted jurisdiction. Assad has now been at war with his own citizens since 2010. He or individuals in his government are likely responsible for a number of war crimes and, at a minimum, they have much explaining to do. UN High Commissioner for Refugees (UNHCR) reports that close to half of the Syrian population (10.6 million out of a country of close to 22 million) has been directly affected by violence since the start of the civil war.[34] Over 6 million people have been internally displaced.[35] Additionally, 3.8 million Syrians have already registered as refugees in the UNHCR.[36] The Syrian Observatory for Human Rights reports that more than 200,000 Syrians have died in the conflict as of January 1, 2015. Of these, 17,719 were civilians, and more than 3,000 were children.[37] Over 1 million Syrians have been wounded.[38]

In addition, the Assad government faces allegations of the use of chemical weapons against its citizens and in its use of barrel bombs,[39] which are said to kill indiscriminately and which, therefore, violate standards of humanitarian law. In addition, there is substantial evidence that members of the Syrian security forces have engaged in torture, kidnapping, and murder.[40] Even before delving into social media resources, the case against Assad can be made out. Take, for example, an Amnesty International report concerning torture and hangings by the Syrian government at its Sednaya prison.[41]

Amnesty International's findings are estimates with wide variability. These findings place executions of detainees at between 5,000 and 13,000 over a four-year period at Sednaya prison (reporting for 2011 to 2015). The prison is located just outside the city of Damascus, and Amnesty International was able to interview a combination of former detainees, as well as former guards and doctors and other staff, to come up with its estimates. The report quotes one prison doctor as saying the prison was operating as a "slaughter house."[42] Nighttime was when the killing would take place. There were reports that killings were done en masse and on a schedule. Groups of 20 to 50 were taken from their cells and walked to the basement of one of the jail's two main buildings. There they were hanged. The bodies of the victims were brought to a hospital for registration before being dumped into mass graves on military land. According to the report, the hangings often took place twice a week, usually on Mondays and Wednesdays.

The Amnesty International report anticipates that the Syrian government might claim these were not political prisoners but terrorists and criminals. In addition to the mass executions, interviewees were asked about whether the prisoners were subject to judicial proceedings. The interviewees reported that most were subject to phony trials, lasting just 1 to 3 minutes. These often occurred shortly before being executed. The blindfolded prisoners only found out about their death sentences minutes before being killed, having initially been told they were being transferred to a civilian prison.

The report says that the night time executions were done as a way of keeping most of the staff and daytime guards from being directly involved in the killings. Of course, they would know something was amiss the next day when the prisoners were gone. Some interviewees reported that while there might be some room for deniability amongst some staff, high-up Syrian officials know about the practice. It would be interesting to know the names of these officials. Perhaps they can be identified for later criminal or other proceedings.

The mass hangings were not the only humanitarian crimes reported by Amnesty International. Their report contains horrific accounts of torture and abuse suffered in the prison. It details detainees being deprived of food and water, as well as being subjected to routine beatings and humiliation. Multiple interviewees also told Amnesty International that prison officials sexually abused detainees and forced them to rape each other.

Although the report only went up to 2015, Amnesty International says that there was no reason to believe the extrajudicial killings and other abuses have stopped. The report argued it was likely thousands more detainees have been killed in the last year. Amnesty's report implores the UN to take steps to ensure that the practices have been stopped. It hoped that issuing the report might cause Assad to change his behavior.[43]

As we will see, the evidence for these acts includes and is enhanced by the use of publicly available social media postings.[44] This is particularly true with the latest incident of Assad's use of chemical weapons. Assad denies having used gas. He says it was done by others: outsiders. But as we discussed at the outset, the videographer filming the cloud of gas noted the sound and sight of government aircraft.

Most damning is the evidence gained from YouTube videos. For Syrians now concerned with how to make peace while not creating impunity for the Syrian regime for these past acts, the exchange is difficult: which is more important, to make peace or to secure justice for past victims? They may be looking for a different process that will provide sufficient guarantees to some of the top leadership to end the conflict but still hold out the possibility of a process that will at least shed light on what had been done by the government and why against its own citizens.

One possibility would be to turn to the process used by South Africa in its transition away from an apartheid government. There, the transition period included the use of a Truth and Reconciliation Commission (TRC).[45] The South African TRC, therefore, merits receiving a hard look to determine whether its use might be appropriate for Syrians.

A Truth and Reconciliation Commission

Between the extremes described earlier (cleaning house and negotiating immunity or effectively giving the military a pass by not taking any action against it) some have argued instead for the transitional structures used by South Africa.[46] In South Africa, the military was not given immunity for past war crimes, but South African opposition groups, led by Nelson Mandela, agreed to give up on a formal criminal prosecution if the South African government agreed to submit to a Truth and Reconciliation process to deal with past criminal acts.[47] The TRC agreement provided for the possibility of amnesty if an individual came forward and told the truth about what happened.[48] South Africa is often held out as the most successful transition between apartheid and democracy, as it was able to maintain its military power structures, and yet its military eventually succumbed to the authority of its new president, Nelson Mandela.[49] South Africa's transitional period was orchestrated through the legal vehicle of an interim constitution, which set up a five-year period of power sharing, but then led to the adoption of a new constitutional democracy when F. W. de Klerk resigned in the third year of the transitional period and Mandela formed his majority government. The South African military stood behind Mandela and submitted to his executive authority even though de Klerk resigned.[50] Some attribute the success of this period to South Africa's immediate use of Truth and Reconciliation Commissions.[51] They attribute to the TRC the impetus for at least delaying somewhat the African National Congress (ANC) and its desire for revenge, leading instead to a gradual reconciliation that is still working itself out in South African's law and politics.[52] Could such a transition be worked out in Syria between the Assad government and the rebel groups?

Potential difficulties with a TRC in Syria

International advisors caution Syria on being too quick to hold up the relatively successful transitions to democracy that occurred in South Africa because of the substantial historical and political differences between Syria and the South African situation.[53] Syrians might worry that there were several additional factors that led to the success of the transitional period. First, the courage of de Klerk to initially seek out Mandela as a bargaining partner is now missing on the part of Assad's governmental leadership. A second reason the South African situation is different from Syria's was Mandela's moral standing from which he could make the claim for himself and for other victims that South Africa needed peace more than it needed justice. Again, who among the Syrian opposition has the standing of a Nelson Mandela? Third was the role that Desmond Tutu and the church played in arguing for an end to apartheid. Finally, South Africa was uniquely left alone during its transition period: the regional powers in the Middle East are unlikely to follow suit in in the case of Syria, where there are a number of regional players with various stakes in the successes or failures of different groups vying for power. The Iranians are said to have too much to lose should Assad fall, supporting the Shia groups and their offshoot, the Alawites;[54] the Saudis support Sunni Salafists;[55] and the Turks and Qataris support the Muslim Brotherhood.[56] Without Russian and US involvement, there is a fear that a removal of Assad will result in a power vacuum and fear all the tragedy which will most likely follow, brought about by the situation created by a failed state.[57]

In any event, what seemed essential to what South Africa achieved was a trade that was made during the peace process between seeking justice against those who had orchestrated apartheid and doing what was necessary to make peace and work for a transition towards an integrated society. As Desmond Tutu famously once said, what South Africa needed was "the truth, more than justice."[58] His intent was evidenced in his leadership in the writing of the South African Truth and Reconciliation Preamble.[59] Importantly, the South African TRC was expressly provided for in the enactment of the new South African constitution.[60] As a result, South Africa's TRC avoided the legal trap that otherwise exists when TRCs are created independent of the nation's founding documents, namely that any later prosecutions arising from the TRC's processes are extra-legal, thus rendering the TRC with no jurisdiction.

The question will be whether the Assad regime will ever agree to a transitional period that uses a TRC. On one hand, it is hard for any rational actor to admit that it is unwilling to face a Truth and Reconciliation process. After all, to refuse such a process implicates that the actors themselves realize that their explanations or confessions are not likely to be met with a sympathetic response. Their refusal to participate might mean that they know their violent acts against civilians to fight terrorists will only take them so far, when their actions had an impact on so many innocent civilians and were applied so indiscriminately as to violate all notions of proportionality and just war theory. Either they should feel like they can explain their justifications for the use of force (they were ordered to take their actions by superiors who have since been granted amnesty, or were so overcome by fear and concern for themselves and their love ones that they hated to do what they did and now ask for forgiveness) or they will likely have to admit that their acts were raw exercises of power that disregarded the dignity of the Syrian population and put their own needs ahead of the needs of innocent Syrians.

The dilemma Tutu poses between *Truth* and *Justice* is one that TRCs have struggled with ever since South Africa. Some have sought justice following the TRC processes, claiming that individuals did not speak the truth, or that they did not do so with remorse, and so it was still the purview of the TRC to recommend subsequent prosecutions.[61] Some even sought to use statements by expatriates, given in confidence, as the grounds for future prosecutions of individuals for war crimes.[62]

Difficulties with TRCs in Liberia, Rwanda, and Kenya

Yet, despite the successes of South African's TRC, subsequent TRC processes in Liberia, Rwanda, and Kenya have floundered.[63] The ability of prosecutors in these countries to bring evidence against defendants has been compromised by the passage of time, the difficulty of getting witnesses to step forward and testify, and for failures in the capacity of the courts.[64] In other words, the dilemma postulated by Desmond Tutu, that truth will be sacrificed for justice, seems to continue to be real because the ability to get justice has been compromised by the atrocities themselves. The dilemma seems to be based in part on the belief that producing evidence of war crimes is a very difficult and time-consuming process that is likely to produce little in the way of what would constitute admissible evidence in a court of law.[65] And so making that tough trade between truth and justice seems required by the very nature of the atrocities: that those in power will be able to either avoid the accounting for what they did, because either there are so few survivors or those surviving will not be willing, or able to come forward to give evidence for what was done to them.

Still the example of South Africa suggests that where the pressures for peace take precedent, (such pressure for peace could come from Russia and/or Iran – would Russia or Iran be willing to grant Assad asylum?), then those left behind may prefer to face a TRC process with the promise of amnesty than the ICC or some existing Syrian court structure that will likely be run by opposition judges. Without such pressure, the Syrian regime will likely insist on some arrangement like that granted to the Egyptian Supreme Military Council, agreeing only to sit on the sidelines and have the right to become involved again should it feel threatened or for the "good of the Syrians generally." One option might be to require that the military leadership submit to some specially designed hybrid military tribunal if they are interested in seeking to maintain leadership positions. That way, each individual Syrian would have to decide for him- or herself whether their continued exercise of power would be able to withstand the scrutiny of a judicial process.

If one assumes a working Supreme Constitutional Court or Supreme Court of general jurisdiction, sufficiently independent of the executive branch, might such a body serve as the arbiter of past or ongoing acts against the state and its citizens?[66]

As we have seen in Chapter 4 use of the existing legal frameworks (1973 or 2012 constitutions) presents significant challenges. Who will sit on such courts? Will these courts have the capacity to try these individuals for past crimes? In answer to the latter question, new developments in modern evidence-gathering techniques suggest that with some minor support by the international community, the capacity of the Syrians to try individuals subjected to the jurisdiction of Syrian courts is not only possible but is even likely to produce both due process for the accused and also the evidence necessary to convict those who committed such atrocities. There are significant risks to the continued peace during the transitional peace process if these national and/or regional courts refuse to prosecute either Assad or his regime leadership or if they simply prosecute but ultimately find no evidence of wrongdoing.

An interim process presents different kinds of challenges. Vital to the success of these interim arrangements are the establishment of oversight mechanisms and a separation of powers structure that protects against a strong man returning to power. It also protects against a minority sect that, once in power, would seek to override the majority/minority rights of other sects or religious groups.[67] At a minimum, some provision in the agreement should rule out the use of "emergency" powers by the executive (or Supreme Military Council) during the interim period.

Zimbabwe is an example of a cautionary tale in this regard. Following its crisis in 2008, it adopted an interim agreement on the model of Kenya, but without a sufficient mechanism for oversight during the interim period.[68] The President had reluctantly signed the agreement and did not abide by its terms and principles.[69] To provide against this possibility, interim arrangements might include the establishment of a Transitional National Assembly and a Transitional Judicial Council, together providing the necessary checks and balances over the Transitional Governing Body.

How these oversight bodies might be constituted is worth a close look. For example, one option for Syria is to use transitional oversight bodies like those used in Cambodia[70] and provided for in the Dayton peace accords.[71] Of course, these transitional bodies were imposed by the international community after there had been a forced regime change.[72] Still, the various regional powers might demand a new power-sharing arrangement to end the conflict, and Syrians themselves could turn to the international community for help. Both of these peace agreements (Cambodia and Dayton) included representation from the international community: from the UN Special Representative of the Secretary-General in the case of Cambodia, or a "high representative" from the international community in the case of Dayton.[73] These served as "guarantors" of the peace agreement.[74] A further recent example of the role that the UN can play in investigating and providing proof for war crimes comes in its investigation into Assad and Hezbollah. The UN tried five Hezbollah members, in absentia, for their killing of former prime minister Rafiq al-Hariri of Lebanon and 21 others.[75]

Of course, President Assad may have significant objections to giving up power in this way during the interim period. Still, the principles for governance during the interim period might provide sufficient guarantees for the safety and security of the president himself. In addition, the agreement should make clear that the oversight body and its members will be both neutral and principled, ensuring that no side use force or violence to bring about its goals. In other words, the principal purpose of the oversight committee would be to provide a forum for the mediation of disputes between the parties by insisting on the (1) non-violent and peaceful resolution of disputes occurring outside of the glare of publicity and (2) moving the parties along to the end of the transition period, when democratic processes and a new constitution can take over. In addition, one option that might be used during the interim is a TRC-like process that is designed for the resolution of disputes involving the leadership of the military and security forces. This might provide enough "truth" about what was done by the military during the civil war to help the country move past the war and to start to take constructive actions toward a peaceful future.

Whatever the dispute resolution system is chosen by the Syrians for disputes between the Syrian people and the military leadership, there still remains to be determined what dispute resolution systems during the interim period should be employed at the local levels. What will be the processes that will deal with Syrians who engaged on behalf of opposition groups, or ISIS, and remain in Syria? In addition, the interim period will need to provide a system for handling disputes that will inevitably arise between those who stayed and those who left during the civil war and to hold accountable any who engage in violence during the interim period.

Syrians who committed atrocities on behalf of opposition groups or who engaged in murder, extortion, or kidnapping for criminal gain may remain in these communities post conflict. The capacity of Syrian courts to handle these disputes will likely need to wait until after a new constitution has been enacted and judges can be appointed. In the meantime, Syria may choose to empower and support its local assemblies, Sharia courts, councils, and governing bodies in handling disputes that occur in those communities. Civil service organizations (CSOs) should ready an effort to train and support these local bodies in mediated solutions, if possible, to deal with the acts committed during the war. One option is to use Rwanda-style Abunzi proceedings that use community standards for determining the facts, use sanctions that emphasize compensation over retribution, and use community rituals that may produce meaningful truth telling, opening up the real possibility of victim forgiveness.[76]

Syria might adopt a dispute resolution process similar to that used in Iraq in the aftermath of the war that removed Saddam Hussein to deal with real property disputes that arose between those who stayed and those who left during the war.[77] A US Agency for International Development (USAID)–backed UN commission called the Committee for the Resolution of Real Property Disputes (CRRPD) was set up to mediate such disputes.[78] The commission trained Iraqis to mediate these disputes with a goal of keeping the parties from resorting to violence.[79] The program has since been integrated into Iraqi governance structures as the Iraqi Real Property Commission.[80] It gives the right to compensation from the Iraqi government to anyone displaced by a returning Iraqi.[81] By all reports, it has resolved most of the real property disputes without the parties ever using violence.[82]

Finally, the interim period might also provide for a back-up dispute resolution system should the informal processes fail to provide adequate resolution of disputes on a local level. A hybrid body might be employed for cases that need the oversight of an appellate review process. This second “backup” judicial body could operate like the old circuit courts, where it travels from place to place to place to hold proceeding on the most egregious cases. This body could be made up of Syrian judges, supported by international prosecutors and defense counsel, ready to step in should the dispute not be resolved to the satisfaction of the parties and to investigate the dispute using international standards of evidence gathering to ensure due process was provided to the accused.

In the end, this two-tiered system of dispute resolution best balances the need for peace against Syrian insistence on resisting impunity for those who committed crimes against civilians. Especially when backed by the ability of international NGOs to provide support to both formal and informal dispute resolution processes, the transition government can both continue to enforce the end of violent conflict and manage a dispute resolution process out of the public eye until the new governance structure is established. It also ensures that in coming out of the transition there will be rule of law processes in place to cabin the decision-making of local mediators. Without rule of law, as shown earlier, the temptation is for mediators to turn dispute resolution into a mechanism for promoting their own self-interests. That is another reason why a hybrid is a preferable system over a straight local mediation system.

Part II

Conflict mapping of social media and its impact on dispute resolution during the interim period

Since the start of the Syrian conflict, both victims and perpetrators of war crimes have been prolific in their use of video postings on YouTube, Facebook, MySpace, and Twitter.[83] In addition, Syrians have sent a large number of videos as attachments in emails to friends and acquaintances.[84] These videos depict not only atrocities committed against Syrians by the government, but also promote various armed group activities and the recruitment of new members.[85] As we have seen in Part I, the evidence provided through public source social media has changed the equation between truth and justice that may exit in any transition period following the Syrian civil war.[86] In particular, video evidence collected by NGOs like Human Rights Watch (HRW), the Organisation for the Prohibition of Chemical Weapons (OPCW), and other NGOs with conflict mapping projects raise important implications for the transition options discussed earlier.[87] Proof might already exist that the Assad government did use chemical weapons and barrel bombs to indiscriminately kill civilians during the war. Similarly, what was done by ISIS, or by various opposition groups, might also be sufficiently documented to prove that members of these groups committed war crimes. As a result of this social media evidence, the truth of what has been done and by who is known even before a peace agreement is reached.

Why a particular bombing, beheading, use of chemical weapons, or other indiscriminate killing was done may be in doubt, but these matters are subject to more discrete items of proof. If the person involved was ordered to commit a criminal act, there should be evidence of such an order. If President Assad denies knowing about what was done, he may be face the burden in court of presenting evidence of what he did to remove those who committed such acts from their leadership positions, or why he didn't investigate what was done and by whom.[88] At a minimum, such failure may subject the leader to criminal responsibility.[89] In any event, a decision to give amnesty to suspected war criminals in Syria in advance of these individuals agreeing to end the violence should not require the same blind trade between truth and justice that may have been required to end past conflicts.

The conflict mapping projects in some respects intensify the difficulties for the peacemakers between ending the conflict and establishing the rule of law in brokering a peace with known war criminals. Now the calculation is the hard-pragmatic choice between continued fighting and loss of future lives. To the extent that such a choice has implications for the victims of these atrocities, it is likely not within the authority of the peacemakers alone to make these difficult assessments or trade-offs. For a lasting peace, some provision needs to be made to hold those who did these acts accountable. As I have argued earlier (see Chapter 6, pp. 155–57), in order for amnesty and forgiveness to be granted in the peace agreement, the victims must know what they are forgiving, and then themselves be the ones granting forgiveness.[90] Without their input, the agreement may only delay questions of retribution, reconciliation, or forgiveness.[91]

One option for peacemakers is to put the choice to the individuals seeking amnesty whether they will submit their actions to an impartial tribunal or whether they will instead defer to the jurisdiction of the Syrian courts and the International Criminal Court as a condition of peace. Otherwise, the leadership of the parties might be given the option of submitting to the processes of a TRC or the local tribunal (like the Abunzi-like tribunals used in Rwanda), to work out reconciliation between those who committed the atrocities and their victims and victims' families.[92]

Because of the conflict mapping data, in setting up these various options for dispute resolution during the transitional period, the UN or an international NGO (like HRW or other human rights organizations not intimately involved in the peace process[93]) can now provide a unique supporting role in the work of both the formal court proceedings and the informal TRC or local mediation efforts. They can help provide the supporting evidence for these alternative forums to make the determination necessary and appropriate to each alternative: to make findings of fact of what happened during any alleged war crime, and to help the parties assess the nature of the act committed in order for the victims to make meaningful determinations of whether forgiveness is in the offing.

First then we will look at how admissible proof that can connect war criminals with their murders and with the victims of their crimes may change the peacemaking equation in dealing with the perpetrators of atrocities in Syria. We will look at admissibility standards in the US, the ICC, and in criminal prosecutions under present Syrian law to see what challenges will likely arise from the use of social media evidence. Then, we will look at how such evidence might also be used in TRC or local community mediation settings to create a greater likelihood that meaningful reconciliation will take place.

Use of social media videos and proof in formal judicial proceedings

Consider evidence recently collected by HRW concerning the Syrian Government's use of barrel bombs.[94] This evidence strongly suggests that Syrian government helicopters dropped barrel bombs embedded with cylinders of chlorine gas on three towns in northern Syria in mid-April 2014.[95] The question is whether such evidence would be admissible if provided to a judicial body like the ICC or a Western-style court. Allegations that the Syrian military used an industrial chemical as a weapon, an act banned by the international treaty prohibiting chemical weapons, would be important in proving a case against Assad, or his military leaders, of committing war crimes.[96] Syria had signed on to the international treaty in October 2013,[97] so it would difficult to deny that it knew such acts were criminal. What would remain for a prosecutor would be to prove whether a particular military leader, or President Assad, knew that the chlorine gas was being used or knew that barrel bombs were being dropped on civilians.

The HRW and OPCW proof is just a small part of the evidence the NGO community has gathered during the Syrian conflict. For example, an organization at Stanford University has taken up the task of mapping militant organizations, including ISIS.[98] Using special mapping techniques, over time it has been able to show the growth of various militant groups and map these groups' activities.[99]

In addition, consider what might be accomplished through a Conflict Mapping Project run by the UN to support later prosecutions regarding the treatment of women and children[100] and of the parties for war crimes or to assist in any process that would attempt to bring reconciliation between the parties and victims. If the UN is able to adequately segregate its mapping projects from it peacemaking efforts, it might be able to support post conflict transition periods, depending on what type of transition is negotiated. Where the peace agreement asks for involvement of the ICC, it can use the information it gathered as evidence, and where the peace agreement will use a TRC or other informal reconciliation process, it can use the data to support more meaningful confessions and possibilities for forgiveness.

Most of the data used in conflict mapping come from public-source social media.[101] There are some reports of over 700,000 videos posted by Syrians on YouTube that have been posted since the conflict began in 2011.[102] By coding and searching these videos, a map of the conflict can produce significant results. For a link to the undated map (checked as of July 2017), go to www.cartercenter.org/syria-conflict-map/.

Such a project would be able to coordinate videos with other reports of events at certain places and locations in Syria and map those reports with the information it is coding from the videos. Take, for example a news report on Al Jazeera News that ISIS had beheaded a Shia Muslim simply for being a Shia.[103] ISIS seemed bent on provoking Shias in Syria into an all-out civil war.[104] A mapping of the conflict would allow the mapper to identify the place Al Jazeera reported as being where the beheading took place as one that ISIS was involved in. It could confirm that another related insurgent group had posted a video of a clash where the Shia was said to have been beheaded.[105] It could then confirm that the video of the place where the clash occurred is consistent with the video of the beheaded body of a young Arab. The clash between the related ISIS group is easily identified by referring to that group's promotional video, as being one against a predominately Shia insurgent group. This would seem to corroborate that ISIS is taking responsibility for a real event: a war crime. An event that not only violates humanitarian law but also, at least for some Muslims, is a misinterpretation of the meaning of "jihad" and violates 75 Islamic verses from the Koran, attributed to the Prophet himself, which forbid such acts against minority groups.[106]

In 2011, a number of other research organizations[107] noticed evidence in social media. This was a relief to the humanitarian based NGOs who did not want to be seen as being responsible for gathering evidence against any one party in particular to the detriment of another. These other NGOs also became aware that there were an enormous number of YouTube videos from Syria that were being posted by various groups that seemed to be documenting various acts of violence in Syria and started gathering social media posts on the conflict. Early on, the quality was not that good. Most videos were taken from handheld devices like cell phones (the videos were poor quality, the camera moved and jerked throughout the video,[108] and the sound quality was also quite bad), but later in the conflict there was more professionally shot video filled with high-quality sound and special effects.[109] In fact, there were approximately 4,000 videos posted per week in 2013 trying to show the world what was happening in Syria.[110] Concerned that many of the videos were from civilians trying to get the world to know what was happening, some NGOs hired staffs of young Arab-speaking researchers to code the videos according to a number of criteria, including the type of group recorded; its mission; the place, time, and date; the weapons shown; and various information about victims.[111] They also did the same with "formation" videos posted by different rebel groups, which were trying to recruit disaffected Arabs and so were claiming responsibility for events that they may or may not have actually participated in.[112]

The problem conflict mappers recognized early on was how to use these videos to help map the conflict, and thereby provide information to the world and to humanitarian groups about what was occurring on the ground. How would mappers go about verifying and authenticating the information in these videos in order to help humanitarian groups determine who should receive funding and help, and who was likely a terrorist group? Of course, one way is to use the mindset of a prosecutor, and set out to code the videos according to time and place, whether they showed a clash (violence), force on force, chemical weapons use, shelling, improvised explosive devices, bombings, aircraft used, instances of crime, and/or killings. An investigator could also code the videos according to whether the videos were of civilians, or of military, the uniforms worn (deserters from the Syrian army?), the weapons they carried, their politics, the symbols they used to identify their group, and the narration that accompanied the video regarding why the group had formed. The higher the number of code factors, the more one can use mapping techniques to explore various relationships between these factors. One mapper has already recorded the existence of close to 6,000 different groups that have formed since the start of the civil war.[113] A conflict mapper could then map the rise and fall or the consolidation of many of these groups up to the present.[114]

Other conflict mappers could then search news stories and activist human rights organizations, as well as Facebook posting and Twitter accounts, to attempt to corroborate and authenticate what can be seen on the videos. They can also map the conflict by coordinating what they are seeing on video with the movement of refugees. These human rights groups might also enlist the help of a computer software maker, such as Palantir, Inc., to help them see the relationships between events, times, and places in the videos of a particular group or groups they are tracking. Palantir's involvement has been crucial in helping The Carter Center, for example, observe various relationships between the groups and the data that was being produced for their ability to give advice for humanitarian purposes.[115]

Much of what has been collected would be admissible in court. To be admitted into evidence, such materials must be properly *authenticated* in a courtroom proceeding by the fundamentals of due process.[116] The mapping project has included the gathering of sufficient evidence to support a finding that particular videos are authentic.[117]

A conflict mapper can potentially help authenticate the videos by providing evidence to identify and locate the witness who took the video, so long as that witness is also able to testify that the video looks like what they observed. That is the method used by Human Rights Watch. Additionally, taking witness's statements may be effective for confirming the authentication of the video by HRW but is not sufficient authentication in a later court proceeding unless those witnesses are also produced for their testimony authenticating the evidence. (The ICC may authenticate the video based on the testimony of unavailable witnesses but recognizes that such evidence is less reliable, and so a court may give the video evidence less weight.[118]) Where, instead, the witness is not produced, or where the video is not posted by the person who took the video, then the proponent of the evidence supports the reliability of the evidence using other evidence to verify the posting.[119] Of course, in the great majority of cases, either the eyewitness of what was taken on the video or the poster of the video may not be able to be located. This is not fatal to the eventual admissibility of the video in that the NGO conflict-mapping project designed to collect such evidence would most likely also gather the circumstantial evidence necessary that will likely still authenticate it as admissible evidence.[120]

When a witness is unavailable or uncooperative, proving that social media content was, indeed, authored by the user can be a slightly more complicated task. Due process, however, provides that circumstantial evidence, including "appearance, contents, substance, internal patterns, or other distinctive characteristics of the item, taken together with all the circumstances," can help to authenticate evidence.[121] Notably, the characteristics of the offered item itself, considered in the light of circumstances, afford a great variety of authentication techniques.[122]

Take for example a promotion video by ISIS that shows a beheading. First, its video posting is often done on a Twitter or Facebook page. Social networking sites can include a wealth of information, such as profile pages, posts, photographs, and video, as well as several types of metadata, some of which are not publicly visible.[123] Different types of social media evidence will require different indicia of reliability. For example, profile pages and posts may require sufficiently distinctive data, such as references about which only the author would have known.[124]

Circumstantial evidence visible on the social media site, if it provides enough content and context, also may be sufficient for authentication. This could include, for example, a combination of photographs, video, comments, e-mail addresses, and posting dates. Related data from other sources also may provide context to aid authentication, including email notifications of posting activity, and computer and account usage logs. Metadata, such as location, user ID numbers, IP addresses, and when messages were created or revised can provide context as well. Moreover, presenting this authenticating evidence through video or interactive demonstration software can help accurately represent dynamic information and provide a solid foundation for authentication.[125]

What would happen if the video has been taken down, or there is evidence that it has been obscured in an attempt to hide the identity of the original taker of the video?[126] Obviously, there are good reasons why victims may want to obscure their identity when initially posting the video. They may worry that the regime may itself be looking for evidence of victims so as to intimidate or prevent them from being able to bring evidence against the regime. How would such videos be authenticated? Again, the primary tools for authentication are the self-authenticating nature of the videos (that barrel bombs look like those in the photo, and chemical plumes look like the ones shown in the video) and then corroboration by other circumstantial evidence (serial numbers on the bomb can be traced to bombs sold by a known arms dealer to the Syrian government before the incident where they were used).

On the other hand, a tech savvy criminal defense lawyer would advise that any video taken by an accused be taken down ahead of any court proceeding. Any video a prosecutor produces for admission such a lawyer may then also attack by raising challenges to the legitimacy of its authentication. The defendant might show how that video can be altered and edited since it has been posted or even at the time of its posting. Application software, for example, can alter the metadata that accompanies any video posted on YouTube from its very first posting. The metadata can put a false time and place and date simply by programming the camera to initially record false meta information.[127] Other applications can be shown to add or remove images in a video by editing out or adding in other pictures.[128]

Circumstantial evidence can help in this regard. Expert testimony that examines the initial downloaded file may provide evidence that no such editing or obscuring software took place in the original posting. The absence of certain metadata tags can prove the negative: that these videos were not altered.[129]

Again, while other circumstantial evidence can likely be offered to overcome these challenges, archivists interested in authenticating a video they may offer at a dispute resolution hearing will do their best to download the original video when they first put it in their archives.[130] Archivists may use software such as Checksum,[131] which gives a proponent of the evidence an ability to provide a mathematical code when they initially download the file, to then show that the file they are offering as evidence is the same as that downloaded one. If the proponent can show that the download occurred before the defendant or someone else had a chance to remove or alter the file, then the proponent has a better case for authentication.

Social media evidence is most likely to be admitted at trial when it is obtained through formal discovery requests made to the opponent or accused subject to a legal search. Where such a process is impossible, thoroughly documenting and verifying the process and results of social media data collection can help the evidence survive authentication challenges.[132] The simplest method is to capture and preserve static images taken from social media sites. In addition, downloading the video to one's own system, and then documenting its download, can also be an important way to preserve it in its original, unadulterated state. However, these images may be difficult to authenticate without testimony based on personal knowledge.[133] A conflict mapper should create a system for downloading such files that will establish the use of a "custodian of records" that would be able to lay the foundation that the video is authentic.

Collecting metadata for use at trial may require specialized software. Printouts, screen captures, video saves, and most archive tools will not provide all the available metadata.[134] Working with Google, a conflict mapper might develop the tools to download and collect content to better capture and preserve the unique metadata fields associated with social media. Google has the technology to help a mapper establish authenticity by, for example, generating hash values (unique document identifiers) for collected social media items and automatically creating collection logs.[135]

Collecting data from social networking sites can also raise ethical concerns.[136] Essentially, NGO researchers should adopt the best-practices approaches in their collection of videos, so that they act like attorneys and take care to avoid conduct that could be considered "pretexting" or deceptive as proscribed by court rules of professional conduct.[137]

Beyond the unique issues of authentication and ethics, social media evidence also must clear evidentiary hurdles such as relevance and hearsay. Such issues, however, are generally more susceptible to traditional reasoning and evidentiary standards.[138] In fact, electronic communications, such as e-mails, lend themselves to novel uses of hearsay exceptions.[139] Hearsay is an out-of-court statement offered to prove the truth of the matter asserted. Exceptions include present sense impressions, excited utterances, and then-existing mental, emotional, or physical conditions.[140] Facebook status updates, public posts, chat transcripts, Tweets, and more lend themselves well to such exceptions. Litigators who keep these exceptions in mind may be able to find creative ways to overcome the hearsay hurdle to admissibility.

It is important to note, as a legal matter, that little help is likely to come from a prosecutor's subpoenaing of third party vendors like Google and others.[141] While the discoverability analysis is a product of the common law, there is at least one statute relevant to the discussion. In the US, the Stored Communications Act (SCA) limits the ability of Internet-service providers to voluntarily disclose information about their customers and subscribers.[142] Although providers may disclose electronic communications with the consent of the subscriber, the SCA does not contain an exception for disclosure pursuant to civil discovery subpoena.[143] The application of the SCA to discovery of communications stored on social networking sites has produced mixed results.[144]

Providers, including Facebook, take the position that the SCA prohibits them from disclosing social media contents, even by subpoena. According to Facebook's website,

> [f]ederal law prohibits Facebook from disclosing "user content (such as messages, Wall (timeline) posts, photos, etc.), in response to a civil subpoena. Specifically, the Stored Communications Act, 18 U.S.C. § 2701 et seq., prohibits Facebook from disclosing the contents of an account to any non-governmental entity pursuant to a subpoena or court order.[145]

The SCA does not override a party's obligation to produce relevant electronically stored information in a criminal proceeding.[146] To the contrary, a party must produce information evidence of a crime that is within its possession, custody, or control.[147] Thus, a US court can compel a party to execute an authorization for the release of social media content. With an executed authorization, a properly issued subpoena, and, in most cases, a reasonably small payment for associated costs, litigants can obtain all information related to a user's social media account.[148] How this plays out in a criminal proceeding is subject to debate.[149] What is left even more ambiguous is the ability of a court like the ICC, or some foreign national court, to exercise jurisdiction over these third-party vendors to turn over their electronically stored evidence as evidence of a crime. One could imagine that in the US, where national security interests were at stake, subpoenas to obtain such evidence might be forthcoming. One wonders whether an interim Syrian court's issuance of subpoena could have the same impact on Google's duty to produce its data.

The ubiquity of social networking sites and the amount of personal information they contain make them a fertile source of potential evidence. However, the cloud-based, transient, and collaborative nature of these sites poses challenges unique to these media. At the start of a case, international NGOs should consider methods of data collection that will help to ensure successful authentication. Carefully documenting the process of data gathering, and using sophisticated software where necessary, will help to ensure that the fruits of discovery are not excluded from evidence due to a failure of authentication.[150]

Under the ICC and under an inquisitorial system of justice, the use of hearsay and other evidence is governed by a broader standard of relevance. The evidence is not rendered inadmissible if it lacks firsthand knowledge, foundation, or authentication but is given less weight if it lacks any of these indicia of reliability.[151] As a result, in proceedings conducted by the ICC, less in the way of authentication for admissibility might be required. In addition, Syrian courts following civil court procedures most likely will also require less in the way of authentication of the videos. The alleged expertise of the court would allow it to make its own determination of the relevance of the video, with as much of a worry that it will be prejudiced by seeing the video before judging finally its authentication.

If the Syrians choose a formal judicial process, by using the ICC, a Supreme Constitutional Court given jurisdiction over those not granted amnesty, or a hybrid court, part Syrian and part international, it will have much of the evidence it may need to connect individual actors with individual acts of murder and indiscriminate use of force.[152] Of course, the defense might raise the "Nuremberg Defense": that the person responsible for using chemical weapons, or beheading a person, or killing innocent civilians, was ordered to commit the act by someone who would kill him or her, or kill his or her family, if he or she did not so act.[153] These will present important issues for the tribunal to decide and will raise the possibility that the defendant will not be found guilty. On the other hand, there would not be the possibility most often raised in past cases where the individual denies any knowledge of or involvement in the act allegedly committed.[154] For example, an NGO conflict-mapping project likely includes the coding and preservation of YouTube videos and their correspondence with evidence of other reports of surrounding events in similar locations. Such evidence presents the possibility that the truth will be known, and therefor that any reconciliation that might occur will be based on a better understanding of who did what to whom.

Use of social media evidence by TRCs or local informal mediation bodies

Just as in cases where a TRC process has gathered witness statements from victims, the use of corroborating evidence can test the truth of what a particular accused says at a TRC proceeding where he or she is allegedly confessing the extent of their past doings and sincerely asking for forgiveness.[155] Here, however, the corroborating evidence comes from public sources and so can be used without violating promises made to the witness during the gathering of the information.

The importance of this kind of evidence in judging the efficacy of an informal TRC or other local mediation process should not be overlooked. One of the most important trade-offs between formal and informal dispute resolution processes is whether the truth really can ever be known through either process, and therefore whether appealing to a person's desire to be reconciled will produce a true confession of guilt. The informal process is chosen in order to provide the individual accused with the choice of a voluntary confession or of facing a formal judicial proceeding. The reality has been that such a choice is often made with the almost certain knowledge that in refusing to testify, the formal process will be sufficiently delayed, and the capacity of the formal prosecution will be thereafter so compromised that that no proceeding will likely take place at all.[156] The ability of an interim period dispute resolution process to use the conflict-mapping information is helpful in two ways. First, it helps Syrians assess the truthfulness of what the individual accused may say they did during a truth and reconciliation process. Second, it allows for the identification of victims of those acts to directly confront the accused and to better create the possibilities of meaningful forgiveness and reconciliation. This is because true forgiveness and reconciliation will necessarily involve the victims of those actors' wrongdoing. The victims need to understand what was done and why to truly be able to choose to set it aside and forgive while not forgetting. The forgiveness cannot be mandated or dictated by the peacemaking process. For true forgiveness to occur it must be freely given. Otherwise, the resentment is likely to remain in the victims and their families and could very well cause a return to violence should the perpetrators stay in the locality.

For Syrian peacemakers, the use of social media may be an important consideration for deciding whether they will grant immunity for certain acts, who they will grant immunity to, and, in addition, what kind of dispute resolution systems they will adopt for what kind of disputes. It may very well suggest that immunity be given to Assad and key military figures in exchange for an end to the conflict and/or a set time for transitioning out of leadership or removal immediately from their involvement in the government and/or their leaving Syria altogether. For those that remain, the question will be more specifically what their individual responsibility was for the use of barrel bombs, chemical weapons, and torture tactics or the disappearance of other civilians. These can be tried according to formal procedures that provide due process protections to everyone involved. In the alternative, these individuals could face a TRC process. The individuals could make that choice knowing that some conflict-mapping evidence might be available that will test the sincerity of their confessions and the impact on victims' willingness to forgive.

For those others – ISIS, Al Qaeda, or other opposition group members – a different dispute resolution process might be employed. First, it must be recognized that the number of ISIS members who would likely remain or survive after the conflict is over between opposition groups and the Assad government is likely to be a small number. Those that do not die in conflict may try to flee to reform in a different setting. Those opposition groups members who remain will likely be those who have participated in the armed conflict in an attempt to fight what they may have thought was an illegitimate government at war with its own citizens. Still, there may be accusations that some of these persons were engaged in criminal acts and perpetrated war crimes during the conflict. Again, these individuals might be subject to dispute resolution processes if victims come forward to seek some sort of justice for what was done to them.

In these cases, a more informal local and/or regional-led dispute resolution process might be employed. The peacemakers might decide that these individuals should be brought before existing Islamic courts and local councils to consider what they did and why they did it.

In either case, what can result from the existence of this evidence is that Syrian courts and mediators can obtain a more accurate and complete understanding of the nature of the accused's acts and the effects on the victims. Armed with such information, the tribunal can better assess the truthfulness of any confession that is given as well as the sincerity of the person's remorse. As a result, victims can also be more readily identified and brought into the reconciliation process. The possibility of meaningful reconciliation can be more readily provided for. In addition, the international community can more readily assist in this reconciliation process without intruding on who is making the decision, or what punishment, compensation, or ritual of confession is provided for.

Conclusion

Any transition that Syria will face will have to navigate through a number of potential obstacles on the way to a sustainable peace. The first obstacle will be what Syrians will decide to do about those who may have committed past atrocities, including both Assad and members of his military and security forces, as well as any of the rebel groups that also engaged in war crimes. A legal strategy that will either require Assad to share power on the way towards a more democratic form of government that is inclusive of all tribal and religious groups will likely have to include both prisoner releases and some sort of amnesty for top leaders. The remaining disputes between Syrian citizen-victims and the perpetrators of violence during the interim period will have to be handled by both informal and then formal means. Perhaps the best mix of dispute resolution will include both informal dispute resolution mechanisms that draw on local leadership to help resolve them, followed by more formal methods – most probably hybrid regional courts run by both Syrians and international players committed to the continued peaceful resolution of these disputes while at the same time remaining committed to building religious freedoms and minority protections to keep the "winners" from seeking retribution or imposing their will on the "losers."

Surprisingly, the role that social media plays will most likely complicate the transition for peacemakers. As we've seen, social media has a positive impact on peacemaking in at least two ways. It helps humanitarian groups identify those rebels who may have engaged in war crimes, to avoid their giving aid and assistance to the wrong parties both during the conflict and during the transition. Second, social media also helps post-conflict to match accused war criminals with their victims in a way that may bring about more truth speaking, and more forgiveness and reconciliation.

What is complicating is that social media also makes possible the more successful prosecution of those who have committed war crimes. How can peacemakers make promises of amnesty to those disputants who are likely war criminals when they know that evidence from social media may lead others to want to prosecute them for their crimes? The "fog of war" may have lifted sufficiently so that the nature of the choices to the Syrians present an overwhelming ethical dilemma to the possibility of making peace. How will Syrians resolve the choice between peace and justice or decide who to give amnesty to in order to make peace and who to insist on prosecuting in order to ensure that in the future no Syrian actor uses war crimes to promote self and tribe?

What is clear is that peacemakers need to be careful not to be seen as gathering evidence exclusively for prosecution lest their role as peacemaker be compromised. At the same time, after the conflict has ended, social media evidence can serve two different purposes in two different phases of the peace process. In the first phase, the evidence from social media can be used to bring about mediations that lead to better reconciliations. In the second phase, where reconciliation has not occurred because the perpetrators are neither forthright nor sincere in their participation in the mediation, evidence from social media sources can be made available to prosecute in more formal judicial settings. Justification for its use comes in the form of classic evidentiary principles based on reliable foundations, relevance, and authentication. Especially where such evidence is produced by recalcitrant groups themselves in the process of their recruitment of others to their side of the conflict, there should be little hesitation by hybrid courts to use such evidence to bring these war criminals to justice.

Notes

1 Much of this chapter has is adapted from an article that I wrote for the *Emory International Law Review*. See Paul J. Zwier, "Social Media and Conflict Mapping in Syria," *Emory International Law Review*, Vol. 30 (2015), p. 171.

2 Syria, Witness for the Prosecution, (describing the work of Abdelkader Mandou, and a group of Syrians, working for Turkey. Abdelkader is the director of the Syrian Institute for Justice). http://www.aljazeera.com/programmes/specialseries/2016/11/syria-witnesses-prosecution-161115091502071.html

3 Reuters in Geneva, "New UN team to collect evidence for Syria war crime prosecutions," *The Guardian*, Thursday, February 17, https://www.theguardian.com/world/2017/feb/16/syria-un-sets-up-unit-to-aid-prosecutions-of-war-crimes

4 Ben Hubbard and Eric Schmitt, "Military Skill and Terrorist Technique Fuel Success of ISIS," August 27, 2014, www.nytimes.com/2014/08/28/world/middleeast/army-know-how-seen-as-factor-in-isis-successes.html. The *NYT* article goes on to report what it has learned from conflict mapping of the war in Iraq and Syria:

> According to a map of the group developed by Mr. Alhashimi, the Iraqi expert, Mr. Baghdadi has 25 deputies across Iraq and Syria. About one-third were military officers during Mr. Hussein's rule, and nearly all were imprisoned by American forces.

5 Richard Barrett, "The Islamic State," The Soufan Group, November 2014, http://soufangroup.com/wp-content/uploads/2014/10/TSG-The-Islamic-State-Nov14.pdf.

6 "Iraq: Building a New Security Structure: ICG Middle East Report N°20," December 23, 2003, www.crisisgroup.org/~/media/Files/Middle%20East%20North%20Africa/Iraq%20Syria%20Lebanon/Iraq/Iraq%20Building%20a%20New%20Security%20Structure.pdf.

7 Barrett, "The Islamic State."

8 The real story is more complex. The US tried to integrate significant numbers of the former military, reportedly paying the salary of close to 40 thousand of these troops. See Timothy Williams, "Sunnis in Iraq Allied With US Rejoin Rebels," *NYT*, October 17, 2010, www.nytimes.com/2010/10/17/world/middleeast/17awakening.html?pagewanted=all&_r=0.

9 Zachary Laub, Online Writer/Editor, and Jonathan Masters, Deputy Editor, "The Islamic State," *Council of Foreign Affairs*, Updated April 1, 2015, www.cfr.org/iraq/islamic-state/p14811.

10 See Timothy Williams, "Sunnis in Iraq Allied With US Rejoin Rebels," *NYT*, October 17, 2010, www.nytimes.com/2010/10/17/world/middleeast/17awakening.html?pagewanted=all&_r=0.

11 Ibid. Most recently there are reports that some of these same Awakening members are willing to now support the efforts against ISIS by forming a new group called Awakening II. See also Zachary Laub, Online Writer/Editor, and Jonathan Masters, Deputy Editor, "The Islamic State," *Council of Foreign Affairs*, Updated April 1, 2015, www.cfr.org/iraq/islamic-state/p14811.

12 One can also compare integration effort by Colombians to integrate the Fuerzas Armadas Revolucionarias de Colombia (FARC) back into its military. Part of the plan to help the FARC fighters includes paying them 90 percent of Colombia's minimum wage as they emerge from their strongholds. The negotiators compared the monthly $200 subsidy to the thousands of dollars spent on each army bombing raid. Helen Murphy and Marc Franc, "Colombia Sends Peace Deal to Congress as Negotiators Defend It," *Reuters*, August 24, 2016, www.reuters.com/article/us-colombia-rebels-idUSKCN10Z2HJ.

13 David D. Kirkpatrick, "In Egypt, Signs of an Accord between Military Council and Islamists," *NYT*, January 23, 2012, www.nytimes.com/2012/01/23/world/middleeast/signs-of-accord-between-egyptian-military-and-muslim-brotherhood-on-new-charter.html?pagewanted=all.
14 Daria Solovieva, "Egypt's Military Takes Control Over Muslim Brotherhood, Supporters," *Special to The Washington Times*, Sunday, August 18, 2013, www.washingtontimes.com/news/2013/aug/18/egypts-military-takes-control-over-muslim-brotherh/#ixzz3XUCpoFbQ.
15 Sarah Leah Whitson, "Egypt Sentences 683 to Death as Military Crackdown Continues," April 30, 2014 06:09 PM – Updated April 30, 2014 06:13 PM, www.msnbc.com/msnbc/egypt-mass-death-sentences.
16 Simon Tysdale, "Muamar Gaddafi's Violent Death Leaves Libya at a Crossroads," www.theguardian.com/commentisfree/2011/oct/20/gaddafi-death-leaves-libya-crossroads.
17 Adam Taylor, "Gaddafi Died 3 Years Ago, Would Libya Be Better Off If He Hadn't?," *Washington Post*, October 20, 2014, www.washingtonpost.com/blogs/worldviews/wp/2014/10/20/gaddafi-died-3-years-ago-would-libya-be-better-off-if-he-hadnt/.
18 Souhail Belhadj, "Tunisia: An Exemplary Political Transition?," Paper prepared for the Norwegian Peacebuilding Resource Center (NOREF). Geneva, September 2014.
19 Ibid.
20 Ibid.; Sarah Chayes, "How a Leftist Labor Union Help Forced Tunisia's Political Settlement," *Carnegie Endowment for International Peace*, March 27, 2014, http://carnegieendowment.org/2014/03/27/how-leftist-labor-union-helped-force-tunisia-s-political-settlement.
21 James Fromson, "Tunisia's Transition," *International Institute for Strategic Studies*, February 27, 2014, www.iiss.org/en/iiss%20voices/blogsections/iiss-voices-2014-b4d9/february-72f2/tunisia-transition-d9e8.
22 Ibid.
23 Discussion of this option in the present historical context may seem somewhat naïve. Why would Assad agree to submit to UN resolutions when he has not been defeated? On the other hand, Assad did agree to submit to chemical weapons inspections when political pressure was applied. He also has denied that he has done anything wrong, and that charges that he has used chemical weapons or barrel bombs have been trumped up by the West. Perhaps implicit in that denial is a logical trap – that if you haven't done anything wrong, why not submit to the UN resolutions and the ICC's jurisdiction? Still great pressure would likely have to be brought to bear on Assad to get him to agree to submit to the ICC. As discussed in the following, more likely Assad will have to be given some sort of amnesty. The question remains how many others in the leadership of the government would have to be given amnesty or how many of these might be made to submit to the ICC. See, *infra*, 18–19.
24 "Comprehensive Peace Agreement between the Government of Liberia and the Liberians United for Reconciliation and Democracy (LURD) and the Movement for Democracy in Liberia (MODEL) and Political Parties, Accra," August 18, 2003, www.usip.org/sites/default/files/file/resources/collections/peace_agreements/liberia_08182003.pdf; See also, "Power Sharing Transitional Government: The Accra Peace Agreement," http://peaceaccords.nd.edu/provision/power sharing-transitional-government-accra-peace-agreement.
25 Ibid.
26 Associated Press, "The Hague: Sarajevo Siege General on Trial," *New York Times*, http://www.nytimes.com/2007/01/12/world/europe/12briefs-haguetrial.html?rref=collection%2Ftimestopic%2FMilosevic%2C%20Slobodan&action=click&contentCollection=timestopics&region=stream&module=stream_unit&version=latest&contentPlacement=32&pgtype=collection

27 Diseree Nilsson, "Crafting a Secure Peace: Evaluating Liberia's Comprehensive Peace Agreement of 2003," www.pcr.uu.se/digitalAssets/64/64071_1crafting_a_secure_peace.pdf.
28 ICC, "UN Assembly of States, Report on Court Activities," www.icc-cpi.int/iccdocs/asp_docs/ASP7/ICC-ASP-7-25%20English.pdf.
29 Lionel Nichols, *The International Criminal Court and the End of Impunity in Kenya* (Cham, Switzerland: Springer International Publishing, 95, February 13, 2015).
30 Ibid.
31 Ibid.
32 Russia has vetoed other resolutions aimed at Syria. Rick Gladstone, "Friction at the U.N. as Russia and China Veto Another Resolution on Syria Sanctions," July 19, 2012, www.nytimes.com/2012/07/20/world/middleeast/russia-and-china-veto-un-sanctions-against-syria.html?_r=0.
33 American Non-Governmental Organization Coalition for the Support of the International Criminal Court, http://amicc.blogspot.com/2014/10/kenyatta-case-at-icc-three-options.html.
34 UNHRC, www.unhcr.org/pages/49e486a76.html.
35 Ibid.
36 Ibid.
37 Ibid.
38 Rick Gladstone and Mohammad Ghannamjan, "Syria Deaths Hit New High in 2014, Observer Group Says," January, 2015, www.nytimes.com/2015/01/02/world/middleeast/syrian-civil-war-2014-deadliest-so-far.html?_r=0.
39 Human Rights Watch, "Syria: Use of Barrel Bombs," www.hrw.org/news/2014/07/30/syria-barrage-barrel-bombs, (containing maps that documented evidence of barrel bombs). See also *Financial Times*, "UN blames Syrian government for chemical attacks," https://www.ft.com/content/db77f7fc-930e-11e7-a9e6-11d2f0ebb7f0 (confirming that Assad actually used chemical weapons and barrel bombs 27 times over the course of the war).
40 Human Rights Watch, "Syria: Political Detainees Tortured, Killed," www.hrw.org/news/2013/10/03/syria-political-detainees-tortured-killed.
41 Nick Robins Early, "Syria Killed Thousands In Secret Mass Hangings Inside Prison, Amnesty Reports," www.huffingtonpost.com/entry/syria-sednaya-killings-amnesty-report_us_5899e32ce4b0c1284f2824bb.
42 Ibid.
43 As of yet there has been no evidence that Assad has taken steps to curtail the killing of prisoners. President Donald Trump may shift US priorities in Syria to increasingly focus on fighting militants of the so-called Islamic State and move away from pressuring Assad's regime. In the summer of 2017 Assad praised Trump's rhetoric on terrorism as "promising" and in November said the new US president could be a "natural ally" against terrorists. Assad has previously denied the disappearances of prisoners and said that the government doesn't detain political prisoners.
44 See, *infra*, Part 2.
45 Note that the ICC did not exist at the time of the South African transition. While an international war crimes tribunal was a theoretical possibility, South Africa decided to take control of its own process for dealing with the past.
46 Nel Marais, *Deconstructing the Conditions That Enabled South Africa's Transition to Power-Sharing: The Transformation Initiative* (Zurich, 2014). This paper was prepared for the Norwegian Peacebuilding Resource Centre, the Carter Center and Swisspeace for a seminar of the "The Syria Transition Options Project of The Carter Center." See also Nelson Mandela Center of Memory, www.nelsonmandela.org/omalley/index.php/site/q/03lv02039/04lv02046/05lv02092/06lv02096.htm.

47 O'Malley, "Multi-Party Negotiation Process leading to Constitution," www.nelsonmandela.org/omalley/index.php/site/q/03lv02424/04lv03429/05lv03438/06lv03439.htm; See also Department of Justice and Constitutional Development of the Republic of South Africa, The Truth and Reconciliation Official Website, www.justice.gov.za/trc/amntrans/index.htm.

48 Marais, *Deconstructing the Conditions That Enabled South Africa's Transition to Power-Sharing: The Transformation Initiative.* This paper was prepared for the Norwegian Peacebuilding Resource Centre, the Carter Center and Swisspeace for a seminar of the "The Syria Transition Options Project of The Carter Center."

49 Jay A. Vora and Erika Vora, "The Effectiveness of South Africa's Truth and Reconciliation Commission: Perceptions of Xhosa, Afrikaner, and English South Africans," *Journal of Black Studies*, Vol. 34, No. 3 (2004), pp. 301–22.

50 See Mariai, *supra*, note 13.

51 Report for October 94, "Independent Board of Inquiry," 16, www.historicalpapers.wits.ac.za/inventories/inv_pdfo/AG2543/AG2543-2-2-44-01-jpeg.pdf.

52 See Mariai, *supra*, note 13.

53 See Marais, *supra*, note 23 and Belhadi, *supra*, note 11.

54 Nathan Gonzales, "Solving the Sunni-Shia Conflict Begins with Tehran," *The Diplomat*, May 23, 2014, http://thediplomat.com/2014/05/solving-the-sunni-shia-conflict-begins-with-tehran/.

55 Ed Husain, "ISIS Atrocities Started with Saudi Support for Salafi Hate," *NYT*, August 22, 2014, www.nytimes.com/2014/08/23/opinion/isis-atrocities-started-with-saudi-support-for-salafi-hate.html?_r=0. Hasain writes,

> Al Qaeda, the Islamic State in Iraq and Syria, Boko Haram, the Shabab and others are all violent Sunni Salafi groupings. For five decades, Saudi Arabia has been the official sponsor of Sunni Salafism across the globe.

56 MEM, "Qatar Emir Support for Muslim Brotherhood Is a 'duty'," *Middle East Monitor*, Tuesday, December 31, 2013, 14:54, www.middleeastmonitor.com/news/middle-east/9000-qatar-emir-support-for-muslim-brotherhood-is-a-qdutyq; Ryan Mauro, "Call in Congress to Sanction Turkey, Qatar for Terror Support," *The Clarion Project*, December 11, 2014, www.clarionproject.org/analysis/members-congress-sanction-turkey-qatar-terror-support.

57 Chase Carter, "The Case for Assad," *The National Interest*, June 20, 2014, http://nationalinterest.org/feature/the-case-assad-10708.

58 Archbishop Tutu's speech was given to the South African press club on October 21, 1997, www.futurenet.org/7Peacebuilding/tutu.htm. Alex Boraine, *A Country Unmasked: Inside South Africa's Truth and Reconciliation Commission* (Oxford and New York: Oxford University Press, 2000): Alexander Boraine, "Truth and Reconciliation Commission in South Africa Amnesty: The Price of Peace," in *Retribution and Repatriation in the Transition to Democracy*, ed. Jon Elster (New York: Cambridge University Press, 2006), pp. 299–316.

59 *The Promotion of National Unity and Reconciliation Act, as Amended, 1997*
The preamble to this act (known commonly in South Africa as the TRC Act) is as follows:

> To provide for the investigation and the establishment of as complete a picture as possible of the nature, causes and extent of gross violations of human rights committed during the period from 1 March 1960 to the cut-off date contemplated in the Constitution [6 December 1996], within or outside the Republic, emanating from the conflicts of the past, and the fate or whereabouts of

> the victims of such violations; the granting of amnesty to persons who make full disclosure of all the relevant facts relating to acts associated with a political objective committed in the course of the conflicts of the past during the said period; affording victims an opportunity to relate the violations they suffered; the taking of measures aimed at the granting of reparation to, and the rehabilitation and the restoration of the human and civil dignity of, victims of violations of human rights; reporting to the Nation about such violations and victims; the making of recommendations aimed at the prevention of the commission of gross violations of human rights; and for the said purposes to provide for the establishment of a Truth and Reconciliation Commission, a Committee on Human Rights Violations, a Committee on Amnesty and a Committee on Reparation and Rehabilitation; and to confer certain powers on, assign certain functions to and impose certain duties upon that Commission and those Committees; and to provide for matters connected therewith.

60 Constitution of the Republic of South Africa Act 107 of 1996. For a textual analysis of the Constitution see Heinz Klug, *The Constitution of South Africa: A Contextual Analysis* (Oxford, England: Hart Publishing, 2010).
61 *Transitional Justice and Peacebuilding on the Ground: Victims and Ex-Combantants*, ed. Chandra Lekha Sriram, Jemima Garcia-Godos, Johanna Herman and Olga Martin-Ortega (New York: Routledge, 2013), 62.
62 See, *for example*, Liberian TRC. Ibid., 181–8.
63 Ibid.
64 Ibid.
65 Ibid.
66 Choosing this option has the potential of keeping the ICC at bay, under principles of complementarity.
67 For example, in during the South Africa transitional period de Klerk agreed to a structure that bound the military to the president and created a constitutional court that would provide the independent interpretation of the South Africa Constitution, including its enforcement of minority rights. Brice Dickson, "Protecting Human Rights through a Constitutional Court: The Case of South Africa," *Fordham Law Review*, Vol. 66 (1997), p. 531.
68 Alexander Noyes, "Securing Reform? Power Sharing and Civil-Security Relations in Kenya and Zimbabwe," *African Studies Quarterly*, Vol. 13, No. 4 (Winter, 2013), http://asq.africa.ufl.edu/files/Noyes-V13Is4.pdf.
69 Ibid., 34.
70 Extraordinary Chambers in the Courts of Cambodia, (ECCC), www.eccc.gov.kh/; These courts are described by the International Court for Transitional Justice website, located at www.ictj.org/our-work/regions-and-countries/cambodia.
71 The full text of the General Framework Agreement for Peace, the Annexes to the Dayton Peace Agreement, and related documents are available from numerous sources, including the Office of the High Representative. The website of the Office of the High Representative is located at www.ohr.int/; See also, Elizabeth M. Bruch, "Hybrid Courts: Examining Hybridity through a Post-Colonial Lens," *Boston University International Law Journal*, Vol. 28 (2010), p. 1 (hereinafter Bruch):

> The Human Rights Chamber was created under Annex 6 of the Dayton Peace Agreement to "assist the Parties in honouring their obligations" to secure the highest level of international human rights protection for the people of Bosnia.38 More broadly, it was conceived as an intentionally hybrid court with the teleology of achieving Europeanized protection of human rights and the rule of law in the specific context of post-war Bosnia. Ibid.

72 Ibid. See also David Cohen, " 'Hybrid' Justice in East Timor, Sierra Leone, and Cambodia: "Lessons Learned" and Prospects for the Future," *Stanford Journal of International Law*, Vol. 43 (2007), p. 1 (evaluating hybrid tribunals in East Timor, Sierra Leone, and Cambodia).
73 Citation needed Bruch, *supra*, note 86, at 4.
74 Citation needed Ibid.
75 Special Tribunal for Lebanon, The Hague, www.stl-tsl.org/; See also, Ronan Bergman, "The Hezbollah Connection," *NYT Magazine*, February 15, 2015. See also, Matthew Shaer, "The Media Doesn't Care What Happens Here: Can Amateur Journalism Bring Justice to Rio's Favelas?," *NYT Magazine*, February 22, 2015, p. 155, (describing the work of a human rights organization called Witness, to train journalists to gather evidence that could later be used in criminal prosecutions in areas such as Rio and in other conflicts around the world. Ibid., 156. The article also described the work by two engineers from the Medical College of Wisconsin, Brian Laning and Bonnie Freudinger, who recently won a USAID grant to work on the International Evidence Locker, a free smartphone app. Photos collected on the app are automatically location-, date-, and time-stamped, encrypted and securely sent to two separate protected servers. They can also be submitted anonymously.
76 The Abunzi process is describe on the Rwanda Ministry of Justice website at www.minijust.gov.rw/services/abunzi/.
77 Statute of the Commission for the Resolution of Real Property Disputes, Order No. 2 of 2006, www.globalprotectioncluster.org/_assets/files/field_protection_clusters/Iraq/files/Iraq_PC_Statute_Commission_Property_Resolution_2006_EN.pdf.
78 Ibid.
79 Peter Van der Auweraert, "Property Restitution in Iraq," Presentation at the Symposium on Post-Conflict Property Restitution, Hosted by the United States Department of State, Bureau of Population, Refugees, and Migration; Bureau of Intelligence and Research; Office of the Coordinator of Reconstruction and Stabilization September 6–7, 2007, http://2001-2009.state.gov/documents/organization/98032.pdf.
80 Statute of the Commission for the Resolution of Real Property Disputes, Order No. 2 of 2006, www.globalprotectioncluster.org/_assets/files/field_protection_clusters/Iraq/files/Iraq_PC_Statute_Commission_Property_Resolution_2006_EN.pdf.
81 Ibid.
82 Peter van der Auweraert, "Iraq Updates Its Approach to Former Regime-Related Land and Property Claims," *Terre Nullius Web Blog*, 2010, https://terra0nullius.wordpress.com/2010/03/11/iraq-updates-its-approach-to-former-regime-related-land-and-property-claims/.
83 See generally, Marc Lynch Deen Freelon and Sean Aday, "Blogs and Bullets III, Syria's Socially Mediated Civil War," *United States Institute of Peace*, www.usip.org/sites/default/files/PW91-Syrias%20Socially%20Mediated%20Civil%20War.pdf. (hereinafter, Blogs). Cf, Lauren Kirkwood, "Study Finds Bias in Internet Postings about Syria's Civil War," *McClatchy Washington Bureau*, February 24, 2014 (finding bias in Internet postings), www.mcclatchydc.com/2014/02/24/219223/study-finds-bias-in-internet-postings.html#storylink=cpy.
84 Blogs, *supra*, note 98.
85 Ibid.
86 See, *supra*, Part I, p. 2.
87 See, for example, "Syria: Strong Evidence Government Used Chemicals as a Weapon, Civilian Casualties in Barrel Bomb Attacks on 3 Towns," *Human Rights*

Watch, May 13, 2014, www.hrw.org/news/2014/05/13/syria-strong-evidence-government-used-chemicals-weapon; Organization for the Prohibition of Chemical Weapons, (OPCW), www.opcw.org/.

88 The International Criminal Court uses the doctrine of *command* or *superior responsibility* to provide it with proof of intent necessary to convict an individual for war crimes. If a leader argues he did not know war crimes had been committed, then once having learned, what steps did the leader take to remove the individual from power. Guénaël Mettraux, *The Law of Command Responsibility* (Oxford: Oxford University Press, 2009); Kai Ambos, "Superior Responsibility," in *The Rome Statute of the International Criminal Court: A Commentary*, Vol. 1, ed. A. Cassese et al. (Oxford: Oxford University Press, 2002), 823.

89 Ibid.

90 Paul J. Zwier, "History, Creative Imagination, and Forgiveness in Mediation on an International Stage: Practical Lessons from Paul Ricoeur's Hermeneutics," *Journal of Law and Religion*, Vol. 30, No. 2 (April 15, 2015); Emory Legal Studies Research Paper No. 16-405. Available at SSRN: https://ssrn.com/abstract=2735882

91 Kristin C. Doughty, "Contesting Community: Legalized Reconciliation Efforts in the Aftermath of Genocide in Rwanda" (2011). *Publicly Accessible Penn Dissertations.* Paper 333.

92 The Abunzi process is describe on the Rwanda Ministry of Justice website at www.minijust.gov.rw/services/abunzi/.

93 Note that some NGOs like TCC refuse to use their conflict mapping for other than humanitarian purposes, in that it could potentially compromise its neutrality in negotiations for peace, if were seen to be gathering evidence against the parties.

94 "Syria: Strong Evidence Government Used Chemicals as a Weapon, Civilian Casualties in Barrel Bomb Attacks on 3 Towns," May 13, 2014, www.hrw.org/news/2014/05/13/syria-strong-evidence-government-used-chemicals-weapon, *HRW disseminated the following documented evidence about barrel bombs*:

> Improvised barrel bombs are typically constructed from large oil drums, various types of metal cylinders, and water tanks filled with explosives and scrap metal to enhance fragmentation, which are then dropped from a helicopter. The heat from the explosion of the barrel bomb would destroy much of the chlorine and any remaining gas would be dispersed in the air by the explosion so the concentration of chlorine would quickly drop to non-lethal levels.

(Others wonder whether HRW is mapping opposition groups use of rockets with the same degree of vigilance it uses to gather evidence against Assad.)

95 "Syria: Strong Evidence Government Used Chemicals as a Weapon, Civilian Casualties in Barrel Bomb Attacks on 3 Towns," May 13, 2014, www.hrw.org/news/2014/05/13/syria-strong-evidence-government-used-chemicals-weapon.

Much of the evidence gathered concerning the use of chemical weapons was gathered through interviews of OPCW and HRW soon after the attacks. Human Right Watch's deputy director Middle East and North Africa went into Syria and interview a number of witnesses, HRW concluded that Syria had used of chlorine gas as a weapon and had targeted civilians. It recommended that the UN Security Council refer the situation in Syria to the International Criminal Court.

HRW started with verification of this fact, during April 2014, that the Syrian government is the only party of the conflict with helicopters and other aircraft. "Syria: Strong Evidence Government Used Chemicals as a Weapon, Civilian

Casualties in Barrel Bomb Attacks on 3 Towns," May 13, 2014, www.hrw.org/news/2014/05/13/syria-strong-evidence-government-used-chemicals-weapon.

But see BBC exclusive interview with President Bashar al-Assad, February 10, 2015, www.bbc.com/news/world-middle-east-31327153, (where President Assad denied that Syria was using barrel bombs or chlorine gas in their war against the opposition. During the BBC interview with Assad, Assad seems to be denying that the Syrian government was engaged in the use of barrel bombs, or, chlorine gas, or at least, that he doesn't know that they are using barrel bombs or chlorine gas). His argument is a little suspect – that he has "no reason to use these types of weapons against Syrian civilians, so therefor he isn't using them." He does not say that he has investigated their use and directed the army not to use these types of weapons. Presumably he could have offered his willingness to investigate as that is the process he went through in helping the UN dispose of other chemical weapons. He does not offer a willingness to investigate whether his military is engaged in the use of barrel bombs or chlorine gas.

96 Organisation for the Prohibition of Chemical Weapons, Convention on the Prohibition of the Development, Production, Stockpiling and use of Chemical Weapons and on their Destruction. https://www.opcw.org/fileadmin/OPCW/CWC/CWC_en.pdf

97 "Syria Officially Joins the UN Chemical Weapons Convention," *The Hindu*, October 14, 2013, www.thehindu.com/news/international/world/syria-officially-joins-un-chemical-weapons-convention/article5233423.ece.

98 Mapping Militant Organizations, Stanford University, http://web.stanford.edu/group/mappingmilitants/cgi-bin/.

99 http://web.stanford.edu/group/mappingmilitants/cgi-bin/maps/view/syria.

100 United Nations CEDAW report: "Seeking Accountability and Demanding Change: A Report on Women's Human Rights Violations in Syria before and during the Conflict," www.law.cuny.edu/academics/clinics/iwhr/publications/Seeking-Accountability-and-Demanding-Change-A-Report-on-Womens-Human-Rights-Violations-in-Syria-Before-and-During-the-Conflict.pdf.

101 Federico Guerrini, "How Researchers Use Social Media to Map the Conflict in Syria," *Forbes*, April 15, 2014, www.forbes.com/sites/federicoguerrini/2014/04/15/how-researchers-use-social-media-to-map-armed-forces-in-syria/.

102 Palantir Technologies provides technologies to map data over time in a variety of settings. Examples of its maps in Syria can be found at Palantir Blog, www.palantir.com/2014/06/mapping-the-syrian-crisis-with-the-carter-center/. It describes how its technology helps in the conflict mapping process as follows:

> The Syrian conflict is notable for the amount of related open source information being published through social media platforms such as YouTube and Facebook. Analysts at the Carter Center have carefully coded over 70 attributes from thousands of videos, which together represent thousands of individual conflict events and the formation of over 5,600 armed groups in which some 100,000 fighters have appeared. Analysts coded information including where and when events occurred, what weapons they observed, symbolism and uniforms that appear in the videos, and evidence of mass atrocities.
>
> The platform used – Palantir Gotham – is one of the best analytical tools in existence today, and has already helped us find meaningful trends in our data that would otherwise have been lost in a series of disconnected network diagrams, Excel spreadsheets, and reports.
>
> By integrating and analyzing this information in Palantir Gotham (as in the video above), the Carter Center can better help humanitarian organizations deliver aid to those who need it most. In a rapidly evolving conflict where

the security of aid workers and civilians is paramount, real-time data analysis provides international actors with situational awareness of the conflict as it unfolds, allowing them to operate both more efficiently and more safely. Furthermore, Palantir Gotham's granular access controls and auditing capabilities allow for both raw data and analysis to be shared responsibly and securely, while ensuring that collaborators understand the sourcing and pedigree of the data in question. Ibid.

103 http://stream.aljazeera.com/story/201408201239-0024088.
104 Ahmed Rashid, "ISIS: What the US Doesn't Understand," *The New York Review of Books*, December 2, 2014, www.nybooks.com/blogs/nyrblog/2014/dec/02/isis-what-us-doesnt-understand/.
105 http://stream.aljazeera.com/story/201408201239-0024088.
106 True Islam, www.jihadwatch.org/2014/08/muslim-cleric-justifies-islamic-state-beheadings-islam-is-a-religion-of-beheading. The Prophet spoke directly against the killing of minority religious groups in negotiating the rights of passage of Muslims to pilgrimage to Mecca. But see, Muslim cleric justifies Islamic State beheadings: Robert Spencer, "Islam Is a Religion of Beheading," *Jihad Watch*, August 25, 2014, www.jihadwatch.org/2014/08/muslim-cleric-justifies-islamic-state-beheadings-islam-is-a-religion-of-beheading.
107 See, for example, Political Geography Now, polgeonow.com; CUNY Law Clinic.
108 John Hall, "ISIS Mass Beheading Video Took up to Six HOURS to Film and Cost $200,000: Forensic Analysis of Syrian Soldier Murders Reveals Clues That Could Help Nail Jihadi John," December 8, 2014, www.dailymail.co.uk/news/article-2865745/Has-EXACT-location-infamous-ISIS-beheading-video-pinpointed-Forensic-analysis-filmed-Syrian-soldier-murders-breaks-filmed-long-took-cost-make.html#ixzz3YKpGgHDR.
109 Ibid. The Carter Center's conflict mapping project mapped some videos that were documented to have been shot and posted around the time that Saudi television was interviewing members of the insurgent group. Their appearance looks like the television studio not only did the news interview, it also then shot a promotional video for the group. These promotional videos apparently used the same kinds of special effects in their new casts, as was used in the video.
110 TCC Syria Conflict Mapping Project, www.cartercenter.org/peace/conflict_resolution/syria-conflict-mapping.html.
111 Syria Justice and Accountability Centre, PILPG, A Global Pro bono Law Firm, Mapping Accountability Efforts in Syria, Prepared by the Public International Law and Policy Group, February 2013, pp. 4–5, www.dchrs.org/english/File/Reports/mapping-accountability-efforts-in-syria.pdf.
112 TCC Conflict Mapping Project, www.cartercenter.org/peace/conflict_resolution/syria-conflict-mapping.html.
113 Ibid.
114 For example, as of 2016 the TCC can still identifying close to 2,000 groups that are active in the conflict, roughly grouped according to 5 different major groups. "Carter Center Makes Dynamic Syria Conflict Map Available to Public," March 9, 2016, www.cartercenter.org/news/pr/syria-030916.html; For data current up to June 2017, see www.cartercenter.org/syria-conflict-map/.
115 For example, see Stanford, Mapping Militant Organizations, http://web.stanford.edu/group/mappingmilitants/cgi-bin/maps/view/syria.

See also Reports, The Carter Center, Conflict Mapping Project, www.cartercenter.org/peace/conflict_resolution/syria-conflict-mapping.html.

To see a video that shows the mapping process go to www.youtube.com/watch?v=9X6GqEAph2E&feature=player_embedded. There you will find an example of a recruiting video for ISIS (see Figure 7.1).

Figure 7.1 Screenshot, Recruitment Video

116 For example, Federal Rule of Evidence 901(a) and its state law analogs require laying a foundation of "evidence sufficient to support a finding that the matter in question is what its proponent claims." Rule 901(b) provides an illustrative list of methods by which evidence can be authenticated.

117 Federal Rule of Evidence (FRE) 901 (a) In General. To satisfy the requirement of authenticating or identifying an item of evidence, the proponent must produce evidence sufficient to support a finding that the item is what the proponent claims it to be. Videos could be authenticated as a process or system. See FRE 901(b) Examples, . . . (9). Process or system. Evidence describing a process or system used to produce a result and showing that the process or system produces an accurate result.

FRE 1001 (d) (1) and (w) makes provisions for use of writings, recordings, and photographs, and FRE 1001 (3) provides a definition of an original, "An "original" of a writing or recording is the writing or recording itself or any counter-part intended to have the same effect by a person executing or issuing it. An "original" of a photograph includes the negative or any print therefrom. If data is stored in a computer or similar device, any printout or other output readable by sight, *shown to reflect the data accurately*, is an "original."

FRE 1001 (4) defines Duplicate. A duplicate is a counterpart produced by the same impression as the original, or from the same matrix, or by means of photography, including enlargements and miniatures, or by mechanical or electronic re-recording, or by chemical reproduction, or by other equivalent techniques which accurately reproduces the original.

118 Michael P. Scharf, "International Decisions," *The American Journal of International Law*, Vol. 91, No. 4 (October, 1997), pp. 718–21. Also see: www.icty.org/sid/7537; 6 Rules of Procedure and Evidence of the ICTY, Rule 89 C, www.icty.org/x/file/Legal%20Library/Rules_procedure_evidence/IT032_rev44_en.pdf.

119 Social media sites are dynamic and complex and may be unfamiliar to many judges. Testimony about how user profiles are created, security procedures, privacy settings, metadata, and general operation may help courts to determine whether a satisfactory foundation for authenticity has been laid. Furthermore, courts have raised legitimate concerns that social networking accounts may be hacked, fictitious accounts created, and accounts left open and unattended. Testimony thus should address those concerns and explain the degree to which the social media in question may have been vulnerable to manipulation. These considerations are important both for proffering evidence and for challenging its admissibility.

Rule 901(b) (1) allows for authentication through testimony from a witness with knowledge that a matter is what it is claimed to be. Most straightforwardly, the person who created the evidence can testify to authenticate it. Testimony also may be provided by a witness who has personal knowledge of how the social media information is typically generated. In such a case, the authenticating witness must provide "factual specificity about the process by which the electronically stored information is created, acquired, maintained, and preserved without alteration or change, or the process by which it is produced if the result of a system or process that does so[.]" The social media websites themselves, law review articles, and experts can all provide this type of information.

120 Witnesses may be fearful to come forward because of retribution by those depicted in the video. Syria Justice and Accountability Centre, PILPG, A Global Pro bono Law Firm, Mapping Accountability Efforts in Syria, Prepared by the Public International Law and Policy Group, February 2013, pp. 4–5, www.dchrs.org/english/File/Reports/mapping-accountability-efforts-in-syria.pdf.

121 FRE 901 (b)(1).

122 See analysis of FREs in footnote, *supra*, 132. H. Christopher Boehning and Daniel J. Toal, "Authenticating Social Media Evidence," *New York Law Journal*, Vol. 65, 248, Technology Today, October 2, 2012 (hereinafter Authenticating). Social media sites are dynamic and complex and may be unfamiliar to many judges. Testimony about how user profiles are created, security procedures, privacy settings, metadata, and general operation may help courts to determine whether a satisfactory foundation for authenticity has been laid. Furthermore, courts have raised legitimate concerns that social networking accounts may be hacked, fictitious accounts created, and accounts left open and unattended. Testimony thus should address those concerns and explain the degree to which the social media in question may have been vulnerable to manipulation. These considerations are important both for proffering evidence and for challenging its admissibility. Rule 901(b) (1) allows for authentication through testimony from a witness with knowledge that a matter is what it is claimed to be. Most straightforwardly, the person who created the evidence can testify to authenticate it. Testimony also may be provided by a witness who has personal knowledge of how the social media information is typically generated. In such a case, the authenticating witness must provide "factual specificity about the process by which the electronically stored information is created, acquired, maintained, and preserved without alteration or change, or the process by which it is produced if the result of a system or process that does so[.]" The social media websites themselves, law review articles, and experts can all provide this type of information.

123 Authenticating, *supra*, note 137. See John Patzakis, "Key Facebook Metadata Fields Lawyers and eDiscovery Professionals Need to be Aware of," October 11, 2011, http://blog.x1discovery.com/2011/10/11/key-facebook-metadata-fields-lawyers-and-ediscovery-professionals-need-to-be-aware-of/ accessed September 17, 2012.

124 Relevant factors include whether the person to whom the proponent of the exhibit wishes to attribute the printout has adopted the username shown on the profile page, whether the person has shared his or her social media password with other

people, whether there is a photograph on the person's or entity's profile page that identifies the person to whom the proponent wishes to attribute the posting, and whether there is personal information on the profile page, such as a birthday, unique name, or other pedigree information that corresponds to known information for the person to whom the proponent wishes to attribute the posting.

125 See Authenticating, *supra*, note 132. See also Authenticating, *supra*, note 137.

126 Umberto Bacchi, "Isis: French Jihadist Mickael Dos Santos 'Denies Appearing in Beheading Video'," *International Business Times*, November 20, 2014 19:14 GMT, www.ibtimes.co.uk/isis-french-jihadist-mickael-dos-santos-denies-appearing-beheading-video-1475833.

127 See, for example, ObscuraCam. Described at https://guardianproject.info/apps/obscuracam/.

128 Ibid.

129 See John Patzakis, "Key Facebook Metadata Fields Lawyers and eDiscovery Professionals Need to be Aware of," October 11, 2011, http://blog.x1discovery.com/2011/10/11/key-facebook-metadata-fields-lawyers-and-ediscovery-professionals-need-to-be-aware-of/ accessed September 17, 2012.

130 Methods of how to download original video found at Interactive Archivist, http://interactivearchivist.archivists.org/technologies/podcasts/.

131 Checksum Checker, Software for Digital Preservation, *Download version 3.0.1*, released March 25, 2014, AEST.

Checksum Checker is free and open-source software developed by the National Archives of Australia. Checksum Checker is a piece of software that is used to monitor the contents of a digital archive for data loss or corruption.

Checksum Checker is a component of the Digital Preservation Software Platform (DPSP).

Features

As part of the Digital Preservation Recorder (DPR) workflow, checksums are generated for each Archival Information Package (AIP). Checksum Checker generates a new checksum for each AIP and compares it against the stored checksum. If the checksums do not match, then the AIP is flagged as being corrupt.

Checksum Checker incorporates the following features:

- Checksum Checker functions as a service.
- Checksum Checker sends automated emails to a nominated administrator email address, coinciding with certain events (such as the start of a checking run or when an error is encountered).

Checksum Checker is released under the GPLv3, and is available for download, http://checksumchecker.sourceforge.net/

132 See statutory analysis, footnote 132, See also, Authenticating, *supra*, note 137.

133 John Patzakis, "Key Facebook Metadata Fields Lawyers and eDiscovery Professionals Need to be Aware of," October 11, 2011, http://blog.x1discovery.com/2011/10/11/key-facebook-metadata-fields-lawyers-and-ediscovery-professionals-need-to-be-aware-of/ accessed September 17, 2012.

134 Ibid.

135 Google, Archivist website.

136 Authenticating, *supra*, note 137.

137 This guidance provided by state bar associations is not binding but does suggest best practices that will help attorneys avoid ethical pitfalls that may taint evidence and destroy admissibility.

138 Authenticating, *supra*, note 137.

139 Ibid.

140 FRE 803(1), (2), and (3).
141 Reprinted with permission from the October 2, 2012 edition of the New York Law Journal © 2012 ALM Media Properties, LLC. All rights reserved. Further duplication without permission is prohibited. For information, contact 877-257-3382 or reprints@alm.com. # 070-10-12-04.
142 Stored Communications Act, 18 U.S.C. § 2701 et seq.
143 Ibid.
144 See cases discussed in footnote 160.
145 One of the earliest cases to address the issue, *Crispin v. Christian Audigier, Inc.*, 717 F. Supp. 2d 965 (C.D. Cal. 2010), concluded that the SCA prohibited a social-networking site from producing a user's account contents in response to a civil discovery subpoena. In that case, the defendants served subpoenas on several third parties, including Facebook and MySpace, seeking communications between the plaintiff and another individual. The plaintiff moved to quash the subpoenas. The court held that plaintiff had standing to bring the motion, explaining that "an individual has a personal right in information in his or her profile and inbox on a social-networking site and his or her webmail inbox in the same way that an individual has a personal right in employment and bank records." Moreover, the court determined that the providers were electronic communication service (ECS) providers under the SCA and were thus prohibited from disclosing information contained in "electronic storage."
146 See Hon. Paul W. Grimm, Michael V. Ziccardi and Alexander W. Major, "Back to the Future: Lorraine v. Markel American Insurance Co. and New Findings on the Admissibility of Electronically Stored Information," *Akron Law Review*, Vol. 42 (2009), pp. 357, 370–1.
147 Ibid.
148 Ibid.
149 Ibid.
150 See also Grimm et al., "Back to the Future: *Lorraine v. Markel American Insurance Co.* and New Findings on the Admissibility of Electronically Stored Information."
151 Scharf, *The American Journal of International Law*, 718–21 Also see: www.icty.org/sid/7537; 6 Rules of Procedure and Evidence of the ICTY, Rule 89 C, www.icty.org/x/file/Legal%20Library/Rules_procedure_evidence/IT032_rev44_en.pdf.
152 President Assad denies use of barrel bombs, using chemical weapons, or targeting in anyway civilians. See Syria conflict: BBC exclusive interview with President Bashar al-Assad, February 10, 2015, www.bbc.com/news/world-middle-east-31327153.
153 Paola Gaeta, "The Defense of Superior Orders: The Statute of the International Criminal Court versus Customary International Law," *EJIL*, Vol. 10 (1999), pp. 172, 74.
154 Ibid.
155 Scharf, *The American Journal of International Law*, 718–21. Also see: www.icty.org/sid/7537; 6 Rules of Procedure and Evidence of the ICTY, Rule 89 C, www.icty.org/x/file/Legal%20Library/Rules_procedure_evidence/IT032_rev44_en.pdf.
156 The use of TRCs in Liberia and Kenya produced no referrals to formal judicial proceedings and impunity for those who choose not to submit to the process. Human Rights Watch, Neela Ghoshal, "Four Years after Kenya's Post-Election Violence, Impunity Reigns," *Huffington Post*, December 9, 2011, www.hrw.org/news/2011/12/09/four-years-after-kenya-s-post-election-violence-impunity-reigns.

8 Conclusion

When I first set out to write this book, I had been struck by what I had noticed in the NGO international peacemaking community about a willingness to strike a deal with Assad. By the end of 2016 leaders in that community seemed to back away from UN principles that Syria should set itself on a strong course toward democracy and the rule of law. There are, of course, good reasons for this. First, there was the hope that the Arab Spring would work its magic in Syria, like it had in Egypt. But then, by 2016, the democracy in Egypt collapsed. Next there was hope that Assad's surrogates, Russia and Iran, wouldn't be able to afford to back Assad, and the economic pressures on Assad would lead to either an internal coup, or a willingness on the part of Assad to make a deal. The UN had just come off a relatively successful intervention in Kenya, and perhaps a similar powering sharing arrangement to lead to a transition to democracy in Syria. But by 2016 the peacemaking situation was hit with a series body blows. Russia had sent its aircraft to fight on behalf of Assad. There was the refugee crisis, flooding Turkey, Jordan, Lebanon, and then Europe with Syrian refugees. Countries in Europe responded with a mixture of fear and desperation about the refugee crisis. Some saw a failure in the US to take a strong stand against Assad as part of the cause of the refugee crisis. Europe was in the midst of its own economic crisis and so became more inclined to back solutions that stopped the flow of refugees. There was a rise of nationalism, both in response to the economic situation and in response to fears of terrorist infiltration out of Syria and the Middle East.

In the light of what was happening my attention turned backward to look for missed opportunities. I conducted research on Assad's decision to back away from his earlier messages that he was interested in reform and on President Obama's decision not to intervene militarily. I thought it important to understand the decisions each made in the light of historical events at the time. I intend to take a litigation approach to identify the competing narrative at play in order to make a more nuanced judgment about the fault that lay at the feet of these two protagonists. My hope was in understanding Assad's slide into more and more repressive and extreme measures to protect his regime, I hoped I would find lessons for the international community that might be learned that prevent similar slides from democracy to dictatorship from occurring the future. I was particularly interested in how religion and religious disputes became part of each party's understanding of the conflict. Assad became more and more willing to use religion to recruit followers to his side. As ISIS had Sunni ties, Assad was able to draw on his historical relationship with Hezbollah, and then Iran, to gather support for his cause.

By way of contrast, I wanted to look at Obama's decisions and how he thought of his religious faith as informing the Obama Doctrine. What I saw was that his faith motivated him, on one hand, to intervene. He had selected as one of his key advisors Samantha Power, who had written the book *A Problem from Hell.* He seemed to want someone at his side to remind him of the US's obligation to use military force to protect against war crimes. He went from an understanding of the need for the US to intervene in the world to combat evil to worrying and wondering about whether intervention in Syria would only make things worse. His religious faith seemed to be turned inward, to question his own motivations, and to worry that having seen evil, he might use it as an excuse to exercise control and impose a US version of democracy and the rule of law in Syria. Would military intervention really work, or would it lead to a situation like Iraq and Afghanistan? There the US had become stuck in countries that did not invite the US to intervene. Their citizen groups would start to see the US as the enemy. If the US intervened in Syria and then left, or bombed and didn't put troops on the ground, would it create a situation like that in Libya? Obama worried that the US's intervention, even with the full support of the international community, would create a power vacuum that would only make things worse.

Ironically (having been accused of not believing in democracy by the former Israeli foreign minister), Obama turned to Congress for support. But they refused to back him.

I thought it would be important to see Obama's decisions in the light of historical events in order to see if there were lessons that could be learned from these decisions. What started to emerge was that Congress itself seemed too mired in its own political infighting. In a sense, Congress had lost the focus of the US, and democracy around the world, in exchange for a chance to gain power through partisan politics. I was divided by what lessons I was learning here. Should the US return to more traditional constitutional positions – one where Congress declared war? Perhaps it was better for the US president to intervene militarily to support democracy movements around the world. I was and am unsure about what lesson should be drawn for the future.

The Trump presidency complicates things. Without congressional advice, Trump has bombed in response to a new use of chemical weapons, allegedly by Assad. He has increased his use of support personnel but ended a "covert" effort to remove Assad. He talks to Putin to try to get more cooperation in the fight against ISIS, yet sanctions are also now on the table to discipline the Russians (freezing $US 200 billion of Putin's assets in Western banks?) for their aggressive actions in US elections and in Crimea.

At first I also wanted to examine the role the UN played in the process. I wanted to chronicle the rise and fall of its ability to mediate peace and move the opposing parties to a peaceful conclusion, built on democracy and the rule of law. Seeing the UN in historical context showed how it had first been constrained following World

War II in its peacekeeping role by having to appear neutral between Communism and the Soviet Union, and the US and its allies. As told through the decisions of the General Secretary, the history of the UN shows its role would change, especially with the fall of the Soviet Union. Its role became not only peacekeeping but peace maintaining as well. As part of peace maintenance, it would also work to create the institutions that build democracy and the rule of law. One of the major stories to tell in the history of the UN is its continued unease about the conditions needed to give rise to the UN's "*Responsibility to Protect*" (R2p). That history shows the UN shares the US's concerns about how to intervene without getting caught in a quagmire of nation building. Complicating this history is the UN's role as a funder and institutional home for the International Criminal Court. I thought it important to see how the rise of the ICC complicates the UN's role as mediator. In Syria, Assad had good reason to question the UN's neutrality in the light of its investigation of his involvement in Harari's assassination. Like early declarations from the US (even if motivated to inspire the democracy movement), it declares the UN's intention to bring Assad to justice. Making peace with Assad's participation thereafter becomes complicated, at best. Perhaps the lesson that is learned is that if the UN keeps its role as the home of the ICC, it will need to turn to NGOs, or groups of states, such as the Syrian Group, to work out peace without its direct influence. Of course, the result is that these other mediation groups can give no assurances in making peace regarding the ICC. The question remains how the UN's dual role will impact its mission and ability to make peace in the world.

The original purpose of the book was to turn to the peacemaking process for insights about what might lie ahead of any post-conflict transition period. I thought that examining the role that constitutions might yet play in building a lasting peace would reveal problem-solving opportunities for the parties to make peace with Assad and yet start a process that could lead to democracy and the rule of law. Seen through the lens that post-Soviet Eastern European constitutions provide, what becomes clear is that it is not so much the constitutions structure that is important: they all possess a declaration of rights and a set of institutions designed to provide checks and balances on the power of the presidency. What is more important to determine who will populate the courts and the institutions set up to provide checks and balances. I thought the major lessons to learn from examining constitutional options were twofold; that all constitutions need to provide some flexibility to not only the executive to act in terms of an emergency but also strong court system to eventually establish a rule of law that would bring that executive into account. What was clear was that voting and elections would not be enough. My focus originally was on persuading Assad to see his accountability to a court as being in his long-term best interests.

What emerged during the writing was the importance of two other forces at work in any transition period: first was the importance of good faith on the part of the president and all implementers during the transition to be committed to democracy and peace. The contrasting examples of Egypt and Tunisia are telling in this regard. I was also startled to learn in a review of post-Soviet-era constitutions how liberal democracies depend on both the capacity of those who occupy the various bodies meant to check the power of the elites and the character of the president and his or her willingness to adhere to, or honor the intent of democratic institution to curb his or her power. The president must have some baseline willingness to restrict the president's decision-making to act out of self-interest. From Hungary to Kazakhstan, the transition from Soviet state to democracy seems to depend not only on the language of the constitution but more so on the will of the various institutions to honor its intent. During the course of writing, Poland has become a prime example of how delicate democracy can be. Hungary seems to have slipped back into dictatorship.

Originally, I thought that I would then further explore the difficult job of peacemaking in post-conflict societies from a more theoretical perspective. In engaging Paul Ricoeur's theories of peacemaking and forgiveness, I hoped to provide some practical advice to peacemakers bent on making peace both at the local level and at the national level. I hoped to show that a one-size-fits-all Truth and Reconciliation process like that used in South Africa and Tunisia was likely to encounter significant challenges in the context of Syria. First such a process needs to take into account not only the reconciliation process with the Assad regime but also be designed to deal with the multiple atrocities that occurred between variously constituted rebel groups (ISIS, and multiple others), some with vaguely connected religious motivations (Sunni, Shia, Yazidis, Kurds, Christians) and some motivated by the economics of proxy warfare. Methods for helping the parties understand what happen might vary from community to community and might be much different from that which is need on a national level. Finally, my original purpose to show how forgiveness in these multiple settings is made both more important and more complicated by the existence of social media. It was my hope that this chapter could provide some important practical advice to mediators on the ground, especially for those dealing with property dispute involving the right of return if and when refugees return to communities during the transition period. I also wanted to make some suggestions that Syria move eventually to a more formal rule of law process for solving conflicts. The importance of building independent courts as a check on corruption and personal power grabs is vital to the future of Syria to resist tyranny, whether it occurs on the national level or on the local level. These would all be lessons for peacemakers looking to TRCs or other alternative dispute making processes as the answer to Syria need for reconciliation going forward.

When I started writing this book two years ago, Trump was the last thing on my mind. I watched the situation in Syria go from demonstrations for democracy to repression to Assad's use of chemical weapons in 2013 to the rise of ISIS to the refugee crisis. The international community became more and more desperate for a solution to the conflict. I was witnessing a change in both the US's attitudes toward peacemaking but also in the attitude of the UN and its NGO partners. At first there seemed to be virtual unanimity that Assad should go. Even Russia joined in a UN resolution condemning the use of chemical weapons.

But with Trump's campaign, and his first six months in office, I started to see new points of emphasis in the story that I was telling about Syria. As a result, part of my purpose for writing this book started to change. On one hand, it is the same story, only made worse by the combination of three things: the role that Russia is playing, Assad's second use of chemical weapons on civilians, and the refugee crisis. The refugee situation seems only to have intensified the need for peace. Still no one from the international community has been willing to put troops on the ground. As various groups struggled against the Assad government, the conflict turned even more into a proxy war. The Saudis backed the Sunnis; the Iranians, the Shia; and Russia, Assad.

In addition, it is not as if democracy and the rule of law have always been seen as the magic ingredient to peace with justice. Its track record in this regard is fairly short-lived. The US, its allies, and the UN only have had a free hand to express their beliefs in democracy and the rule of law since the fall of the Soviet Union. Moral philosophers and political scientists have long struggled to find a sufficient grounding for democracy as a system of government, to insist that it be part of post-conflict nation building. Some economists have argued that a liberal democracy produces the optimum conditions for economic growth and prosperity. On the other hand, other nations that have risen to prominence over the last 50 years that seemed to have raised some significant counter-examples to whether that is indeed the case. In addition to China, what emerges, at least in the short run, is that controlled economies run by either a single party system, or an oligarchy, or by a dictator, can produce conditions that help bring populations from poverty into some type of prosperity. Acemuglu and Robinson, in their book *Why Nations Fail*,[1] argue that democracy is less important to national success than whether the country has institutions run by leaders that see their jobs as being first and foremost about benefiting the citizens of the country as a whole, rather than as acting for themselves. A benevolent dictator can produce good economic growth in the short run.

In addition, the world watches as liberal democracy struggles to combat extreme differences in wealth between different segments of society. Maybe democracy only provides a more elaborate cover for the elites to promote their wealth over the good of the nation itself. Maybe, control by the elites in liberal democracies is just as pronounced as with dictatorships. Each system uses wealth to impact legislation. The legal system becomes the means for those in power to avoid paying taxes, and to grow their investments. Perhaps using elaborate tax shelters available and understood only to specialized lawyers paid by wealthy, the elites turn their backs on those without health care, or basic education, or services, by escaping paying their "fair share." They argue that to be taxed by governments causes dependencies and drains the people of incentives to fend for themselves. Wealth disparity is a good thing, they say. Liberty takes precedence over equality.

But common citizens notice and start to wonder whether the system is rigged against them. How do they and their children compete when those with wealth from luck, effort, or inheritance have such an advantage in the market? The common citizens turn nationalistic in their outlook. They prefer the meaning they feel they are a part of in a "nation first economy," whether it is Brexit, or the US, rather than maximizing opportunities for everyone. They want the government to favor them over those not like them. The need to protect the immigrant, the refugee, and the outsider is set aside.

In the US, de Tocqueville's worry about the *tyranny of democracy* seems to be prescient. He worried that the elites would create status and class in the US through their control of law, and the courts and lawyering. This is what he saw happen in the aftermath of the French Revolution. It is what led to the rise of Napoleon, and he feared the same would happen elsewhere in the aftermath of revolutions followed by democracies. Tocqueville marveled that in the US, there did not seem to be habits of classism. Instead, he saw a potential for tyranny to develop through the courts but saw also beliefs that pervaded the population: that anyone could get ahead if they worked hard. While Nancy Isenberg, in her book *White Trash, The 400-Year Untold History of Class in America*, has argued that this "by your bootstraps mentality" was based more on myth than reality, the very fact that the book is news to most citizens demonstrates the power of the myth. Once the myth is revealed, faith in the political system, and whether the US truly provides a level playing field, is called into question.

Perhaps it is better for the US to be led by a member of one's own tribe, fighting for the tribe, and favoring the tribe than to place much faith in equal opportunity or equal rights under the law. And protections of minority rights or free speech or religious freedom are less important. These are the laws of the elite and for elite to help them distance themselves for the rest, as the different groups of the poor infight for the scraps left over by the elites. (At least this is the way the Poles seem to be thinking. And according to *Hillbilly Elegy*,[2] this is the way a good number of people in Appalachia and the Midwest view things in the US). Liberal democracy and the rule of law seem not all that important anymore.

Perhaps then, Trump is just riding this wave of democracy's deeper discontents in its understanding of itself. Democracy's flaws are that it can turned into an instrument of oppression, as elite groups fix society and the rule of law to favor the elites in the market place of life. Democracy can became made a tool of tyranny by enabling those who win elections to impose its will on others. These flaws appear all the more clearly during this first time with Trump.

Here is what Yascha Mounk writes in a recent *New York Times* opinion piece titled "Trump Is Destroying Our Democracy":[3]

> America is on its way to a full-blown constitutional crisis.
>
> Over just a few days last week, President Trump and his allies stepped up attacks on Robert Mueller, the special counsel investigating the campaign's connections to Russia. They tried to push Attorney General Jeff Sessions out of office. They thought out loud about whether the president can pardon himself.
>
> . . .
>
> There have, in fact, been a few times and places when the villains were quite as villainous, and the heroes quite as heroic. (Think Germany in the 1930s.) But in most cases, the demise of democracy has been far more gradual and far easier to overlook.
>
> In their first years in office, Vladimir Putin in Russia, Recep Tayyip Erdogan in Turkey and Viktor Orban in Hungary claimed that they wanted to

> fix, rather than cripple, democratic institutions. Even as it became clear that these strongmen sought to consolidate power, most of their opponents told themselves that they were saving their courage for the right moment. By the time the full extent of the danger had become incontrovertible, it was too late to mount an effective resistance.
>
> In some ways, the United States seems far from such a situation today . . .
>
> But in other respects the United States is already well on the way to what I have, in my academic work, called "democratic deconsolidation." Mr. Trump is increasingly emulating the playbook of popularly elected strongmen who have done deep, lasting damage to their countries' democratic institutions.
>
> "
>
> No flashing light will announce that the very survival of democracy is now at stake if Mr. Mueller is fired. And since nobody can say for sure that the Constitution will become toothless if congressional Republicans let yet another infraction pass, their instinct will be to defer their patriotic duty to some more opportune moment in the future. But that moment may never come. There may never be a time when we know for sure that this decision, today, will determine whether the American republic lives or dies.
>
> In Hungary, democracy did not end when Mr. Orban staffed the electoral commission with his cronies, or when he put loyalists in charge of state television stations or even when he changed the Constitution to expand his powers. But now that he has taken all these steps, the opposition has little chance of ousting him at the next elections. Slowly but surely, Hungary has ceased to be a real democracy.
>
> The temptation to delay opposing Mr. Trump until the right moment comes along is understandable. It's also very dangerous. Even if congressional Republicans abdicate their duty, the Constitution may turn out to be unusually resilient. But the only sure way to save the Republic is for them to start standing up to the president's authoritarian behavior – not next week, or next month, but today.[4]

As a result, then, of these events, I feel I need to add my voice of concern to what is happening in the US. Through the lens of Syria and Assad, Putin, Erdogan, Orban, and Poland, and, in the hands of Trump, democracy does seem to be losing its moxie. This book then is my attempt to add a warning to the US, as well as to democracies around the world. Democracy is more than just an election. Working democracy requires persons and institutions that act consistently with the norms of democracy, the rule of law, and good faith interpretation of its power, not for personal gain but for the good of the country as a whole. Democracy is fragile, as is peace, if there is no willingness to put one's power in check to the greater good of the people.

For peacemakers, this exacerbates the stress that will be put on transition periods in post-conflict societies. The time to build habits in the citizens, and norms of behavior in the leaders, will never be long enough. And yet the building blocks are still the same. It will be in a combination of electoral accountability and dispute resolution processes that people will turn from violence to civil discourse. Education will need to play a role. Faith in its principles will need to take root. What is required for democracies to work are people who understand these lessons and are willing to play by the rules to those ends.

Courts, as well as legislatures, need to be populated by people willing to look past short-term gains and put the good of the people first. Otherwise, the needs for security and order may be used justify emergency powers and the usurpation of the rights of the minority. Otherwise, leaders may use religion to stoke fears between groups, which eventually lead to violence. Otherwise, frustrations in times of scarcity and fear will lead to the election of leaders who believe their followers have delegated arbitrary and unlimited authority. Once the leader believes in his or her own right to dictate and issue decrees, the slide away from democracy may have been put in motion.

I hope that this is also the lesson that emerges from the book, not only about peacemaking in other settings but also for peace with justice here at home.

Notes

1 Daron Acemuglu and James Robinson, *Why Nations Fail* (New York: Crown Publishers, Random House, 2012).

2 J.D Vance, *A Hillbilly Elegy, A Memoir of a Family and Culture in Crisis*, (New York: HarperCollins Publishers, 2016).

3 Mounk isn't the only one to issue a call to arms in the *New York Times.* David Brooks expressed similar concerns but tried to rally Republicans to the cause:

> Do you ever get the feeling we're all going to be judged for this moment? Historians, our grandkids and we ourselves will look and ask: What did you do as the Trump/Scaramucci/Bannon administration dropped a nuclear bomb on the basic standards of decency in public life? What did you do as the American Congress ceased to function? What positions did you take as America teetered toward national decline?

Brooks then quotes for Senator Flake's new book, *Conscience of a Conservative*, which asks conservatives the following questions:

> Is it conservative to praise dictators as "strong leaders," to speak fondly of countries that crush dissent and murder political opponents . . .? Is it conservative to demonize and vilify and mischaracterize religious and ethnic minorities . . .? Is it conservative to be an ethno-nationalist? Is it conservative to embrace as fact things that are demonstrably untrue?

4 Yascha Mounk, a lecturer at Harvard, a columnist for *Slate*, and the host of the podcast "The Good Fight," is the author of the forthcoming *The People Versus Democracy.*

Index

Note: Page numbers in italic indicate a figure and page numbers in bold indicate a table on the corresponding page.

Abrahamic religions 145
actions, intent (ascribing) 4–5
adjudication, mediation (contrast) 168–170
adjudicative process, usage 157
African National Congress (ANC) 190
agency problems 161; mediating theory, impact 160–161
aggression, GA definition 78
al-Assad, Bashar 13–14; asylum, granting 192; chemical weapons usage, Obama red line (drawing) 51–56; conferring 86; exit, requirement (Obama announcement) 50–51; external conspiracy 20–22; father, relationship 40–41; hardline diplomacy 15–19; heinous actions, Obama fault (Trump accusation) 22; iron fist terrorism promise 20; military, war crimes 187–189; oppression strategy 47–49; political challenges 106–107; promises/outcomes 14–25; regime, transitional period agreement (question) 191; religion, role 24–25; role 3; Russia, relationship 18–19; security forces, war crimes 187–189; Shi'ite militia, assistance 58; victims 188; war crimes case 5–9; war crimes investigation 193; war crimes responsibility 4–5
al-Assad, Hafez: coup 12–13; power, seizure 103; sins 9–12; son, relationship 40–41
Alawites: al-Assad protection 134; political force 106; Shia, affiliation 117
al-Bashir, Omar 187
Aleppo: fighting 21; violence, resurgence 91
Al-Hajj, Ali (assistance) 17
al-Hariri, Rafik: al-Assad meeting 15–16; assassination 16; murder, ITCL investigation 80; resignation 16
Allah, beliefs 142
al-Maliki, Nouri 185
Al Qaeda: Al Qaeda-affiliated groups, atrocities 114; opposition group members 204; predecessors, impact 133
Al-Sayyed, Jamil (assistance) 17
al-Shabat 113
Al-Zalqa, Promenade Hotel (explosion) 17
Amnesty International report 188–189
amnesty, peacemaker option 196
anger, management 161
Annan, Kofi 70–72; contact group, assembly 87; power-sharing arrangement, negotiation 83; UN efforts 86–87
apartheid, negotiation (Botha refusal) 161
application software, impact 200
Arab League 86
Arab revolution movement 109
Arab Spring 83–84; democracy demonstrations 100; impact 219
Arabs, recruitment 198
Aridi, Ghazi (resignation) 16
Ashraf, Abu 163
Ashrafieh, explosion 17
Assad *see* al-Assad
atrocities, experience 169
Audacity of Hope, The (Obama) 45

authentication 202; issues 201
authority, grounding 142
Awakening 185–186

Ba'ath Arab Socialist Party, coup 103
Balance, Fabrice 132
bargaining process 168
barrel bombs, Syrian government usage 196–197
Basheer, Omar 80
Beirut: industrial zone, explosion 17; Kuwaiti information office, explosion 17
blameworthiness 157–158
Botha, Peter 161
Boueiz, Fares (resignation) 16
Brahimi, Lakhdar 168; UN interaction 87–89
Bush, George W. 58

cabinet meetings, convening (presidential ability) 110
caliphate, declaration 49
Cambodia, transitional oversight bodies 193
Cameron, David 58
Carter, Jimmy (role) 113
Chandler, John 46
chat transcripts, usage 201
Checksum, usage 200
chemical arms, claims 49
chemical weapons, usage 195
Chidiac, May (injuring) 17
circumstantial evidence, visibility 200–201
cities, blockading 21
civilians, collateral damage 156
civil service organizations (CSOs), training/support 194
Clapper, James 58
Code of Crimes 78
Cold War 78; proxy fighters 81–82
collateral damage, occurrence 156
Committee for the Investigation of Post Election Violence (CIPEV) 83
Committee for the Resolution of Real Property Disputes (CRRPD), setup 194
Comprehensive Peace Agreement 187
conciliation procedures, establishment 121
conflict: cessation, peacemaker difficulty (intensification) 195–196; history/complexity, acknowledgment 161; international conflict, mediation 165; NGO mapping 169; post-conflict complications 163; resolution, long-term system 77–78; transition process setup 185
conflict mapper: file downloading system 201; function 198; video authentication 199
conflict mapping 195–196; NGO conflict-mapping project 203; projects, impact 195–196
Congress, focus (loss) 220
Constituent Assembly: Article 40 creation 121–122; decisions 186
Constitutional Court, authority 105
constitutionalism, doctrine 118
constitutional options, examination 221
Constitution of Al-Jihad 163
contact group, Annan assembly 87
Convention on the Prevention and Punishment of the Crime of Genocide: GA adoption 78; violations 78
conviction, ethics 136
cooperation, strategies 168
Corniche, explosion 80
Crane, David 183, 184
Creator God: belief 144–145; usage 144
credibility, fetish/preservation 59
criminal prosecution, Rome Statute (impact) 78–79

DAESH 89
Darke, Diana 163
data collection: ethical concerns 201; methods 202
Dayton Peace Accords 80, 193
de Klerk, F.W. 81–82; decision 111; power, sharing 161
de Mistura, Staffan (UN interaction) 89–91
democratic deconsolidation 225
Democratic Republic of Congo, urgency 79
Dickinson, Emily 145
diplomacy, teachings 165
disappeared 160
disputants, security threat (mediator identification) 167
dispute resolution: proceedings 184; processes, management 194–195; processes, requirements 134–135; social media, impact 195–196
disputes: mediation, challenge 153–159; non-violent/peaceful resolution 193
disruptive projection, utopian role 144
Dreams from My Father (Obama), Oren criticism 41–42

egocentric view, expansion 161
Egypt: Supreme Military Council, arrangement 192; Supreme Military Council, Muslim Brotherhood negotiation 186; transitional structures 186
el-Sisi, Abdel Fattah 84
emergency powers, usage 192
enlightened self-identity, cultivation 140–141
Erdogan, Recep Tayyip 224–225
etat de droit doctrine, Russian acceptance (evidence) 117–118
ethical memory 141
ethics, issues 201
ethics of conviction 136
ethics of responsibility 136
"Ethnic Cleansing Threatens Syria's Unity" (Balance) 132
evidence, gathering 197–198
evil: phenomenon, hermeneutics (impact) 143; understanding 143

Facebook: status updates, usage 201; user content, disclosure prohibition 202
Faith-Base Policy (Chandler) 46
faith, non-rationality 158
Farhat, Abdullah (resignation) 16
flourishing, ideas 136
force, usage 156
forgetting, noninvolvement 157
forgiveness 152; appeals 158; conditions, forgiving conditions (contrast) 155; examination 154–159; future 140; heroic proportions 142; implications 153; impossibility 156; justice, contrast 153–159; meaning, requirements 168; origin 154; possibilities, consideration 159; possibility 166; religious origins 155; Ricoeur theory 222; victim selection 160
forgiving: process, representative risks 161–162; voluntary act 157
formal judicial proceedings, social media videos/proof (usage) 196–203
formation videos 198
Franco-Syrian treaty (1936) 6
French Resistance (World War II) 135
Friday of Departure demonstration 84
Future Movement 17

Gabriel, Mark A. 162–163
Geneva Communiqué 87–88, 91; basis 89–90
Geneva Conventions 78
Geneva I 98, 101
Geneva II 88–89, 98, 101
Germany, Versailles obligations 102
Getting to Yes (Fisher/Ury) 167
Ghouta, chemical weapons attack 49, 88
God: act/command 155; forgiveness 154–155; laws, following 142; sign of approval 139
Google, conflict mapper interaction 201
gosudarstvennost (statehood) 116, 119, 124
Great War standards 36
grief, airing 161

Hamadeh, Marwan: assassination attempt 16; resignation 16
Hariri *see* al-Hariri
Hariri, Saad 17
Hawi, George (assassination) 17
hearsay, out-of-court statement 201
hermeneutics 131; impact 143
Hezbollah: al-Assad, relationship 220; war crimes investigation 193
Hillbilly Elegy (Vance) 224
historical events, uniqueness 140
history: hermeneutics 137–145; imagination, relationship 131; narrative history 140–141
Holocaust 140–141
Homs sit-in, security force raid 20
Hong Kong, Chinese governance 122
hostility-control strategies 92
human condition, forgiveness (impact) 155
human forgiveness 157
humanitarian aid, delivery 46
humanitarian groups, funding receipt 198
human rights 168; organizations, peace process involvement 196; violations 21
Human Rights Watch (HRW) 195, 196; proof 197
Hussein, Saddam 134; removal 194
hybrid constitutions, adoption 116

identity mediations 165
Idlib Province, Jaish al-Fatah (Army of Conquest) Islamist rebel alliance control 49
Idlib Province, Khan Sheikhoun (nerve gas attack) 22
imagination: action 138; hermeneutics 137–145; history, relationship 131;

metaphoric imagination 139; poetic imaginations 167
imperialism: danger 108; fight 103, 109
indeterminancy, result 156
informal TRC, efficacy 203
initiative, vision (impact) 144
innovation: behavior form 142; semantic innovation 144
interest-based negotiation 141–142, 166
interim constitution-transitional governing body 111–114
interim period, social media (impact) 195–196
international conflict, mediation 165
International Covenant on Economic, Social, and Cultural Rights (1968), Syrian ratification 106
International Criminal Court (ICC) 187, 202; absence 71; Assad military/ security forces, war crimes 187–189; establishment 79; investigations 18; investigative arm, impact 170; jurisdiction 79–80; peace condition 196; statutes, ILC drafting 78
International Criminal Court for the former Yugoslavia (ICTY) 187
international criminal prosecutions, implications 183
International Criminal Tribunal for Lebanon (ITCL) investigation 80
International Criminal Tribunal for the former Rwanda (ICTR) 79, 187
International Criminal Tribunal (ICT) for the former Sierra Leone 79–80, 187
International Criminal Tribunal for the former Yugoslavia (ICTY) 79–80
International Law Committee (ILC), ICC statutes 78
international NGOs, data collection methods 202
International Organization for Migration 131
International Syria Support Group (ISSG): labelling 89–90; meeting, reconvening 91; negotiations forum, reopening 92–93
intervention strategies, changes (meaning) 91–93
Iraq, Socialist Ba'ath Party 117
iron fist terrorism, al-Assad promise 20
Isenberg, Nancy 224
ISIL, rise 89
ISIS 113, 193–194; atrocities 114; attacks 132–133; dissolution, appearance 114; enemy of the state 117; loyalty 132–133; opposition group members 204; proselytization 119; recruitment videos 183; rise 89, 183–184; Shia Muslim beheading 197; suicide squad, attack 133; Sunni/ Hussein military leaders, involvement 185–186; Sunni ties 220; targets, air strikes 46; videos, tracking 184
Islam: defining 117; West war 134
Islamic Front formation announcement, recruitment video *215*
Islamic State, air strikes 49
Islamic State of Iraq, caliphate declaration 49
Islamists, rise 49

Jaish al-Fatah (Army of Conquest) Islamist rebel alliance, control 49
Jdeideh, explosion 16
jihad, waging 162
Jounieh, explosion 17
Journey into the Mind of an Islamic Terrorist (Gabriel) 162
justice 152; forgiveness, contrast 153–159; truth, dilemma 191
just war theory, principles 156

Kahneman, Michael 136
Kant, Immanuel 139
Karame, Omar (government formation) 16
Kaslik shopping center, explosion 16
Kassir, Sami (assassination) 17
Kennan, George F. (impact) 37–40
Kenya: Annan negotiation 83; TRC difficulties 191–195
Kenyatta, Uhuru 83, 187
Khan al-Assal, sarin attack 22
Khan Sheikhoun, nerve gas attack 22
Kibaki, Mwai (mediation) 83
kidnapping 188
Ki-moon, Ban 86
Kobane, Islamic State (exit) 49
Kurdish Popular Protection Unit 23
Kurdish question 123

labor movement, impact 186–187
Lahoud, Émile: Hezbollah support 16; term extension 15–16
language shift, party understanding 168
League of Arab States (Arab League) 76
League of Nations, sanction 102
Lebanon: Syrian troop exit 17; Syria/ Palestinians, relationship 9–12
legal processes, evolution 158–159

legislative power 121–123
liberal democracy, struggle 223
liberation, achievement 107
Liberia, TRC difficulties 191–195
liberty, equality (contrast) 223
Libya, transitional structures 186
life events, sequence (transformation) 139
local informal mediation bodies, social media evidence (usage) 203–204
Ludwikowski, Rett 118

Maghed, Assim Abdul 163
Mandela, Nelson 81–82, 85, 169; appearance 169–170; bargaining partner 190; election 88; neutrality, role 113; power, sharing 161; principles, usage 111
mass hangings 189
meanings, structure 137
mediating: hazards 160–161; theory 159–170
mediation: adjudication, contrast 168–170; identity mediations 165; implication 140; international conflict 165; local informal mediation bodies, social media evidence (usage) 203–204; process, party involvement 159; strategy 81–82; UN efforts 86–91
mediator complications, management 156–157
mediator decision making 194–195
Menkel-Meadow, Carrie 167
Merkel, Angela 58
metadata: application software, impact 200; collection 201
metaphoric imagination 139
Middle Eastern suffering, alleviation 36
Mikati, Najib (parliamentary election announcement) 17
Milošević, Slobodan 80, 81; war crimes 187
minarchist school 116
minority groups, violence 164
moral hazard, recognition 157
Moreno-Ocampo, Luis 79
Morsi, Mohamed 84
Mounk, Yascha 224
mourning, impact 141
Mubarak, Hosni 83–84; repressive state 112
murder 188; excuse 156
Murphy, Jeffrie 155
Murr, Elias (wounding) 17
Muslim Brotherhood 124; buy-in 112; Supreme Military Council, negotiation 186; Turk/Qatari support 190
mutual destruction, cycle (overcoming) 142
mutual questioning 138
My House in Damascus (Darke) 163
mystery site 19

narrative: dialogic nature 167; role, understanding 141; usefulness 140
narrative history: impact 141; literary elements 140
National Assembly: implementation decisions 114; members 123
National Democratic Party (NDP) 83–84
nation first economy 223
negotiation: interest-based negotiation 141–142; power-sharing arrangement, negotiation 83; reframing 141–142
Niebuhrian needle 44
Niebuhr, Reinhold 45; checks/ balances 46
night time executions 188–189
nongovernmental organizations (NGOs): assistance 163; community 111; conflict mapping 169; conflict-mapping project 203; international NGOs, support ability 194–195; partners, opposition side 115; peacemaking efforts 66; supporting role 196; video evidence 195
non-rational belief, sharing 159
Nuremberg Defense 202–203
Nuremberg Judgment 78

Obama, Barack 135; *Audacity of Hope, The* 45; congressional support 220; decisions 47; doctrine, assessment 60–61; *Dreams from My Father*, Oren criticism 41–42; intervention failure 49–56; military intervention, avoidance 219–220; punitive strikes, request 22; red line, drawing 51–56; religion, impact 42–47; Syria relationship 34; thinking, unpacking 53–54
Odinga, Raila (mediation) 83
Oneself as Another (Ricoeur) 136
opening statements, forgoing 165
opposition groups: atrocities 194; interaction 193
oppression: strategy (al-Assad) 47–49; witness 168
Orban, Viktor 224–225

Oren, Michael 35
Organisation for the Prohibition of Chemical Weapons (OPCW) 195; proof 197
Organization for the Prohibition of Chemical Weapons, chemical weapons removal 22
otherness, respect 140
Ottoman Empire 163; fall 103; rule 101–102

Palantir, Inc. 198–199
Palestinians, Syria/Lebanon (relationship) 9–12
Pan-Arabism 103
pardon, possibility 141
past: opening 137–138; otherness 140
past narrative, present (meaning) 137
peace: condition 196; meaningfulness/sustainability 170; process 153; survival 167
peacemakers: amnesty option 196; difficulties, intensification 195–196
peacemaking 221; choices 74–76; difficulty 165; efforts 66; Ricoeur theory 222; Rome Statute, impact 78–79; social media/conflict mapping, impact 183
People's Council, reservation 104–105
Peoples Protection Unit (YPG), arming 23
People's Protection Units (YPG), displacement accusations 132
perpetrators, victims (matching) 163–168
phenomenology: approach 138; grounding 137
pluralism, discovery 158
poetic imaginations 167
poetic narrative 140
poetic, role 144
"Points of Commonalities" list 91
Poland judiciary, independence 122–123
"Police Day" holiday 83–84
possible, power 144
Post-Cold War surge 70
post-conflict peace building, UN practices (problems) 84–85
post-conflict societies, peacemaking job (difficulty) 222
post-Soviet strong statist constitutions 119
post-traumatic stress, cause 160–161
Power, Faith, and Fantasy (Oren) 35
president: guarantor role 121; mediator role 121
pre-transition process 114–115
Principle of Accountability 111
Principle of Effectiveness 111–112
Principle of Freedom 111
Principle of Healing 111
Principle of Participation 111
Principle of Peace 111
Principle of Respect 111
printouts, usage 201
problem solving: description (Menkel-Meadow) 167; language 142; language, usage 166; mediations 159; mediators, impact 166; usage 141–142
Progressive Socialist Party 17
Promenade Hotel, explosion 17
proof, usage 196–203
propaganda, prohibition 119
Prophets, teachings 162–163
proxy war (Russia) 56–61
public posts, usage 201
Putin, Vladimir 224–225; Trump interaction 220

Qornet Shehwan Gathering 17
quasi-Kantian idealist project 137

Rafik Hariri Martyr List, government win 17
Rahman, Hamdi Abdul 163
Ramadi, assault 131
rationality, choices 158
rebels, non-lethal support (US/Britain suspension) 49
reconciliation 169
records, custodian (usage) 201
recruitment video *215*
regime change, transition process setup 185
religion: freedom 167; impact 42–47; role 24–25
religious courts, concept 105
religious organizations, equality 118
representatives: agreements 163–164; capacity 161; forgiving process risk 161–162
Resolution 1559, UN Security Council adoption 16
Resolution 2254, UN Security Council adoption 90
Resolution 2268, UN Security Council adoption 90
responsibility, ethics 136
Ricoeur, Paul: binary alternatives 142; hermeneutical mediation 162; hermeneutical process 161; hermeneutic philosophy 144;

hermeneutics 131, 154, 158, 165–167; hermeneutics, moral critique 169; history/imagination, hermeneutics 137–145; legal/psychoanalytic theory 136–137; mediating theory 159–170; peacemaking/forgiveness theories 222; personal background 135; philosophical support 167; symbols, types 139
Rome Statute 78–79, 187; signing, deadline 79
rule of law 77–78, 223
Russia: backing, unlikelihood 187; draft, religion/rights (relationship) 118–120; *etat de droit* 117–118; history 116–117; intervention/proxy war 56–61; involvement 22–24; negotiation opportunity 114–116; post-Soviet strong statist constitutions 119; problem-solving approach 98; rhetoric, softening 99–100; role 77
Russia, al-Assad (relationship) 18–19
Rwanda: atrocities, prevention/intervention 88; TRC difficulties 191–195; war 78

Salafi-Jihadist opposition, war 91
San Remo Conference 102
sarin, usage 22
saying-as/being-as 139
Scowcroft, Brent 54
screen captures, usage 201
seeing-as 139
self-constancy, informing 141
self, notion (party rehabilitation) 141
semantic innovation 144
shared humility 159
shared interests, usage 85–86, 167–168
Sharia law 164; institution 84; reference, absence 116
Shia: Alawites, affiliation 117; beheading 197; militias, motivation 134; Sunnis, religious reconciliation 124
Sierra Leone, International Special Tribunal 183
Sikes-Picot division 166
Six-Day War, God's sign of approval 139
slaughter house, prison operation 188
social identity, grounding (ideological role) 144
social imaginary 144
Socialist Arab Ba'ath Party, leadership 107–108
social media: conflict mapping 195–196; evidence, TRC/local informal mediation body usage 203–204; evidence, trial admission 200–201; impact 183, 195–196; site, circumstantial evidence visibility 199–200; usage 203–204; videos, usage 196–203
social networking sites, data collection (ethical concerns) 201
South Africa, Truth and Reconciliation Preamble 191
Soviet state/democracy, transition 222
Soviet Union, fall 82–83, 122
Special Advisors for the Prevention of Genocide and the Responsibility to Protect 76
square table assumption 85
state power, function 121
static images, capture/preservation 201
statism, predominance 118–119
statist school 116
Stored Communications Act (SCA) 201–202
Strong Statism 116; post-Soviet strong statist constitutions 119; tradition, impact 124
Sufism 163
Suleiman, Omar 84
Sunni Salafists, Saudi support 190
Sunnis/Shia, reconciliation: examples 162–163; religious question 124
superpowers, comparison 53
Supreme Constitutional Court 192
Supreme Council of Armed Forces (SCAF) 84
Supreme Court (general jurisdiction) 192
Supreme Islamic Constitutional Court, design 113
Supreme Judicial Council (SJC): control 110; impact 109
Swinburne, Richard 155
symbols, types 139
Syria: atrocities 114, 194; ceasefire, Russia/Iran/Turkey enforcement 22; chemical attack, suspicion 23; conflict, context 67–69; conflict mapping 183; conflict, UN situation 74; Constitutional Court, authority 105; constitutional history 101–103; constitutional instability 102; context 35–40; cruise missile attack (2017) 23; dispute resolution processes, requirements 134–135; division, French administration (impact) 6–9;

draft constitution 116–117, 121–122; events, chronology (2004–2005) 15–17; executive branch 104; formal judicial process, selection 202–203; governance structure, interference (international community role) 100–101; government bombings 183; government jet, US attack 23; interim constitution-transitional governing body 111–114; iron fist terrorism, al-Assad promise 20; judicial branch 105–106; Lebanon/Palestinians, relationship 9–12; legislative branch 104–105; militant struggle 108; military force, usage (Obama intervention failure) 49–56; military, interaction (absence) 186–187; military, removal/ignoring (question) 185–186; non-compliance, UN Security Council threat 22; nonintervention, Obama reasons 58; operations/challenges 72–74; Organization for the Prohibition of Chemical Weapons, chemical weapons removal 22; Ottoman Empire, rule 101–102; peacemakers, difficulty 188; peacemakers, social media usage 203–204; People's Council, reservation 104–105; political options 184–185; presidency 120–121; presidential powers 104; pre-WWII map *7*; reality, mediating theory (relationship) 159–170; reassessment 70–72; rebel groups, military support (US discontinuation) 23; refugees 219; refugees, flight/expulsion 132–133; revolution (1963) 107–108; Russia, involvement 22–24; Russia, role 77; sanctions, UN Security Council veto 22; sectarian distribution *133*; secular Syria, Russia demand 99; security forces, removal/ignoring (question) 185–186; security leadership, interaction (absence) 186–187; Socialist Ba'ath Party 117; social media, impact 183; Supreme Judicial Council (SJC), impact 109; transition, mediation (pitfalls) 100; TRC difficulties 190–191; truthfulness, assessment 203; UN actions 76; UN Human Rights Council, executions evidence 21; United Nations, Annan (involvement) 86–87; unity (notion), Alawi community (tension) 6; UN mediation efforts 86–91; UN peacekeeping choices 74–76; uprisings, religious dimensions 92; YouTube videos 189
Syria Accountability Project 183
Syria-A Decade of Lost Changes (Wieland) 20
Syria constitution: constitution-based transition, options 98; revision 115; suspension 103
Syria, constitution (1950): flaw 106–107; reinstatement 106
Syria, constitution (1973) 103; flaw 106–107; opposition 105–106
Syria, Constitution (2012) 107–110; amendment/adoption 98; Article 3 118; Article 8, repeal 107; Article 15 123; Article 40, impact 121–122; Article 53 110; Article 55 121; Article 85 110; Article 103 110; Article 111 109, 110; Article 132–33 110; Article 144 109; Articles 81–84, provisions 120, 123–124; Articles 97/113 109; Articles 133/136 109; preamble 107–109; principles 108–109
Syria Deeply group 183
Syrian Observatory for Human Rights 90–91; report 188

Tahrir Square (Liberation Square), mass demonstrations 83–84
Tal Abyad Arabs, YPG displacement 132
Tantawi, Mohamed Hussein 84
tat de droit, ideas 118
Taylor, Charles 80, 81; international prosecution 187
temporalization, process 142
Territorial/Constituent Assembly 122
terrorism: acts, deterrence 157; Syrian Sunni support, absence 131; threat, inflation 46
text, language 138–139
The Carter Center (TCC) 163, 197–198
theodicy, scandal 140–141
third-party vendors, jurisdiction 202
thought experiments 139
torture 188; pervasiveness 21
towns, blockading 21
traditionality 137–138
traditions 138
transitional government/executive body, formula (absence) 105–106

Transitional Judicial Council, establishment 193
Transitional National Assembly, establishment 193
Transnational National Assembly: executive power assembly 113; Tunisia example 112
Trump, Donald: complications 220; negative impact 222–223; statement issuance 22; strongman mentality 225; Syria relations 34
"Trump is Destroying Out Democracy" (Mounk) 224–225
Truth and Reconciliation Commission (TRC) 189–195; difficulties (Liberia/Rwanda/Kenya) 191–195; difficulties (Syria) 190–191; failure 161–162; hybrid process 170; processes, implications 183; setup 82; social media evidence, usage 203–204; success 169; usage 197
Truth and Reconciliation process 153, 159, 169
truth, justice (dilemma) 191
tselostnost (state integrity) 116, 117, 121
Tunisia: transitional structures 186; Transnational National Assembly example 112; UN role, problem 85
Tutu, Desmond: appearance 169–170; dilemma 191
Tweets, usage 201

United Arab Republic, Syria joining (attempt) 103
United Nations: actions 76; Brahimi, interaction 87–89; Charter, Article 33 82; de Mistura, interaction 89–91; Diplomatic Conference of Plenipotentiaries 79; evidence, collection 184; International Independent Investigation Commission, UN Security Council formation 17; involvement 170; mediation efforts 86–91; mediator 82–86; peacemaking choices 74–76; peacemaking efforts 66; peacemaking force, history 67–69; peacemaking operations 74; resolutions 187; *Responsibility to Protect* (R2p) 221; role, problem 85
United Nations Declaration of Human Rights (UNDHR) (1948) 119–120
United Nations General Assembly (GA): *Convention on the Prevention and Punishment of the Crime of Genocide* 78; Preparatory Committee (PrepCom) establishment 79; resolutions 76
United Nations High Commissioner for Refugees (UNHCR) report 188
United Nations Human Rights Council: executions evidence 21; resolutions, passage 76
United Nations Security Council: Resolution 1559 adoption 16; Resolution 2254 adoption 89–90; Resolution 2268 adoption 90; sanctions veto 22
United States Agency for International Development (USAID), UN commission 194
US-Syrian relations: context 35–40; history 3, 34; Obama, role 34; Trump, role 34
utopia: a-historical utopia 167; imagination 142

Versailles Peace Treaty (1919) 102
vicitmization, horror 140–141
victims: forgiveness, selection 160; incapacities, mediating theory (impact) 160–161; perpetrators, matching 163–168; saving 170
videos: authentication 202; conflict mapper authentication 199; coordination 197; formation videos 198; postings, use 195; recruitment video *215*; shooting 198; usage 196–203
violence 164; cycle, overcoming 142; perpetuation 159
visée de l'histoire à faire 137

Waldheim, Kurt 70
war crimes, al-Assad responsibility 4–5
water supplies, destruction 21
White Trash (Isenberg) 224
Why Nations Fail (Acemuglu/Robinson) 223
Wieland, Casten 20

Yabroud, Syria/Hezbollah force recapture 49

Zedong, Mao 104
zero-sum game 144
Zimbabwe, interim agreement 192–193
Zionism: danger 108; fight 103, 109
Zohdy, Karam 162
Zoummar, Abod 163

For Product Safety Concerns and Information please contact our EU
representative GPSR@taylorandfrancis.com
Taylor & Francis Verlag GmbH, Kaufingerstraße 24, 80331 München, Germany

www.ingramcontent.com/pod-product-compliance
Ingram Content Group UK Ltd.
Pitfield, Milton Keynes, MK11 3LW, UK
UKHW020010200926
475702UK00014B/1811
* 9 7 8 0 3 6 7 5 9 3 5 8 2 *